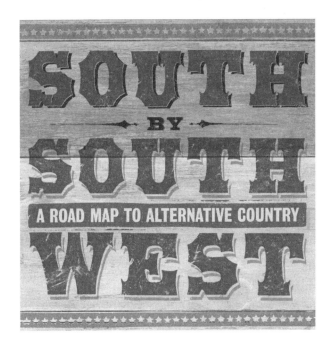

SOUTH
BY
SOUTH
A ROAD MAP TO ALTERNATIVE COUNTRY
WEST

Printed and bound in Great Britain by Butler & Tanner Ltd, Frome, Somerset

Distributed in the US by Publishers Group West

Published by Sanctuary Publishing Limited, Sanctuary House, 45–53 Sinclair Road, London W14 0NS, United Kingdom

www.sanctuarypublishing.com

Cover: Ghost Design

Photographs courtesy of Michael Ochs Archives/Redferns; Ebet Roberts/Redferns; Graham Knowles/Redferns; Charlyn Zlotnik; Redferns; Michael Ochs Archives/Redferns; Amanda Edwards/Redferns; Michael Ochs Archives/Redferns; Gems/Redferns; Martin Philbey; Carey Brandon/Redferns; Nicky J Sims/Redferns; Olivia Hemingway/Redferns; Paul Bergen/Redferns; Tabatha Fireman/Redferns; Olivia Hemingway/Redferns

While the publishers have made every reasonable effort to trace the copyright owners for any or all of the photographs in this book, there may be some omissions of credits, for which we apologise.

ISBN: 1-86074-461-3

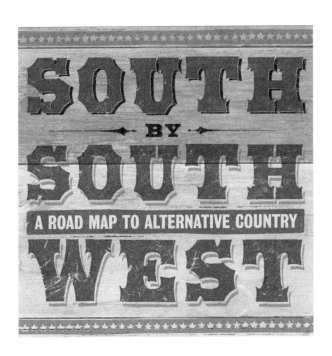

A ROAD MAP TO ALTERNATIVE COUNTRY

Brian Hinton
Sanctuary

In memoriam
Johnny Cash
1932–2003

Contents

Acknowledgements

I'd like to give a big *South By Southwest* thank you to Iain MacGregor, who commissioned this book – not originally from me, but I'm good at stepping in at the last minute. To Clinton Heylin who told me exactly where I was going wrong in his usual cheerfully acerbic manner and lent me rare tapes to prove his point. To Roger Careless (a walking history lesson in himself) and his retail outlet Rear View Mirror, the best mobile Americana record stall going. To Vic King and many others for being so generous with their own Americana collections. To Geoff Wall for helping me through the transition from my trusty old Amstrad to a gleaming laptop, and to the ever-calm Dave Griffin for rescuing much of this book from the bowels of that very machine. And to Maurice Wilson, the Irish pedal-steel enthusiast who responded so positively to *Country Roads*, and became a friend (though I've yet to meet him face to face).

Thanks to the manager of the Oxfam Music Shop in Portswood, Southampton, where I bought the super-rare Leon Payne album and whose manager used to road manage The Clash and came up with all kinds of interesting anecdotes. One of them was even printable. Regards also to Jeff Lewis, whose stock of rare vinyl fills the basements of the Victorian arcade in Union Street, Ryde, Isle of Wight.

Greetings to my own favourite Texan, Will Ware from Houston: poet, attorney at law, and an expert on music in the Lone Star State; and to Arthur Brown, who could well be a hellfire preacher in another life when not being a neglected genius in this one. Greetings too to Malcolm Morley, perhaps Britain's finest translator of Americana into English country music and a man whose music should be in everyone's CD rack.

To Alan Clayson, who has turned pedantry into a rare passion, and Dick Taylor, one of the greatest guitarists alive, who has stretched from the snarl and thrash of The Pretty Things to the whine and clatter of the Mekons and bejewelled both, and with whom it has been my immense privilege to play keyboards in front of a handful of bemused audiences as Alan acted out his narratives of English life – Anglicana, anyone?

Heartfelt thanks to people like 'Captain America' on Virgin Radio and Bob Harris, Andy Kershaw, John Peel, Nick Barraclough and Johnny Walker – who was so great when I chatted to him live on Radio 2 – and whose enthusiasm for different aspects of the music shines through. Good wishes to Grant Alden and the *No Depression* crew – not that I've ever met or talked to them, it just feels like it sometimes.

Thanks also to the great, and doomed, Norfolk revivalist singer Peter Bellamy who (in the late '70s) looked disparagingly at my record collection that stretched floor to ceiling, and bemoaned the lack of any Carter Family material. 'There are ten albums still in print, so just go out and buy them'. Peter, you were right! I will also never forget a day spent with the English traditional singer Shirley Collins as she recalled her early song-catching trips out to the Appalachian mountains with Alan Lomax.

My musical education owes a great debt too to Fairport Convention who first introduced me – though I didn't know it at the time – to the music of Johnny Cash and the Greenwich Village singer songwriters recast as screaming rock 'n' roll. Fairport brought the Americana sensibility into their lovely mix of celestial harmonies and twangy lead guitar, courtesy of a shy young lead guitarist who some years later with his wife Linda Thompson used to pepper their acoustic sets with all kinds of obscure country classics. Though both have performed wonders since, that pairing is still sadly missed – and unlikely ever to be reconvened – except that I hear their influence in all kinds of current American music.

And thanks finally, of course, to Ashley Hutchings, the first Englishman I ever saw in a bootlace tie, and who, with one of the earliest of his Albion bands, played a great live version of Leon Payne's 'Don't Make It 54'. Little did I know that 30 years on I'd be writing a book about such wonderful stuff. And still spending at least half my spare time listening to it.

Introduction

'As I travel through this world of woe/with a bible and a gun.'

– Jason Rindenberg

A Sense Of Place

Born and raised in Austin, the State Capital of Texas, Nanci Griffith is a bit musically mixed up, which makes her records and live gigs all the more interesting. Brought up on '60s psychedelia, as her parents were friends with Roky Erickson, as a teenager she fell in love with The Clash. Nanci's own music developed into a polite blend of country and folk, but with something haunted just below the surface. It is a surprisingly common musical trajectory for many of the artists who now comprise the worlds of 'Americana' and 'alt country'.

South By Southwest is full of such strange musical journeys. It traces a series of concentric circles, all united by one thing, an antipathy to what has become the dead hand of the Nashville country-music industry. And the basic plot, time and time again, is of contemporary musicians delving back into the past to make something brave and new and strange.

South By Southwest centres on a whole geography of places, and the sounds that are part of their musical landscape, each as distinct as a regional accent. Later in this book we will be circling America on a kind of magical mystery tour. There is old-time music from Appalachia, there is that typically Texan blend of the outlaw mentality and twangy guitars, with something even more indefinable creeping in from the desert and across the Mexican border, there is soul music from Memphis – and the real Nashville – plus some mighty strange transplants reared in the urban wastelands of LA, Chicago and the East Coast. If there is a common denominator, it is something powerful and mysterious arising from the no-hope towns and the forgotten enclaves of the West and the tin tabernacles and back porches of the hills – from the still-beating heart of old, weird America.

As Nanci Griffith puts it, 'In Texas and New Mexico we feel we're from the Southwest, not the South. Texas is more rebellious and renegade.' So, in their own ornery way, are the Blue Ridge Mountains. This book zigzags between the two: Jimmie Rodgers and The Carter Family, rockabilly and bluegrass, country rock and mountain harmonies, cowpunk and newgrass, alt country and 'old time'. From hillbillies and singing cowboys right up to Ryan Adams and Gillian Welch. And then finds that, at the core of their being, they are all one.

Austin's Annual Music Festival

But 'South By Southwest' is also the name of an annual 'Music and Media Conference and Festival', first held in 1987 in Austin, Texas, Nanci Griffith's home town. Taking place in mid-March, it was originally a modest attempt to highlight regional talent. The word 'festival' now hardly describes it. This is a showcase for Americana, and much else besides. There are over a thousand live gigs – both as part of the official festival and as fringe events, plus talks, workshops, discussion groups and record-industry receptions, all packed into just one week.

In 1993 'South By Southwest' added a film festival, and the parent event has gradually grown to a crowded week of the utmost importance to the roots music industry. One of its instigators, Roland Swenson, now comments that, 'We helped expand the world's view of Austin as a place that was mostly about country music to something different. It's unusual to have 40 different nightclubs that all book original music without bad mouthing each other. I can't really think of another place like that.'

But things move on. Brent Grulke, currently Creative Director, added that Texas-based roots music by the likes of Willie Nelson and Lucinda Williams – whose joint show was one of the highlights of the 2003 event – was once the only kind of music SXSW was designed to showcase.

'Now it's just part of an expanding mix of sounds emerging from the Texas capital.' Also included are Latin acts and DJs. 'The overall Austin music scene is fundamental to the success of "South By Southwest".'

As to the industry conference, 'The music biz is in freefall, but for indie labels specialising in music typically ignored by the majors, these are boom years. Probably because the majors are having such a tough time, the indies have been able to find niches.' Most of these niches are the ones we are going to cover in the later chapters of this book.

In 2002 Jeanne Fury visited the *NY Rock* website and was most impressed by The Boggs. 'The backwater-blues band combined deep wailing and moaning with some of the most impressive finger-pickin' guitar and banjo this side of the Delta. Oh Brother, thou art from Brooklyn.' 'Buzz names' that year, neither alt or old country, were Norah Jones and the Yeah Yeah Yeahs, both of whom have gone on to worldwide fame.

The keynote address in March 2003, which kicked off the event, was by Daniel Lanois. When Lucinda Williams spoke some years earlier, her theme was perseverance and that everyone should ride the 'little bumps in the road'. 'South By Southwest' officially opens with inductions into the Austin Music Hall of Fame. Nominees for 2003 included the challenging singer/songwriter Eliza Gilkyson, while live highlights of included Clem Snide, Tony Joe White at Antone's, Ray Benson at the Austin Music Hall, Chris Knight at BD Riley's, the Gourds, Alejandro Escovedo and the Derailers taking part in free open-air events at the Town Lake Stage – near the Congress Avenue Bridge. Willie Nelson, Lucinda Williams and The Jayhawks, all of them with new albums to promote on the Lost Highway label, take turns to share a rowdy stage at the Austin Music Hall; and if three acts encompass this book, it is them, especially as between sets the massive video screens played Johnny Cash's almost unbearably poignant 'Hurt'.

Sylvie Simmonds reported back on the evening for *Mojo*. 'The Jayhawks were previewing *Rainy Day Music*, which actually owes more to The Beatles than to Americana, but the real crowd pleasers were songs from earlier, and more twangy albums like *Tomorrow The Green Grass*. The Music Hall is a standing-only venue, just the place to see live music at its best – with queues of hopeful punters still trying to get in.

Lucinda Williams was introduced by hippie veteran Wavy Gravy with the immortal words, 'Fuck Woodstock, man, I get to introduce one of the great singer/songwriters of our age' and she quit the stage some 50 minutes later, snarling 'Welcome to the music business. Music and business have somehow managed to come together and fuck each other – but thank you, you're the only reason I'm doing this.' Now that's what I call Americana, the very obverse of Music Row's patent insincerity. Lucinda's music is made-to-match, 'full-on sexy' and ranging through the emotions, 'between slow, sultry "Ventura" – Williams' drowsy voice smeared over the mellow melody – and big-mama belting hellfire blues "Atonement", or country rock ballad "People Talking" and full-on sexy "Righteously"'.

Willie Nelson might be almost 70 years old, but he comes on stage after midnight and performs for two-and-a-half hours with his five-piece band. Willie's 800-acre farm is just down the road and if anyone counts as a naturalised inhabitant of Austin it is him: after all, it was his move here in 1971, and the massive 4th July 'Picnics' he established that helped Austin's rise to musical prominence. He opens, as ever, with 'Whiskey River', and covers songs by the likes of Bob Wills and Kris Kristofferson, while keeping self-written classics like 'Crazy' with his jazzy inflections, and those wonderfully soulful acoustic guitar breaks, which Nelson tosses off as if in his sleep. Simmonds captures exactly the look of the man, as important as the music in defining Americana, 'dressed, hat to boots, in black, plaits grazing his waist, a cross between a Mount Rushmore sculpture and a road-tanned Patti Smith'. Needless to say, the place erupts as soon as Willie sets foot on stage.

No single human being could take in every event at 'South By Southwest', but Mac Randall tried to sum up the mayhem for *Word*. He finds Austin a madhouse, 'thronged with indie-rock geeks, hip-hoppers in track suits, cowboy-hatted yokels and countless halter-top wearing femmes fatales'. Walking down East Sixth Street is like listening to eight radios all on full blast, and at 2am, when the bars close, the crush on the street climbs to comic proportions. He recalls seeing Tom Waits here in 1999 at the old and 'lavishly appointed' State Theatre as being transcendent, and plunges into a series of gigs in theatres, nightclubs, bars and backyards.

Among the highlights is the 'impassioned, intelligent roots rock' of Alejandro Escovedo. Another is the traditional Bloodshot Records party from noon to six, held at Yard Dogwith, which is accessible through a boutique, with virtually their entire roster playing 30-minute sets. The excitement of this crowded week is best captured on the many breathless websites devoted to audience reports. One of the best comes from Duke University, whose Greg Bloom reports that, for a host of anonymous bands, whether invited or not, this is 'their best chance to be seen and hopefully signed to a deal'. Every journalist is scrambling to discover the next White Stripes. 'Though it is guitar-centric, "indie-rock" doesn't begin to describe the variety – hardcore punk and heavy metal, singer/songwriter pop, traditional country and others that are rather indescribable. Last year's hit was Petty Bookah, a Japanese girl duo with grass skirts and ukeleles. We spent 20 minutes just looking for a place without music blaring.'

There is now a sister festival, 'North By Northeast', held in Toronto in late Spring, but there is something about Austin, a cosmopolitan city with thousands of students and old hippies among its population, located symbolically between Dallas and the Alamo, and a hotbed of radicals and free thinkers in a state best known for its traditional values. The city is crammed with live-music venues for the other 51 weeks of the year, from Threadgills to the Broken Spoke, though the legendary Armadillo is now long gone. As we will see, Austin has a long and proud tradition of music making, and of going its own way, creatively.

Americana

'South By Southwest' indicates something profound playing under the surface of the music industry. The Americana Music Association was set up in 1999 as a pressure point for 'real' music in the USA, in its own jargon 'a professional trade organisation whose mission is to provide a forum for the advocacy of Americana music, to promote public awareness of the genre and to support the creative and economic viability of professionals in this field'.

Since March 2003, the AMA has produced a weekly 'Americana' airplay chart, and hosts an annual conference in Nashville, enemy territory in many ways. No less than Johnny Cash was among the guests last year. It also hosts a musical showcase for the best of roots music at 'South By Southwest': the 2003 line-up included Rosie Flores and Ray Wylie Hubbard. A Lifetime Achievement award went to T-Bone Burnett, whose work has ranged from playing on Dylan's *Rolling Thunder* tour to putting together the musical soundtrack for *O Brother, Where Art Thou?* The inaugural President's Award, as chosen by Grant Alden of the peerless *No Depression* magazine, went to the late Doug Sahm, one of Austin's finest sons.

Grant and the AMA are also responsible for planning a series of compilation CDs, each titled *This Is Americana* and each put together by a small and vital record label. *Volume One* comes courtesy of Sugar Hill, and runs the gamut from Doc Watson to the Gourds. Alden asks himself what exactly is 'Americana', and even if 'we tend to run quickly from the room when asked for that endlessly troublesome definition', this album is 'offered as the beginning of an answer'.

The whole series should stack up as a multi-volume anthology, and this CD alone encompasses 'alt rock' and bluegrass, hillbilly boogie and driving country rock and new old timey. Exactly which artists can be rightly termed 'Americana', and which can't is certainly less a matter of place of origin than of state of mind.

Definitions

Justin Tubb once defined Americana as 'the music of the working man, the farmer, the trucker, the factory worker'. The dictionary definition of 'Americana' is a plural noun describing 'things associated with the United States', but it is far more specific than that.

The fine-art photographer Holly Pedlovsky, who teaches at Yale but spends much of her time taking haunting images of ancient stone angels in Torcello ('old Europe') reckoned in an e-mail to me during the Iraq crisis that I was 'the only guy on the planet these days to want to know more about Americana. When I hear the word I think of plastic Jesuses and US flags on every mailbox, and I want to reach for my revolver.'

But 'Americana' tends to have a more specialist meaning – that of the folklore and history of the United States. And that in turn reflects the landscapes and people who create it. You need look no further than Ornette Coleman's orchestral suite *Skies Of America*. At times bracingly atonal, at others spirited and lush, it homes in on an epic grandeur that you will also find in photographs by Ansel Adams, or the epic poetry of Walt Whitman, or the movies of John Ford. The sense of endless vistas, of a new land in which the sky is the limit, matched by a kind of folksy tolerance of others. The key word is optimism, which is the quality I most admire about the Americans I meet in England. As Ornette writes in his sleeve notes, for all the suppression of its original inhabitants, the racial wars, drugs, assassinations , there is a 'goodness' too, a country that has 'the essence of mankind and the blessing of the skies'.

The guitarist Michael Chapman is a proud Yorkshireman, but he named one of his finest albums of guitar instrumentals *Americana*. It evokes the landscape of the Southern States, as experienced on a recent road trip, as one review puts it 'from the swamplands of the South via roadhouses and food shacks, trying to find the town of Unclear, Texas'.

But we need to focus in even more closely. The defining mood of what is now usually described as 'Americana' – in purely musical terms – is something deep and folksy and slightly creepy, about family and nostalgia and blood and sex and religious faith and death. By itself that would be well nigh unbearable, but there is a matching and extremely deadpan sense of humour, born of fatalism and all the funnier for it.

This is down-home music, intimate – sometimes too intimate, or too close to home – and often sung close to the mic. It can be played on loud guitars – often slightly out of tune or at the very least 'twangy' – or on instruments as ancient as the hills. It is music that needs close attention. It often sounds bare, or rough around the edges. It is never merely for effect. Like the instrumentation, the lyrics are always interesting, never over-sophisticated and often downright weird. 'Americana' is kinda twisted. It is the opposite of contemporary Nashville and its heartless gloss. Real music for real people, in an uncertain time.

Leon Payne

As an example, what could be better than Leon Payne's LP *Americana: Rare Ballads And Tall Tales*, released in 1963 on Starday, as part of their 'Country-Sacred-Bluegrass-Western-Old Time INTERNATIONAL from Nashville, Tennessee, the Musical Heart of America.' This is the kind of music that contemporary Nashville would throw in the trash, It now sounds very much of its time. Even so, it still entertains, and is an early and brave attempt to put music to the history and legends of the South.

Payne was the blind songwriter whose creepy song 'Psycho' was memorably covered by Elvis Costello. Leon also wrote 'Lost Highway', which is cause for his immortality. The session musicians here, who jog trot through these songs as if half asleep, include Wayne Moss on 'open-gut string guitar'. He later played on *Blonde On Blonde*, proof in action of how this music mutates and yet stays the same.

Payne's songs deal with the likes of Butch Cassidy (who'd 'pillage each village'), Sam Houston, Billy the Kid and Daniel Boone. He narrates one song in the role of Joe Lopez: as he writes on the sleeve almost half of the men who led the 'Texas revolution' were Mexican by 'birth, race, religion and culture. Texas is proud of her Latin American descendants'.

The most memorable song here is 'Don't Make It 54', a plea to John Wesley Hardin not to kill any more victims. 'He removed men from temptation, but he done it Texas style.' Leon sings lines like 'He had a method, but he was no Methodist' – totally deadpan, which makes them all the funnier. Conversely, the creepy 'Cory Belle' is a murder ballad that dates back to the time when 'rails were laid across the Nebraska prairie', sung in a disturbingly soft voice. It ends with a threat that if anyone hurts poor dead Cory, he will 'send his soul to hell'.

Overviews

Forty years on, 'Americana' is a marketing term, in its own right, though no-one has ever precisely pinned down what kinds of music it encompasses. Let's look at some of the best recent compilations to employ the term. *Both Sides Now, The Spirit Of Americana* is the most adventurous, a wonderful double CD that dwells on such alt-country mavericks as Josh Rouse and the Silver Jews, and Jay Farrar who started the ball rolling with Uncle Tupelo. We go from Bob Dylan's invocation of the rural blues of Charley Patton to the crooning of Raul Malo and the smoochy oddness of Lambchop. But look a little deeper, and you have the quiet psychedelia of Mercury Rev, the driving blues rock of Wiskey Biscuit and the LA cynicism of Warren Zevon. Let alone Norwegian postman St Thomas, the Be Good Tanyas from Vancouver, Manchester's Grand Drive, and Big Steve Arlene, who got closest to the prairie on the 'Lincolnshire flatlands where he grew up'.

Global Roots Americana is a 'collection of classic American songsmiths', which ranges from Joan Baez to Lone Justice, Joni Mitchell to John Stewart, Edie Brickell to Robbie Robertson. I would argue that the former of each pair has nothing to do with Americana by any known definition, whereas the latter represent its breadth. Again, the likes of Vince Gill and Don Williams are, to my mind, strictly Nashville not Americana, indeed the very kind of artist Americana would run a mile from, while the likes of Tom T Hall can happily encompass both. It is something to do with storytelling, and staying true to one's roots.

Uncut magazine issued three 'state of the art' compilations all labelled *Sounds Of The New West*, although the first is subtitled 'The Best Of Alternative Country' – and lives up to its billing – and the two issued this century have changed this term to 'The Best Of Americana'. The artists on all three remain much the same, only the category used to describe them has changed. There is a shared spirit, if only that each artist inhabits their own weird and unique inner world.

So, if the marketing terms can't be trusted, we need to look briefly at some of the myths and archetypes behind 'Americana.' Extremely briefly, I promise. Then a rapid run through how its music evolved, from Appalachian ballad singers through Nashville in the '50s, Haight Ashbury in the '60s and LA in the '70s to the 'big bang' (early '80s) when punk rock fused with old-style country to form something new. Two of the architects of that music appear on *Both Sides Now*, Steve Earle and Jason Rindenberg of The Nashville Scorchers. But they are the tip of the iceberg.

1 Roots

'For a transitory enchanted moment, man must have held his
breath in the presence of this continent, face to face for the last
time in history with something commensurate with his capacity
for wonder. His dream must have seemed so close. He did not
know that it was already behind him, somewhere back in that
vast obscurity beyond the city, where the dark fields of the
republic rolled on under the night.'

– *F Scott Fitzgerald: The Great Gatsby*

i) Making Tracks

A steam train winding its way across a prairie landscape is one of the
central images of Americana. Oddly reassuring, with human ingenuity
conquering this 'vast obscurity', yet also slightly foreboding. People look
very small, set against a continent. Here lies danger, a hint of the supernatural, as in Elvis Presley's 'Mystery Train', or the Grateful Dead's engine
driver 'Casey Jones' as he thunders along the tracks, high on cocaine.

In the movies, the coming of the railway marks the point when
civilisation comes to town, bringing the rule of law and family values to
what was previously a place for outlaws and misfits. And yet to take a
train ride is to visit another place from here – even if, as with Hitchcock's
Strangers On A Train, it is a ride into nightmare. It links us with one of
the deepest mythic archetypes, the journey of the soul.

Compare the sleeve note to Hank Snow's concept LP *Railroad Man*:
'No matter how fast man travels, nothing will ever replace the peaceful
reassurance of a lonesome whistle crooning through the night' with Bob
Dylan's notes on the back cover of *Highway 61 Revisited*, 'on the slow

train, time does not interfere'. The spookier side of rail history is rich
with its own folklore, hence numbers here like 'The Crazy Engineer',
'Ghost Trains', and 'The Wreck Of The Number Nine'.

Johnny Cash's concept album from 1960, *Ride This Train: A Stirring
Travelogue Of America In Story And Song* does not celebrate the steam
locomotive just for itself but as a vehicle to take him on an imaginary
journey through rural America. Cash takes stock of its history and culture
and the people who are building this nation. 'I'm a million different
people, from all over the world.' He changes persona for each deep-
voiced spoken monologue, as an intro for each song: there are subtle
differences in the way he sings each one, just dragging a note long enough
to make it personal. We visit a Kentucky miner, the outlaw John Wesley
Hardin, a young Oregon lumberjack – and inhabit each from the inside.

It is remarkable how the young Cash can so convincingly portray a
child at a county fair, a cotton planter, or an Irish immigrant to Iowa –
he seems to get right inside their skins. He creates a marvellous portrait
of a new country, rough and alive and full of romance, which melds the
varied races who come to settle into their new identity, Americans all.

'Ride this train up and down a strange, wonderful land.' Cash lovingly
recites the place names of this new world, and does not forget either the
original population, 'already millions of people living in teepees along
the rivers', and puts their names to the same rhythm as the train he is
travelling on, like a poem. He feels assured enough to update a traditional
song for his own 'Dorraine Of Ponchartrain', about an Acadian settler
in Louisiana who falls in love with a Creole girl, or to turn 'Old Paint'
into his own 'Slow Rider'. The end result is 'markedly grown-up and
gutsy for a man who had forged his popularity in teenish rockabilly'.*

Merle Haggard's nostalgic elegy for steam engines, *My Love Affair
With Trains*, sums up why Americana is so compelling, 'The train is
called America, your ticket is a dream.'

There are other archetypes that help define America, none more potent
than the idea of a life out on the range. On his latest album *Shining
Brother, Shining Sister*, the Scottish singer Jackie Leven writes a lament
for Dusty, a small-scale heroin dealer in North London, who dreams of
escaping to the prairies. He took out a large amount of heroin powder

* *No Depression*

and spread it out on a mirror. 'With a razor blade he organised it into what he described as a desert landscape, with a little cabin (a razor blade) at one end of the mirror and with a small town (two matchboxes) at the other.' He plans to move to America and sit out on his porch watching the setting sun. A week later, Dusty is shot dead in Kilburn High Road.

'Heroin Dealer Blues' ends with a snatch of the song 'I Wish I Was A Cowboy', performed by SE Rogie, a 'palm-wine guitarist' from Sierra Leone, and laid down in a tiny African studio sometime during the 1960s. Rogie tells his mother that his chosen career is 'roaming with my guitar all day, with the prettiest women around me, singing my little cowboy songs'. His parents are horror struck, until a letter arrives offering him 'thousands of dollars outright' to do just that. The family celebrates. Rogie sings with a sweet conviction, accentuating all the 'wrong' words. A fantasy – like Dusty's vision – but for that brief spell, normal time stops.

The cowboy really came into his own after the Civil War, and owes much to the Spanish rancheros of New Mexico. On *Ballads Of The True West*, Johnny Cash followed western trails in his Jeep and by foot, sleeping under mesquito bushes and in gullies. 'I heard the timber wolves, looked for golden nuggets in old creek beds, sat for hours in an ancient Indian burial ground, breathed the West wind, and heard the tales it tells only to those who listen.' The result is Johnny talk-singing stuff like 'Stampede', 'Mean As Hell' and 'Bury Me Not On The Lone Prairie'.

This sense of foreboding and transcendence is a counterpart of the 'high lonesome sound' of mountain music. It is there too in *The Great Gatsby*, as urban and 'sophisticated' a novel as you could find. It is there in the music of Bruce Springsteen, a man born and raised in New Jersey. A songwriter obsessed with being trapped in his own back yard, and then the unbearable excitement of escape. But to what?

Both the Wild West and the Appalachians, with their murder ballads and blood feuds, are landscapes defined by violence. The landscapes of the West – real or imagined – echo through the lyrics and music of 'alt country', just as the revival of 'old time' dwells in the Appalachians of the mind. It is in the timbre of the voice, or the rhythms of the music – Will Oldham rather than Willie Nelson, terror rather than grace. And it was there from the start of American popular music.

ii) Old Time Music

In 1916, when the songcatcher Cecil Sharp first visited the Southern Appalachians he travelled between remote mountain hollers by pony and trap, and later wrote that 'although the people are so English, they have their American quality. They own their own land, and have done so for three to four generations, so that there is none of the servility that unhappily is one of the characteristics of the English peasant'. Such praise was unusual for a people more usually referred to as 'mountain whites' or 'poor white trash' at the time.

Sharp and his assistant Maud Karpeles were treated with great hospitality. He noted down songs and dance steps, and his account of the expedition seems oddly dreamlike, as if this upper-class Englishman had been entranced by rural Americana. During an 'American Square Dance', 'the moon streamed fitfully in, lighting up the mountain peaks, casting its mysterious light, seeming to exaggerate the wildness and break-neck speed of the dancers, as they whirled through the mazes of the dance'.

Practically all the songs collected by Sharp can be traced to English or lowland-Scots sources, but in the Appalachian mountains they have become something new, 'more austere, possibly less mellow, but no less beautiful... Many of the tunes have a primordial intensity of expression, which strikes at the very root of our being.' Here is the first written account of the high, lonesome sound that later moved on through blue-grass to the soundtrack of *O Brother, Where Art Thou?*, and on to the airwaves of the world.

Cecil Sharp went on to collect the cream of his findings in *English Folk-Songs From The Southern Appalachians*, two volumes of prime Americana. He writes these are the produce of people 'immune from that continuous, grinding, mental pressure due to the attempt to make a living, from which nearly all of us in this modern world suffer'. Tell that to Dolly Parton, who has written many songs about her own impoverished rural childhood. It does explain, though, why the likes of Gram Parsons, Mike Seeger and Gillian Welch plunged back from their existence as students at some of America's best universities to devote their working lives to updating this music, and the lifestyle it encompasses.

In the careers of all three, we can see further confirmation of Sharp's theory of Continuity, Variation and Selection, as his explanation of the way that folk songs evolve. Of 16 variants of 'Little Musgrave And Lady Barnard', collected during this trip, the most fascinating is that performed by Doc Pratt of Knott County, in which the tiny adulterer is invited to 'strike the very first lick'. Having chopped off his errant wife's head, Lord Darnel 'stove it' against the ground. Most startling of all are the lines 'it's just my uncle's negroes/herding my sheep to the barn', which certainly appear in none of the Scottish versions.

Things have moved on again from Cecil Sharp's time, and the song was put to a subtle rock beat by Fairport Convention, while its US variant 'Shady Groves' was recorded 20 years on, by the Blood Oranges as a crunchy slice of electric folk rock, with Thompson-esque lead guitar.

Here is a songbag still available for re-interpretation. 'The Death Of Queen Jane' gives birth to Bob Dylan's 'Queen Jane Approximately', and 'Gone To Cripple Creek' to The Band's song of almost the same title, and same sense of happy contentment: 'gone…to have some fun'. And here is just the kind of down-home surrealism that will resurface in the *Harry Smith Anthology* as country blues, and the Basement Tapes as drugged humour. 'Sally in the garden was shifting sand, all upstairs with the hog-eyed man.' Pure innuendo. Scholars have since found that many of the ballads that Sharp collected were not unique to the southern Appalachians, as he himself thought. Many have also since emerged in New England and the plains of Mississippi and Texas.

Cecil Sharp divided the songs he found in into ballads, songs, hymns, nursery songs, jigs and 'play-party games', while scholars like Francis Childs identified other forms too. Broadsides were an early, cheap form of printed literature, the equivalent of popular newspapers today. They were often told by a narrator – 'My name is Daniel Martin/I'm borned in Arkansas' – they related a real-life event, usually a murder or a hanging, with a moral drawn at the end. It was a technique honed to genius by Woody Guthrie. The form is as old as speech, and can be traced right up to something as contemporary as Steve Earle's 'Ballad Of John Walker'.

In the middle of the 19th century, 'The Buck's Elegy' appears as a broadside, set in Covent Garden, about a young gentleman who dies from a sexually transmitted disease. When the song crosses the Atlantic, and travels West, it becomes known as 'The Dying Cowboy'. Sharp notes down a version in 1918 in Bedford County, Virginia as 'St James Hospital', where the young man dies after a bar-room brawl. The same plotline becomes the blues song 'St James Infirmary'. Over in the logging camps of Pennsylvania, it becomes 'The Wild Lumberjack'. In 1957, the folk singer Rosalie Sorrels tapes a variant, which her husband has learnt from a colleague in the telegraph industry. 'The Lineman's Hymn' has the hero ask six 'splicers' helpers to mud-in my grave'. By now the whole thing is an in-joke, but it retains some of the original chill, with a young man facing his funeral, 'all wrapped up in white linen, and cold as the clay'.

When Maud Karpeles returned to the Appalachians 40 years later she found that much had changed. 'The log cabins have nearly all disappeared. People no longer ride mule-back, but they go spinning along the roads in motor cars. The serpent, in the form of the radio, has crept in, bearing its insidious hill-billy and other pop songs.' The term 'Hillbilly' first appeared in print at the turn of the century, to describe inhabitants of the southern backwoods. When Al Hopkins' string band was recording for Ralph Peer, in 1925, and were asked for a suitable name for the group, Al answered 'Call the band anything you want. We are nothing but a bunch of hillbillies from North Carolina and Virginia anyway.' Their publicity shots play on this, with overalls, funny hats and neckerchiefs.

Maud Karpeles despaired too soon. Collectors in the '60s like Mike Seeger, Frank Warner and Alan Lomax who trawled these same hills found much the same songs as Sharp, still as part of a living tradition. Now on magnetic tape, not just music transcriptions, Dock Boggs' 'Sugar Baby', Frank Proffitt Jr's 'Pretty Polly' and Norman Edmond's 'Bonaparte's Retreat' fuelled a new generation of ballad singers, swapping songs in the pastures of Harvard or the confines of New York's Washington Square.

Jacques Vassal once described the hillbilly style as a 'nasal tone in a constricted and high-pitched accent. The final syllables of each line are often stretched out and exaggerated to produce an effect that is partly comical, partly insistent.' Adding to the strangeness are 'cries in the form of yodels, common to certain mountain peoples of Europe, as in the Tyrol, designed to exploit the echo effects produced by the mountains.'

The singer Jean Ritchie is a bona-fide traditional singer, and wrote a beautiful account of growing up in Viper, Perry County. She was the youngest of 14 children, and 'there weren't even any instruments, we didn't even have a dulcimer. In the old days they just sang'. This was partly due to a fear that banjos or fiddles were 'instruments of the devil'.

In the spiritual wake of the 'Great Awakening', travelling evangelists would teach the word of God at huge outdoor meetings. This impetus spread. All-day 'singing conventions' would be held at the local court-house, a tradition now taken up by bluegrass festivals. Further back still, a collection of 'shape-note' tunes published in Georgia (1844) and titled 'The Sacred Harp' gave its name to a whole tradition. These are songs that can still pierce the heart, and that were sung at maximum volume.

Settlers brought the fiddle over from Europe in the late 17th century. Distinct fiddling styles evolved in different regions, and players were in great demand for dances, which would often follow 'work gatherings' or 'moonlights'. Some fiddlers sang as they played, or called out the dance steps, a tradition carried on by the eccentric Jon Hartford.

Another instrument best associated with America, the banjo, probably came over from Africa. Early examples still survive, made out of groundhog skins. A fifth string was added in the 1830s, by the minstrel entertainer Joel Sweeney – this variant became closely identified with mountain music, to 'lend pathos to a lonely lament, or give driving excitement to the wild hoedown'.*

Originally an upmarket instrument, the guitar became widely available in the States through mail-order firms like Sears Roebuck. The dulcimer probably came over with German immigrants, while the mandolin arrived with its Italian owners. As to the autoharp, it was originally a child's toy. From such unpromising material, untutored musicians virtually off the map in the rural USA began to evolve a music that now sounds even more remote and savage than the wildest country blues.

By the early 20th century, Southern musicians, often members of the same family, had begun to form adhoc string bands, usually fiddle, banjo and guitar. The savagery of such music, made by combos with names like Walker's Corbin Ramblers, still crackles out on historic 78rpm singles. It is music just caught on the brink of recorded history. Communal music,

* Bill Malone

but like a mad thing released. It is easy to read back into it the pulse behind early rock 'n' roll, or the anarchy of punk. There is a driving quality that seems to have come from nowhere, which can be traced on as a direct line through Hank Williams, Gram Parsons and Uncle Tupelo – with a sideswerve into Bill Monroe – and beyond.

In the early 1920s, US record companies began to seek out the ethnic music of their own homeland. Texan fiddler Eck Robertson turned up at Victor Records in New York in June 1922, and his solo version of 'Sallie Gooden' is still startling. Texan singer Marion Slaughter took the name Vernon Dalhert and sold a million copies of 'The Wreck Of The Old 97' – followed up by other tales of railway disaster, like the childrens' favourite 'The Runaway Train'. His voice now sounds corny, but the performance, with jew's harp solo and a convincing train whistle, has enough verve and bounce to make it a keystone of Americana. Meanwhile New York-based talent scout Ralph Peer had gone off in the reverse direction, and in June 1923 recorded the much more 'authentic' sound of Fiddlin' John Carson in a portable studio he had set up in Atlanta.

Carson was in his 50s, born and bred in Georgia, where he had won many 'old-time' fiddling contests, and Peer's view of his voice and violin scraping as 'pluperfect awful' has gone down in history. Even so, an original pressing of 500 copies of 'The Little Old Log Cabin In The Lane', backed on the 78rpm shellac with 'The Old Hen Cackled And The Rooster's Going To Crow' sold out within a month. Not for the last time, the public displayed a taste for 'the sort of music that people really wanted to hear sung by one of themselves instead of the dreary crooners and dance band versions foisted on them by record companies'.* Nothing changes. Suddenly hillbilly was firmly on the national agenda. Just to list some of Fiddlin' John's repertoire of tunes – 'Cotton Eyed Joe', 'Old Joe Clark', 'Fire In The Mountain', 'Turkey In The Straw' – is to hear the sound of history. His version of 'When The Saints Go Marching In' is joyful with lots of scrapey fiddle, until you listen more closely to lyrics and realise that it is about the end of the world.

In the wake of Carson, several singles appeared that demonstrate the wildness and grace of mountain music. Photographs of the musicians show them sitting, stiff as boards, with shoes well polished and ties tight

* Folk Roots

25

on the collar. Only the presence of fiddles and banjos and harmonicas and mandolins and cellos and mountain dulcimers, mostly held like weapons, indicate that these men are set to unleash musical mayhem.

The Cornshucker's Frolic: Downhome Music And Entertainment From The American Countryside mixes and matches white and black performers. Here are the likes of the Red Headed Fiddlers, Walter Coon and his Joy Boys and the Binkley Brothers Dixie Clodhoppers. This is a stream that has constantly refreshed successive generations of musicians.

Freeny's Barn Dance Band features two cousins on duelling fiddles, and there's an unsettling series of gruff shouts, directing the dancers. Stoneman's Blue Ridge Cornshuckers open with a bit of staged banter, so full of ancient slang that it could be in a foreign language. In comes the fiddle of Uncle Eck Dunford and the banjo of George Stoneman, with 'Pop' on mouth-harp and guitar, and what sounds like somebody else kicking an old fence. A woman shouts out from another room, 'Don't break that light', and they all swing into 'Love Somebody'.

In comparison, Bascar Lunsford has a voice as deep as the ocean but full of joy, and set to a rippling banjo so that the love song 'Kidder Cole' is as happy as could be. There seem to be no barriers between the singer's inner emotion and the music he produces. This is music without self-consciousness. Listen to a performance like 'All Night Long' by Earl Johnson's Clodhoppers, where everyone sounds drunk – the lyrics are about a wild night on the tiles – with queasy fiddle and a wild woman on backing vocals to match, and the whole thing taken at an unfeasibly rapid lick. It is exhilarating and strangely primitive. The only live bands I have seen who compare would be The Damned doing 'New Rose' or The Clash on their *White Riot* tour.

Another trawl of rural musical talent took Ralph Peer to Bristol, Tennessee in August 1927. He discovered two new acts. Between them they helped to define American music – The Carter Family showing where it had come from, and Jimmie Rodgers where it could go to, if it dared.

AP Carter came from Maces Spring in rural Virginia, at the heart of the Southern Appalachians. As a fruit-tree salesman, he used his travels to search for material, noting down traditional folk songs like 'Cowboy Jack' and 'Rambling Hobo' then reworking them for mass consumption.

Any great 'traditional' folk singer – Martin Carthy comes to mind – quietly reshapes and rewrites their apparently timeless material. Carthy is fond of saying that the only bad thing you can do to this music is to ignore it: otherwise anything is possible. However much you bend it out of shape, 'it bends back'. Among the grateful recipients of such rewritten classics from this archetypal Londoner, have been prime exponents of Americana from Dylan to Cordelia's Dad.

Unlike Carthy, AP Carter would first rewrite then copyright these songs to himself. In turn, songs like 'Will The Circle Be Unbroken' entered the popular imagination and became classics of the genre. Without The Carter family, a whole civilisation could have been lost to us. Here on crackly shellac are cowboy ditties and the blues, gospel tunes and scaffold songs, murder ballads and tunes dating from the Civil War, plus AP 's own songs written in the traditional style, so that you just can't see the join. 'Wildwood Flower' and 'Little Log Cabin By The Sea', 'Cowboy's Wild Song To His Herd', 'The East Virginia Blues' and 'See That My Grave Is Kept Green'. Americana, all sung plaintively to a rural strum.

Alvin Pleasant Carter, his (then) wife Sara and Maybelle, ten years younger than Sara and her cousin and AP's sister in law, travelled to meet Ralph Peer in AP's Model-A Ford. Maybelle was pregnant, and AP and Sara took their 8-year-old daughter and baby along. From the start, the Carters were a family affair. And the antidote to showbiz. 'They wandered in. He's dressed in overalls and the women are country women from way back there. They look like hillbillies.'* That word again.

But then Sara started to sing, and, for the big city talent scout, 'as soon as I heard Sara's voice, then I knew it was going to be wonderful'. She has the country twang, but also a haunted sound. A later review of her work noted that over time 'Sara's beautifully plaintive voice – politely exuberant on the trio's earliest recordings – gets heavier and thicker as she eases into middle age. That natural process is egged on by the fact that she was losing interest in both her musical career and her husband.'† The two are really one and the same.

It is an early example of feminism in action, with AP relegated to backing vocals and songcatching. He was a true poet though, whether adapting the old music or recreating it anew, with 'a feel for the perfect

* Ralph Peer
† *No Depression*

line that would echo down the years', with their mix of 'gospel songs, old love songs, just everything, they paved the way'.*

What still astounds is the nimbleness of Maybelle's guitar playing, and the impassive nature of Sara's vocals. Implacable, almost. As Gillian Welch, who dresses and sings like their kid sister, told *Mojo*, 'imagine how powerful it must have been to hear The Carter Family on the radio and think, "This is my music, this is speaking to me." Then to go out and buy the record and play it again. That's part of why it exploded, that people heard it and thought, "These people are singing about my life."' Just as important was Maybelle's discovery of how to pick out the melody on the lower strings of her guitar while strumming chords on the higher ones, thus inventing what Johnny Cash describes as 'the most influential guitar style in country and folk music'. And in alt country and new old time too.

We will trace The Carter Family lineage through Maybelle down through June Carter Cash, on to Rosanne – who subjects personal relationships with a rigour learnt from Sigmund Freud – to Carlene, who once claimed to have put the first syllable back into 'country' music, and whose early albums feature the best of British pub rock musicians, on the cusp of the new wave, which Carlene's own wild character exemplifies.

It is a dynasty worthy of a book in its right, and Johnny Cash devotes much of his second autobiography *Cash* to his family connections. Marrying June was his entry into the royal family of Americana. He owns The Carter Family house in Maces Spring, now on the Virginia Registry of Historic Homes. Just down the road is The Carter Family Fold, a performance space dedicated to mountain music. Cash's own band is the only unit ever allowed to use amplification there.

Cash writes with great affection of Mother Maybelle in old age 'a truly humble person, almost absurdly so'. He describes music revered by everyone from Bob Dylan to Emmylou Harris, Michelle Shocked to Gillian Welch, as 'just stuff I did a long time ago'. He also reveals that she played guitar on a couple of Jimmie Rodgers' final records, when he was not well enough to play himself.

A tribute album like *Songs Of The Carter Family*, by Jody Stecher and Kate Brislin, is more palatable listening than the originals, yet nowhere

* Gillian Welch

near as 'magnetic and hypnotic', * even if Jody is a more exuberant singer than either Sara or the others ever dared or wanted to be.

This is something different in kind to the urgency of bluegrass or indeed even the ancient modal music of Appalachia. Probably because of the 'reserve and reticence' of Sara's vocal style. It even sounds like boredom on some of the later recordings, but it might be sheer exhaustion.

So from what musical roots did the Carters themselves derive? *The Doc Watson Family* was released by Folkways as an LP in 1963, and has since been augmented on CD with many extra songs from the same recording session. In either format, it is a near-miraculous throwback to what family music gatherings must have sounded like a century ago, recorded at the same time as The Beatles were beginning their recording career. Combine the two, and you have the template for alt country. Unlike The Beatles, though, at this time all smiles and stage costumes, 12 family members gather on the front porch in their working clothes, the kids sitting down with young Doc, and the Watson elders standing behind, with fiddle, mandolin, guitar and banjo. No one is smiling.

These are not so much performances as something overheard. Things don't get much more frightening than Annie Watson's crackly 'House Carpenter', to spooky solo violin, a Child ballad she learnt in her childhood. Even the jovial, fatherly tones of Doc himself turn apocalyptic on the ancient hymn 'The Lost Soul', as the womenfolk tonelessly repeat every threat. When Dolly Greer totters up and sings 'Pretty Saro', you feel you are right at the mysterious heart of mountain music. 'I came in this country, 18 and 49, I thought myself lucky to be alive.'

Bob Dylan once talked about his own links with traditional music. 'My songs, what makes them different is that there is a foundation to them. Those old songs are my lexicon and prayer book.' As to his own successors, the likes of Bruce Springsteen right up to Beck Hansen. 'They weren't around to see the end of the traditional people – I was.'

When the call came to Jimmie Rodgers to audition in front of Ralph Peer, it was as a solo singer, just voice and acoustic guitar. On CD and DVD, he still looks and sounds contemporary: witty and sly as a possum. Jimmie was perhaps the first of the singer/songwriters, steeped equally in cowboy songs, railway lore and the blues, a man who taught Americana

* Jody Stecher

how to be literate. 'Waiting For A Train' is still a life-affirming experience, even though it exudes a deep sense of loss – it seems impossible that the man who recorded it is long in the grave. (AP Carter always seemed to sing from six-feet below.) The emotion you would usually associate with him is cheerfulness, yodelling, as if for sheer joy.

Rodgers was a self-conscious artist who recorded with jazz bands, a Hawaiian band, and Louis Armstrong. In his songs, he could adopt at will the persona of a jovial railroad man or a cheerful cowboy or a lovelorn drifter. He died young, of a disease common in the rural heartlands. 'I've been fighting like a lion, looks like I'm going to lose/'cause there ain't nobody ever whipped the TB blues'. During his final recordings (New York, 1933), he was so weak that he had to sing sitting down, and rest between takes. The next day he lapsed into a coma, and never awoke.

Bob Dylan released a tribute album on his own Egyptian label, saying that Rodgers 'may very well be the man who started it all'. Among those he reckons have been 'affected by Jimmie like no other' are Steve Earle, who provides a rowdy cover of the totally appropriate 'In The Jailhouse Now', Alison Krauss, and Iris Dement with a keening 'Hobo Bill'.

If Jimmie Rodgers took the blues into the country mainstream, then Dock Boggs took it straight down to hillbilly hell. Dock 'sounded as if his bones were coming through his skin every time he opens his mouth'.* Just look at Boggs' cold eyes in old photographs. It is a look much aimed at by various modern alt country troubadours, but this is the real thing. Dylan reckoned that Boggs' music was just about 'as deep as it gets'.

Moran Lee Boggs was born in West Norton, Virginia, and worked as a miner. His religious-minded wife regarded his banjo as an instrument of the Devil – and in Dock's hands it certainly sounds like it. Dock re-emerged in the 1960s, 'rediscovered' by Mike Seeger. The song that defines his whole repertoire is 'Oh Death', an extremely unsettling dialogue with the grim reaper: 'I'll fix your feet so you can't walk, I'll fix your mouth so you can't talk.' Dock passed over in 1971, on his birthday. He could never have even imagined that a young band of New York boys would mimic his sound, and even take over his name. But then you put on The Boggs' debut album, close your eyes, and you are slap bang in a timeless Appalachia of the mind, with all the music's ragged glory.

* Greil Marcus

The kind of spooky music made by Dock Boggs and his 1920s counterparts had gone right off the public agenda by the 1940s, when warehouses were being cleared of ancient 78s, and a few (very) odd collectors began sifting. The oddest of all was Harry Smith, and his release in 1952 of the sumptuously packaged *Anthology Of American Folk Music*, 6-LPs and a booklet, not only predated the CD box set by some 40 years, but gave this music a public authority it had never before had. This is classic Americana, distilled.

Harry Smith rescued a 'great roar of voices' from the inter-war years, many of whom, almost beyond belief, were still alive. Greil Marcus sees its release, at the height of McCarthyism, as a form of mute resistance to the cultural status quo. Its raising of lost music – and musicians – from the dead turned 'the forgotten into a collective memory'. He also notes that Smith ignored 'all field recordings, Library of Congress Archives, anything validated only by scholarship'. Harry was not some dusty folklorist, he was a cultural terrorist who had tipped the dustbin of popular taste before the Depression all over the back porch, and was picking out the strangest items. Smith erected his private horde of rare shellac into a monument to the forgotten. Here, wittily annotated and sequenced into a kind of rural soap opera, with occult significance – Rudolph Steiner and Aleister Crowley are given name checks – was a whole secret tradition of American life.

By going onto library shelves under the guise of anthropology, the *Anthology* was out there in the public domain for whoever wanted to take it as their own. Through it, a new generation of folk troubadours found a repertoire and a voice. With the *Anthology* now on CD, the music is once again ripe for recycling. Artists from Beck to Nick Cave, Freakwater to The Handsome Family, have done just that.

One of the darkest songs of the whole anthology is Bascom Lamar Lunsford's 1924 recording of 'I Wish I Was A Mole In The Ground', with its picture of a railroad man who will 'kill you if he can, and drink up your blood like wine', and of the singer wishing to 'root that mountain down'. But do not think that such primeval things came to a halt once committed to old 78s, for Harry Smith to bring back to light. Lunsford continued as a performer right up to his death in 1973, performing in front of the Queen of England at the White House, and passing the old music on to younger musicians.

Lunsford wrote 'Old Mountain Dew', about moonshine whiskey, and built up a 'memory collection' of songs from the Appalachians, which he laid down for the Library of Congress in the late '40s. Like Cecil Sharp before him, he respected the people he met on his songcatching trips. 'They are sturdy, and they are fine, and they have held on to their tradition. When you go to see a man about playing, you take your hat off. You go in there and treat them like ladies and gentlemen.'

Meanwhile, the country-music industry was moving in a new direction, away from the wellsprings of the music. The future was Nashville.

iii) Modernisers

In 1925, George D Hay moved to the Nashville station WSM, and put together a down-home variety show called the *Grand Ole Opry*. Many singers started to write their own songs, and make money from selling picture songbooks. For record-company scouts, the catchment area shifted west, and a craze for cowboy songs began. John A Lomax's *Cowboy Songs And Other Frontier Ballads* offered a large body of western folklore. It was time for acts to commercially exploit this material.

'Tex' Ritter was indeed Texan, but he studied law, not cow punching, and then became a professional actor, winning an Oscar for his appearance in *High Noon*. He was a rightly acclaimed interpreter of cowboy songs, on tracks like 'Blood On The Saddle', the weird sound of which predates the experiments of Joe Meek, as the tape is artificially speeded up and slowed down. It also gave perhaps the most extreme of all the '80s cowpunk bands a fit name to call themselves. Tex made a speciality of 'talkin' songs', with a voice like 'a lonely wind blowing across a landscape populated only by tumbleweeds, rattlesnakes and human vermin' Cue Will Oldham. 'Western' quickly replaced 'hillbilly' as a sales term.

Marty Robbins started as a teen star, but changed his image and his musical style to record three albums of tough and cinematic 'gunfighter' ballads, steeped in the folklore of the Wild West. 'El Paso' boasted

Mexican-style guitar and became the central tale of 1959's *Gunfighter Ballads And Trail Songs*, closely observed short stories set to music. Robbins credits songs like 'Billy The Kid' and 'Utah Carol' as traditional. The latter became the name of one of the best, and most obscure, alt-country acts. A later single, 'El Paso City' brought the saga up to date, with a flash forward to death.

In the '30s, old-style string bands out in the West developed a unique style by soaking up local influences, in particular the Tex-Mex. What emerged was a sound that became known as 'western swing', dominated by fiddles and guitars. By adding a polka beat, and lots of jazz, the music put on muscle: it was gutsier, sexier and with a stronger beat than early Appalachian string bands. The style was made famous by Bob Wills, founder of the Texas Playboys. He acted as bandleader, leaving lead vocals and lead fiddle to others, whooping them along in a high-pitched manner: you have a breakneck version of 'Cotton Eyed Joe' or a smooth take on 'Corrine, Corrina' next to ragtime and two-steps. Gibson had began to market their electric guitar in 1936, and Wills brought Eldon Shamblin into the band to play it, alongside a brass section, steel guitar and drums. Shamblin wrote down arrangements for this augmented line-up – again making the old new. 'You can change the name of an old song, rearrange it and make it swing'. The result was at first called 'Okie Jazz'.

When Wills came into town with his $100 boots and shiny band bus with logo on the side and steer horns on the front, the rustling sound in the background was that of country singers throwing away their dungarees. His spirit remains unquenchable, even after his death.

Darker shadows intrude on an album from Bloodshot Records of Chicago. *The Pine Valley Cosmonauts Salute The Majesty Of Bob Wills*, and its bar-room renditions and studio backchat, catch the rough-and-ready nature of Wills. Jon Langford writes on the back cover, 'Bob Wills was the first man to use drums on the *Grand Ole Opry*. When asked what he thought of rock 'n' roll – Bob said he'd been rockin' since 1928.' The presence here of alt-country stalwarts like Jimmy Dale Gilmore, Alejandro Escovedo and Robbie Fulks confirms his continuing influence.

Wills tended to play dance halls, but another new development in Texas and the rougher parts of California was the rise shortly after the repeal of Prohibition of 'honky tonks' – roadhouses selling cheap beer. For Glen Campbell, honky tonks are still 'the fightin' and dancin' clubs'. Music was more often than not supplied by jukeboxes, though those that survive are now some of the best haunts of 'real' country music.

Meanwhile, under the auspices of the Archive of American Folk-Song, John Lomax and his son Alan began to make field-recordings of traditional musicians. President Roosevelt targeted government relief into projects, which sent researchers throughout rural America to record its musical heritage in words, on tape, and on camera. Some intellectuals also began to use folk songs – the music of the people – as a tool for political change. The greatest of them all was Woody Guthrie.

However one defines Americana, Woody is one of its architects. Listen to the Library of Congress recordings , with Alan Lomax leading Woody through his memories of bootleg whisky, 'house parties' – he plays 'Old Joe Clark' and recalls the frequent fist fights – the Dust Storm of 1935, hobos and flood, labor unions and Government camps. Guthrie, born in Oklahoma, learnt traditional folksongs from his mother, then formed a hillbilly band of his own in Texas, basing his guitar style on Maybelle Carter. Even his own songs tend to be put to traditional tunes. 'This Land Is Your Land' is set to the melody of 'Little Darling, Pal of Mine'.

The young Bob Dylan, a Woody Guthrie 'jukebox', paid homage to the older man as a 'link in the chain, the same as I am to other people'. 'Tom Joad', the 17-verse retelling of the movie version of *The Grapes Of Wrath*, was written by Woody and set to the tune of the outlaw ballad 'John Henry'. This sparked off Bruce Springsteen 50 years on. But Woody was a marginal figure at this point: his album *Dust Bowl Ballads* was issued in an edition of 1,000 copies at most, though each copy was treasured. The most extraordinary resurrection, though, was when Wilco and Billy Bragg collaborated on two albums of Woody's unused lyrics, titled *Mermaid Avenue*, Woody's latter-day Coney Island home.

The problem is stripping away the air of sainthood that has been built around Guthrie and getting back to the man who was once imprisoned for sending obscene materials through the mail, and who 'every time money or fame was a handshake away, he'd get drunk at a showcase, disgrace himself, press the self-destruct button'. The Guthrie who emerges from Joe Klein's magnificent biography is much more believable (horny and streetwise and a man who didn't wash too often) than the myth. This is the Woody who rises from the Billy Bragg/Wilco collaborations, writing songs about a night of passion with a girl who might or might not have been Walt Whitman's niece, Ingrid Bergman and flying saucers – the opposite of po-faced: lustful, ironic, having fun.

Wilco's bar-room renditions second all those emotions, as do vocal contributions from Natalie Merchant, and by the time they reached the follow-up CD, released a year or so later but dipping into the same recording session, the gloves were really off. A video documentary had suggested growing creative tensions between Bragg and Jeff Tweedy, over mixes of the first album. Certainly Tweedy is far more prominent here, turning romantic on 'Someday Some Morning Sometime', while Bragg hollers out 'All You Fascists'. But Tweedy and his band mimic *Highway 61*-era Dylan on 'Feel Of Man' and Tom Waits on the chain-gang stomp of 'Meanest Man'. Wilco even transmute into The Byrds on 'Secrets Of The Sea', a superb mix of twangy guitar and rich organ chords and Tweedy singing with the utmost joy.

Guthrie's wonderful approximations of living voices in his songs intersects with the Beat poets who a decade later went much the same way, rediscovering America by getting out on the road, and sleeping rough. Just play *Mermaid Avenue Vol II* back to back with *Kicks Joy Darkness*, a tribute album to Jack Kerouac put together by the likes of Patti Smith, Michael Stipe and Morphine. It is far more wordy, but shares the same rough verbal energy and sense of urban rhythms. Sexy too.

During the war, and seemingly in another world, Bill Monroe's Blue Grass Boys had been quietly changing from the old string-band style to something new. With the addition of guitarist Lester Flatt in early 1945 and banjoist Earl Scruggs a few months later, they found it.

When Elvis Costello caught a gig in a hotel ballroom by an elderly Monroe, the angry young punk was amazed by the sheer savagery of Bill onstage, how he attacked his mandolin like a man possessed. You can hear bluegrass evolve and solidify through the 1940s, in Monroe's capable hands, into a slice of pure Americana. Just listen to an early recording like 'Dog House Blues', with yodels and (imitation) dog yelps, then compare it to the maturity of expression in 'Blue Moon Of Kentucky'.

The keynote to bluegrass is restraint. The arrangements are subtle and carefully worked out, with everyone featured but no one actually soloing. Stage clothes are Sunday-best, not flashy. Everything is subservient to the overall vibe, there's a deliberate quietness going on. Egoless music, not least in Bill's singing, which wastes no emotion yet is full of it. A subtle use of dynamics is central to bluegrass, and is achieved by the way the singer and players stand, controlling their pitch and sound by the way they approach a central microphone.

It was the revolutionary banjo playing of 22-year-old Earl Scruggs that really ignited the flame, his three-finger roll as rapid and jaw-dropping as the three-card trick. Bill Monroe later told *Acoustic Music* that 'I wanted to have a music of my own to start with where I could say I wasn't copying no man. So I went to putting different sounds, from the time I was a kid. I put some blues on it, a little bit of jazz, Scotch bagpipe, Baptist-Methodist and the Holiness way of singing in it. I really put a solid beat in it, a driving beat, so it would be different, a driving music.' His range of influence is clear from the memorial concert held in the Ryman Auditorium in 1997, with John Hartford and Dr Ralph Stanley – who would both return for the *Down From The Mountain* show – and Del McCoury, Tim O'Brien, Ricky Skaggs and Marty Stuart.

Stuart's emotive album *The Pilgrim* was inspired by the passing of Bill Monroe, together with Nicholas Dawidoff's book *In The Country Of Country*, based on interviews with the great pioneers of Americana, captured near the end of their lives. The album also samples voices like Johnny Cash, George Jones and Ralph Stanley, which help dramatise Marty's honky tonk, a drama in three acts based on a true story that involves a love triangle, steam trains, suicide, loss and redemption, and ends with a reading from Tennyson, no less, and an instrumental version of 'MrJohn Henry, Steel Drivin Man' with Earl Scruggs. The whole thing is framed by Stuart's song 'The Pilgrim', dedicated to Bill's memory.

Peter Rowan paid tribute on his album *Bluegrass Boy*. 'Bluegrass is a moment that happens, and sustaining that moment is a real challenge. The quality of bluegrass that raises the hairs on the back of your neck has always been in the music waiting to happen.' Bill was the 'ultimate

Zen-bluegrass man'. You had to 'let his fire infuse and enthuse you.' As the Appalachian singer Jean Ritchie says, 'Bill used the old music, but he invented bluegrass with it… He took the old music and made it new'.

Flatt and Scruggs soon formed their own bluegrass combo, the Foggy Mountain Boys. Earl Scruggs used his left hand to add a cascade of grace notes and, as a further trick, he would sometimes 'pinch on', simultaneously plucking two strings at once. By adding 'drone' notes, Earl learnt how to put together a flowing melody. Earl went on to heavily influence the 'newgrass' movement and played a major part in gathering the veteran contingent for The Nitty Gritty Dirt Band's *Will The Circle Be Unbroken?*

In quite a different firmament, though, is the spectral music left by two brothers from a mountain village in Virginia. Ralph and Carter Stanley could not have had more impeccable traditional roots. After the war, the Stanley Brothers recorded music that combined the influence of Bill Monroe with ancient material like 'Little Glass Of Wine', a 'murder and suicide ballad' that went down well with their hill-country audience.

Ralph's tenor voice, in the classic back-country pinched-throat style, soared over Carter's lead vocals. When they moved on to Columbia Records, Carter began to write songs that evoked loss. Typical is his 'Lonesome River': 'the lonesome wind blows and the water rolls high'. The duo recorded a surprisingly rocky 'Blue Moon Of Kentucky' shortly after Elvis, but there is no flash of teenage rebellion here. Sheer happiness is part of their world view, offsetting the gloom. Here a banjo plucks and a violin dances, and the song slows down just where Elvis speeds up.

Carter died at 41, but Ralph kept going, emphasising that 'what he sings is old-time mountain music – not bluegrass'. Ricky Skaggs explains, 'When you hear Bill Monroe you hear the fire of the music. When you hear Ralph Stanley, you hear the high lonesome sound of the mountains.'

iv) Going Electric

Over in Nashville, an industry was being built, although one that barely concerns *South by Southwest*. When Billboard changed the name of its chart from 'Hillbilly' to 'Country and Western' in 1949, it was part of a sweetening process, drawing out the music's sting. Our interest, though, is with the mavericks and the wild boys.

Merle Travis is now best known for his 'thumb-style' guitar, but when it was suggested that he should record some 'back home' folksongs, he decided instead to write his own. The results, on the solo and acoustic 1947 album *Folk Songs From The Hills* are prime Americana. The quest for God on the adapted hymn 'I Am A Pilgrim', or lyrics sung from the point of view of a miner, as his father was, on the 1962 album *Songs Of The Coal Mines* are serious, despite Merle's light and easy singing style.

Merle played a guitar built by Paul Bigsby and developed by Leo Fender: 'I got the idea from a steel guitar, I wanted the same sustainability of notes, and I came up with a solid body electric guitar with the keys all on one side.' Fender had by now perfected the Telecaster, with its piercing tone and staccato bursts like automatic gunfire, and an electric bass to match. Rickenbacker had also developed a solid-bodied guitar.

The electric guitar is well in evidence on recordings by Hank Williams. As Marty Stuart puts it, 'he's part of the fabric of America, he's as important as Miles Davis or Stephen Foster, any of those guys. Hank's there'. He grew up singing sacred music in the Baptist churches of Alabama, and that style of rural gospel singing is buried deep in his music. So is the sense of damnation. As to the old music 'It can be explained in one word, sincerity. When a hillbilly sings a crazy song, he feels crazy. When he sings "I Laid My Mother Away" he sees her a-laying right there in the coffin. He sings more sincere than most entertainers, because the hillbilly was raised rougher than most entertainers.

Hank joined the cast of a new radio show, the *Louisiana Hayride*, and shot to stardom. Hank is the first *King of Americana*. He could take the wit, sadness and vision of the best hillbilly music, and compress it to the core. When he sings 'I'll Never Get Out Of This World Alive', a fiddle scrapes and a steel guitar sobs, and Hank sounds playful, jaunty almost, with a whoop to his voice, and every syllable carefully enunciated.

As a musician, Hank was largely self-taught: 'I have never read a note or written one. I can't.' As a lyricist he was about as functionally illiterate as Shakespeare. Everybody who came after is in his debt, cutting things down to the bone. 'You Win Again' starts at a lively trot, but Hank seems to drag the pace backwards as his voice plunges deeper into melancholy, spiralling down to the word 'sin', then rhyming it with 'again'. The same voice can express pure lust too, in songs like 'Hey Good Looking'.

Hank was himself in the ballad-making tradition. 'A song ain't nothin' in the world but a story just wrote with music to it.' Emmylou Harris, thinks that 'he brought that real high lonesome sound to country music'. Which promptly mislaid it again as soon as he had gone. Long prey to a diet of booze and amphetamines, Hank passed out for good on the back seat of a car on New Year's Day 1953, on the way to yet another gig, at the age of 29. Gone, but never forgotten. Lucinda Williams, born the same month that Hank died, remembers her own father's story of how he had met Hank after a show, and Hank telling him not to drink whisky, 'cause you got a beer-drinking soul'. 'I always related to this story in a way that would help me form my view of the world, and the way my music reflected that. Hank was one of us'.

Jason Rindenberg of The Scorchers was working on his father's farm, when he heard 'Cold Cold Heart' 'coming out of the barn and...over the cornfields'. Ever since, he has included 'hopped up versions', 'to rock and roll and punk audiences all over the world, and they never fail to rock the house'. For Mike Mills of REM, 'simplicity, honesty and pain run like rusty trains through a very dark night; nobody said it like Hank Williams'.

Matt Johnson of The The came out of the London badlands like an electronic hillbilly. Matt was never a country fan. 'I wanted to come at it from the viewpoint of a guy from London a couple of generations later.' He condemns the way Nashville re-wrote Hank's life story after his death, to make him commercially palatable. The The return him to the gutter, 'I think he was a very dark guy, very intense, but sensitive and brooding.' The oddest thing is that the graveyard guitar and lonesome harmonica take these songs back to the Appalachians. 'Honky Tonkin' becomes a dirge while 'I'm A Long Gone Daddy' turns psychotic.

Hank Williams Jnr's musical tribute to his father is a lighter beast: he principally remembers his father as a practical joker. Hank Jnr had just released a hard-rocking album with Charlie Daniels and other Southern boogie-merchants, and a largely unspoken influence on the alt country that followed 20 years later. For Hank Jnr, the mid '70s were 'polarising times, and the music was cutting edge. If you listened to country music, you were a redneck, and if you listened to rock 'n' roll you were a hippie freak. So what happened to the Allman Brothers, in Macon, Georgia, was of no concern to the pickers in Nashville, Tennessee, just a couple of hundred miles up the road. But it was important to me because those Georgia boys were trying to tell me something'.

Just before the 20th century ended, Steve Earle and friends turned up at the Lisner Auditorium, Washington to perform a tribute concert to Hank – 'When Steve turns up wearing a freshly pressed shirt and looking downright respectable, you know something unusual is going on.'* Lucinda Williams and Kathy Mattea were there too, alt country and new country at their best, and Kim Richey stole the show: 'all this uptempo stuff just pisses me off when I'm in a bad mood'. She sang her own song 'Home', a gospel song in the Hank tradition.

By this time the Dark Empire was already on the rise. The chief architects of the 'Nashville Sound' were Owen Bradley and Chet Atkins: they played down the country twang, lost the banjo, and replaced scraping fiddles with mellifluous string sections. Supper club music.

Far more influential on 'alt country', 30 years down the track, was the sound being pioneered in the early '60s at Muscle Shoals, a couple of hours drive north from Nashville. Dan Penn and Spooner Oldham were white Southern boys who had grown up on a mix of Hank Williams and bluegrass. At Muscle Shoals, they began to specialise in slow bluesy ballads in 6/8 time, for the likes of Percy Sledge and Joe Simon. Gerri Hirschy saw such songs as 'part church, part hills', part of an unspoken heritage, all the weirder because, as fellow songwriter Donnie Fritts put it, 'I can't explain how the country feel crept into our songs, cos apart from a few guys like George Jones, we didn't like country music'.

The essential difference was that while Nashville musicians played 'on the beat', the Muscle Shoals style was to lay behind it a fraction. Country soul later osmosed into the likes of the Allman Brothers, 'balancing Gregg Allman's blues against Dicky Betts' bluegrass'. It is a dialogue that echoes back and forth, so that Janis Joplin started singing Carter Family songs with a bluegrass band in Austin. She ended up as a white blues shouter, having mixed in a little psychedelia on the way.

* No Depression

Other musicians were learning how to rock up country music, under another name. Bill Haley And The Comets came out of western swing to make a new sound that was 'not quite r&b, not quite hillbilly, not quite pop'. 'It's a kind of shaking, rattling and rolling music that shakes a lot of people, rattles others and rolls along all the time'. It re-emerged 25 years later, alongside cowpunk, as a back-to-the roots sound.

Meanwhile, a young country gospel fan, Elvis Presley, toured with Bill Haley, as a support act. At the Sun studio in Memphis, Sam Phillips put Elvis together with two 'hillbilly musicians' Scotty Moore (electric guitar) and Bill Black (string bass). No drums. All five of Presley's Sun singles combined a blues tune on one side and a country song on the other. On 'Blue Moon Of Kentucky', Bill Monroe's bluegrass anthem, Elvis hustles things along. He sings over the beat, around it, even inside it, and by the time he has finished bluegrass has been taken on a generation. You can still hear the ramifications, in the likes of the Bad Livers. When Johnny Cash had just signed to Sun, he was present at a Carl Perkins session when Elvis sat in on piano, 'and he was asking me if I knew any Bill Monroe songs. So a lot of those songs on there are old bluegrass things'. Bluegrass was one of the many rough edges that Presley's handlers sanded off in moulding him into an all-round entertainer.

Cash also talks about what a 'fabulous rhythm guitar player' Elvis was. Equally underrated was Buddy Holly as a lead guitarist. On his one UK tour, Buddy played his Fender louder than anyone had previously ever imagined. Fellow Lubbock boy Joe Ely likes the way that 'all the guitar leads are almost like Northern Mexican leads. That's a real Texas thing'. But Holly was even more, 'he was one of the first singer songwriters. He wrote and arranged 'em, and played guitar and sang. He kinda changed the course of music'. Holly's time in Lubbock was a 'well kept secret', but his memory fuelled a new generation of singer songwriters there too, Ely prominent among them.

Meanwhile, gospel – or something quite like it – was blessed with the sharp voices and close harmonies of the Ira and Charlie Louvin. The keystone to their vision is the 1959 album *Satan Is Real* on which the singing is interrupted with short sermons. Gram Parsons' 'Hippie Boy' is a direct parody of the title song.

Ira was killed by a drunk driver in 1965. He was a man of sudden rages who would smash his mandolin on the floor. The paradox is that the music he left is like a trip to heaven. Just listen to the sacred waltz that is 'The Christian Life', slow and stately with lovely splashes of piano. Later albums incorporated electric guitars and secular lyrics but still sound weird to modern ears, which is why so many of the alt country crowd love them. The difference is that the likes of The Handsome Family or Beck would sing lyrics like 'Dying From Home, And Lost' or 'Insured Beyond The Grave' with a certain irony. The Louvins meant every word.

Charlie Louvin remembers a 'poor kid' with overalls but no shirt, tanned as a 'moon pie', who came to a show in Arkansas. It was the young Johnny Cash. On *Country Love Ballads*, their voices are like a man and woman duetting. When Gram Parsons first introduced Emmylou Harris to their music she asked who the girl was 'singin' the high part'.

Ira and Charlie were consciously passing on a musical baton, and it was grasped next by a couple of brothers from Kentucky. The trick was to use their youth and good looks – one dark-haired, one light – to disguise their country roots and send their music shooting up the charts, so that session men like Chet Atkins suddenly found their work in the Top Ten.

The Everlies dropped a musical bucket into a deep well on *Songs Our Daddy Taught Us*, a quiet and largely acoustic affair, with old mountain songs performed sweetly, but straight. No drums. An extraordinarily bold move for a pop duo. Their harmonies bring 'these ageless songs of a family fireside to the jet-propelled age of today'.

Roots (1968) presents gentle country-rock versions of songs by the likes of Merle Haggard and Jimmie Rodgers, and is topped and tailed by a home tape of the Everly Family in 1952, segued into songs from an earlier strain of country music. They sing heartfelt versions of 'Kentucky' and 'Shady Grove', an 'old time toe tapper' as Pop Everly calls it.

v) The '60s Folk Panic

In 1958 the clean cut Kingston Trio had a number one hit with 'Tom Dooley', loosely based on an Appalachian murder ballad. Trite rubbish, but suddenly folk music was hip. In the undergrowth the kind of music that we are tracing through *South By Southwest* was once again stirring.

Tom Paley, a postgraduate in maths at Yale, hardly fitted the stereotype of the ignorant moonshiner. He sang and played banjo and guitar, searching New York record shops for the old music. 'I got interested in old time country string band music as opposed to what most of the people were doing in the so-called 'Folk Revival.'* A favourite was Charlie Poole And The Carolina Ramblers: 'they had this interesting syncopated way of playing those runs: the way the fiddle took the melody...and those runs going off the bass strings of the guitar'. Such influences fed direct into The New Lost City Ramblers, a trio of young upper-class zealots for 'old time' music– Paley, Cohen and Mike Seeger, Pete's half brother.

A description of a 1958 concert mentions 'a peculiar nostalgia for 1932... Their music is kind of dishevelled...not pretty like the greeting card pictures painted in song by other "folk" singers. Rough around the edges, kind of gritty, kind of real. Kind of old timey'.

Mike Seeger has continued to put out albums of solo banjo playing as well as continuing to collect American music out in the field. He sees the music he loves in a constant state of development – 'One doesn't need to go outside the field to have evolution or even revolutions. People like the Horseflies reach outside, and I find that entertaining.'*

So what exactly is 'authenticity'? Let's return to Arthel 'Doc' Watson, discovered in the Appalachian heartlands in 1960 by Ralph Rinzler of the Greenbriar Boys, as part of the crowd of musicians surrounding Clarence Ashley. Watson was playing an electric Gibson Les Paul, much to Rinzler's disappointment, but when the young man started picking at a banjo, Watson climbed out of the truck, grabbed the instrument off him...and 'ripped off some of the best mountain picking imaginable'. Within a year, Doc Watson was guesting at the Newport Folk Festival.

Doc was born blind, and he learnt to play literally at his father's knee. His music might sound simple, but it is a cunning musical construct in which blues, dixieland and new-style country lend a riff here, a lick there. His 1964 debut album for Vanguard has Doc taking murder ballads, country blues and songs by the likes of the Delmore Brothers in his stride. Doc makes it all seem so easy. Even more exciting from this distance is

* *Folk Roots*

43

the release of his first solo residency at Gerdes Folk City in 1962. Here, in astonishing sound quality for the period, is that deep, warm voice, singing songs of love and murder, and acoustic guitar dexterity – and taste – plus some onstage badinage to bring it all down to earth. As the fiddler Mark O'Connor points out, 'Bill Monroe and Doc Watson are as progressive as anybody I've ever heard of.' Doc's son Merle was a perfect rhythm guitarist, and companion on the road, until death took him young. Thankfully, their albums together are numerous – wonderful collision points of blues, country and folk.

Doc later recorded with Michelle Shocked on *Arkansaw Traveller*, and immediately put her at ease, 'I said "I'm just people, I'll make a lot more mistakes than you will."' Watson 'brought an open-mindedness to the folk world by being both the real thing and a genuine innovator. He was one of the first people to play real country music for the city crowd.'* When Jimmy Dale Gilmore plays supper sessions at Threadgills, 'at least four songs a night' are drawn from Doc's repertoire.

Over in Greenwich Village, the Holy Modal Rounders, and similarly weird acid-fuelled acts took American folk music into a fourth dimension. Technically speaking, Harry Smith was the producer of the Fugs' first album, *The Village Fugs – Ballads Of Contemporary Protest, Points Of View And General Dissatisfaction*. Smith's contribution, though, was simply being there, the guardian spirit of this collage of weird sounds, plus smashing a wine bottle against the wall on 'Nothing'. The Lower East Side was the Fugs' natural habitat: disease and drugs and bad rock 'n' roll. It was also the haunt of Woody Guthrie and Pete Seeger – who lived on East 10th Street – and the natural habitat for the coffee-house scene, where old-time music was given artificial resuscitation, with not a mountain in sight.

The Holy Modal Rounders comprised Steve Weber and Peter Stampfel, who, in 1963, came up with the idea of 'combining *Harry Smith Anthology* era music and rock 'n' roll – the basis of much of the music I've been doing ever since'. It just took the rest of the world about 40 years to catch up with him. Check out at least half of the bands I discuss in the final chapters of this book, and spot the influence. Stampfel started playing banjo in 1958, and learned fiddle by playing along with the

* Jimmy Dale Gilmore

Anthology, where he found that, while 'post bluegrass fiddlers tend to sound similar, these guys sound like they come from different planets'. Like Bob Dylan, he put new words to these old songs, but even Dylan never went this far.

The Holy Modal Rounders used the *Anthology* 'to explore long-forgotten, mouldy corridors and dirt paths, heedless of place and time'. Classic songs like 'The Cuckoo' are rewritten to accentuate Stampfel's zen wisdom. He writes, 'this song is very old. It's about everything'. The 'standard' words gradually mutate into a personal observation about Peter and his woman moving to the mountains to die together, while the banjo and vocals could be straight out of a mountain holler.

This is music far better suited to the stage than the studio, as the idea of chance happenings is all part of the charm. *On Live In 1965* is full of string scrapings and wobbly vocals and you wonder exactly what deranged mind composed the songs, until you realise that they are almost all drawn from traditional sources. One tune comes via an ancient string band 78. 'Hold The Woodpile Down' combines the poet William Blake and Uncle Dave Macon. They also revive 'Going To Memphis', a Johnny Cash song from 1960, and give a special salute to Charley Poole.

The band temporarily split up, then came back together for *The Moray Eels Eat The Holy Modal Rounders*, where they spiral from eccentricity into madness. No '60s band ever went further out, psychically, than 'My Mind Capsized'. The 'Bird Song' turned up on the soundtrack of *Easy Rider*, where its mood fit perfectly into the sense of druggy excess. The Rounders were 'the first really bent traditional band. And the first traditionally-based band who were not trying to sound like an old record.'* He re-emerged recently with a similarly risk-taking guitarist Gary Lucas – whose musical CV ranges from Captain Beefheart to Jeff Buckley to resurrecting keltzmer tunes – as the Du Tels.

John Fahey was just as defiantly eccentric as a person, but his music is far easier on the ear, even when later mixing electronics and *musique concrète* with acoustic guitar drones, and influencing the likes of Sonic Youth. *Spin* argued that 'Fahey's musical influences match those of John Coltrane and Harry Partch for sheer transcendental American power'.

Drawing his tunes from impeccably authentic sources, Fahey played

* Peter Stampfel

extended works for guitar that drew together country blues, bluegrass, ragtime and classical to develop their own logic, as did their titles, poetic constructs like *Death Chants, Breakdowns And Military Waltzes*. The word 'death' appeared a little too often, and Fahey's first release, as the bluesman Blind Joe Death fooled lots of people before he came clean.

Fahey once told John Tobler about the American fingerpicking tradition – the Mississippi John Hurts, the Merle Travises, the Leadbellies – and how it could be 'the fountainhead of a whole new realm of music'. He spent years looking for musicians who could 'take that sound and expand its vocabulary, much as Bach expanded the vocabulary of German sacred music, or Armstrong that of New Orleans Jazz'. He never found them, so in the end he had only himself as a music laboratory.

Fahey acknowledges a massive debt to The Carter Family and the Episcopal Hymnal, plus of course the Harry Smith 'miracle', which 'justifies, by itself, the existence of Folkways'. He also set up Revenant to re-release archive material like the Stanley Brothers that 'vividly recast the past, not as nostalgia but as American Primitive or Raw Music'.

Fahey's conceptual masterpiece remains the ambitiously titled *America*: his native land is polluted, so he goes back to the country blues, to sacred songs like 'Amazing Grace' and Fahey's own 'Jesus Is A Dying Bedmaker', via Charlie Patton, plus the 14-minute instrumental 'Mark 1.15', about the end of time. It doesn't end there. 'Voice Of The Turtle' is about peace reigning over the world, while the final track, 'The Waltz That Carried Us Away And Then A Mosquito Came And Ate Up My Sweetheart' is a tune that stops and starts, like an old car on a frosty morning.

No Depression sees an America evoked on this album that is 'older and wiser than its founding fathers', and a world that has 'both enchanted and forsaken him'. Even the turtle obsession of early album sleeves turned out to be a metaphor for the sexual abuse John was subjected to as a child. No wonder he seemed to lose his way in life, and become little more than a tramp, an embittered man who treated audiences and promoters with equal contempt, Fahey's final album, *Red Cross*, saw a return to simplicity, from its handmade cover to the music inside, a unique mixture of religious dread and the transcendental, mainly played on six unamplified strings. Haunting and mysterious as hell.

John Sebastian grew up in Greenwich Village, and played with Doc Watson before forming The Lovin' Spoonful. Their music still sounds fresh, a mixture of blues and folk with a country tinge, and electric auto-harp whisps (rocking up the Carters) over a solid beat. There's something wistful about Sebastian's persona, a man who continues to mess blues and folk together. That's the essence of the alt rock attitude – steal what you like, and if it sounds good, it can't be bad.

Happy Traum admits that 'We all gravitated towards Manhattan, and formed the nucleus of a folk revival in America'. Some members of the New York scene were 'genuine', and none more than Jean Ritchie, whose family had been visited by Cecil Sharp in 1917. Her 1962 album *Jean Ritchie Singing Traditional Songs Of Her Kentucky Mountain Family* was the first folk album to be released by Elektra, and she has since recorded and published multiple volumes of Child Ballads and dulcimer tunes. Indeed, perhaps the most lasting influence on Americana of all this feverish activity was the fruits of the song-collecting excursions by the likes of Mike Seeger, John Cohen and Anne and Frank Warner, songs that then fed straight into the folk-song revival.

Elektra was already a very special record label. Started by Jac Holzman in the early '50s, it was legendary for the quality control of its vinyl, crystalline recording techniques and striking album sleeves. It developed a trademark sound of harpsichords, strange lyrics and a drugged subtlety. A recent series of double CDs by artists like Judy Collins and Tom Rush catch the pivotal time when such essentially interpretative singers moved from Appalachian ballads to the work of coffee-shop troubadours.

Only a few need bother us here. Eric Andersen started as a mixture of Guthrie copyist and beat poet who sat at the feet of Allen Ginsburg, then moved to New York and into the influence zone of Bob Dylan, even going as far as to re-record his acoustic album *'Bout Changes And Things* with a folk-rock band. *Blue River* is one of the saddest albums ever made, a suite of love songs that Eric's uniquely bruised voice makes almost too intimate. Now relocated to Europe, Andersen has had a late flowering, with a series of richly textured albums like *Ghosts Upon The Road* and the deeply emotional *Memory Of The Future, You Can't Relive The Past*, featuring collaborations with Lou Reed and Townes Van Zandt.

SOUTH BY SOUTHWEST: A ROAD MAP TO ALTERNATIVE COUNTRY

The double CD, *Beat Avenue* (2003), whose 26-minute title track recreates a doomed night in San Francisco with the likes of Neal Cassady and Lawrence Ferlinghetti, when news comes in about the assassination of John Kennedy. A performance that incorporates beat-box rhythms and sound effects, and takes you back to that night, with chilling realism.

Place it in the same uneasy musical territory as the burst of classic Americana produced by Richard Farina before a motorbike crash wiped him out far too young – gambler songs like 'Reno Nevado' and political satires – and the poisonous fruits of Phil Ochs' final years, classic albums like *Pleasures Of The Harbour*, which lay bare a whole civilisation on the verge of dissolution. 'The Crucifixion' is also based on Kennedy's death, written when emotions were still raw and bloody. Ochs reckoned that he learnt how to 'take pictures with my mind', and – like Tom Rapp, another paranoic with a cinescope imagination, or the ornate despair of David Ackles – he snapped those troubled times, for all time.

The saturnine Bob Neuwirth was Dylan's sidekick for much of the '60s. He re-emerged 30 years on and made *Look Up*, of which *Bucketfull Of Brains* reckon that 'anyone whose heart was touched by Son Volt would be at home with it'. Even better was *Friends Of Mine*, the swansong of Ramblin' Jack Elliott, a beautifully warm series of duets with the likes of Nanci Griffith, Guy Clark, and Peter Rowan, on the frankly bizarre 'Me And Billy The Kid'. But not the skinny little kid from Minnesota who plundered Jack's cowboy repertoire wholesale.

vi) Bringing It All Back Home

When Bob Dylan first blew into New York in 1961, those in the know saw him as an amalgam of Dock Boggs, Woody Guthrie, Rabbit Brown, Hank Williams and just about every American roots singer, mixing blues and folk and country into one raggedy voice and songbag. There was no great sense that he was any good as a songwriter, except as yet another Guthrie copyist. Peter Stampfel watched Dylan put a bunch of lyrics 'to tunes on Harry Smith's *Anthology* just as a way of teaching himself to write songs'. Smith himself had just released an album of peyote rituals.

48

Stampfel first saw Dylan in a Greenwich Village coffee house. 'He was the first person who really knew traditional stuff, whose phrasing was rock 'n' roll.' Back in Minneapolis, a couple of years earlier, Dylan's repertoire had been a mixture of blues, Woody Guthrie, and traditional folk. A grab bag of Americana. A boy with the voice of a weary old man gives us 'Wild Mountain Thyme' – 'a Texas song, I learned from Woody Guthrie'. The trademark laugh and words cut short suggest a mountain retard, not the pampered son of a smalltown Jewish shopkeeper.

No-one since, until Beck perhaps, has dared as much, or moved on so quickly. But Beck is always tongue in cheek and self-regarding, whereas the young Dylan seems unafraid to give himself up to his material. He certainly knew the *Harry Smith Anthology* inside out, and mimicked performances from it note perfect, songs like like 'Ommie Wise', 'The House Carpenter' and 'See That My Grave Is Kept Clean', which concludes his debut album. More important, he used it as a picture book of images, so that Bascom Lunsford's line about railroad men who 'drink up your blood like wine' resonates into a whole new song. But he was not just a record collector – Dylan saw the likes of Lunsford and Dock Boggs in concert, and at the Newport Folk Festival, plus a whole range of his contemporaries, from whose repertoire he was always ready to pluck out musical treats. Most of them just grinned and forgave him.

Speaking in 1997, Dylan described how he was drawn to folk music 'at a time when it was totally off the radar screen'. As to Woody Guthrie, Roscoe Holcomb or The Carter Family, 'they were free spirits who took chances, and I never wished to annul any of that spirit'. When he duetted with Ralph Stanley, another such, on 'The Lonesome River', Dylan claimed it as the highpoint of his career.

Dylan gave his own view of the folk tradition at the height of his amphetamine haze, in the mid '60s. 'Traditional music...comes about from legends, Bibles, plagues and it revolves around vegetables and death... Nobody's going to hurt it.' The same truth is put more wittily – and nastily – in the famous confrontation with his Scottish copyist Donovan. 'You know I haven't always been accused of writing my own songs. But that's one I did write.' 'I didn't know, man. Thought maybe it was an old folk song'. 'No, it's not an old folk song yet'.

By the mid '60s, Dylan was busy remaking everything in his path. It was as if he had tapped into an unstoppable flow of words. One with roots deep in the tradition. For *Blonde On Blonde*, Dylan booked a recording session in New York, with his road band, an untried and nameless group who had until recently been backing Ronnie Hawkins. In February 1966, Dylan moved his operations across to Columbia Music Row Studios, Nashville. Thus it was that in the very epicentre of what was generally perceived as the most hidebound and backward musical force in America, Dylan created the first truly psychedelic album.

Greil Marcus takes us back to Cardiff 1966, with Dylan and Johnny Cash – 'at 33 he looks like cancer' – jamming on Cash's 'I Still Miss Someone'. Dylan looks like an insect. He suddenly begins a new song, 'I bought me a ticket, for a one-way train', and 'the song he's now singing sounds older than the grandparents of anyone in the room and more familiar than anyone's own face'. The music literally of his grandparents' generation – via Harry Smith – will guide him back home.

He stepped away from the madness of the road and retreated to Woodstock, with The Band just down the road in a house called Big Pink. Here, taped in rough stereo – just a kind of aural home movie – is a music by turns ribald and stately and quite insane. Outside it was the summer of love, with wild electric guitars and singer/songwriters exploring the cosmos. Here, as an antidote, is a bran tub of Americana.

Dip in at random and you find songs by Flatt and Scruggs, Hank Williams as 'Luke the Drifter', Sun era Johnny Cash, Marty Robbins, Roscoe Halcomb the Skillet Lickers, Hank Snow and The Carter Family's 'Wildwood Flower', plus sea shanties and Appalachian ballads. Dylan chooses a different voice for every one, and The Band chug along like the finest-ever string band, crossed with a mad church organist. They swap instruments like a school band giving everyone a turn.

Dylan's own new songs partake of a vast knowledge of musical history, but delivered with a sly wit. 'Clothesline Saga' was originally called 'Answer To Ode', as a riposte to Bobbie Gentry's 'Ode To Billy Joe', but you would hardly guess it now. The sound is something else, warm and intimate. As Robbie Robertson explained, because of the room's acoustics, 'we played in a little huddle: if you couldn't hear the singing you were playing too loud'. Even so, the recording process is far from random, with false takes ruthlessly erased. 'You're wasting tape,' Dylan tells Garth Hudson, who is masterminding the stereo mix using state-of-the-art recording apparatus. There is a sense of the five participants as emigrants in a strange land, holed up in the hills, slightly stoned, remembering the good old days, recreating American music from scratch.

This is not to say that there is not a huge sense of fun, with Dylan laughing out loud during 'Get Your Rocks Off', or his mumble in 'Lo And Behold!', 'I'm going down to Tennessee/get me a truck or something'. The albums to emerge after both parties surfaced from the basement were far more sombre affairs. *John Wesley Harding* was supposedly written back in Dylan's study with a large family Bible open on a lectern and Hank Williams albums scattered around. These semi-acoustic mysteries were recorded only a few days after the death of Woody Guthrie, and update his plain style. 'I Dreamed I Saw St Augustine' is based on 'The Ballad Of Joe Hill', but the Old Testament – that Hebrew primer of so much Americana – is the dominant influence here, with all kinds of half quotations. Even the short story on the back is deliberately opaque. 'Nothing is revealed'.

When Dylan talked to Mikal Gilmore in the mid '80s, he pounced on Gilmore's record collection. 'This Hank Williams thing with just him and guitar – man, that's something, isn't it? I used to sing those songs way back, a long time ago, even before I played rock 'n' roll as a teenager.' *Under The Red Sky* was a surprising return to the rustic surrealism of the Basement Tapes, and the Harry Smith magic show behind it. The whole album is a collection of nursery rhymes. 'Back Alley Sally Is Doing The American Jump'. A folk song, no less.

Dylan was beginning to sing traditional songs again during the acoustic part of his concerts. Two albums of acoustic folk, blues and country dutifully arrived, all written by other people. His vocal on 'Blackjack Davey' is terrifying, like a sly and deranged mountain man. These are songs that draw you in like a seedy carnival huckster. Even the seemingly light-hearted 'Froggie Went A Courting', taken from Mike and Peggy Seeger's album *American Folk Songs For Children*, is sung as if each word is costing Dylan his lifeblood.

Talking to *Mojo* in 1998, Dylan recalled that he heard the *Harry Smith Anthology* 'early on, when it was very difficult to find those kind of songs'. 'It's all poetry, every single one of those songs, and the language is different than current popular language.' If you can learn songs like those, from the inside, 'then there's nowhere you can't go'. It was a process that resulted in *Time Out Of Mind*, in which Dylan once again creates something new from the roots of Americana. These are songs written by a man who has come back from the other side of death, and he sang them just like that in the first UK tour after his illness.

Dylan has taken to opening his endless set lists with traditional songs like 'I Am The Man Thomas'. It is the same terrain as the urgent gospel songs he was writing, and performing live with terrifying intensity at the tail end of the '70s. Cue Ira Louvin. A 9-CD bootleg of the *Genuine Never Ending Tour*, from 1988 to now, sorts these cover versions into categories like 'Folk Rot' and 'Rock Of Ages', which reveals the depth of these borrowings. 'This World Can't Stand Long', taped in California just after the Millennium, is sung lovingly, with a kind of resigned sadness, and to a jingle-jangle backing.

When I last saw Dylan, in a concrete leisure centre, the back of his natty suit drenched with sweat, he moved like a rock 'n' roller. When he resurrected 'Wheels Of Fire', from the Basement Tapes, the stage seemed to levitate. The ghost smiling at the back of the hall was Harry Smith, seeing his investment returned, a thousandfold.

Levon Helm was born on his father's cotton farm near Turkey Scratch, Arkansas, and he would sing along with his father, 'a fountain of music'. The first live show he saw was Bill Monroe And His Blue Grass Boys – 'They took that old hillbilly music, sped it up, and basically invented bluegrass music; the bass in its place, the mandolin above it, the guitar tying the two together, and the violin on top, playing the long notes to make it sing.'* The banjoist – Earl Scruggs – 'backed the whole thing up, answering everybody'. It really 'tattooed my brain'.*

The first time he saw Elvis, it was just with Scotty Moore and Bill Black on 'doghouse' bass. No drums, as by law you could not have a drummer in a place where alcohol was served. Johnny Cash was also on the bill: 'It was fantastic, early rockabilly, always circling and real bouncy,

---

* Levon Helm, *This Wheel's On Fire*

with an almost jazz feel to it.' The second Presley sighting was about six months later, at a high-school auditorium, and by now Black was playing electric bass, releasing Scotty to make his guitar strings 'cry'. DJ Fontana 'played like a big-band drummer – full throttle. DJ set Elvis free'.

Local hero Ronnie Hawkins was another early rock 'n' roller, and Levon joined his backing band, the Hawks, watching new members arrive, including a young Canadian guitarist called Robbie Robertson. Levon's stories and reminiscences led Robertson to shape a whole mythology drawn from American history and folklore.

The Band aimed to sound as if they were 100 years old, and even dressed like mountain men. They produced music that sounds richly odd, almost static. Their voices drip age and passion, with old-time harmonies and enigmatic lyrics, music that consoles, and yearns. Richard Manuel's singing on 'I Shall Be Released' is other-worldly, a plea for tolerance, but he sounds lost and lonely as a ghost.

Their second album, with the working title *Harvest* and recorded in LA, inhabits its own universe, a template of Americana, created from their own guts by a band of whom only Helm was born south of the Canadian border. Here their voices are more differentiated, with Levon a raconteur, Richard still questing for release and Rick Danko the cowpoke, honest but embittered. Robbie is silent, talking through his reined-in guitar. The music spans from primal rock 'n' roll to 'Rocking Chair', which sounds like it was taped on a back porch high in the hills.

The Band learned to start 'halving the beat', slowing things down. Then they got urgent, over the top. Just listen to 'Rag Mama Rag', with Levon's laconic tale telling refusing to be rushed by the musicians behind him. They fuse into one, with 'Honey Boy' Garth Hudson staying behind late into the night, sweetening the sound, adding brass and woodwind. What Robertson brought was verbal precision. There's something playful about the way they go to work, and something spooky too, barely human. No wonder that Levon, the farm boy, uses an agricultural metaphor when he writes that 'we were reaping this music from seeds that had been planted many years before we'd even been born'. This might explain why the album hasn't dated a second from its moment of release.

vii) Sweethearts Of The Rodeo

The *Johnny Cash Show* brought Bob Dylan and cajun fiddler Doug Kershaw to a family audience, as well as featuring Mother Maybelle Carter and a history section, 'Stop This Train', 'a combination of history and song', which included archive film and photos. Johnny Cash was still pursuing his lifetime's quest, to give America back to his people.

At Folsom Prison (1968) is as good a place as any to start. Under the harsh strip lights, he looks as hard as anybody present, guards or inmates, and his voice is granite, unmelodic but remorseless. Steve Earle certainly recognises a father figure: 'in 1991 I dropped off the edge of the earth, resurfacing in '95 by way of the Davidson Criminal Justice Centre'. Later that year, he met Cash, who offered him a piece of steak, 'as if nothing had happened'. The punchline holds the sting in the tail, 'to either one of us'. Cash then repeated the trick in 1969 at San Quentin, with Shel Silverstein's 'A Boy Called Sue' and Dylan's bespoke song 'Wanted Man', plus the traditional 'Wreck Of The Old 97'. If anyone is entitled to sing about American history and myth, it is Cash. He was born in Arkansas in 1932, and has traced his family tree to 17th-century Scotland. As a child he broke fruit jars 'just for meanness'. His older brother Jack walked into a saw blade, and Johnny watched him die.

Cash was raised in rural poverty in Dyess, a community created by the New Deal to resettle farmers on productive land. This later fed directly into songs like 'Pickin' Time' and 'Five Feet High And Rising', about the flooding of the Mississippi. Cash would make up songs where he stood, on spec. As we have already seen with his imaginary train ride through America, his concept albums from the '60s have been hugely undervalued. They reveal an ambition and a love of his native land that surely makes him the Godfather of Americana. *From Sea To Shining Sea* finds genuine excitement in his voice as he describes finding primitive flint arrowheads.

He writes new folk songs for his native South on *Songs Of Our Soil*. There is a truth to experience on a song like 'Five Feet High And Rising' – check out his half laugh – or his version of 'The Great Speckle Bird', which only bitter experience, or a deep religious faith, can teach. Elsewhere there are the worksongs of *Blood, Sweat And Tears*, and the history lesson that is *America*. He now reckons, proudly, that they 'brought out voices that weren't commonly heard at the time, and they addressed subjects I really cared about. I was trying to get at the reality behind some of our country's history'. Not bad for a one time rockabilly on Sun.

Here is a man who dresses in black as message to the hard done by, to 'carry off a little darkness on my back' And who to get away from being recast as 'new country' gave CBS a record called 'Chicken In Black', and even got them to shoot a video in New York with Johnny in a chicken costume. The same record company later repackaged some of his greatest songs under three headings, *Love, God* and *Murder*, but it was Johnny himself who chose the tracks, and wrote the sleevenotes.

Just by being there, and surviving it all, Cash has become an icon. At the 1994 Glastonbury Festival, he electrified the main stage with the power of his songs and that voice straight out of the school of hard knocks. 'That night I realised I'd come full circle, back to the bare bones of my music, pre-stardom, pre-electric, pre-Memphis. I could have been back singing with just Momma to hear me on the front porch under the clear night sky of Arkansas.' With 100,000 young converts, sitting at his feet. No wonder that he attracts tribute albums from the likes of the Pine Valley Cosmonauts on *Misery Loves Company*, or post-punk bands like Kill Switch on *Americana*, while the likes of U2 come calling whenever they need a world-weary voice to add to the mix.

With rap producer Rick Rubin, whose label American Records was more used to releasing the Red Hot Chilli Peppers and the Beastie Boys, Cash went way outside the Nashville envelope.

The first instalment of *American Recordings* saw Cash unplugged, without annoying choirs or that endless two to the bar rhythm section, recorded simply in Rubin's living room in Southern California, the singer's cabin in Tennessee and the super-cool Viper Room, hangout of Johnny Depp and the like. They cheer Loudon Wainwright's line about being 'bullied and buggered', for the sheer joy of the way in which Johnny spits it out. It is as if Cash has started to free associate, so that his whole musical heritage spills out, folk and blues and country and lots of gospel.

It is a heritage that he proudly passes on. Talking to Barney Hoskyns, Cash describes the young Dylan as 'one of the best hillbilly singers I'd ever heard', and reckons much the same of Beck, 'He had that Appalachian music like he really felt it and loved it.' As to Americana, 'I've always loved folk music. It's the backbone of country, or it used to be'.

Over in early 1960s in Bakersfield, at the heart of the oilfields, the 'California sound' was taking over, a rocking noise like the sound of a beer bottle breaking on a barroom table, with piercing steel guitar. A blue-collar town if ever there was one, Bakersfield back in the 1930s had been a natural migration point for the Okies, who put their rural folk songs into the mix. The tenor voice of Alvis 'Buck' Owens and his band the Buckeroos will be forever associated with the place. Don Rich on lead Telecaster was one of the progenitors of country rock.

The most interesting music they played – in the context of this book – was on some of their side projects, Buck's tribute to the great songwriter Harlan Howard or *Dust On The Bible*, an album of 'joyous inspirational songs'. *Ruby* sees Buck going bluegrass, but as he grew up on a dairy farm in Texas, he would listen on XELO radio to the Monroe Brothers. As the sleeve notes say, '*any* song can be bluegrass, if it's treated right'.

The hottest dog in Bakersfield, though, was Merle Haggard. He knows exactly how to hit a vein of working-class pride. Two tribute albums were issued almost simultaneously. One was largely mainstream Nashville, and needn't concern us. The other is essential listening. *Tulare Dust* on Oakland's tiny Hightone label, has roots singers like Lucinda Williams and Iris Dement, the Joe Ely and Peter Case. They seem to dig deeper into these songs. Producers Tom Russell and Dave Alvin – alt-country stars in their own right – reckon Haggard as 'the last of a breed of great Country songwriters. His kind ain't coming around again'. Maybe not, but over in Austin, The Derailers have recently revived the Bakersfield sound – and look – on albums like *Full Western Dress*.

But we still haven't cracked how exactly this all cohered into alt country some 30 years down the line. Johnny Cash supplied the mythology and the guiding spirit – but with a strong dose of sentimentality and a limited musical palette. The Bakersfield sound provided guts and subject matter, but remains a music of fairly basic emotions, even in the hands of sophisticated imitators like The Derailers. What was needed too was another tradition that we have been following down the years, the troubadour, telling twisted stories set deep in the American heartland, but understandable wherever human beings live and breathe.

Before we see how a new and wilder strain of bluegrass mutated into country rock, it is time for some brief detours via a handful of mavericks whose music represents a unique and ornery world view, and which is still avidly collected and listened to today. Jimmy Webb might have had his songs re-interpreted by Glen Campbell, but even Glen can't disguise the nagging unease at the heart of them – poetic hymns to the American outback. Webb's own more untutored voice digs out the vein of sadness at the heart of 'Galveston' and the ghostly 'The Highwayman'.

Bobbie Gentry is one of those singers who has got lost along the way, something that in her case appears to have been deliberate, but she remains a role model for many of the women singer/songwriters to emerge in the last decade, from Iris Dement to Kate Campbell. She is a poet of place, the people and landscape and even the bugs of the Mississippi Delta. Add sophisticated arrangements by Jimmie Haskell on her debut album *Ode To Billy Joe*, and we have music that endures in its own private world. Was it a baby they threw from that bridge? After the fractured guitar intro and spooky strings and with the unnatural calm in Bobbie's voice, this is pure American gothic. A later album, *The Delta Sweete* ends with a sinister, unresolved chord. 'What you do in the dark will be brought to light', as Bobby writes on the back sleeve.

Tom T Hall also wrote about small-town life. On his boldest record, *In Search Of A Song*, Hall took a guitar, notepad and tape recorder and went out to find America. The songs are the aural snapshots. 'Who's Gonna Feed Them Hogs' has a farmer fretting in hospital and staging a miraculous recovery. 'Trip To Hyden' revisits the site of a mining disaster. It is sunny 'but somehow the town was cold'.

No Depression says he reshaped country music, 'deepened details, complicated narrative and followed colloquial voices further than they'd ever gone'. *Real, The Tom T Hall Project* sees these songs done by current alt-country stars, as if they are already part of the tradition. Joe Henry puts a charge under 'Homecoming', sampling a classic intro from Charley Pride, and adding 'staccato guitar, drum loops and scratchy moans'. The results are menacing, over which Henry acts deadpan, and defeated.

Just as weird are the late '60s albums of country exotica by the gruff-voiced Lee Hazlewood. *Cowboy In Sweden* is a deranged c&w album recorded during Lee's self-imposed exile in Scandinavia, with swathes of violins 'sweetening Hazlewood's creepy, weather-beaten baritone'.*

Trouble Is A Lonesome Town (1963) centres around the inhabitants of a mythical Wild West town called Trouble. Each song (and character) has a spoken introduction. 'You won't find it on any map, but take a step in any direction and you're in trouble.' Hazlewood kick-started country rock when he released the debut album by the International Submarine Band on his own label, LHI. He invented cowboy existential-ism all by himself. *Total Lee* is a tribute album by the likes of Lambchop.

Van Dyke Parks is just as enigmatic a figure, and anyone who collaborated with Brian Wilson on the still-unreleased *Smile*, is de facto a pioneer of Americana. Who else but Parks could write a concept album around the Brer Rabbit stories, or set off to discover America through calypsos. He can't sing of course, but nobody's perfect.

An even more skewed vision emerges from Randy Newman's album *Good Old Boys*, an exploration of the Southern point of view, which Randy was bold enough to premiere with an orchestra at the Great Southeast Music Hall, Atlanta. 'Rednecks' establishes the tone. Here is a song of the south, for those who drink too much and laugh too loud. But Randy suggests that such racism is just as prevalent, but quieter, up North. As usual Newman performs a monologue of a person far from himself, whom he both skewers and pities. The whole album is a catalogue of the Southern dispossessed. 'A Wedding In Cherokee County' describes a back-porch bride surrounded by freaks. In 'Louisiana 1927', Newman sympathises with the poor white trash, 'crackers', down in the flood.

All this is far from Newman's own life, as the resolutely middle-class LA-based son of a Hollywood composer, but it rings true. Back on his debut album, 'Cowboy' was a richly orchestrated elegy for the pioneer spirit. 'City faces haunt the places I used to roam'. He suggests that the cowboy is too worn out and disillusioned, 'too tired', even to resist.

The influence of country rock is still expanding, from a low initial base, as an outgrowth of bluegrass and old-time music. The music of choice of Randy Newman's targets in *Good Old Boys*. Mountain music

* *Mojo*

might sound like it is preserved in aspic, but it is like a living force, even if the basic repertoire remains much the same.

When Ralph Rinzler of the Greenbriar Boys became Bill Monroe's manager, he began booking him into folk clubs and colleges. Young musicians got hooked on this weird, purist sound. Among those to work their apprenticeship as Blue Grass Boys were Richard Greene and Peter Rowan. The true musical revolutionary, though, was Bill Keith.

A Bostonian, Keith only played with Monroe for nine months, but during that time developed a 'chromatic' style to enable the super-fast yet precise playing of fiddle tunes on his banjo that then fuelled 'progressive bluegrass'. The music began to spread far from its mountain strongholds, proving most at home in Washington DC. The Country Gentlemen were founding fathers of progressive bluegrass. They brought a punk-like energy, speeding things up and relying on visceral energy.

Long before Woodstock, fans of the music chose to OD on their favourite music at open-air festivals. Elder statesman Ralph Stanley began to add unaccompanied singing to his repertoire, looking back to the vocal phrasing of the Primitive Baptist Church. Ralph's standing among a younger generation was shown when Dylan and Gillian Welch and Dwight Yoakam and Hal Ketchum jammed live in the studio on Clinch Mountain Country. Gillian Welch later reckoned 'it was one of the scariest things I've ever done – to sing with your biggest influence.'

Ricky Skaggs came from Eastern Kentucky, and by the age of seven he was guesting on Flatt and Scruggs' TV show. With his friend Keith Whiteley, they auditioned for Ralph Stanley. 'Keith and I grew up the same way the Stanleys did, in fundamentalist Baptist churches and in rough country'. On the way back from gigs, and to keep themselves awake, 'we'd sing those old Baptist hymns. They came out as natural as can be for us'. Stanley invited them onstage, and 'told us that our singing really brought back a lot of memories, just to hear people sing old songs'.

During the early to mid '60s, bluegrass saw a blast of energy from the West Coast. Brothers Doug and Rodney Dillard left Salem, Missouri in 1963 to head for California. The Dillards proved too irreverent for the serious fans and yet too rough and ready for the mainstream. The solution came with a live album recorded in 1964 at the Mecca in Los Angeles.

On Dylan's 'Walking Down The Line', they sing for sheer joy, and the acoustic instruments circle round each other as only bluegrass can.

Doug went off to play electric banjo with The Byrds, then join Gene Clark for a while in the Fantastic Expedition. The Dillards hired Herb Pederson and went on to make two ground-breaking albums, 1968's *Wheatstraw Suite* – with snatches of Southern talk between tracks – and *Copperfields*, with songs from the likes of Eric Andersen and The Beatles.

The Kentucky Colonels were even wilder, with Roland and his brother Clarence on mandolin and guitar. They recorded the legendary 1964 album *Appalachian Swing*, without vocals as they were too expensive to record. The Kentucky Colonels played 'with an intensity that bordered on chaos'. *Acoustic Guitar* magazine described Clarence's style as the next step on from Doc Watson: 'he deconstructed these phrases, punching holes in them, twisting and stretching them, and making them perform acrobatic feats of unequalled grace and daring'. It can be heard in full flow on *Livin' In The Past*, a rag bag of live recordings introduced by a soft-voiced Jerry Garcia in 1964, notably a hysterically fast 'Fire On The Mountain'. This music makes punk sound geriatric. It feels like the strings are on fire, and, like Hendrix, Clarence is so extraordinary a player that you somehow feel he is not long for this world.

The band went electric much at the same time as Dylan, 'to get work', with Bart Henry on drums and Clarence playing a Fender Telecaster. As Bush recalls, 'we just played country music but we rocked it up a little bit'. They drew their new repertoire from Hank Williams mainly, with rock 'n' roll drums. 'Clarence was being influenced by session musicians like James Burton and a really wild guitarist from the Paul Butterfield Blues Band, Michael Bloomfield'. Clarence described how difficult it was at first for him to transfer his to electric guitar: 'when I switched to electric, I found I had far too much strength and power in my right hand. I was making the strings jump and rattle, which led to distortion. I had to learn to use a more delicate touch in conjunction with the tone and volume controls'. He went on invent the Stringbender, a device that enabled him to imitate a pedal steel, by pulling down on the guitar neck.

Next Clarence formed Nashville West, with Gene Parsons and Gib Gilbeau. He was offered a demo recording of Dylan goofing about on

'Mr Tambourine Man' with Jack Elliott, 'like a drunk man singing', but the others turned it down. So it went to The Byrds...

The Kentucky Colonels were not the only bluegrass band to come out of Los Angeles. The Golden State Boys featured Chris Hillman on mandolin, and the Gosdin brothers. They subsequently renamed themselves the Hillmen, after their 17-year-old boy genius. Their music makes easier listening than the Colonels, less supercharged, and mournful. Hillman grew up near San Diego, and came to the music through the New Lost City Ramblers: 'I loved Mike Seeger's mandolin playing'. He began to frequent LA's Ash Grove, and take in sets by Flatt and Scruggs and the Stanley Brothers. His producer, Jim Dickson promoted another band, the Jet Set – also known as the Beefeaters – to cover 'Mr Tambourine Man', and brought Hillman in on electric bass. The new band – soon to be again renamed, as The Byrds, was unusual in being drawn from a bunch of hardened professionals, mostly from an acoustic background.

While still at school, Jim McGuinn painstakingly learned five-string banjo and 12-string guitar at Chicago's Old Town School Of Folk Music. He signed up with the Chad Mitchell Trio, playing acoustic folk, then joined Bobby Darin to spice up his cabaret set. He also served an apprenticeship at the Brill Building, as a 9-to-5 songwriter. Jim – as he was known until he joined the Subud faith, and renamed himself Roger – was already a folkclub legend: his voice a one-off, dreamy and bored. Commuting across America , he became a resident at LA's Troubadour. Then one night, he was woodshedding a song on the stairwell with his new friend Gene Clark, when teenage tearaway David Crosby turned up and added a third vocal harmony. The result was instant magic.

Gene Clark was born in Missouri, and raised on bluegrass. He too became a folk fanatic, briefly joining the New Christie Minstrels. Crosby had been a spoiled brat in Hollywood, albeit with the singing voice of an angel. Soon he joined commercial folkies Les Baxter Balladeers. The Byrds, perhaps the most American-sounding band of all, started out copying British beat combos. The film A Hard Day's Night made the three young folkies suddenly want to go electric. A studio tape sees the band burst into a spontaneous bluegrass jam. Their country 'n' traditional roots did begin to peep through, eventually sprouting a whole forest.

Fifth Dimension went about as far out as was possible in 1966, but also present was the safe haven of traditional song, 'Wild Mountain Thyme'. The Byrds' version wavers between cowboy theme tune and Indian raga. On *Younger Than Yesterday*, Hillman's old friend Clarence White plays on 'Time Between', a country shuffle. Hillman 'sort of grew up with Clarence. Then, around the end of 66, I found him again – living way out of LA and playing in country groups in bars and things'. *The Notorious Byrd Brothers* sees a viciously slimmed down group. Clarence White picks bluegrass style on Goffin-King's 'Wasn't Born To Follow'.

For the next album McGuinn 'wanted to use elements of early music, progressing to Celtic music, showing how that was distilled in North America to produce various forms of folk music, then to show the origins of country music and bluegrass, r&b and rock music, and finally going into the future and exploring the synthesiser and computer music'. Here, never achieved, is the story of Americana, over the last two centuries.

To carry out this plan, McGuinn needed more than the two Byrds, so 'when I hired Gram Parsons, it was as a jazz pianist. I had no idea he was a Hank Williams character too.' Hillman says he first met Gram in a Beverly Hills bank in late 1967, but already knew of 'the young upstart who'd beaten me to the punch' by uniting rock music and country. At the audition, he broke out into a spontaneous rendition of a Buck Owens song, and Hillman stopped and ran over and caught the tenor part. 'I'd found an ally, and quite possibly my future.' When his cousin Kevin Kelley came in on drums, Hillman virtually controlled the group. McGuinn's plan was put on hold, 'so we did a country album in Nashville instead'. For him, this was just an interlude, 'something we were doing for kicks… It was a role-playing thing for me'. And then the mask stuck.

Gram Parsons was a true Southern aristocrat, heir to a citrus-fruit empire in Florida. In the sleevenotes to Sundazed's *Another Side Of This Life – The Lost Recordings Of Gram Parsons 1965–1966*, Parson's school-friend Jim Carlton says: 'Gram was influenced by such artists as Fred Neil, Buck Owens, Don Rich, Albert King, George Jones, Gene Pitney, Van Dyke Parks and even country pop star, Jim Stafford. Stafford was the lead guitarist in our High School rock band The Legends and was the one who encouraged Gram to play country music.'

Gram started playing in teen bands like the Legends, whose 'Rip It Up' is pure rock 'n' roll with a wild guitar break, then unplugged with the Shilohs, whose work survives on *Gram Parsons: The Early Years 1963–65*, all neat matching suits and haircuts. Gram plays down his southern accent – he sounds like a young James Stewart when he instructs the rest of the band during 'Surfinanny'. There is little here to suggest his boast that, 'I'm sure my music is going to be as big as Dylan's.'

Parsons briefly attended Harvard, then put together the International Submarine Band, to fulfil his vision of 'Cosmic American Music'. Not a pedal steel in sight. Gram moved to LA, where he mimed in Peter Fonda's drug movie *The Trip*, and played the Palomino Club, in a rhinestone suit, singing Merle Haggard covers. Everyone from Rick Nelson to the young Bernie Leadon was trying to fuse country and rock. For Chris Darrow, later of Kaleidoscope, 'There was a different vibe about Gram, particularly because he wrote his own songs.' Meanwhile the International Submarine Band split. Gram kept the name to record *Safe At Home* (1968), undoubtedly the first country-rock fusion to make it onto album, mixing and matching new Parsons songs like 'Luxury Liner' and classics by Merle Haggard and Johnny Cash, rocked up.

Stanley Booth noted: 'He happened to meet David Crosby's fiancée, take her away from Crosby, and replace Crosby when The Byrds fired him.' Now Gram was in The Byrds he could try again. Byrds' roadie Jimmie Sieter flew down to prepare the Nashville studio, 'we had two 8-tracks plugged together in sync, and no-one had ever seen that before. All the players like Ernest Tubbs' band came from miles just to look at our machines.' On March 15th The Byrds appeared at the *Grand Ole Opry*, having been booked to sing two Merle Haggard songs. A redneck audience sat suspiciously through 'Sing Me Back Home', some calling out 'tweet tweet'. Just as it seemed that some of the audience might unbend, Parsons announced a change of plan – Tompall Glawer had announced 'Life In Prison' – and launched into 'Hickory Wind', dedicated to his grandmother. They were immediately banned from the *Opry*, for singing the greatest song to emerge from the South for decades.

Sweetheart Of The Rodeo was no sooner recorded than legal pressure from Lee Hazlewood forced McGuinn to re-record Gram's vocals himself, in a fake southern accent, leaving only 'Hickory Wind' as at first intended. McGuinn brings a kind of raised eyebrow to his renditions, which helps rock 'n' roll refugees ease themselves into this alien listening experience.

A brisk note on the acoustic fiddle, and we're into bluegrass gospel, sung by Hillman like a lost soul, with McGuinn on Rickenbacker banjo. An outtake of 'The Christian Life', opens with McGuinn urging 'Let's just clean the whole song up, get the accents right.' On the released version, McGuinn takes lead vocal with a pronounced twang, like a comic hillbilly. For the country soul of 'You Don't Miss Your Water', Roger is back to his sweet Byrds' voice, with marvellous clunking piano from Earl Ball. Gram sings 'You're Still On My Mind' with steel guitar and piano predominant. The Byrds are hardly here at all. It's back to McGuinn's folk roots for his laconic yet passionate retelling of Woody Guthrie's 'Pretty Boy Floyd', with stand-up bass and sawing fiddle.

Parsons' vocal was kept on 'Hickory Wind', as even McGuinn couldn't sing this tenderly. Country rock starts here, and it doesn't get any better than this, the way the piano climbs and the sighing violins and whispering steel, or the weary way Gram almost prays for the wind to follow him home. McGuinn's genius as an arranger is in full flight.

All kinds of interesting material has since surfaced from these sessions, including the traditional ballad 'Pretty Polly', sung by Roger, and presumably a track from his proposed concept album of 'old-time music, not bluegrass but pre-bluegrass, dulcimers...nasal Appalachian stuff'. He gives the song just the pitiless treatment it needs.

The Byrds now went on the road, and their gig in May 1968 at Rome's Piper Club opens with a slow, intense 'You Don't Miss Your Water', with musical embroidery on the electric banjo by Doug Dillard in the absence of a steel guitar. Alt country 30 years early – it's wonderful.

Next up is a passionate 'Hickory Wind', with bluesy grace notes on the banjo and lovely harmonies. Then the set list suddenly veers towards older material like 'Feel A Whole Better' with bluegrass trills from Doug, then McGuinn soloing over the top. Dillard goes beserk on 'Chimes Of Freedom'. 'Turn, Turn, Turn' is almost The Byrds of old, but that banjo just won't give up its insane chuntering, bringing the song down to earth. 'My Back Pages' sounds particularly appropriate in the circumstances, with stunning bass from Hillman. Last up is 'Mr Spaceman', announced to loud cheers, and the banjo performs a jig over Roger's super-cool vocal. As befits so fresh a musical experiment, Dillard has trouble getting his banjo into the right key. 'We tuned these things down on the airplane – it's hard to get them back.' The same band, minus Dillard, appeared at London's Middle Earth club, and is much heavier on the country material, including a sprightly reading of the Buck Owen's song 'Under Your Spell Again'. More psychedelic guitar, slipping and a-sliding. 'Hickory Wind' is more melancholy than in Rome. 'Sing Me Back Home' is a dying man's wish, with a bass-heavy lead break, and a pedal steel sound on electric guitar. The country material is now a section by itself.

Next day, Gram played his final gig with the band, at 'Sounds 68' at the Royal Albert Hall, then the rest went off on a disastrous South African tour, and Gram went to take over control of the Flying Burrito Brothers.

viii) Taking Wing

McGuinn was left to put together a brand new Byrds, and signed up Clarence White. On 'This Wheel's On Fire' on *Dr Byrds And Mr Hyde*, Clarence sketches out a nervous breakdown on fuzzed electric guitar. His aim was 'to play honest music in an honest style that I believed in'. The last line up of The Byrds saw McGuinn's jangle surrounded by sweet country picking. *Ballad Of Easy Rider* plunged deeper into America's folk roots. The title track expanded a few words scrawled by Dylan on the back of an envelope into a song seemingly as old as the hills.

The live half of (*Untitled*) sees The Byrds stretch out on a 16-minute 'Eight Miles High', with McGuinn and Clarence White trading guitar licks. The studio half contains songs from *Gene Tryp*, a rock opera, never completed, which aimed to transpose Ibsen's epic drama to 19th-century America. The hypnotic 'Chestnut Mare' corresponds to Peer Gynt's attempt to catch 'a reindeer or some animal like that'. In 'Lover Of The Bayou', 'the scene was set during the Civil War, and our hero smuggling guns to the confederates'. The Byrds slowly drifted to a close, with a final album named after the traditional bluegrass lament 'Farther Along'.

The same song was sung over Clarence White's coffin by Gram Parsons and Bernie Leadon. One night at Hammersmith Odeon in 1977 – heyday of punk – a shiny-eyed McGuinn, a laid-back Hillman and a stumbling, heavily bearded Gene Clark joined together for a short but explosive set, culminating in 'Eight Miles High'.

Meanwhile, Gram Parsons hung out with Keith Richards. Ever the musical pickpockets, the Stones learnt the method from Gram to compose 'Wild Horses', 'Dead Flowers' and 'Sweet Virginia', on which Parsons is said to sing harmony vocals. Parsons then talked with Ritchie Furay about forming a country-rock band, to be called Pogo – who actually became soft rockers Poco – but instead reformed the Flying Burrito Brothers, a Southern soul group playing country and gospel-orientated music with a steel guitar. He was transfixed by Delaney and Bonnie. 'That's where the idea for big-time country music started hitting me... There was a little bit of room for funk.' Unfortunately, many of Parsons' own later live performances, both with the Burritos and the Fallen Angels, were relaxed and unrehearsed to the point of chaos. Only on the edge of personal disaster could he finally find the inner energy to produce a sound that was new to the world, and whose echoes still resonate.

Immersing himself in the emotional pain of his hero George Jones did him no good. What Gram added to Jones' tales of self-inflicted failure was the ability to write some of the greatest country songs ever, the voice of a bruised angel – totally without the edge of aggression of the older singer – and an intellectual agenda. Gram's childhood in Georgia saw country music regarded as 'the corn-poke outpourings of hillbillies and hayseeds'. During their annual summer vacation at Beaver Dams Springs, Tennessee, they would listen to fiddlers at the local square dance, and that was that. Gram started as an Elvis Presley fan, and worked back.

Now he tried to divest country music of its old-time past, and substitute black music. 'We are playing roots music. It's a form of love music, a binding type of music between people. We're playing with white soul, and soul is universal.' One could argue that Parsons' project was ultimately disastrous, both for the dilutions of country rock, and for Gram himself. But it was a hell of a ride! The first step was the Burrito's debut, *The Gilded Palace Of Sin*.

The music is ominously prophetic. Sneaky Pete's pedal steel is put through all kinds of special effects to make it virtually unrecognisable from the plaintive sounds of yore. The songs too take an oblique view of country obsessions. The 'proud to fight' song turns into a young man escaping the draft in 'My Uncle', woman as temptress becomes a 'devil in disguise', and comic vengeance turns to hellfire at the door. 'Hot Burrito #1' opens up a vein of tenderness that others had been too 'manly' to dare. 'I'm your toy, I'm your old boy' has a playfulness new to the genre.

For Sid Griffin, 'Gram gave country a new catalogue of subjects: long hair, drugs, the city, Vietnam. He didn't play country rock, he played country with a rock 'n' roll attitude.' Elvis Costello was just one new-wave musician for whom the Burritos were the gateway to country: 'I just liked the guy because he liked Aretha Franklin too.' When the Burritos hit the road, their live sound, a ragged mix of 'Dixie rave ups and emoted, ragged, raw country soul'* – fell between every imaginable musical stool. As Hillman remembers, 'it was too country for FM rock radio, and Nashville hated us'. One witness recalls more people onstage than in the audience at one gig. Even so, some people were taking careful note. Hillman remembers a gig at the Troubadour when Glenn Frey watched Gram like a pickpocket sizing up a client. 'I think he was looking at the Burritos as this very raw, soulful but loose aggregation of guys and thinking "we could do this but better".' Which The Eagles did, as a very successful, slick version of the Burritos'.

Parsons was unmarketable, 'doing this mild cross-dressing, playing these redneck country bars where people just wanted to kill us'. When the Stones came to town, Gram in effect left the Burritos. They persuaded Parsons and his band onto the bill at Altamont, where hellfire really did seem to be coming down to earth. They even appear briefly in *Gimmie Shelter*, playing some sweet country tunes. By now, they had a new guitarist, Bernie Leadon, another Eagle to be.

A surviving tape from the Avalon finds the music is a little sloppy, true, and this is nothing like the free-jamming Byrds with Clarence White. Parsons' voice dominates, with Sneaky Pete all over the instrumental sections. The music sounds alive and passionate. 'We'd like to do some country songs' Gram slurs in an almost comically exaggerated Southern

* *No Depression*

accent, after 'Dark End Of The Street', which is anything but. 'It's really great the way everybody sits around and listens. This is what it all comes from, nostalgia and sweet country music'. 'We are so simple', he comments later. There is a wonderful free flow to the sound, a lively simplicity.

Shortly after the release of *Burrito DeLuxe*, a tuinol-soaked Gram was asked to leave his own band. The undoubted highlight is Parsons' reading of the Jagger/Richards song 'Wild Horses'. Gram sings it with sweet sadness, as if lost. But Gram's ace card was a young and unknown harmony singer, Emmylou Harris. She had grown up around military bases in Virginia, moved to Greenwich Village as a folk singer, then on to Nashville where she failed to break through as a country star, and then back home, where she played bars with a repertoire that stretched from Joni Mitchell to bluegrass, barely making a living. Rick Roberts came in one night, was bowled over, and for a time Emmylou was seriously considered as the first Flying Burrito Sister. Chris Hillman urged Gram to go see her, and in front of an audience of three people he joined her for a duet on 'I Saw The Light', which seems wholly appropriate.

To hear them duetting was to encounter love in action. She recalls going out on the road with Gram, touring the hippie haunts and honky tonks. 'They came to see this young man and to hear the voice that would break and crack but rise pure and beautiful and full with sweetness and pain.' As to herself, 'I feel like I swallowed a piece of Oklahoma – and a big ol' moon comes rising out of my throat.' Shivers of light from that moon touched Gram's final recordings, a blessing from above.

A radio broadcast of Parsons and the Fallen Angels live in 1973 is a revelation. Everything is relaxed, even 'Drug Store Truck Drivin' Man', and the duet with Emmylou on 'The New Soft Shoe' reaches a luxuriant sweetness that no-one else in country has ever touched. 'A great breath of fresh air', the DJ reckons. Gram carefully places each of the Angels in their geographical context. Emmylou from Birmingham, Alabama. He's still mixing up the medicine, so that 'Cry One More Time' is by the J Geils band, as r&b as white men can get. It's the duets that really hit home: 'Just by singing with him, I learned that you let the melody and the words carry you. Rather than this emoting thing, it will happen on its own. You have to have restraint in how you approach a song.'*

* Emmylou Harris

'Gram said, 'Let's just voice it down. Basically, less is more.' – the secret of all great country music, from Jimmie Rodgers to The Handsome Family. Gram introduced Emmylou to 'a vein of music I call the High Lonesome – the beautiful heartbreak harmony duets you hear in songs by the young Everly Brothers, Charlie and Ira Louvin, Felice and Boudleaux Bryant'. It is that sound that seeps through their work together.

On *GP*, 'She' puts Gram into the body of a poor, black woman from the Delta, leading people to the Lord. He emotes over slow piano chords and mournful fiddle as if singing in church, a desperate hope in his voice. Steve Earle saw them in Houston: 'it was loose but it was tough. Gram's hair was frosted and his fingernails were painted red. He sang through his nose with eyes closed while the band played catch-up for most of the night. I saw and heard Emmylou for the first time…I left a little bit in love and absolutely certain what I was going to be when I grew up'.

Gram only ever received one royalty cheque – via Joan Baez. John Lomax III recalls that, towards the end, 'He was blasted out of his gourd. He was putting everything into his system you could get, without regard to anything'. Gram wouldn't even reach Hank Williams' brief span. 'Death is a warm cloak,' he told *Crawdaddy* in a last interview, 'an old friend'. *Grievous Angel* came out posthumously and sounds like a goodbye note. It opens with the sheer joy of 'Return Of The Grievous Angel', an immersion in the c&w myth, where truckers and cowboy angels meet in porch or parlor. 'Cheyenne To Tennessee' is written on a night train: Dylan himself appears as a king with 'an amphetamine crown', set to unbuckle the bible belt. A glorious outtake, which surfaces on *Sleepless Nights* is the Louvin Brothers' 'The Angels Rejoiced Last Night'.

Emmylou floats over Gram's voice like a swimmer. The whole album is an arrow straight to the heart. 'Love Hurts' sounds here too intimate to be allowed out in public. Emmylou uses her folk background to be both spot-on and slightly out of sync – it's all very modal – and a country fiddle adds a third voice to the equation. The middle verse of the album's closing song, the singalong 'In My Hour Of Darkness', is supposedly about Clarence White, but Parsons too was 'just a country boy' at heart.

When Parsons died in room 8 of the Joshua Tree Inn, Emmylou felt like 'I'd been amputated, like my life had just been whacked off'. Phil

Kaufman honoured a pledge he had made to the singer, and having kidnapped his coffin at LA International Airport, built a funeral pyre out at Cap Rock, where Gram had once watched for UFOs with Keith Richards. Gram burnt like 'an unbelievable fireball'. As a later song pledged, Emmylou did indeed become 'the keeper of the flame, till every soul hears what your heart was saying'.

Mark Olson and his wife Victoria Williams now live out at Joshua Tree. There is a 'well-kept book to document messages his fans write in' at the hotel, an annual Gram Fest, and regular concerts at a nearby cafe, where 'Emmylou's daughter recently sat in with musicians from Dig Your Own Cactus'. Gram has become his own legend.

When Emmylou organised the 1999 tribute album *Return Of The Grievous Angel*, she deliberately chose new-wave country acts and others outside the genre to pay testimony. This is only appropriate, as alt country is far more in tune with Gram's true intentions than contemporary Nashville. *No Depression* reckons that the difference between Music Row and the alternative is that the latter 'are much more likely to be influenced by Gram Parsons'. Here, The Cowboy Junkies carefully leech out any sign of life from 'Ooh Las Vegas'. Beck sings 'Sin City' relatively straight, and the Mavericks glide through 'Hot Burrito #1'. Wilco play a saloon-bar 'One Hundred Years From Now', and Whiskeytown slow strut through 'A Song For You'. Whiskeytown got the slot because Emmylou, who knew nothing else about them, heard that while looking for a deal they would cross-examine A&R men how much they knew about Parsons. 'And I said OK, that sounds like something Gram would do, only he would ask about George Jones or Webb Pierce.'

Most interesting is the way that strong-voiced women have now come to take the lead role, not just the harmony vocal. Here, the highlights are Gillian Welch's stern and haunted old-timey 'Hickory Wind', Chrissie Hynde on a tough 'She' and Lucinda Williams slurring the title track – David Crosby, of all people, soars above her on harmony vocals. Sheryl Crow and Emmylou Harris duet on a sweet-voiced 'Juanita', like sisters.

Elvis Costello now hears Gram's sound in rock bands like Son Volt. Hillman, who should know, reckons that Wilco have really captured the early Burritos' sound, 'nobody was doing it then, it was so out of left field. It was loose but it was full of energy and life'. Talking to Nigel Williamson, Emmylou concurs, not hearing much of Gram's influence in Nashville, 'but I hear it outside in the more diverse pop and alternative musical worlds. I went for people who are innovators in their field'. Beck 'does it even more traditionally than Gram. He sang it from more of a country place'. Talking to Pete Doggett, she adds that the album is less a tribute than an introduction, 'because few people in the United States have any clue who Gram was, though I know it's different over here.'

Harris now looks back to her collaboration with Parsons as 'regressive country. You have to draw on the past and you have to come up with something new.' She herself came to the music late: 'It was like I discovered this treasure that was under everybody's noses, and it overwhelmed me'. But she has never wanted to 'restrict myself to what people called country'.

When Emmylou started up with the Angel Band, 'I was definitely gathering up everything that Gram had touched, almost like musical relics'. Emmylou writes few songs herself, so goes to outsiders for material. *Profile*, a superior 'best of' compilation has songs by AP Carter, the Louvin Brothers, Don Gibson, Dolly Parton and Billy Sherrill – all 'country' – but also r&b offerings from Chuck Berry and Delbert McClinton. Her voice is a hybrid too, with country vowels but a folky glissando. Unlike Judy Collins whose vocal purity she most resembles, there is never a sense that Emmylou is skating over the meaning of the lyrics. She lives every word.

A tape of a show at London's New Victoria Theatre in 1975, the year of her debut album *Pieces Of The Sky*, reveals a sound not that far removed from the Nashville mainstream, with pedal steel and piano, and songs that alternate between weepy and uptempo. She is still most used to performing 'with people sitting at tables and beer in front of them'. Emmylou brought honky-tonk intimacy to the concert halls of the world. There is a real twang to her voice, lots of Gram Parsons songs, and, best of all, her lament for the dead singer, 'Boulder To Birmingham'.

She describes the Hot Band, put together to back her, as 'the greatest country band in the world', with heavyweights like James Burton, pianist Glen D Hardin and Rodney Crowell, 'a real good old boy from Austin, Texas'. Here, they glide beneath her voice with no apparent effort. It is the very antithesis of rough mountain music. The Hot Band powered a succession of regal albums, which straddle soft rock and country.

With the help of bluegrass star Ricky Skaggs on fiddle, Emmylou began a sharp left turn towards traditional sounds on 1979's *Blue Kentucky Girl*. Western swing is in the air. Emmylou appears in front of a painted stage set of an old Wild West saloon, wearing antique clothes and with rose-engraved boots 'n' matching guitar. She sings with even more of a rural tremor, and 'Hickory Wind', slowed and toned right down, sounds like a fond farewell to more than her favourite singer. Flip the disc and you have Jean Ritchie's 'Sorrow In The Wind' – with the White Girls on harmony and an old-timey sound, alongside material mainly written in the '60s. Even Rodney Crowell's contribution here, the sprightly 'Even Cowgirls Get The Blues', is deliberately old-fashioned.

The following year brought *Roses In The Snow*, and really broke the mould, mixing bluegrass with Appalachian material. Violins weep, acoustic guitars pick out simple riffs, and the whole thing is driven by God. Even Paul Simon's 'The Boxer' is incorporated into the tradition, though Emmylou's voice is perhaps a little too pure, too carefully tuneful, to really dig out the painful joy at the rough heart of these songs.

Again she was doing what she's always done best, interpreting an off-centre music for a mass audience, but with respect. Her voice flows smooth, but never bland. Emmylou won a Country Music Assocation award for this album as female vocalist of the year, but as she told John Tobler, 'they don't have a category for bluegrass, they just ignore it. It's getting to where they're finally starting to recognise Bill Monroe.' The later *Angel Band* is a collection of acoustic country-gospel, in the steps of the Stanley Brothers.

Emmylou swopped husbands and producers, leaving Brian Ahern and an album of farewell scraps in Evangeline. She then married Paul Kennerley, the English composer of concept albums of Americana, like *White Mansions*, which refers both to Southern architecture and the skulls of the dead on Civil War battlegrounds. Together they wrote *The Ballad Of Sally Rose* a final expunging of Gram Parsons' memory, whose story it tells, even if 'The Singer' is never named. Typically subtle is her long awaited declaration of love, set to the AP Carter tune 'You Are My

Flower'. Emmylou is 'The Sweetheart Of The Rodeo', out on 'the longest road'. Some facts are changed, with Sally Rose the daughter of a Sioux Indian. Later 'she gives up everything and settles down' alone in a broadcasting tower, sending out 'the sound of the Singer' for the rest of her days. Like a ghost 'she's just waiting for you to tune in'...

Emmylou went back further, and dropped a rapidly cooling Hot Band for the Nash Ramblers, an incandescent bluegrass band with Sam Bush on mandolin. The 1991 live album *At The Ryman* looks forward as well, opening with a Steve Earle song, but poor reviews led to her being dropped by her record label. She had stepped too far outside the expectations of her core audience. To be more exact, she had outpaced them.

Each of her albums has its own inner logic, and Emmylou went on to record some of the greatest of her career. Producer Daniel Lanois sculpted *Wrecking Ball* with U2's drummer and his own guitar textures, using lots of antique instruments to achieve a haunted and mysterious sound. Just as he filtered out every extraneous noise from Bob Dylan's voice on *Oh Mercy*, and helped take Robbie Robertson back to his Indian roots, so he helps Emmylou to look deep into herself, and the result is the highest, most lonesome sounds she has ever uttered.

Here too is a repertoire of songs by heavy friends like Lucinda Williams, Gillian Welch, Rodney Crowell, the McGarrigle Sisters, Neil Young, Lanois himself, Bob Dylan... Rock, folk and new country: not a Nashville hack in sight. A radio broadcast of her 1995 appearance with the Lanois band at the Shepherds Bush Empire prove that this sound is not the product of studio trickery. Live, it's even more extreme, with Daniel's effects-laden guitar work pushing Harris seemingly to sing with a new voice, like a woman possessed. 'Poncho And Lefty', and the Burritos' song 'Wheels' join songs from the record, which is based around one theme. 'Yearning. That's probably always been a driving force in what I look for. If yearning had a sound it would be Daniel's production.'

'Sweet Old World' is a 'love letter to a friend who has committed suicide', while 'All My Tears' is 'an elegy written in the voice of the deceased'. No wonder the disc sounds so haunted, so close to Appalachian ballads in spirit if not in sound, but Emmylou reckons that if anything from it gets played on country radio, 'it'll be nothing short of a miracle'.

She intends to make records, regardless. 'I still love country music, but the mainstream is just so squeaky-clean right now. I think people need to get a little dirty.' More recently, Emmylou has collaborated with the alt-rock band *Spyboy*, featuring Buddy Miller on lead guitar. It was 'the sound of a band reconstructing country rock with a passion the young pretenders might well envy.'* Emmylou is also a harmony singer of genius still, as recent collaborations with Linda Ronstadt and Dolly Parton show. The two *Trio* albums centre on, in turn, mountain ballads like 'Rosewood Casket' and love songs. Co-producer of the second, is John Starling of progressive bluegrass combo The Seldom Scene.

Nanci Griffith reckons Emmylou's secret as a harmony singer is that 'she has a great capacity to listen', that and 'the amount of heart she puts into it'. Likewise, Emmylou's Nashville home has provided a refuge for the likes of Nanci Griffith, Steve Earle and Lucinda Williams, for whom she remains a surrogate mother, a 'connoisseur of songs' in Earle's phrase. Nothing in current Nashville strikes her as 'mysterious or creative'. To her, a rock star like Bruce Springsteen is far closer to the country tradition 'because of the way he phrases, the simplicity and passion of what he does – it's country even if he doesn't have a pedal-steel guitar. Merle Haggard doesn't always have pedal steel, you know.'

Bob Dylan, too. In 1975 he revisited his musical roots on the *Rolling Thunder* tour. With conscious symbolism, the first concert was to be held at Plymouth, Massachusetts, where the Pilgrim Fathers had came ashore. The sprawling four-hour show traversed the nation, carefully choreographed by Jacques Levy, Roger McGuinn's partner in *Gene Tryp*. 'The thing was to make it appear like a spontaneous evening... There was no tuning up between songs, there were no pauses. Big chunks of the show were the same every night'. It was a final gathering together of so many of the coffee-house traditionalists, like a parade of ghosts.

In the bursts of live action captured on the movie *Renaldo And Clara*, Dylan himself wears a cowboy hat and white paint on his face, his eyes blazing like burning coals during 'Isis' and other new folk-tales. Each singer – Ramblin' Jack Elliott, Joni Mitchell, Bob Neuwirth, Kinky Friedman – has their own guest spot. The tour is an attempt to rediscover a lost, mythical America, from the Pilgrim Fathers to a Shaker Village

* *Mojo*

to Jack Kerouac's grave. Each night starts with David Mansfield on pedal steel leading the tour band through 'Flint Hill Special', an example of electric bluegrass. The final song is a mass rendition of Woody Guthrie's 'This Land Is Your Land'. Mansfield's country-steel wailings and mandolin trills, along with Scarlet Rivera's electric violin and the ramshackle rhythm section ties this music firmly to the string bands of the '30s, rocked up and coked out. Such was the air of excess that many of the musicians converted to evangelical Christianity shortly afterwards, Dylan included.

As to The Byrds, they came back into fashion in the '80s thanks to bands like REM and the Long Ryders. That mix of laconic vocals and jangly guitars fed straight through into 'alt country'. Chris Hillman returned to his bluegrass roots with the mainly acoustic *Morning Sky* for Sugar Hill, a label that rapidly became the brand leader for the genre. *Desert Rose* was more of the same, with added electricity. Even so, Hillman does not now consider himself a bluegrass player. 'I'm so out of practise. I can play the music but I can't keep up if they play a fast song'.

Gene Clark had been the first ex-Byrd to embrace country rock, on his 1967 album *Gene Clark With The Gosdin Brothers*, full of good playing, sad songs and sweet country harmonies. Next Clark teamed up with Doug Dillard. Clark's primal melancholy seeps through via his questing voice and songs like 'She Darked The Sun', offset by Doug's cheerful picking. 'Don't Come Rollin' has the swing of mountain music, but an excess of words, a Clark speciality.

When the *Fantastic Expedition Of Dillard And Clark* debuted the album at the LA Troubadour in late 1968, the line up was Gene, Bernie Leadon on lead guitar, Doug on a custom-made Rickenbacker electric banjo, another former Byrd, Michael Clarke, on drums and David Jackson on electric bass. One reviewer wrote, 'They play country music with a rock beat. I hope it isn't immediately classified as country rock'. Something was in the air. The new rock magazine *Crawdaddy* had already reported in October 1967 that 'Los Angeles is getting interested in country & western music. The Byrds, the Buffalo Springfield are groups that already show a strong country influence; the possibility of c&w getting into the heads of a group like Love, or some of the blues bands, is very exciting indeed'. A Byrds reunion proved disastrous, and Gene Clark went on to release his masterpiece, *No Other*. Gene has filtered out country music for a kind of multi-dubbed drone, with lyrics rich in mountain wisdom.

It is a long way from bluegrass, but the emotional power and transcendent singing are a common denominator. Cosmic American Music. Clark starts fully confident, jaunty almost, on 'Life's Greatest Fool', though he is staring into a void, 'the darkness of the day'. Rich acoustic guitar, and we're into 'Silver Raven', with Gene's voice bucking and cracking with the sheer majesty of his vision. Bell-like bottleneck guitar from Jesse Ed Davis recreates the flight of 'wings that barely gleam', then almost weeps. 'Strength Of Strings' is a return to the medieval idea of the music of the spheres. 'From A Silver Phial' starts with a 'cocaine burn-out', according to Byrds fanatic Johnny Rogan: if so, it certainly sums up what eventually happened to country rock.

Gene sings about these mysteries with his country-boy twang, which makes them all the more believable. Just when you think you might be completely leaving the known world, along comes the cooling country breeze of 'The True One' – 'I used to treat my friends as if I was more than a millionaire, but what's been flying high must always touch the ground'. The album ends with the age-old image of a breeze that 'whispers through the trees', the same presentiment of death that Gram Parsons heard in a hickory wind.

No Other was finally re-released in 2003 with beautifully crisp sound, and six early takes 'before the full-scale arrival of backing singers and additional musicians'. In this barer context, the beauty of the songs, and Gene's singing, shine through all the more clearly.

The two strands of Gene music, country boogie and folk prophecy, existed uneasily side-by-side on *Two Sides To Every Story*. After the mental storm of the zen album, he is left here 'coming down' to the crying sound of a pedal steel. Newly emerging cowpunks like the Long Ryders took Gene as an icon, and having guested with them on disc, he returned with *Firebyrd*, but 'Gene wasn't there mentally', living in one room and hitting the bottle. He died in 1991, just as he was starting to resurrect his career with the young singer Carla Olson, of new-wave band the Textones. John York remembered 'a sweet guy who had to die to get the world to start taking him seriously. His Missouri meets Elizabethan sensibilities, his courtliness versus his drunkenness – it adds up to a real Hillbilly Shakespeare'.

There has been a big reissue programme, with an augmented *No Other*, and lots of studio sessions, though the painful and frustrating account so brilliantly outlined in John Rogan's latest book on The Byrds reveals all kinds of aural magic still held up in legal red tape. If anyone deserved a proper 'box set' tribute it is Gene Clark. *Full Circle* is a respectful 2-CD tribute by largely unknown acts, from the alt-rock end of the spectrum, the likes of the Finkers and Happydeadmen, and with Steve Wynn and Sid Griffin lending a helping hand.

Peter Rowan and mandolin player David Grisman had played together in various teenage bluegrass combos. They later joined Seatrain, an attempt at fusing bluegrass with classical music. It now sounds as dated as the band look. Not so Muleskinner, a band of young musicians put together for a TV special starring Bill Monroe. Bill's tour bus broke down, and after three hours of rehearsal this sparkling combo – guitarist Clarence White and four former Blue Grass Boys, Rowan, Grisman, banjo player Bill Keith and Richard Greene on fiddle – set to work. When the same bunch reconvened in the studio to record *Muleskinner* something else happened. The music shoots out of the speakers with a fierceness that takes the breath away. Part of this must be due to Rowan's energetic voice, a kind of feral yelp when he gets excited, but these players have brought the energy – and the noise – of rock music to the subtleties of bluegrass, with Clarence's Telecaster 'cracking like a bullwhip' and a heavy rhythm section. They play so fast on the title track that there seem to be notes missing. As Rowan puts it, 'Clarence's gentle soul was our unifying force, holding the music together.' All kinds of history collide on this record. The lonesome 'Rain And Snow' is a traditional song that Rowan learned from Obray Ramsey, 'the great Appalachian singer', and made famous with the Monroe band, from whom the Grateful Dead learnt it and put it on their first album.

Rowan then took off on a strange odyssey that shows no sign of coming to any firm conclusion. *Texican Badman* has a set list that ranges across the Texas-Mexico border, and the album is a weird update of western swing, but with lyrics like 'come see the dragon chase the autumn moon', Bob Wills on peyote, perhaps. The final track is that old country stand-by, the roll call of dead heroes, but here it is Eric Dolphy, John Coltrane, Otis Redding and Charlie Christian on the 'blue horizon'.

This sense of another world haunts all of Rowan's best work. He and his wife went looking for 'a spirit of American history and myth'. They found it in Monument Valley, the landscape endlessly revisited by filmmaker John Ford. Here they found dinosaur bones and wall paintings. 'You look at your feet and there are fossils of seashells, and you realize that you're standing on the bottom of an ocean that is now the top of a mountain'. No wonder that the album *Walls of Time* is one of his finest.

Rowan was careful not to over-rehearse his musicians, among whom are maestros like Sam Bush and Ricky Skaggs, so that they capture the 'spontaneous feel' of true bluegrass. The underlying narrative is of a former jailbird who goes up to the mountains on a quest for spiritual redemption. He meets a mysterious woman, and his troubles really begin. As Rowan explains it, 'Maybe "Walls Of Time" is him finding the grave of his sweetheart and maybe she didn't really die. Maybe it was love that was dead.' Certainly the title song, credited jointly to Rowan and Bill Monroe, is about love beyond the grave, in the best mountain tradition.

As Rowan told *Folk Roots*, 'there were certain things that Bill Monroe passed on to me. It has a lot to do with feel, it's what Bill used to call the "Ancient Tones".' His 1996 CD *Bluegrass Boy* is a fine tribute, entirely self-composed, with an ageing Peter silhouetted against a darkening sky.

Back in the late '60s, Rowan and his long-time musical compatriot David Grisman had formed Earth Opera, one of the best of the psychedelic bands, with two classic albums on Elektra as their memorial. A song like 'Death By Fire' is somehow archetypal, a strange tale told in anguish with instruments and singer on full intensity. At first, psychedelic sounds seemed to have nothing at all to do with old-timey music, and its buttoned-up sound and players. Mountain music dealt with limitations while this new sound was about the very lack of limits. Scratch below the surface a little, though, scrape away the long hair of the new psychedelic bands, and the faces that emerge are long-term inmates of the '60s folk scene. Listen carefully to the repertoire of bands at the Fillmore, West and you will hear songs or ideas or atmospheres from the *Harry Smith Anthology*, given a new twist. It was as if Smith's vison of that old, weird America was coming true, with adventurous light shows, and through a haze of dope smoke. His one-man resistance to the 1950s had borne fruit.

Though stoned Texans, the Thirteenth Floor Elevators, have a strong claim, as do garage rockers with a weirder edge than most, the Seeds, most rock historians trace the music that burst out of San Francisco like a love bomb in 1967 to the historic Red Dog Saloon in the ghost town of Virginia City, Nevada – on the Comstock Lode – two summers earlier. The youthful clientele dressed self-consciously in Wild West clothes and listened to a weird jingle-jangle bunch, called the Charlatans, whose self-mocking glee was part of the joke. It was the new Wild West. 'We were all post-adolescents playing at Cowboys and Indians.'

When George Hunter first met Mike Wilheim, 'I used to hang out at his house, listening to Johnny Cash.' What evidence survives of the original line-up shows a barely adequate, country-ish combo, but with strange undercurrents. Listen to Buffy Sainte-Marie's 'Codine Blues', with its weird echo and clunking backing, over which Wilheim sings deadpan and slightly off-key about his helpless drug addiction. There is a guitar solo in the near distance, with an unsettling edge. If one word describes the mix of blues, folk and country the Charlatans purveyed, it is 'Americana'. A reformed line-up recorded an album for Philips, long after the magic had evaporated. Songs by the likes of AP Carter indicate their roots, and the band gradually mutated into the jovial western swing of Dan Hicks And His Hot Licks, with the singing drummer now in sole charge. Meanwhile, other off-centre bands were emerging, taking the music into a warped-world entered through the prism of LSD.

A scruffy group of ex-bluegrass and jugband players went electric, and called themselves the Warlocks. Just after the Charlatans' residency had been cancelled following the inevitable drugs bust, a strange bus rolled through Virginia City on its way from Ohio to San Francisco, painted in day-glo and with the legend 'Further' on the front. The new frontiersmen were rolling in. In December 1965, they held the first Acid Test, with a soundtrack by the Warlocks, at this point still a heavy r&b band with a heavy following among the Hells Angels. As they began to play hippie hangouts like the Fillmore and the Avalon, the band began to loosen up, and to incorporate some of the music they grew up with. The Grateful Dead – as they soon became – is a name taken straight from the twilight zone where folklore and the occult meet. Ditto the Warlocks, and the skull and roses motif that the band took. Growth from decay. Had the Dead been an obscure '20s hillbilly band, Harry Smith would have had them straight into his *Anthology* for the strange atmosphere and wayward playing of their early songs, a code to which the listener does not quite have the key. Robert Hunter was one of the first volunteers to undergo trials under LSD, and it opened up the whole of Americana, its legends and landscape and movies – as a kind of cosmic playpen.

On their first album, Garcia's weedy voice ploughs through an unemotional update of 'Cold Rain And Snow', credited to the band rather than the public domain where they found it. A lecherous-sounding Pigpen takes most lead vocals, and goes through the gutbucket blues repertoire. By 1968, though, Hunter's baroque lyrics had blossomed into the rich incomprehensibility of 'Dark Star' and its likes. Garcia's picking is country-clean, interacting carefully with the rest of the band, so that the music ebbs and flows. As he himself said 'I would describe my own guitar playing as descended from bar-room rock 'n' roll, country guitar'. Bakersfield, in other words. Garcia's bluegrass heritage was also starting to pay dividends, as his maimed fingers conjured endless runs of electric magic. His notes dance an endless duet with Phil Lesh's energetic bass, over Pigpen's rich organ chords and two drummers.

Jerry had been 'an absolute ferocious five-string banjo player' in his youth, and described the Dead as a 'mutated bluegrass band: as in bluegrass, the instruments talk to each other'. Jerry began soloing 'in paragraphs rather than riffs and licks', in the slipstream of Scotty Stoneman from the Kentucky Colonels. 'This is a guy who took an ABBA fiddle tune, and extended it out for 15 minutes, with 17-bar phrases and unbelievable expressive shit. I couldn't believe what I was hearing.'

Garcia had become 'kind of froze up in bluegrass'. Once the Dead had moved from Haight-Ashbury into the wilds of Marin County, Garcia and Hunter began to discover how to write tight and sharply focused songs about getting back to the country. At much the same time, the likes of Merle Haggard's prison song 'Sing Me Back Home' were entering the

Grateful Dead's live shows, as they mutated from freak-outs to selections from a cosmic American jukebox. It is wonderfully ironic that just the kind of musicians whom the mythical Okie from Musgokee would most distrust, fear and spurn – wild men on drugs playing atonal hour-long jams – were now taking Merle seriously as a national bard. Under the tie-dies and long hair, they are kith and kin. As Garcia points out, 'Hunter and I always had this thing where we liked to muddy the folk tradition by adding our own songs. It's the thing of taking a well-founded tradition, and putting in something that's totally looped'.

Another great psychedelic band with more than a trace of country music were Moby Grape, though their speciality was short, sharp songs. The roots influence came through on later albums like *Moby Grape 69*. Central to the band was 'demonic' Skip. He was responsible for the cod '30s number 'Just Like Gene Autrey; A Foxtrot', which played at 78rpm. Quite what the singing cowboy had done to get a namecheck remains unclear – yet another example of Americana imagery floating in the wind, thanks to the collision between stoned minds and childhood memories.

Skip Spence finally went over the top when he threatened fellow Moby Grape member Don Stevenson with a fire-axe, and was committed to Bellevue mental hospital for six months. Once he was discharged, Spence went off to Nashville in late 1968, and recorded *Oar* 'the sort of haphazard folk music that might have been made around campfires after the California gold rush burned itself out – sad, clumsy tunes that seem to laugh at themselves'.* Just listen to 'Cripple Creek', in which an ancient song is updated through 'streams of fire', and is now both 'daydream' and a modern legend. Through Skip's weird inner alchemy, the song now has the stamp of reality.

Skip sings everything slightly out of tune. Officially diagnosed as a paranoid schizophrenic – the US war casualties of the late '60s were not all in Vietnam – Columbia were generous enough to give him 6 days recording time in that same Nashville studio. The latest *Oar* reissue contains ten tracks recorded on that final day, though nothing compares to the spectral drone of 'Grey/Afro', about the furthest from country music that anything recorded in Nashville has ever got. At one point it sounds like he's playing the didgeridoo. Skip provides a kind of ghostly

* Greil Marcus

commentary to *John Wesley Harding*, recorded in the same place a year before. The slow lament 'Weighted Down' is pure Johnny Cash.

Shortly after Spence's death in 1999, a tribute album *More Oar* was released with the likes of Beck and Alejandro Escovedo providing sympathetic covers. Jay Farrar sings 'Weighted Down' with feeling, but loses its funereal sadness and Skip's stoned, dying croak.

There are other albums that seem to inhabit a weird and unsettling landscape, which later outlaws like Will Oldham or Beck were to make their home of choice. No one could claim Mad River as a direct influence on 'alt country' – no fond name checks or tribute albums – but they made the edgiest album of even those strange times. Matters were not helped when the initial pressing was accidentally speeded up. Lawrence Hammond's keening wail of a voice cuts like a scalpel, not least on the horror story of 'War Goes On'. It is as if Vietnam has come home to the prairies. Odd scrapings – this is the kind of record where the drummer is also credited with playing 'fence and worms' – then atonal guitars snap into a brisk beat, and Hammond is telling his story of a 15-year-old girl tethered in a truck, 'her hair tied to her knees'. After one of the wildest West Coast guitar solos ever unleashed, Lawrence returns to find birds picking the veins from her hands 'like they were worms'. He props her upright in a cornfield 'to scare away the crows, I guess.'

Hammond grew up in Nebraska, and as a teenager was a keen fan of bluegrass combo The Blue Southern Ramblers, whom he saw 'in a ragged honky-tonk'. He would place his face right up against their instruments and mutter 'I wonder how d'you do that?' Later he became a folk singer in Greenwich Village, opening for Jesse Colin Young, and later duetting with the likes of Mike Seeger. As for Young, he formed the Youngbloods and, seduced by the California ballrooms, they moved west and recorded *Elephant Mountain*. Mysterious and welcoming, with lots of studio chatter, the disc combines jazz and country and bluegrass and white soul into one seamless whole. Songs break down (literally) and then pick themselves up off the floor – again a rough-and-ready approach that turns the recording studio into a front porch, which is now almost the alt-country norm. And yet, at the heart of *Elephant Mountain* is 'Darkness, Darkness', with a guitar solo that scrapes at your brain.

Meanwhile, the next generation was coming through. Johnny Ciambotti had started his career playing bass with a bluegrass act, The Valley Boys, who had a residency at the Ash Grove alongside the Kentucky Colonels. He jumped ship for San Francisco, met John McFee and founded Clover, a perky bunch with songs about lizards playing rock 'n' roll. They later moved to England, just as punk was starting to rear its ugly head, and played as a session band on Elvis Costello's early records.

Austin, Texas too proved to be a seed bed for the next musical wave. It was a town that had earlier sired Roky Erickson and his band the aforementioned Thirteenth Floor Elevators: 'We had the cops after us wherever we went'. On *Bull of the Woods*, Erikson performed his own mournful take on 'May The Circle Be Unbroken'. He repeats the title phrase over and over, sad but hopeful as he waves goodbye to his mind.

Doug Sahm was an altogether more cheerful creature, who as a child had appeared onstage with Hank Williams at Austin's Skyline club in 1952. As he told Ed Ward, Hank 'was wasted. He was so skinny he had to perform sitting down, so they made me get up on his lap and his legs were so bony they were hurting my ass.' After a spell with the Sir Douglas Quintet, he went solo and became a regular at venues like the Armadillo World Headquarters, as well as helping to launch Roky Erickson back on an expectant world. Doug himself was the spirit of western swing personified – always good for a polka – and as a teenager he received encouragement from no less a figure than Adolph Hofner. He in turn later reformed the Sir Douglas Quintet with two of his sons, one of whom went on to join the Meat Puppets. The circle is, indeed, unbroken.

The Bottle Rockets recently put out their own tribute, *Songs Of Sahm*, with a little more crunch than the original, but some of that cheesy Tex Mex organ, amiable vocals, and the odd yelp and howl that made Doug's music so unique. Sahm himself put out a huge range of material. His refusal to leave Texas for long, after that first initial foray to '60s San Francisco, led to sporadic gigs, and one-off albums, which include *Texas Rock For Country Rollers* with songs like 'You Just Can't Hide A Redneck (Under That Hippy Hair)'. *Groover's Paradise* sees him with the Creedence Clearwater rhythm section on a 'tex-mex' trip. 'Austintatious' music, like the sleeve says. No wonder that Grant Alden chose Sahm, posthumously for his inaugural President's Award of the Americana Music Association. It was a fitting tribute to a career that covered 'almost every conceivable edge of Americana, from the 1960s garage rock of 'She's About A Mover' to the celebrated Tex-Mex of the Texas Tornados'.

ix) From Country Rock To Southern Boogie

Though they only made three albums, one a retrospective, *Buffalo Springfield* led the way for what became known as 'country rock', a fresh and still potent brew of good songs and duelling lead guitars – from Steve Stills and Neil Young – and shared roots that saw Doc Watson, Hank Williams and The Dillards all namechecked. Young would often dress as a native American onstage, an image that fed into his early song 'Broken Arrow', and more generally into images of darkness , paranoia and defeat.

The songs on his first solo album are those of a recluse, lost in luxuriant backings courtesy of Jack Nitzsche, and the Poco rhythm section. His own voice is buried deep in the mix, as if he is trying not to be there at all. This strange, dream-like atmosphere seeped into the quieter sections of *Everyone Knows This Is Nowhere*. He found his band playing roots rock in a bar, and renamed them Crazy Horse, after the rebel chief. On that same album, two long guitar workouts are imbued with the spirit of the Wild West, a gunshot slaying in 'Down By The River' and a cowboy's lament on 'Cowgirl In The Sand'.

But Young's subsequent career, dipping in and out of the soft harmonies of Crosby, Stills And Nash, alternating between acoustic quietude and full-on rock, facing up to his inner demons whatever it might cost him, helped establish the template for alt country, too. No wonder that the Neil Young tribute CD *This Note's For You Too!* is a double. The bands chosen – Slobberbone, Big in Iowa, the Golden Watusis and so on – are themselves impossible to categorise, but tend to come from the wilder shores of alt country and alt rock, not the country rock mainstream.

Here too are cowpunk veterans like Steve Wynn and Chris Cavacas, Richard Lloyd from Television, roots rockers The Walkabouts and avante-gardists like Mushroom, on the instrumental 'Emperor Of Wyoming'.

Not to mention his greatest ever stylist, Dutchman Ad Vanderveen who sometimes seems more in-tune with Neil's early muse than Young himself.

Having immersed himself in TV shows like 'Rawhide and all that cowboy stuff' when growing up, once Neil had moved to California, he began to live the myth. *After The Goldrush*, was based around a film screenplay by Dean Stockwell, 'all about the day of the great earthquake in Topanga Canyon'. Most of *Harvest* was recorded in Nashville, with a new backing band The Stray Gators . The music is certainly less frenetic than Crazy Horse, and Neil's voice has the right kind of whine for c&w, but it's somehow too edgy, too individual. Pedal steel is probably its nearest aural equivalent, scraping at your sinapses. He came back, 20 years on, with much the same musicians and a mournful harmonica for *Harvest Moon*. 'From Hank To Hendrix' is the killer, tracing a relationship through the music they listened to together, and full of bitter wisdom. 'I never believed in much/but I believed in you'. *Silver And Gold* was publicised as the third part of the *Harvest* trilogy, but as *NME* noted, 'it is now the 'alt country' crowd who nod dreamily in his direction'.

Neil himself continues to plough his own eccentric furrow, and *Are You Passionate?*, besides a typically angry and strangely upbeat response to the events of September 11th, 'Let's Roll', boasts long jams with another bunch of veterans Booker T And The MGs. Both have retained their early fire. Ever restless, Young's 2003 solo UK gigs previewed vast swathes of *Greendale*, a CD with an 80-minute movie in which every character speaks in Neil's voice to match, about a fictional family in a fictional California town. Classic Americana for our times, with Neil's own favourite Sun Green, an eco-activist who hauls a truckload of hay up a hill to form a giant anti-war slogan.

Back in 1985, *Old Ways* was largely recorded in rural Tennessee, and reprises the favourite song of his childhood, with Bela Fleck on banjo, with Willie Nelson and Waylon Jennings sharing vocals.

Certainly, Crosby, Stills And Nash used country music as a colouring, rather than as a spur to creativity. This is largely true too of many other bands now pigeonholed as 'country rock', whose music now sounds pleasant but nostalgic, without the bite and snap of contemporary alt country, or the weirdness of new old time. Poco's Rusty Young remembers that when he first got to LA, 'there were a lot of little bunches of people getting together' and one of these was the original conjunction between Gene Clark and Doug Dillard with a string bassist and Bernie Leadon. 'They had their band together and they were going to be real bluegrassy. The record was so different. I was disappointed because it didn't have the magic that the little tapes they made in their house did. Boy, that was the closest thing to what I would consider country rock that I have heard, ever, and it's never made it to a record.'

As so often, it is the left-field mavericks whose work has lasted the longest, and still sounds freshest. Ian and Sylvia were a Canadian folky duo who formed an early country rock band, the Great Speckled Bird, whose 1969 debut was produced by Todd Rundgren. It features a surprisingly tough sound, with Buddy Cage's home-made pedal-steel duetting or duelling with Amos Garrett on lead guitar, string bending as good as Clarence White. The vocals are soulful, and the whole thing still sounds urgent and up to the minute. Drummer ND Smart II later joined Gram Parsons' Fallen Angels.

The LA band Kaleidoscope mixed and matched bluegrass, cajun and Cab Calloway, then added in r&b and Eastern sounds. Chris Darrow heard a record by Earl Taylor and his Stony Mountain Boys, which 'sent me into outer space – especially the mandolin sound that just tinkled my brain'. He formed the Re-Organised Dry City Players, and these merged into David Lindley's Mad Mountain Ramblers, to play 'hot bluegrass with old timey music thrown in'. This developed in live performance into a unique mix of long far-Eastern jams interspersed with fiery psychedelia and old-time Americana. Their debut album, *Side Trips* follows a weird drug song like 'Pulsating Dream' with the truly sombre 'Oh Death'. A fiddle scrapes, percussion sounds like earth clods dropping on a coffin, and a man pleads for his very soul. 'Oh death, can't you spare me over for another year?' 'Egyptian Gardens' suddenly veers from harem music to a banjo-led jig from the Appalachians. On *Incredible*, 'Cuckoo' – a traditional song found on the *Harry Smith Anthology* – is given a heavy electric thump, sung with venom, or then ornamented with a liquid, West Coast guitar solo from Lindley. The third verse brings things round to Vietnam, and past and present coalesce.

David Lindley continues to come at you out of left field. *Live In Tokyo (Official Bootleg)*, a recent CD taped in Japan, with Lindley and Hani Naser on electric guitar and drums, ploughs through cajun and trad folk. *Twango Bango Deluxe* is another prime-time Americana album that's issued by an obscure label in Berlin.

Michael Nesmith escaped from The Monkees to pioneer a sweet form of country rock, with only a small cult audience for his pains. Nesmith played a mix of folk and country under the name Michael Blessing, even before he put on his woolly hat, and acted the John Lennon figure in teen TV. It was a style that ended up influencing the likes of Travis Tritt rather than, say, Wilco. Thank God!

Nesmith recorded in LA, and built his sound around local pedal-steel hero OJ 'Red' Rhodes. The first album with the First National Band, *Magnetic South* still sounds amazingly fresh, with Nesmith's light vocals over a sprightly backing sounding live in the studio, playful and even cuddly. *Loose Salute* is more of the same, self-written apart from his jog-trot version of Patsy Cline's 'I Fall To Pieces', sung without a trace of irony. Then suddenly he's singing 'Conversations' as if his life depended on it. 'Listen to the Band' starts very quiet, and gets louder like it's coming in from another room, but it's still background music when it comes to full strength. On *Nevada Fighter*, which completes the trilogy, the band has been augmented with musicians from Elvis's Las Vegas combo. The opening number 'Grand Ennui', turns out to be a Dylanesque tale of escape. Nesmith's influence is seen at its best on later British pub-rock bands like Deke Leonard's Iceberg and Help Yourself. Light but funky.

In 1972 Nesmith got friendly with Jac Holzman, founder of Elektra records, and the result was the Countryside Record label, whose assets included a studio with a house band including 'Red' Rhodes and some fearsome pickers. The Countryside label was what might be considered the earliest version of today's so-called No Depression mini-industry of alternative country, which Nesmith intended to kick-start with releases from Graland Frady, 'Red' Rhodes and Steve Fromholz. Austin fit right in Nesmith's game plan, with both its musicians and KOKE radio (which was pioneering a progressive country format). The project was axed when David Geffen replaced Jac Holzman at Elektra.

Another maverick who escaped the mainstream for the margins was John Stewart, whose album *California Bloodlines* is pure Americana. At times Stewart sounds just like John Wayne – 'Boys, hell they were men.' When he gets patriotic on the title song, you'll laugh at him through your tears. As the class of 1902 sings, 'Oh Mother Country, I do love you'.

In High School he formed a band called Johnny Stewart And The Furies that played Elvis Presley, Little Richard and Buddy Holly covers. His style shifted to folk music while he was in college, and two songs he wrote were recorded by the Kingston Trio. At the urging of the Trio's manager, John moved to SF and formed the Cumberland Three, a Trio-styled group that recorded an album for the Roulette label.

When Dave Guard left the Kingston Trio in 1961, Stewart was his logical replacement. After seven years and 16 albums with the Trio, Stewart left the group in 1968 and recorded *Signals Through The Glass* with his wife-to-be, singer Buffy Ford. The following year, Stewart went to Nashville to record his first solo album, the aforementioned classic *California Bloodlines*. More albums and more cover versions followed: his songs have been recorded by everyone from Harry Belafonte and Pat Boone to Joan Baez and Nanci Griffith, from the Four Tops and The Lovin' Spoonful to the Beat Farmers and the Violent Femmes.

Stewart went on to make *American Sketches*, a project with the working title of 'Centennial', and heavily influenced by classical ballet suites by Aaron Copland. 'I have always been a big fan. His image of America struck a common chord with me the first time I heard his *Appalachian Spring*, and *Billy The Kid*. To hear the same kind of moods on a guitar project seemed like a true challenge.'

Stewart has spent more than 40 years and over 40 albums helping to change and channel the direction of American popular music. He has created his own distinctive style of Americana, a mixture of folk, country and bluegrass, and a repertoire of memorable original songs and provided hits for artists such as The Monkees, Anne Murray and Rosanne Cash.

Linda Ronstadt was heavily influenced by Mexican music. Another factor behind the sound of Linda's band, the Stone Poneys, was Hearts And Flowers – an LA harmony band that evolved out of bluegrass buffs the Scotsville Squirrel Barkers, and whose 1967 debut still sounds vibrant.

They played what they described as 'Georgia country-folk meets Hawaiian ukelele folk-rock'. Apart from them, 'nobody was doing country rock, and I was sure it could cross over and take off, but nobody believed it except me'. Literally a few weeks later, Gram Parsons joined The Byrds, and the floodgates opened.

Ronstadt 'used to see the Flying Burrito Brothers when they first started off', and she had known Clarence White since she was 16. One night at the Troubadour, she heard an unknown band called Shiloh and was 'flabbergasted'. Soon Bernie Leadon, Randy Meisner, Glenn Frey and Don Henley were backing her on stage and in the recording studio. Henley was a singing drummer from Texas, and when they first met, Frey thought him 'just a fucked-up little punk'. Even so, they planned a new band, The Eagles. Rather than being used as a link with 'authenticity', New Lost Rambler style banjo and pedal steel would now be used as musical colouring, over a hard-driving West Coast rock group.

Producer Glyn Johns ensured that they played virtually live in the studio, part of the reason why the album still sparkles. What The Eagles lost as they turned into a stadium act was the witchy, Carlos Castenada element so carefully reflected in their name. The Eagles plunged totally into the Wild West For *Desperado*, a subtle concept album where themes and tunes repeat and mutate. There is far more acoustic playing, with banjo and slide guitar and dobro. As Frey observed, 'the thread between outlaw and rock star that we were trying to get across was working'. Sam Peckinpah optioned the storyline for Hollywood, but the album sold poorly, and The Eagles started to move towards more guitars and less twang, Joe Walsh coming in and Bernie Leadon going out.

Walsh was on board for the modern folk tale that is 'Hotel California', an encounter with the realm of the dead, from which 'you can never leave'. 'The Last Resort', is an embittered history of California. Henley sings it as a slow lament. 'Someone laid the mountains low, while the town got high'. Don Felder plays pedal steel, and it sounds like someone weeping. *Common Thread* is a recent tribute album by contemporary country musicians. It shows The Eagles as a template for the smart but casual dress, soft rock sounds and well-crafted lyrics that characterise new Nashville. But certainly not alt country, for which The Eagles – or their stadium rock incarnation, at least – represent everything from which they are revolting.

The largely forgotten band Cowboy are a good case study. Tougher sounding than the latter-day Eagles, they beat a path to the Capricorn studio in Alabama, which would see a stampede of Southern boogie merchants over the next decade. Their debut *Reach For The Sky* (1970) draws on their time in a hippie commune – back-porch music with bluegrass trimmings. In 1971 *5'll Getcha Ten* sees more experiment, but by the mid '70s any freshness and sense of adventure was gone. The band's final album, *Cowboy* came out in 1977, a year that tolled the death knell for anything like this: laid-back, well-played, lacking in excitement. But when founder member Tommy Talton made his own album *Happy To Be Alive*, its best track 'It Might Be The Rain' starts quietly, weary and washed out and ends totally magnificent. This way alt country.

June 1969 saw a gig by a pick-up band called Bobby Ace And The Cards, at San Francisco's California Hall, with most of the Grateful Dead, alongside John Dawson and David Nelson, plus Peter Grant on pedal steel, but without Pigpen. The acoustic set comprised versions of traditional mountain songs, plus the debut of Jerry Garcia and Robert Hunter's 'Dire Wolf', about a desperate game of cards and a murderous animal spirit coming for its due. It was a new song that clutched at all kinds of old folk memories. Sombre yet oddly joyful.

Hunter had been turned around by Robbie Robertson's songs for The Band, imbued with Americana. For Jerry, it was just another facet of their vast repertoire of musical voices, 'one of the possibilities'. As he told Elvis Costello, 'I was thinking, let's try a really close-to-the-bone approach, like the way they recorded c&w records. .'

Workingman's Dead is a parable about America, and how it almost fell apart. Backings are unobtrusive, with a strum of acoustic guitars, pedal steel, lightly played drums and electric bass. Each song is like a campfire tale. Here are songs about surviving Altamont – 'this darkness gotta give' – and how the '60s sense of community is fraying, tested to destruction by greed and drugs.

'Uncle John's Band' supposedly describes the proprietor of a flea circus, and his charges, 'little critters in uniforms you could only see under a magnifying glass', but The New Lost City Ramblers were also in Hunter's mind. 'Cumberland Blues' takes its cue from Appalachian tradition. 'Casey Jones' is based on accurate research, but is one of many Hunter/Garcia songs that then lift off from a detail of US legend or history, like a sky-rocket. The real Jones foreswore alcohol, let alone cocaine and speed, but the song also invokes the ghost of Neal Cassidy. 'Trouble ahead/and trouble behind'.

The next album, aptly named *American Beauty*, was an attempt at 'heartland music', and 'there's a lot of heartbreak on that record', especially Garcia's singing on 'Brokedown Palace', about the spirit leaving a dying body. 'Box of Rain' was written to order for Phil Lesh to sing to his dying father.

American Beauty is about how they found the courage and talent to stick together. For Hunter, 'The Band, The Byrds, Poco, CSNY and Dylan were all exploring traditional music augmented by the power of rock 'n' roll, and we were continuing to evolve what we believed to be the logical next step in American music.' The cover painting reads either 'beauty' or 'reality', depending on how you look at it. A third album was planned to complete the trilogy, but never materialised, though much of the material is captured on the live triple *Europe '72*. 'Jack Straw' is an Appalachian murder tale, but the name also belongs to a key figure in the Great Revolt of 1381, and his memory in turn inspired a children's game, and the description of any man of no consequence.

What the Dead now set out to do, in a seemingly endless series of live CDs and night-long concerts, was to put together an epic America, where black and white knew no distinction. The live double album *Dead Reckoning* (1981) is an all-acoustic look backward at the band's folk dimensions, mixing in traditional material like 'Dark Hollow' and 'Jack-A-Roe' with songs by Charlie Monroe. Ken Hunt wisely points out that the Dead have always specialised in American music, of all genres. 'They will just as easily quote from Miles Davis' "Sketches Of Spain" as perform the Child ballad "Jack-A-Roe" or Marty Robbins' "El Paso".' Their own song 'Black Muddy River', with the last rose of summer leaving its mark as it 'pricks my finger', was aptly enough the last song Garcia ever sang in public. Robert Hunter wrote that 'it's just a good look into the deep dark well'. The Dead played their last concert in the summer of 1995, and Eric Pooley beautifully describes how Jerry's 'courage was something to see. He no longer knew if his fingers would do his bidding, but he played on, like Clarence Ashley, or ol' Lightnin' Hopkins or Duke Ellington…because playing music for people is what these gentlemen did'.

The tribute album *Deadicated* (1991), saw David Lindley help Warren Zevon out on 'Casey Jones', while Lyle Lovett croons 'Friend Of The Devil' and The Cowboy Junkies dig into 'To Lay Me Down' as if with a scalpel. Elvis Costello is featured too, repaying a debt.

Jackson Browne was working on a 'concept album of sorts, a tribute to bandits and desperadoes' when the project was handed over to The Eagles instead.

The Nitty Gritty Dirt Band came from Long Beach, and they invited Browne to join them in February 1966 – he stayed with them for six months – and they were 'a real fun band to be in', playing jugband music. 'John McEuan replaced me, and within weeks they had a recording contract.' Liberty Records demanded they sing more contemporary material. 'It was years before they returned to the kind of folk-based music that they felt most comfortable playing.'

The band headlined gigs at the Fillmore, over the likes of Buffalo Springfield, though they were barely amplified onstage. To toughen up the sound, Chris Darrow was brought into the band from Kaleidoscope. The band broke up in early 1969, with Hanna and Darrow joining Linda Ronstadt's tour band, long before The Eagles. Jeff also played with Mike Nesmith. Within six months they were back together. *Uncle Charlie And His Dog Teddy* opens with mountain banjo, and a Mike Nesmith song. The whole thing sounds live, what Jeff Hanna described as a kind of 'Appalachian Mountain surf music', combining a rock rhythm section with traditional acoustic instruments like fiddle, banjo and harmonica. There is even a chicken impersonation. The lynch pin was the Dirt Band's recording of Jerry Jeff Walker's 'Mr Bojangles'. The real Uncle Charlie sits proudly on the cover with his dog and his guitar, and appears on the record playing and reminiscing, on his front porch in Springville. Side Two opens with his rendition of the cowboy myth 'Jesse James', then he talks about his life, with Teddy singing along on 'The Old Rugged Cross'.

Then it's straight into 'Mr Bojangles', never before so heart-warming. 'I ain't too good on B flat'. He sounds fine on everything else.

After Earl Scruggs heard the album, he sought the band out backstage in Nashville one night, 'and that sowed the seed of doing an album that would bring together the traditional and contemporary sides of country music'. Thus evolved *Will The Circle Be Unbroken*. Then 'he got Doc Watson along, and it sort of snowballed from there'. It took just over a week to lay down the whole thing. They first planned a double (vinyl) album, but it ended up a triple: 'a portfolio of traditional country music'.

The album cover proclaims 'Music forms a new circle', and we start off with a history of Nashville in 'Grand Ole Opry Song', sung and played joyfully. That is the keynote here, a harmony between rednecks and long-hairs, with Mother Maybelle Carter working out 'Keep On The Sunny Side' in the studio. 'On the old record, I started it like this ...' The format is relaxed enough to take in a range of traditional material, plus songwriters from Hank Williams to Merle Travis. 'I Am A Pilgrim' is much more cheerful than The Byrds, with a real country swing. The whole thing is wonderfully spontaneous. The affability of Doc Watson acts as a bridge between youth and age. Performances are relaxed and respectful, but never consumed with their own importance, and everyone piles in at the end on another Carter family song, 'Will The Circle Be Unbroken'.

Most people would have ended things there, but this is followed with Randy Scruggs – son of Earl who himself seems to have been reborn on these sessions – playing an instrumental version of Joni Mitchell's 'Both Sides Now'. An extra grace note to the original album is the recent issue of a live concert, tight but loose from 1984 as the 2-CD set *Unbroken – Live*. The likes of Doc Watson and Earl Scruggs are present only among the writing credits, but it just reminds you how good The Nitty Gritty Dirt Band are, quite apart from any special guests, as a kind of jukebox of Americana. The music ranges from covers of Del Shannon's 'Runaway' and Buddy Holly's 'Rave On', to a bluegrassy 'Rocket Top' and retellings of 'Cosmic Cowboy' and 'Mr Bojangles'.

Will The Circle Be Unbroken Vol II (1989) opens with the voice of Johnny Cash, but as so many of the original participants had already moved on to the great hootenanny in the sky, the participants here represent, literally, the next generation of country musicians. Johnny is accompanied by his daughter Rosanne, bassist Roy Huskey Jr repeats his father's role on the original album, and Chet Atkins brings the Nashville stamp of authenticity. Here too are singer/songwriters John Prine and John Hiatt, and former members of the Band and The Byrds. The latest generation of bluegrass pioneers is represented by Sam Bush and Bela Fleck: other guests range from Ricky Skaggs to Emmylou Harris. *Volume III* updates the project yet again, with veterans like Earl Scruggs and Doc Watson having a musical encounter with Iris Dement, Tom Petty and Taj Mahal, and stars of modern bluegrass like Alison Krauss. Once again, John McEuen wanted 'to leave the edges as they were, like human beings playing and singing. Earl Scruggs rehearsed a tune one way, then once in the studio 'started a completely different song. Such chance events illuminate the project, with Tom Petty and Willie Nelson duetting on 'Goodnight Irene' and two of the Nitty Gritty's sons – Jaime Hanna and Jonathan McEuen duetting, and Richard Watson joining his grandfather, Doc. Just as the original album helped bridge the chasm, 30 years before, between long-haired draft protesters and flag-waving, pro-Vietnam-war Nashville, so this too was recorded during a new mood in the US. 'The post-September 11th era is a time of national unity, rather than division. The chasm increasingly to be faced now is one of years, those decades and epochs that stretch ever further between country music's present and a past fading into the mists of history'.

At around the time of the first *Circle* package Americana began to surface in the work of some leading West Coast mavericks. A veteran of Captain Beefheart's Magic Band, Ry Cooder hand-crafted the Western movie soundtrack, using musicians like David Lindley and Van Dyke Parks. Director Walter Hill called Ry 'a uniquely American artist, the work displaying recurring patterns, moods and attitudes that are distinctly his own'. On the *Paris, Texas* soundtrack Cooder seems to be able to sum up a whole, haunted landscape with just a bottleneck and six strings.

Cooder was working at Americana before anyone even gave it a name. *Ry Cooder* – with orchestrations by Van Dyke Parks – *Into The Purple Valley* and *Boomer's Story* form a trilogy, which centre around the blues and folk songs of the Great Depression, back in the '30s, dealing with poverty – among both black and white – and the undertow of the American dream. Dustbowl ballads are a speciality, in a direct line from Woody Guthrie. He resurrects popular songs of the time, like 'One Meat Ball'. 'Do Re Me' and Guthrie's 'Vigilante Man', and sung in Ry's anonymous voice, they sound like the common man talking. It is a form of archaeology, for Cooder, 'you listen to a song and get such a clear picture of how it must have been'.

Much the same could be said of Little Feat, who slithered on the edge of Lowell George's slide guitar, seemingly without effort and with a terrifying power, so that every night saw the same songs taking off in a different direction. George was the enigma at the band's heart, and his skewed songs explore modern America, and turn its backwaters into myth, exploring the 'grubby flipside' of trucking music.

Jesse Winchester was literally on the margins of Americana – raised in Memphis, he fled to Canada to evade the draft for Vietnam then spent his exile years crafting songs of sweet nostalgia. In 'Brand New Tennessee Waltz' the lyrics are undercut by paranoia, 'they'll catch you wherever you're hid'. His tour band later became the Amazing Rhythm Aces, country boogie merchants who influenced the likes of Elvis Costello.

Stranger by far is Michael Hurley, a man who has drunk deeply from the well of old-time music, and approaches it without irony or affectation. On *Armchair Boogie* he becomes that werewolf 'stepping along', with a howl in his throat and a tear in his eye. Acoustic fiddle adds just the right touch of pathos, and Hurley's unearthly, wordless chorus makes the blood run cold. He is a master of lulling you into a sense of false security, then throwing in a line like 'When I learned to drink your blood, friend it took years.' More to the point, Hurley has kept going, recycling his greatest hits through a succession of off-centre record labels, from Folkways to Raccoon to Eugene Chadbourne's Fundamental.

Another man steeped in old-time music who then bent it to his own weird personality was John Hartford, who hit Nashville as a session player, then established his own unique territory with songs like 'I've Heard That Tearstained Monologue You Do There By The Door Before You Go.' Live he was unforgettable, with a hat perched crazily on his head, his feet dancing on a wobble board and his fiddle at right angles to his shoulder, singing out of the side of his mouth. John's much-covered 'Gentle On My Mind' flows dreamily, and bankrolled a whole sequence of uncommercial albums that now sound timeless. On *Aero-Plain*, he entered the studio with a crack acoustic band, and told them to play whatever came to mind. 'A tune would start, and I would stand there and then I would look down and discover my hands busy at the music'.

Sam Bush was just one young bluegrass musician turned on by this experiment in musical anarchy. He saw the band play live. 'Some may call it newgrass. I call it a mind blowing musical experience'. This free-flight jamming carried over to the album, and captures a moment in the post-hippie era when 'musicians were breaking boundaries, just for the love of the music'. In Hartford's last great starring role, as the ironic, seemingly lazy but musically pin-sharp fiddler in *Down From The Mountain* the man is already in fatally ill. As captured by Pennebaker, his grace and courage is there forever, and he has become the worldly wise, slightly untrustworthy mountain man whom he once impersonated. The mask has turned into a vulnerable and much-loved human face.

Paul Siebel was once described as sounding like Gene Clark fronting a lounge band with two ace Nashville pickers – it makes him sound like a precursor of Lambchop. *Woodsmoke And Oranges* is as evocative as its title, with stellar fiddle from Richard Greene. Siebel was country's answer to David Ackles. Both men were too sensitive for their own good, burning out where lesser talents marched on. And both are – or should be – patron saints of Americana. A version of 'Louise' where everyone acts drunk is one of the highlights of *Dixie Fried*, a wild and long-lost album by Southern white soulman James Luther Dickinson. Here too is the traditional carney song, 'O How She Dances', with what sounds like tom-toms. A dry run for Tom Waits, once he got over his barfly fixation. Nick Tosches wrote of *Dixie Fried* as 'a dark, gale-force reworking of some ancient Southern lyrics, warm, visceral graftings of Dock Boggs and a thousand more drunken voices of an older, more tenebrous South'.

John Prine is made of the same tough cloth. He does not so much sing as growl like 'bulldog chewing a holly bush'. He learnt how to play guitar in the style of the New City Ramblers. 'When you play a Carter Family tune, you feel like a master. Right away, I started making up words and writing quasi-Carter Family songs'. His songwriting, from the sad junkie 'Sam Stone' with the hole in his arm 'where all the money goes' to 'Lake Marie', with a couple trying to save their marriage – 'and catch a few fish' is about 'leaving out what's not supposed to be there'.

Prine recorded his debut album in Memphis, not Nashville, and it suits the toughness in his voice. Prine might have grown up in Chicago, but his parents had emigrated from Western Kentucky, and John spent his summers back there, in a small town called Paradise. It was close to Beechcreek, where Johnny Cash came to record the coalmining section of his *Ride This Train* concept album. 'Paradise' is also the bitterly ironic title of Prine's song about a 'backwards old town', where a mining company arrived with 'the world's biggest shovel', and Eden disappeared, 'Mr Peabody's coal train has hauled it away'. Prine is a romantic at his savage heart, and the song ends, 'When I die, let my ashes float down the Green River'. It is now a bluegrass classic.

Prine's determination to make every album sound different confused his audience, though it makes him more interesting now. The highlight of a messy and much-interrupted recording career was 1986's *German Afternoon*, largely acoustic, and a return to his Kentucky roots. He recut 'Paradise', and revisited The Carter Family. He battled with cancer, then came back musically even stronger than before, sounding just as wild and determined. No wonder his band is called the Lost Dogs.

The Missing Years was 'a collection of wry, dusty tales that helped define the genre of alternative country'. *No Depression* was among the magazines to heap praise on *In Spite Of Ourselves*, an album of duets with the likes of Dolores Keane, Lucinda Williams, and Emmylou Harris on what Prine describes as 'these meetin', cheatin' and retreatin' songs'. He toured with Iris Dement in support (and joining him for the title song), a saga of the modern everyday couple, muddling through, with Dement getting the best lines. 'He ain't got laid in a month of Sundays/caught him once and he was sniffin' my undies'. *Lost Dogs And Mixed Blessings* is more of the same, mixing pain and laughter as only Prine can.

There was a matching rough humour in a musical movement concurrent with Prine's emergence from the Chicago folk clubs. Country swing re-emerged through the eccentric delights of Dan Hicks, with his

Hot Licks. It was another route out of the '60s, through America's musical past, back into the future. Born in Little Rock, Hicks felt a little 'detached' in Haight Ashbury, where he first found fame as drummer for the Charlatans. As he told *Relix* 'I wanted to play guitar more' and to play the kind of music where you could hear the words. The Hot Licks started by playing coffee houses, and Dan called his new sound 'folk swing', though others reckoned it 'sarcastic, harmony-ridden 1930s soft shoe rock', with smooth female voices in the chorus. Dan delivers the simplistic lyrics tongue-in-cheek, with a twang and a yodel, and as he said of the bitterly ironic 'Where's The Money', 'This is an instrumental, but it's got some words to it'.

Another good-time act were Commander Cody And The Lost Planet Airmen. They formed in Michigan, then moved to San Francisco, where their easy-flowing mixture of western swing, truckers' songs and rockabilly now sounds like an early try-out for contemporary Americana. It is music that works best live, and is thus best captured on *Deep From The Heart Of Texas*, recorded at the Armadillo World Headquarters in Austin.

Asleep At The Wheel moved to Austin from West Virginia in the early '70s, and were a more controlled bunch, dominated by the smooth voice of Ray Benson, who subsequently compiled two tribute albums to Bob Wills, his mainman, with the likes of the Squirrel Nut Zippers. Benson remains a great enthusiast for the old music – real folk music that 'folks sing' – and makes no grand claims for his music. Deeply communal, deeply American. 'You're not a star, you're just a dance band. You provide music for social gatherings: the tribe gets together and you play the music'.

Meanwhile, the cutting edge of American rock moved down south to Capricorn records, and guitar-fuelled boogie. A mix of blues and country that looks back to '60s pioneers like Creedence Clearwater Revival and the swamp rock of Tony Joe White, but which attains epic majesty in long guitar workouts like the Allman Brothers' 'In Memory Of Elizabeth Reed'.

The greatest influence on alt country though was Lynryd Skynyrd, from Jacksonville, Florida, with their unique mix of driving guitars and laconic but emotion-packed vocals. *Skynyrd Frynds* sees covers by the likes of Steve Earle, as well as more mainstream acts. The 1977 air crash that wiped out half the band gives them the same mythic status as Gram or Hank: youthful promise cut short. Singer Ronnie Van Zant wanted to write songs that took pride in everyday life in the South, and for his band to sound like a cross between Free and The Rolling Stones. Three lead guitars. Muscle and intelligence combined.

There is a direct line from all this to the Drive By Truckers, from Alabama, who have self-consciously taken the tradition onwards. Their double CD *Southern Rock Opera* is an exhilarating retelling of the Lynyrd Skynyrd story, with some facts changed, but the truth intact. Betaxax Guillotine is a fictional rocker who grows up in Alabama to a soundtrack of Skynyrd, Neil Young, CCR and the rest, becomes a punk rocker, then begins to dream about a time when rock music was still made by 'big, masculine looking, hairy men with beards and guts and sweat and spit', a time before MTV. They consign George Wallace to hell, along the way. Act II opens in the present day, but in an alternative universe where you can 'stand tall, turn your three guitars up real loud and do what you do', then moves implacably towards an air crash, and the wreckage of 'angels and fuselage'. The music is made to match, rough but soulful vocals and crunchy electric guitars. Nothing could be better.

Another band keeping boogie alive into the world of alt country is the Bottle Rockets. 'So that was our big plan, to get down in the trenches and decide to be country. But we didn't want to learn country songs, we wanted to take what we knew and write our own country songs.'*

The Bottle Rockets' *The Brooklyn Side* is a catalogue of life on the margins. The opening track sets reality against media images. A young mother living on welfare cheques is demonised by politicians and 'an angry fat man on the radio, even though all she really needs is 'help in this mean old world'. Who could not empathise with someone who buys Carlene Carter cassette tapes in the cut-out bin? Brian Henneman sings with weary compassion, to driving mandolin and fiddle. Producer Eric Ambel gets a lovely crunchy sound out of the Bottle Rockets in his New York hellhole, 'as refrigerated semis loaded with meat idled out front in the July heat of a man's street', and the evening sun lights 'urban mountains'. 'We ate, we drank, we made some music. Here it is'. Forever.

* *No Depression*

99

x) Texas

Under the smooth surface of Nashville in the '70s, all kinds of tensions were simmering. Country & western Lolita, Tanya Tucker was once described as 'American Gothic's last stand'. On 'Would You Lay With Me (In A Field of Stone)', she turns seductress, over a typically cloying string arrangement by Billy Sherrill. But the song itself was written by David Alan Coe, and is indicative of a whole new breed of outlaws and mavericks, on the outskirts of Music Row.

Mickey Newbury made a series of albums for Elektra in the '70s, which work on an epic scale, a masterful blend of Nashville players, huge orchestras, sound effects, and plaintive vocals. He wrote a perfect example of Americana in 'An American Trilogy', which links three fragments from the folk tradition of the Civil War: being Dixie born, glory in battle, and a peaceful death. The same sense of history seeps though the album cover of *The Outlaws*, an old tattered and frayed 'wanted' poster, featuring the bearded and unsmiling trio of Willie Nelson, Waylon Jennings and Tompall Glaser. What had started as a nickname, drawn from Lee Clayton's song 'Ladies Love Outlaws', became a lifestyle.

Now the grand old man of Americana, it was only when Willie Nelson left Nashville for Austin, and began to record with his own tour band, that he began to find fame as a singer. His rough-hewn magnificence was there from the start, if you listen to the original demos for *Crazy*, but Music Row complained that 'he's not singing, he's talking'. Willie explains that, though 'a lot of people think I sing nasal, actually it's the sound that comes from deep down in the diaphragm. That's where you get the most strength.' It is also deeply hypnotic, as Willie plays off the rhythms of his band, clipping the notes short, and interspersing his vocals with improvisations on his acoustic guitar, like another form of speech.

He was already the thinking-person's country star, taking risks that no-one else then dared. *Yesterday's Wine* was a concept album about life and death. The original vinyl release of *Phases And Stages* has side one of a love affair told from the woman's point of view, side two from the man's. *Red Headed Stranger* tells the tall tale of a preacher who shoots his unfaithful lover dead, then takes off on the road, recycling cowboy songs from between the wars as he goes. It could be a movie script, it could be a parable. Willie shows himself to be a master of narrative, switching between observer and participant as he tells the story.

Red Headed Stranger still sounds fresh, largely due to Nelson's decision to ask the band to play only where they felt necessary, to get the barest feel he could. There's some great honky tonk piano, straight out of an old saloon, and nicely out of tune. CBS wanted to cover the raw sound with a string section, but sense prevailed when the album began to sell. The record proved influential, a baton taken up by a new breed of literate singer/songwriters, the likes of Tom Russell and Ray Wylie Hubbard.

Willie has further developed his Tex-flamenco guitar playing since, on albums like *Spirit*. *Teatro* benefits from production by Daniel Lanois, while *Tougher Than Leather* is again about the Wild West and reincarnation, and *Stardust* re-imagines the American popular song, taking Tin Pan Alley out onto the prairie. Unexpected names – Jello Biafra, Steel Pole Bath Tub et al – turn up on the alt rock 'non-tribute' *Twisted Willie*.

Fellow Outlaw Waylon Jennings gave up his seat to the Big Bopper on Buddy Holly's final flight, and it seems to have haunted him ever since. On the records he made in Nashville in the early '70s, backings darken to match, notably on *Singer Of Sad Songs*, produced by Lee Hazlewood. Like Nelson, Waylon began to demand that he record with his tour band, virtually live in the studio, and the triumphant result is *Honky Tonk Heroes*, with heavy bass guitar, and a wonderful take on 'We Had It All'. Certainly Waylon's later albums have a real sense of those wide open spaces. An album like *Dreaming My Dream* has what Jennings himself describes as a 'relentless four-on-the-floor rhythm, phased guitars and eerie drones'. See-sawing between two chords, this is a new form of country music, and one that proved hugely influential.

No wonder that the inevitable tribute album, *Lonesome, On'ry And Mean*, features the likes of Dave Alvin, John Doe, Alejandro Escovedo and Norah Jones, before she became a superstar. Waylon's 1971 album *The Taker/Tulsa* featured songs by Kris Kristofferson, former Rhodes scholar at Oxford but more importantly one-time janitor in a Nashville recording studio. He too was part of the welcome trend to bring tough sense to country lyrics, and a sexuality too: this was the man once said to have 'brought the bedroom to the *Opry* stage'. On the *Old Grey Whistle Test* duet with Rita Coolidge, 'Help Me Make It Through the Night', they looked like they could hardly keep their clothes on long enough to complete the song. Kristofferson made a series of fascinating albums, but it is difficult now to play any of them all the way through, largely due to his singing limitations. *The Austin Sessions* turns this to his advantage by taking his greatest hits, slowing them down even more, then partnering his old-timer growl with the voices of Jackson Browne and Alison Kraus. Even Steve Earle sounds like Caruso here, by contrast.

By the same token, one of the albums that best defines the contemporary sound of alt country – or whatever – is *Don't Let The Bastards Get You Down*, a twang-rich tribute album graced by such luminaries as John Doe, ex of X, slurring out 'Me And Bobby McGee' like Shane McGowan's American blood brother. Paul Burch from the real Nashville talk/sings '*The Pilgrim* (Chapter 33)' – there is a great instrumental jam at the end – and Chuck Prophet gets deep voiced and epic on 'Loving Her Was Easier'. Ditto Stephen Bruton, on a closing 'Border Land', which is truly epic. Things gets weirder, though. Polara add strange electronic noises to 'Just The Other Side of Nowhere'. More genre busting still, Tom Verlaine from Television gives an edgy reading of 'The Hawk', letting his lead guitar do most of the talking. Jon Langford joins Chip Taylor for 'Help Me Make It Through the Night', with lots of mandolin but none of the sexual frisson of Kristofferson's own version.

It's hard to say exactly who or what he has influenced, except the ability to be effortlessy offensive, but another Outlaw who refuses to go away is Kinky Friedman, the self-styled leader of the Texas Jewboys from Palestine – in the Lone Star State. Albums like *Lasso From El Paso*, got him a billet on the *Rolling Thunder* tour, with songs like 'Ride 'Em Jewboy', and 'They Ain't Making Jews Like Jesus Anymore', which challenge just about every stereotype going. In the '80s he went solo, and set up shop in New York's Lone Star Cafe. He also began to write murder mysteries: one, *Road Kill*, features Willie Nelson at threat from an old Indian curse.Asleep At The Wheel, and the likes of Lyle Lovett and Guy Clark from the next wave of Texas songwriters all take part in 1998's *Pearls in the Snow: The Songs of Kinky Friedman*.

Austin

Something strange was stirring in Austin, that home of true outlaws and lost causes. Years before 'South By Southwest', the cosmic cowboy singer Michael Murphey blew in from the Mojave desert, with a new style of poetic idealism on albums like *Americana*, replete with mystic longings, 'the high uncertain singing of the unknown rider's song'.

There were other Austin-based minstrels. Jerry Jeff Walker was once described as the joker in the pack of cards that is progessive country, and with the Lost Gonzo Band he established himself on record and in Austin clubs as an amiable interpreter of other men's songs. His fiddle-led version of Guy Clark's 'Desperados' is magnificent, like an old-timer reminiscing on his death bed. Jerry Jeff, noted for his laid-back and liquid lifestyle – at least as it is presented on disc – once said that 'My goal is not to be on VH1 as one of the great tragedies of all time'. Townes Van Zandt was just that, though it took him a long time to die. His voice sounds a thousand years old, 'like Dock Boggs, he was obsessed with death'.*

Townes started as a tuneful singer songwriter, but even by 69's *Our Mother The Mountain* there is an odd intensity, as he sings lines like 'maybe I'll go insane, I've got to stop the pain' not as a conceit, but a simple statement of fact. His songs hymned a life apart from the rest of humankind, and by the time of *The Late Great Townes Van Zandt*, he was living in a tin-roofed shack in the remotest part of Tennessee, eating raccoon meat. It was the sort of lifestyle that Will Oldham or Beck might pretend to. But the songs said it all. His most famous, 'Pancho & Lefty' is a cowboy ballad set near the border. Pancho, the outlaw who dies quick and silent and enters myth, is happier than Lefty, hanging on to existence like a rat. 'He just did what he had to do, and now he's growing old.' Nothing can beat the matter-of-fact way Townes suggest the federals let Lefty go 'out of kindness I suppose'. The kindness of the torture rack.

Townes had been born to a rich family, with his father the vice president of an oil company, but, after he dropped out of college and became a full time troubadour, there was nothing phoney about his lifestyle, getting just enough from an endless round of live gigs to pay for the drink and food and drugs that kept him going. He lived for a while with Roky Erickson, hardly a force for stability, then toured the

* *No Depression*

south, half a hobo, half a musician. There is an extraordinary interview in which he talks about spells of 'total loss of meaning and motivation', the feeling that 'if I had a machine and could just chop my hands off, then everything could be fine'. His songs come hotlined from his subconscious. 'Bukka White used to call them sky songs. It seems they just come through me.' Doc Watson was one of the first to recognise their worth, and made a cover version. Later came the famous quote from Steve Earle that Townes was the best songwriter in the world, 'and I'll stand on Bob Dylan's coffee table in my cowboy boots and say that'. Except that Townes is brilliant, but on one emotional note, while Dylan's body of work encompasses a whole orchestra of feelings and emotions.

Van Zandt became increasingly confined to his cabin. *No Depression* carried a graphic account of his final days: 'he was in incredible pain' and in a wheelchair for those final sessions. 'Sanitarium Blues' is about his teenage breakdown, and rhymes away the pain. 'They hose you down, make sure you're clean, shoot you full of Thorazine'. A mesmerising performance at London's Borderline proved to be his last gig. Townes had long claimed that he would die on New Year's Day, just like Hank Williams, and at the age of 52, like his father. He was proved right.

At least there is irony in the title of his postumous album *A Far Cry From Dead*, though the music sounds sombre enough, sung by a man seemingly without emotion, a man who has seen the very worst but, even if living is 'mostly wasting time' at least he notices. 'People will only know who I am after I am dead.' Certainly, his cult is now growing. Townes reckoned, rightly, that 'I'm the mould that grunge grew out of.'

Van Zandt's reputation continues to feel out of focus, despite an excellent double retrospective, *Anthology 1968–1979*, and *Poet, A Tribute To Townes Van Zandt* – which features a Southern roll call of honour: Guy Clark, Nanci Griffith, Lucinda Williams, Steve Earle, the Flatlanders, Robert Earl Keen, John Prine and so on. Drawn by genuine respect, there is a unity to the proceedings that so many of these projects fail to attain.

Unfortunately, a whole slew of live Van Zandt performances dragged out from the vaults and posthumous reissues seem often to duplicate each other, and a much anticipated 4-CD, 60-track box set *Newology*, which was set to feature duets with the names listed above, plus Johnny

Cash, Bob Dylan, Doug Sahm and Neil Young was held back due to record company politics. What did go ahead was a series of tribute shows held in Los Angeles, New York and Austin. The large number of websites dedicated to his memory further attest to the Texan troubadour's power to move people and involve them in his peerless storytelling.

Townes appears alongside Guy Clark, John Hiatt and a young, slim Steve Earle in *Heartworn Highways*, a mid-'70s documentary recently re-released on DVD. The movie's original working title was *New Country*, then *Outlaw Country*, which better reflected the status of the musicians featured – 'by the early '70s Nashville had become very rigid. But the young guys wanted to do something different. A lot of them had gone through the '60s and experienced the whole explosion in rock and pop music and wanted to open it up a little.'* And yet 'the music they were making connected more to a generation older than the one in place in Nashville; there is little plot, but a series of essentially unconnected scenes'†, from Van Zandt touring his backyard to David Allan Coe performing at a Tennessee state prison. It might look like a home movie, but it remains an authentic visit to a world that seems changeless, and so is 'a welcome piece of Americana'. Allan Jones saw a preview in 1976, and notes that 'what seemed odd about the film then and even odder now is its complete lack of context'. Even so, one of its highlights is 'a fabulous sequence in the pool room of old geezer's hangout the Wigwam Tavern, that looks like something from a David Lynch movie'.

Guy Clark was a friend of Townes. On the recent *Cold Dog Soup*, Emmylou Harris glides in on harmony vocals on Steve Earle's 'Fort Worth Blues', a lament for Van Zandt. The title track takes Clark back to Mission Beach in the '60s, with Tom Waits collecting the money, and Townes at the bar, 'full of angst and hillbilly haiku'. Clark himself is different songwriter to Townes: one who claimed that in everything he wrote 'there's a chuckle, a ray of hope. They may be sad, but it's not doomsday'.

Guy is also a Texan native, and his recording debut *Old No 1* fell somewhere down the crack between rock and country, with his twangy, voice softened by Johny Gimble's fiddle. *No Depression* once called Clark 'the Lone Star State's Ernest Hemingway' for his ability to get to 'the cruel radiance of what is'. Guy somehow evokes the epic grandeur of

---

* James Szalapski
† *Austin Citizen*

the old West. Clark's album *The Dark* benefits from string-band accompaniment, and a more accepting, less tragic view of life than his old friend Townes: when he dies, he asks to be buried in a muddy creek, 'let the crawfish have their way/it's mud to mud and that's OK'.

Lubbock might still be best known as the birthplace of Buddy Holly, but it has spawned a more recent breed of Texan singer songwriter, rooted in country music, but open to a range of influences. Terry Allen moved there after spending his childhood in Wichita, where he saw Hank Williams and Hank Snow, passing through. Terry's songs are similar, best described as a Texan Randy Newman with a sunnier disposition, even if the way he delivers them is the opposite of melliflous. One clue to his approach is his other profession as an art teacher. 'The idea of story-telling affects everything I do.' Here is a truly Southern trait, where 'the highlight of any relaxation in a week's work would be going to church, or eating supper with people telling stories. It also comes out of a culture that isn't very literate, so verbalising things becomes even more colourful'.

In 1975 Allen cut *Juarez*, 'a simple story' about four people who migrate from California to Mexico, the soundtrack to an imaginary movie. Allen – who now lives in New Mexico – tells Kershaw the border is central to him. 'The fantasy that's there a line that you can cross, and every-thing's going to be great. It was like a magnet to me. It's like a mirror of American culture, but it's a funhouse mirror that's very distorted'. Allen's pitch-imperfect voice and clunky piano playing are a little hard to take.

Lubbock On Everything is a more ambitious, a story cycle that seems to encompass all American life. Rednecks, sleazy businessmen, lovelorn waitresses and goodtime girls, they're all here, brought down – or perhaps up – 'an individual human level'. Tall tales, each with a hidden moral. A collection of cameos that add up to more than the sum of their parts. Good natured and optimistic, Terry is a master raconteur – the way he finesses a rhyme like 'I don't wear no stetson/but I'm as big a Texan/as you are' is priceless. The backing musicians match every ebb and turn of the lyrics, so that the whole album builds up to a masterpiece.

On *Human Remains*, there are deadpan duets with Lucinda Williams, plus musical contributions from the usual cast of thousands, including Joe Ely and Dylan sidekick Charlie Sexton, and a barbed description of modern Nashville superstars, 'some cowboy fake who thinks that all it takes is a hat on his head and a Grammy in his hand'.

Later albums turn to themes of faith and retribution: *Bloodlines* opens with a secular hymn, slow and heartfelt, with the singer's family imagined as part of an idealised landscape: mountain and sky and river. Next is a jaunty song about being mugged by a Christ lookalike, then straight into some Tex Mex and the tale of a US businessman arrested south of the border. The album concludes with the hope that Southern California will succumb to ashes and brimstone, put into the mouth of a heartless mass murderer. This is not exactly John Denver. In his parallel life as an award-winning sculptor, a gargoyle he crafted for Denver airport was attacked by fundamentalist Christians for casting a 'demonic' spell.

Not that this stops him. *Salvation* deals with the Second Coming, and ends with the funereal 'Give Me The Flowers', first performed by Flatt and Scruggs 'basically it's gospel with a limp and a lurch'.* No wonder, with musicians of the quality of Richard Bowden of the Austin Lounge Lizards and the Bad Livers' Mark Rubin on stand-up bass and tuba.

Terry worked with David Byrne on the soundtrack of *True Stories*, again looking at the loopier side of Americana. He was even commissioned to write a new US anthem, with Joe Ely, Butch Hancock and Jimmie Dale Gilmore. They did a 15-song set at the Smithsonian, but the nearest they got to their brief was the tongue-in-cheek 'Slow Boat To Tokyo', about how America was becoming a Japanese colony.

Allen went to the same High School as Gilmore and Hancock, two years his junior, and Ely, whom he did not meet until the late '70s. He had been gone for some years, teaching art in California, when in 1971 the three younger men formed the Flatlanders. The band was so named because Lubbock is at the centre of the Great Plains. David Halley remembers that they 'dressed up like hayseeds, playing this really strange and interesting stringband music'. Ely adds that 'We'd joke about being a band that never played a paying gig'. Only one single emerged at the time, Gilmore's 'Dallas' credited to Jimmie Dale And The Flatlanders.

The music is old-timey, with dobro, string bass and fiddle, strictly acoustic. Steve Wesson's musical saw adds a bizarre sound, like the wind whistling through the trees, and there is a mystical edge to the lyrics. The

* *No Depression*

Carter Family meet Eastern religion. Jimmie Dale Gilmore sings lead vocals, with the others on harmony. Fellow musician James Mastro later described it as 'like a hippie Burrito Brothers...cruder but hipper.'

Wesson now works as a carpenter, and 'uses his saw for building houses', but the other three went on to become professional musicians. They have occasionally convened since, and at a recent show at the Barbican, they took the stage in matching cowboy shirts but radically different hairstyles – a quiff for Joe, neat and well barbered for Butch and a long silver mane for Jimmie. Playing mainly new songs from the recent *Now Again*, what really glowed that night in London was the good-natured banter between the three and the obvious affection.

Ely later told Omaha Rainbow that it was the birth of the Outlaw movement that most inspired him. 'I was excited about the sound that Waylon was getting, stuff that was in that nebulous country realm.' He mixed this in with an early interest in the Tex-Mex style, learnt from the ground up at his dad's clothing store. 'The Mexican labourers would come and buy these ten-cent pair of shoes and stuff. I fell in love with the romance of Spanish guitars and accordions and all that.' He left school at 16, and went straight on the road as a musician. 'We'd be stomping up and down those old Texas plains...playing those old joints.' His debut album was the live set, laid down in the studio fresh and steaming, and it is a brilliant achievement, that still sizzles with energy.

The sound is tougher than the Flatlanders, more electric in every way, and led by pedal steel and honky tonk piano. Country filtered through rock 'n' roll, with Ely enunciating every word. His take on Hancock's 'Tennessee's Not The State I'm In' is slow but punchy, contrary to the Music Row ethos. 'MCA made it known to me that they didn't want me to do a country album, just to do what I normally do. Since Steve Earle and Lyle Lovett recorded with MCA Nashville, the label had begun to take a wider view of things. They're interested in rootsy American music, instead of just straight country music.' It was not to last, but some great music resulted at the time, and when the bars came down again, Lovett and Earle escaped to mainstream acceptance: Ely just seemed to get lost.

But his influence was most crucial when least expected, when he turned up in the UK, just as punk rock was breaking through. Texan accordion star Ponty Bone and pedal-steel maestro Lloyd Maines joined Joe on *Live Shots*, taped during some wild late-'70s London gigs: Carlene Carter on guest vocals adds to the high-energy sound, which is vibrant to this day. Just check out 'Long Snake Moan', his take on Blind Lemon Jefferson, pure rockabilly with wildness in his voice. Literate, too. It set a lot of forest fires raging among punk fans who had previously thought of country music as Jim Reeves on their parents' radiograms.

Meanwhile, 1978's *Honky Tonk Masquerade* seemed to plunge Ely back to his roots – it sounds astoundingly rich now, with killer songs from Gilmore and Hancock, and Ely's own title track. Joe himself went back to play the night spots of America, usually as second on the bill, and felt himself turning into 'a piece of meat'. Back in Austin, he returned to acoustics, began writing again and then formed a hard-rock band and resumed his recording career, as if nothing had happened. *Mojo* described *Letter to Laredo* as 'a triumphant return to form,' and as 'country music's answer to novelist Cormac McCarthy'. Here is a series of short stories set where Tex meets Mex, with flamenco guitar (giving a south-of-the-border feel to the title track) plus a stripped-down acoustic band.

Joe met Teye during 'South By Southwest', and still performs there: a 2000 gig at the Broken Spoke 'lit a firecracker under the crowd'. The same year saw the release of *Live At Antone's* and permanent proof about what Joe can do to an Austin audience, with epic takes on 'The Road Goes On Forever' and the bilingual 'Gallo Del Cielo' – a refutation of that early Butch Hancock song 'She Never Spoke Spanish To Me' – along with the perennial 'Me And Billy The Kid'. Outlaws still rule.

As to the other Flatlanders, what sets Jimmy Dale Gilmore apart is his voice, a soaring, beautiful thing. *Braver New World* saw producer T-Bone Burnett add Vox organ and sound effects to pedal steel and horns, and on the strutting blues of 'Black Snake Moan' Gilmore's voice skitters, like a stone over water. Gilmore sounds at one moment like a '50s throwback, at the next like an old mountain man. Lucinda Williams says of him that he has an ability to 'transform sadness into beauty. He's got that ability to reach deep inside. He's got soul'.

Jo Carol Pierce was married to Gilmore in the '60s, and moved to Austin in the '70s, where she wrote plays and sang in local clubs. Gilmore,

Ely and Terry Allen are among those who paid tribute to her work on *Across The Great Divide; The Songs Of Jo Carol Pierce*, and the same crew – plus Jo herself – acted and sang in *Chippy*, a play written by Terry and his wife Jo Harvey Allen, based on a diary kept by a Texan prostitute during the Great Depression.

Rolling Stone once described the third Flatlander, Butch Hancock, as 'at heart a West Texas mystic with an equal affinity for romantic border balladry and Zen paradox'. Maybe so, but on the surface he is a far more engaging and less intimidating presence than Gilmore, and without the live flash – or voice – of Ely. Butch is as nasal a singer as the young Dylan, but with perky harmonica interjections, and clever wordplay. He released a series of acoustic delights on his own Rainlight label, with resonant titles like *West Texas Waltzes & Dust-blown Tractor Tunes*. These songs of rural life, are worthy of Woody Guthrie, a working man's poetry: 'if you ain't been down a dirt road on your own feet/there's little common ground between you and me'. He is also extraordinarily prolific: a 14-cassette set preserves a 140-song gig at Austin's Cactus Club.

Firewater is far more compressed, featuring fiddle, electric guitar and Jimmie Dale Gilmore on harmonies, recorded live at the Alamo Lounge in Austin – since demolished – and it has the force and thrust of the very best bluegrass.

More recently, Hancock toured his *Health & Happiness Show* – in tribute to Hank Williams – with lead guitarist Richard Lloyd, once of Television. For one reviewer, their album *Instant Living* drops 'front-porch instrumentation in favour of an intuitive, wilfully wobbly and endearingly scruffy roux of American roots', paying homage to Crazy Horse and The Band.

Ray Wylie Hubbard is another Texan mystic, and *Crusade Of The Restless Knights* sees him growl out songs about death and redemption, like 'After The Harvest', which he describes as 'a mythological bluegrass Buddhist Gnostic gospel hymn'. Quite a way from his Outlaw anthem '(Up Against the Wall) Redneck Mother', which Jerry Jeff Walker covered back in 1973. But humour undercuts the mysticism, so that when Ray tours hell with the Devil, he finds 'Country program directors and Nashville record executives', which is just as it should be.

xi) New York

Something was certainly stirring in the mid-1970s, far away from Music Row, in New York's Bowery. Country Blue Grass, Blues and Other Music for Uplifting Gourmandisers was soon shortened to CBGBs, and certainly never featured Bill Monroe, but there is a kind of weird logic to this small and run-down venue being so named. It encompassed everything from dumb-ass impersonations by the clever Ramones, to wild guitar pyrotechnics by the likes of Television, to improvised wild poetry, not so far away in spirit from Ray Wylie Hubbard. But with a very different agenda.

As Patti Smith said, 'we felt that we were carrying on a tradition that groups like the Fugs had begun'. Post-punk bands like Bongwater similarly seemed in tune with the likes of the Holy Modal Rounders. It was when reviewing a Holy Modal Rounders gig that Patti Smith met playwright Sam Shepard: 'Sam wrote this song "Blind Rage", which he sang while playing drums. Patti heard him perform this song…and he cocked her entire mind.'* The two collaborated on a play, *Cowboy Mouth*, and Patti also became close to Bob Neuwirth, who first noticed that her walk was modelled on Dylan's in *Don't Look Back*.

Patti began to fuse poetry and rock music on stage. Her debut album *Horses* was largely improvised in the studio: what comes through in retrospect is her early immersion in the Bible – images of grace and dread. More to the point here is the music that Patti made after her return to the public arena after half a lifetime spent with her husband Fred 'Sonic' Smith, up to his final illness. *Gone Again* (1996) is elegiac, largely acoustic and contains a weird dustbowl ballad, 'Dead To The World', and a cover of Dylan's 'Wicked Messenger' – the two had toured together the previous year. *Gung Ho* includes the Appalachian inspired 'Libbie's Song', voice, acoustic guitar, mandolin and fiddle, as if told by a widow from the Civil War. 'Flower of the Cavalry, you swept me off my saddle'.

At a recent performance at Charleston Farmhouse, one-time home to the Bloomsbury Group, Patti and guitarist Oliver Ray gave a stellar display of modern Americana. 'Piss Factory' has never sounded so determined, and 'Because The Night' was dedicated to Virginia Woolf and her husband. Best of all was an as yet uncompleted poem, which melded

* Peter Stampfel

memories of her mother's migraine attacks with the night of the full moon when the invasion of Iraq began, live on CNN. That night, in a polite English setting, the American voice rang out, clear and vital.

Certainly the spirit unleashed by early punk – questioning, urgent, unimpressed by what the media tried to tell it – continues to infuse the best of of alt country, and every other art form worth its salt. A new, irreverent mood stalked the land. R Stevie Moore, a Nashville bassist, issued literally hundreds of cassettes from his home studio in New Jersey, part of the cottage industry that pure punk crystallised. Moore played c&w songs like 'I Love You So Much It Hurts' with mock seriousness, It was the tip of an iceberg.

Musical gentres began to fray and dissolve. Just look at Steve Forbert, 'born too late' – to quote one of his finest songs – looking like a young Dylan with acoustic guitar, harmonica and a denim jacket, playing a gig at CBGB's and going down a storm. Forbert later moved in a rootsier direction, using members of Wilco on the vibrant *Rocking Horse Road*, and his own band The Rough Squirrels on the live *Here's Your Pizza*.

John Hiatt is similarly uncategorisable. He started as a songwriter in Nashville, but he had a second bite of the cherry, courtesy of the new wave. Sharp songs, an odd stage manner, where he looks genuinely in pain, and snappy electric backing. His sound, though, was perhaps closer to country blues than to anything that could be called 'country' – straight or alt, but his craft with words puts him firmly in the orbit of this book.

Bring The Family was cut over a mere four days in a LA studio with Ry Cooder's lonesome slide guitar, drummer Jim Keltner and Nick Lowe on bass, keeping things simple, and the result is a masterpiece. Hiatt is best when he laughs at himself. On one song, he wants to trade his cowboy boots in for some flash Italian footwear, and tells his sweetheart to 'forget the mousse and hairspray'. The song turns back on itself too, with Hiatt admitting, with some relief, that after this excursion into city style, they can put the cow horns back on the Cadillac.

After the musical disaster that was the 'supergroup' Little Village, Hiatt adopted a hard-rock sound on *Perfectly Good Guitar*. The Jayhawks helped him back to the semi-acoustic territory where he is best, on 1995's *Walk On*. Recorded in Franklin, Tennessee, with lots of mandolin and strong drums, Hiatt's voice has got deeper and richer with the years. There is a surprise at the end, an unlisted bonus track, 'Mile High', then three minutes of sound effects. Crickets chirp over the rumble of a distant thunderstorm, then there is a frighteningly loud hum, which turns out to be an approaching train. Pure Americana.

His *Beneath This Gruff Exterior*, features the Goners and lead guitarist Sonny Landreth, and opens with 'Well I Do My Best Thinkin' Sittin' On My Ass'. The album is full of his trademark wit and wisdom and clever way with rhyme: 'I'm not getting old, I'm slowing down time, stopping it cold.' No wonder that the latest tribute album to him, *It'll Come To You: The Songs Of John Hiatt* features artists from Buddy Guy to Buddy and Julie Miller, alongside Rosanne Cash, Nick Lowe and Willie Nelson. Hiatt has grown respectable, but his late-'70s albums still pack a punch.

And yet there was another, and perhaps even more long-lasting influence on punk. It might have been wild on the surface, but as David Byrne told Clinton Heylin, Talking Heads, along with many other bands of the punk era, were 'very self aware about where they perform, what they look like, how they appear to the press. It could seem very contrived, but I think that's the way people are now'.

And so it goes. Just think of Gillian Welch, or Will Oldham or even the brusque Uncle Tupelo – all knew exactly how to present themselves in public, and who to namecheck, which does nothing to invalidate the music they make. It just helps put it onto the media agenda.

xii) London

To move on, we need to backtrack a decade, and cross the Atlantic. Before they discovered British folk music Fairport Convention were a North London band who exemplified Americana. When I first saw them, I thought that they were American – from their name to the strange mix of (then) obscure US singer/songwriters and old-timey music they reinvigorated with a warm wash of guitars, subtle drumming, lyrical bass patterns – from which the Bangles learnt their craft – and a dash of psychedelia. On stage, they even dressed and looked American.

When I recently asked original band leader Ashley Hutchings if early Fairport knew much bluegrass and old-time American music, he explained that the band members were immersed in exactly that music, and had then moved not so much beyond it as further into its spirit. Simon Nicol was their young acoustic guitar whizz, as he proves on the sadly prophetic 'M1 Breakdown'. It is both a bluegrass instrumental and a van shuddering to a halt. A chilling foretelling of death, as it happens.

When the original band members gradually peeled off for solo careers, they took this freshness of response with them. Singer Iain Matthews has always had a good ear for American songwriters – from Richard Farina to Jules Shear, to whose work he dedicated an entire album – but it is with Richard Thompson that the early live sighting of Gram Parsons with The Byrds at the Middle Earth seems to have sunk in the deepest. He has long paid tribute to the wisdom and verbal restraint of Hank Williams as a songwriter. On stage, he and his then wife Linda would suddenly break into 'Wild Side Of Life' and other country obscurities.

The fatalism of old-time music fuses with Islamic zeal in Richard's late-'70s work, as if he was looking at the human condition from outside. When the two split up, the songs that resulted were golddust in Nashville, with Linda's accusatory 'Telling Me Lies' appearing on the first Trio album, and Richard's funny but bitter, 'Tear Stained Letter' becoming almost a country standard in 1982, when Linda would rush across mid song and kick her errant husband. More recently, Del McCoury took his song 'Vincent Black Lightning '52' to the top of the bluegrass charts.

Lazily labelled as 'folk rock' during their ten-year career together, Richard and Linda were as attuned to Americana as anyone living in a Sufi commune in rural Norfolk could ever hope to be.

There were all kinds of crossovers between Britbeat and US country; Ronnie Lane left the Faces and crafted a rootsy, gypsy sound with his band Slim Chance, then moved to Austin, before succumbing to MS. A live album taped in Austin presents easy-going versions of songs like 'Ooh La La' and 'The Poacher', which sound fully at home in their new location, even if still sung in a cockney accent.

If a British band was ever in tune with itself in the same way as The Band or the Grateful Dead, it was Mighty Baby. Even Clarence White did not play electric guitar with the elasticity of Martin Stone. The UK equivalent to bluegrass, that mix of cold expertise and warm feeling comes through on their semi-acoustic second album, *A Jug Of Love*. Stone went on reinvent himself as a country musician, first in Chilli Willi then as part of Almost Presley, a Paris-based band who reprise the likes of 'Cotton Eye Joe' and 'Orange Blossom Special'.

Purely as a British roots band though, Help Yourself reign supreme. On their second album *Strange Affair* is a long instrumental, 'Excerpts From "The All Electric Fur Trapper"', pure Quicksilver Messenger Service. Their mainman Malcolm Morley shines on his own song 'American Mother', a picture of a native woman, by turns erotic, abstract, spiteful and majestic. 'Richard Treece's guitar shivers in the background, and a police siren wails. Morley played briefly with bands like Plummet Airlines, on the cusp of pub rock and new wave, then disappeared.

Particularly welcome, then, was a reissue programme for the Help Yourself back catalogue, and the extremely positive reaction saw a long belated release for Malcolm Morley's solo album from 1976, *Lost And Found*. It could only be him, warm and melancholy and funny and easygoing. But a year before, Morley had broken his long silence with a new album, *Aliens*, a chilling affair released a month or so before September 11th, and full of screams and bone-chilling vocals.

Back in the early '70s, you could walk into a select handful of London pubs, all of them outside the West End, and hear bands playing rock classics and short, sharp new songs. It certainly made a change from stadium rock. When he first saw Eggs Over Easy, Nick Lowe was amazed at how they could choose from a hundred or so songs, half of them not even their own. Cue Uncle Tupelo, a decade or so later. It set the whole scene alight. Bands and the audience both rediscovered that music could be fun, and as Ian Hoare puts it, 'they got back in touch with the physical aspect of the music, got people dancing'. Eggs Over Easy closed their set each night with Commander Cody's 'Home In My Hand'.

People started smiling on stage again. Chilli Willi announced that 'we don't have no psychedelic show' and *Bongos Over Balham* is a blast of country swing, with fiddles and pedal steel and banjos and upbeat songs. Issued years after the event, the ragbag of transported Americana that is *I'll Be Home* brings together radio sessions and recordings long-thought lost produced by Michael Nesmith, with songs ranging from Jesse Winchester's 'Midnight Bus' to truckers' favourites, 'Choo-Choo Ch'Boogie', or a wild, live, fiddle-crazy 'Fire On The Mountain', followed by their own 'Drunken, Sunken Redneck Blues'. Phil 'Snakefinger' Litham later moved stateside, and recorded with The Residents.

Meanwhile, Chilli Willis's terrifying manager Jake Riviera helped set up Stiff Records, with the help of former Brinsley Schwarz singer Nick Lowe, who went on to marry Carlene Carter, and write 'The Beast In Me' for his then father-in-law Johnny Cash.

As to Carlene, she recorded in London with Graham Parker's spiky band The Rumour. Jake Riviera radically repackaged her for his new label, F-Beat. Maybelle Carter's band might have claimed to produce 'morally-improving' music, but her grand-daughter now combined fishnet tights with cowboy boots and provocative poses. The album *Musical Shapes* saw Rockpile – with both Lowe and Dave Edmunds – give old-time music a new-wave twist. Carlene's own song 'Appalachian Eyes' is a back-porch two step, as if reinterpreted by the Glitter Band. 'Foggy Mountain Top' adds pedal steel to a rockabilly beat. Carlene is only doing what The Carter Family did back in the '30s, bringing 'old-time' music up to date. F-Beat and its satellite labels like Demon and Zippo would later put out swathes of US country punk on the British market, from the Blasters to Green On Red, Thin White Rope and True West.

Closer to home, and back in 1977, Stiff Records had discovered singer/songwriter, Declan McManus, singing country rock in London pubs, and renamed him Elvis Costello, putting him into the studio with Clover. 'Radio Sweetheart', the flipside of his debut single, is updated honky tonk, with John McFee on spectral pedal steel. Costello soon put together his own band, The Attractions, playing vengeful new wave, but if you looked closer, the rhythm section was Pete Thomas from Chilli Willi and the John Stewart band, and Bruce Thomas, from Quiver. Early copies of *This Year's Model* came with a free single – cover versions of The Damned's 'Neat, Neat, Neat' and country classic 'Stranger In The House'.

There was a further connection. The early Costello albums were produced by Nick Lowe, who had recorded the debut single on Stiff, and after a brief spell as the 'Jesus Of Cool' refocused his solo career on country rock where the Brinsleys had left it. On *The Impossible Bird* he got back to what one reviewer termed 'rustic, Alan Lomax-style arrangements...his Cockney-inflected phrase tempered with tart Tennessee-isms'. His own description of the musical landscape he now inhabits is 'a mix of country/western and rhythm and blues. There's a funny little grey hole where those two styles meet, and that's where pop music really lives, or at least where you find the good stuff'. Sounds a neat enough description of alt country to me.

Meanwhile, back in the new-wave haze, Costello began to throw in the odd Hank Williams song onstage. As he told Pete Doggett, 'around 1970, I was interested in this strand of Americana, groups like The Band and the Grateful Dead...they were covering, George Jones and Merle Haggard. I liked the plainness of the chords, the churchy harmony. It was a natural step to write something in that style'. Elvis later worked with The Confederates, a scratch Nashville band whose members had played with Gram Parsons, and indeed with Presley, and together they produced *King Of America*, which, of all his many albums, is the one that deals most self-consciously with Americana. A bonus disc sees them playing live on Broadway in 1986 with James Burton on lead guitar and Jim Keltner on drums. T-Bone Burnett guests on rhythm guitar, and Elvis's assumed American singing voice has never sounded more at home than on 'The Big Light' or 'The Only Daddy Who Will Walk The Line'.

The project that really started a forest fire was *Almost Blue* back in 1981. The real shock was that such a surly and uneasy new waver should choose to take his band over to Nashville and lay down other people's songs, and, even worse, songs mainly associated with beloved entertainers of his parents' generation, the likes of Charlie Rich and George Jones. Surely he could write better himself. On the hugely enhanced reissue CD, two tracks stand out, neither of them from the original album, his softly sung psychopath's confession in Leon Payne's 'Psycho', and the live 'I'm Your Toy', a retitling of Gram Parsons' 'Hot Burrito #2' with Steve Nieve's tinkling grand piano, and the Royal Philharmonic Orchestra.

Costello's edgy but passionate voice reworks Parsons' country croon – a more listenable equivalent of Sid Vicious's aural assault on the Frank Sinatra chestnut 'My Way', or the Pogues shaking up Irish trad folk – and it brought a whole new, spiky-topped audience to the Parsons songbook. Suddenly, it was cool to listen to American country music.

The Clash too had their roots in pub rock – Joe Strummer had briefly played with Martin Stone in the 101ers – and took in London gigs by the Joe Ely band, then 'showed me all places I never knew existed'. In turn, during The Clash's 1979 US tour, Ely found them some gigs in West Texas, and they travelled around in a tour bus, playing Marty Robbins tapes. As Ely later told Pete Doggett, he invited them to play in the kind of out-of-the way places that 'would not normally be on a rock band's agenda – San Antonio, Lubbock, Laredo. They reminded me of the '50s James Dean thing, and they thought us Texas guys were kinda outlaws in our own right. So we hit it off pretty well.' The echoes from those gigs are still reverberating.

There was no more talk from The Clash about being so 'bored with the USA'. They returned to London and put together *London Calling*, the album that, in turn, would establish them in the US, where their debut album had already sold 1,000,000 on import. *Uncut* reckons that it was in the States that Strummer's hippie idealism and Jones' guitar-hero status could develop fully: 'they would become protectors of the very tradition they had set out to destroy'.

Back in England, the Joe Ely band joined dub-man Mikey Dread on The Clash's 1980 tour. Doggett says 'they thundered through their Texas rock 'n' roll, all subtlety lost in the assault of noise and tension'. Ely states, 'the people we were playing for had never heard our songs, and didn't know where in the hell we came from, or why we were on the bill'. New-wave country went into the lion's den, and came out unscathed.

In turn, once The Clash were dust, Mick Jones' subsequent band *Big Audio Dynamite* sampled all kinds of Americana as part of their aural soundtracks, and Joe Strummer went on to explore a twisted kind of Tex Mex music in his final years.

A memorial to Joe Strummer was unveiled in the green fields of Glastonbury during 2003, Billy Bragg fondly described Joe Strummer as the natural heir of Woody Guthrie and Bob Dylan in his time and place, a singer who encapsulated the thoughts and day-to-day experiences of his generation in his songs, and his own lifestyle. And then encouraged others to do the same. A good man in a bad world.

In 1978, at much the same time as The Clash were first hooking up with Joe Ely back in London, Elvis Costello took his new band out to the States to promote their first album together, *This Year's Model*. When they arrived in Nashville, they made the mistake of opening their set with a Hank Williams medley, but soon found that 'the kids there didn't want us to be country. They wanted us to be even more punk than we were perceived to be elsewhere in America. We were accepted wholesale as the real thing, because for many people in America we were the first thing that was anything like a punk band.' And to listen to tapes of those shows, the politeness of Costello's early demos with Flip City, or Pete Thomas's ponytail days with Chilli Willi has given way to a visceral attack that still leaves you breathless. Sham 69 it is definitely not, but the whole point about early punk – both in New York and London – was the variousness: it was an attitude, not a four to the bar and snotty vocals straitjacket, and The Attractions at that point were thermo-nuclear.

Even more to the point, princes of punk-rock darkness The Sex Pistols – another great band, even if saddled with a bass player who was better at chopping at his arm with a broken bottle onstage than actually playing the notes – chose to fall apart, spectacularly, at the end of a short tour of the South. Johnny Rotten's own account is that 'the cowboys took it for the joke it was meant to be'. The Prince of Anarchy admits to liking the people he met in Georgia and Texas, 'they're very individualistic, not a uniformed lump'. He does admit, under-exaggerating wildly, that there were fights in some of the redneck truckstops they visited. But some of the mentally sharper of the audiences for this musical chaos were taking note, as to how the primal energy and ragged violence of this musical anarchy could be attached onto country music and boogie. The results were akin to a nuclear reaction.

The rest of *South By Southwest* will be devoted to looking at the debris, and what then emerged.

2 Branches

'There might be a safety pin in the nose,
but there's a hillbilly in the heart'

– Dolly Parton

i) Cowpunk

In the wake of punk and its do-it-yourself ethos, barely trained musicians gleefully took up instruments they could hardly play, just like the old string bands had done in the 1920s. Shane McGowan was an early punk fan – and performer – but with The Pogues he chose to trash the Irish folk tunes of their collective childhoods. Their early gigs could be truly frightening to someone not of their bootboy tribe, or draped in green.

Their approach proved infectious. Scotsman Champion Doug Veitch combined the influence of Jimmie Rodgers and dub reggae, played at the speed of punk. He called in the Mad Professor to remix pedal steel and fiddle at his Peckham home studio. The term 'cowpunk' became attached to this new movement, but what they played was really skiffle reborn, with punning album titles like *From Lubbock To Clintwood East*. Lash Lariat And The Long Riders played 'hillbilly boogie', and dressed like a western swing band, but their acoustic sound draws mainly on string bands from the 1920s, mixed in with bluegrass. When Matt Black started playing that style, 'it was very unfashionable, fascist and redneck, so I kept quiet about it. But now banjo is in vogue'. A 1985 cowpunk anthology contains the first known use of the 'a' word – *Leather Chaps And Lace Petticoats: Welcome To Alternative Country*.

But weirder things were stirring outside the capital, on provincial college campuses, where Marxist theorising collided with student high jinks. The Mekons were a Leeds-based collective who started their career as the most musically illiterate post-punk band of them all, making a virtue of their ineptitude. Then they met recording engineer John Gill, who had worked with both The Sex Pistols and English traditional folk singers and 'the ineptitude of the playing became stylised and eventually...part of the music'. Having studied art history under TJ Clark – a former member of Situationist International, an anti-philosophy that resists boredom and capitalism through turning work into play, stereotypes into in-jokes – they began to dress on stage in cowboy boots and stetsons . It was a conscious choice to embrace Americana.

The Mekons first achieved this artful feat on *Fear and Whiskey*. The album appears on their own Sin label, and its sleeve is a perfect parody of classic Sun 78s from Memphis. As to the sound, there are scratchy violins, ragged punk guitar and a rockabilly vibe 'inept and rough as barbed wire'.* On their version of Hank Williams' 'Lost Highway' 'Jonny Boy' Langford sounds like a football hooligan. Honorary member Dick Taylor, original bass guitarist with The Rolling Stones, plays one of his 'not a note wasted' guitar solos, and the whole thing seems to levitate. It was not so much a tribute to country music as a wilful deconstruction.

On their next album, *Edge Of The World*, now with the wonderfully disconnected-sounding Sally Timms as part of the collective, Hank Williams' 'Alone And Forsaken' is set to a Velvet Underground style drone, with impassive vocals. In a northern accent, of course.

Sophie Bourbon from Chicago proved to be the Mekons' saviour, and key members of the band relocated there as the Waco Brothers, 'half Clash, half Johnny Cash'. They also started Bloodshot Records, and began to copyright a new style, that of 'insurgent country'.

Back in America, a new form of roots music began to evolve, played by bands like Jason And The Scorchers, Lone Justice and The Blasters. All three continue to illuminate alt country, but back then this music went largely unregarded. The first two bands were so watered down by their record companies, that it has taken years for their early gigs to percolate through to record buyers. The third, was until recently, extremely hard to find on CD. What we can now hear in all three is the rawness of punk clashing with Nashville tunes and country chords.

* *Folk Roots*

There were those, though, who never lost their spirit, and can be traced through cowpunk to the present day. Post CBGBs, the New York punk scene is best exemplified by a band like Tev Falco's Panther Burns, who played a kind of speeded-up rockabilly from the late '70s onwards. What resulted – often now termed 'psychobilly' – leached out all the music's original country elements. But whereas in New York the taste was for one style only, in the South, the audience was made up of 'punk rockers, new wave kids, hillbilly kids, black kids'.

It was in the South that the best musical conjunctions began to occur. LA's punk scene was far more interesting in the early '80s than New York's. In 1980, the term Americana might not have yet been invented, but the Blasters – a punky LA band – released an album called *American Music*. The title track sounds like updated Chuck Berry, with a lead guitar that rings like a bell, and stuttered vocals. This is rockabilly, but with more of a sense of light and air than the contemporary New York variant.

The Blasters were led by two brothers, Dave and Phil Alvin. Dave wrote the title track for *American Music*, an alternative national anthem like a cross between Chuck Berry's 'Rock And Roll Music' and 'Back In The USA', here sung so fast that you can hardly hear the words. Who could deny Dave's proud boast that 'We've got the Louisiana boogie and the devil's blues / We've got country swinging rockabilly too/we've got jazz, countrywestern and Chicago blues/its the greatest music you ever knew'. It barely lasts two minutes, and it sounds like a revolution.

Dave Alvin also wrote 'Long White Cadillac', which Dwight Yoakam made his own. Dwight evolved a note-perfect approximation of the Bakersfield sound, but he was also a close friend of LA punk band X, with whom Dave Alvin later played. X too were inventing a potent brew of '50s music and punk: lead guitarist Billy Zoom was a Gene Vincent fanatic. As to the Blasters, their debut was recorded in a San Fernando garage: 'The simple fierceness of Dave's playing, the shapely urgency of Phil's singing',* and most impressive of all, Dave's original songs that 'sounded as righteous as the covers the band essays'.* Just listen to 'Lone Wolf'. In a different time and place, it could be a country hoedown.

Dave Alvin has since made a line of distinguished solo albums. 'My mother's family have been here since 1870, and my grandparents ran a

* *Uncut* magazine

dance hall back in 1902, so I knew all about California history.' Another major influence on his work is that of the Beat writers, who took intense, poetic language out of the lecture room and put it back in the bars and flophouses. Alvin studied modern American literature at Long Beach under poet Gerard Locklin, and later got involved with the *Illiterati Press*.

His solo career is a series of delights. *Out In California* is one of a series of live albums, taken from a series of West Coast gigs with his band the Guilty Men, and an aural feast of pedal steel and organ and accordion. 'American Music' is three times the length of the original garage version, with pumping bass and barrelhouse piano. The guitar break is wilder and more ecstatic, and Dave sings with a kind of throaty pride. Here he revisits his most famous song, 'Fourth of July' as a touching ballad.

Studio outings have shown yet another facet. *Blackjack David* is steeped in the passage of time, from ancient ballads – the sombre title track, an ancient British ballad about a gypsy stealing a lord's wife, is a universe away from the Blasters – to the story of a Vietnam vet. The playing is relaxed and richly textured, a measured dose of maturity after the adolescent flash of those garage rockabilly years.

Issued at the start of a new millenium, the Grammy-winning *Public Domain* is subtitled 'Songs From The Wild Land', and all the songs are drawn from American folk song. Dave sings deep, and the sound is largely acoustic and respectful. There is a wondrous mixture here, Appalachian ballads and Tex Mex and country blues and murder songs and cowboy tales and railroad tunes: all vital elements of 'American Music', too.

Six years earlier, brother Phil released *County Fair 2000*, which is a series of snapshots from American musical history, from ragtime to good time to Blasters' style rockabilly, with lots of comic asides..

X were a high velocity band, featuring John Doe and Exene Cervanka, battling over an urgent backing, and making political points. By the time of *See How We Are*, Dave Alvin had replaced Billy Zoom on lead guitar, and was contributing songs like 'Fourth of July'. The band showed their acoustic and rootsy side as the Knitters – referring to Pete Seeger's group the Weavers – on the album *Poor Little Critter On The Road*, with covers of The Carter Family's 'Poor Old Heartsick Me' and a song by the Delmore Brothers. Bloodshot issued *Poor Little Knitter On The Road*:

A Tribute To The Knitters, with the likes of Robbie Fulks, Whiskeytown and The Handsome Family. The original band briefly reformed in 1999 and exuded bonhomie on stage: 'In 1985, the Knitters meant that punk rock could be reconciled with historical, grown up music: today they mean that punk rock has become just that.'*

John Doe once claimed that he was seeking the common ground between punk and roots music. 'The positive side of roots music is it gives your lyrics a simplicity, an honesty and a humour that they need. It also acknowledges the past...' The negative side of all this is if you start believing that 'someone else's culture is more valid than your own'.

Originally as San Francisco punk-thrash band, The Dils, Rank And File's first album remains a thing of wonder. Tony and Chips Kinman had relocated to Austin, joining up with a young guitarist called Alejandro Escovedo to make *Sundown* (Slash, 1982). Nothing in their earlier work prepared anyone for the music here, urgent and melodic and extremely odd. The last thing anyone expected to kick off proceedings, was a love song to 'Amanda Ruth'. It boasts harmonies straight out of the Everly Brothers, and slightly off-kilter lead vocals. The lead guitar work sparkles, care of Escovedo, but it emerges out of a punchy mix of strummed six strings on the opening track. Rock music at heart, with a real punky thrust. There are train songs, ballads, and hymns to the highway, 'on Highway 81/we're headed for the sun'. It all sounds wonderfully optimistic, but with something strange at the margins, like an update of the Velvet Underground's 'Train Round the Bend'.

The Kinmans went on to form noise merchants Blackbird – a drum machine and a Jesus And Mary Chain fixation – then right back to their roots as the acoustic Cowboy Nation where they quietly retell dusty tales like 'Remember the Alamo' and traditional songs about life in the saddle such as 'Old Paint' and 'Cowboy's Lament'. Tony plays bass dobro, and Chip lonesome harmonica and the two harmonise like old pardners out on the range, It is no wonder that they attracted some hostility from the professional cowboy music scene. As Tony says, 'they much prefer Gene Autrey movies to John Ford movies. We're exactly the opposite.'*

Live, the brothers wear cowboy hats as wide as sombreros, and employ a drummer who plays mostly bass drum and hi-hat. As to Escevedo, he

* No Depression

went on to form The True Believers with his brother Javier, a band that set Austin alight. The real missing link, though, were the Dallas band Killbilly, who trod the rocky road that led from *Sundown* to Uncle Tupelo playing a 'brand of music that crossed Bill Monroe with Motorhead'.

Back with cowpunk, which *still* sounds great, someone once described LA's Lone Justice as Dolly Parton backed by the Blasters. One hopes it was meant as a compliment. Certainly the early demos they laid down for Geffen in December 1983 show a clattering and exciting combo, with Maria McKee on lead vocals. Here are songs like 'Grapes Of Wrath' and 'Dustbowl Depression', banged out like a US equivalent of the Boothill Foot Tappers with a stronger beat. A few songs from this session surfaced on a retrospective, *The World Is Not My Home*.

Lone Justice had been formed earlier that year by McKee with guitarist Ryan Hedgecock in 1983, and Benmont Tench, from the Tom Petty band, on keyboards. Something happened in the studio and when the band's debut album appeared two years later, produced by Jimmy Iovine, it had the hysterical, boxed-in sound of '80s pop. On the record, 'Soap, Soup And Salvation' is shrill and muffled but with great washes of organ, driving drums and Maria testifying like a hellfire preacher, while the demo is sweeter, more rackety, with chattering guitar and no keyboards.

After recording a second album, *Shelter*, with a new bunch of musicians and declaring that 'I didn't want to be in a country punk band forever,' McKee moved on to a solo career with albums like *You've Got To Sin To Get Saved*, with help from members of The Jayhawks. Drummer Don Heffington joined the disturbing Parlor James, and produced records by the likes of Kieran Kane.

In 2003, McKee is still puzzling out her true direction, and resisting the term sometimes used of her, 'the queen of alt country'. In 1993, having sacked her band, she went on to make *You Gotta Sin To Get Saved*, the same year as Lucinda Williams' *Sweet Old World*, The Jayhawks' *Hollywood Town Hall*, and Uncle Tupelo's *Anodyne*. The four albums were soul brothers, but at a point when McKee seemed to find her way, she took a career-breaking left turn to the art-rock extremes of *Life Is Sweet* – in her teens, she was fixated with Lou Reed – and jumped off the 'no depression' bandwagon just as it was starting to roll.

On *High Dive*, she models on the cover like a farmer's wife from the Great Depression – or Gillian Welch in a wig – and one reviewer compared her to a 'cowpunk Marianne Faithfull'. The album is dedicated to her half-brother, Bryan McLean, and the string and horn arrangements pay homage to *Forever Changes*, Americana on LSD, and with a mariarchi band. There are elements of high opera, and echoes of Bruce Springsteen at his most florid: 'I love the *Born To Run/Darkness* era'. Her singing is miles away from that awkward young cowpunk back in 1983, but there is something edgy too – the high dive here is one that she takes 'into an empty pool'. In her combination of toughness and vulnerability, and soul inflections, Maria is far closer to Dusty Springfield than to Laura Cantrell.

On the side, McKee has made far rootsier contributions to the *Songcatcher* soundtrack, and to Cajun tribute, *Evangeline Made,* and has left a swathe of unreleased recordings in her wake. A bootleg CD of her at Dingwells – an emotionally naked experience – bears the title *Absolutely Barking*. Live, she makes each show a 'cathartic experience. I have this way of performing where I lose myself in a song. It's weird.'

Rosie Flores started singing 'psychedelic country rock' in the late '60s with Penelope's Children at high school in San Diego. Rosie formed Rosie And The Screamers in 1978, playing a mix of rockabilly and hard-core country. By the mid '80s she was a member of the Screamin' Sirens, an all-woman cowpunk band who released *Fiesta* in 1984, then again went solo and worked with California producer Pete Anderson, as part of the Town South of Bakersfield crew. Finally, this strange odyssey culminated with her moving to Austin. As to the future, she has faith in younger artists who are bringing the old music back: 'they appreciate things like bluegrass or rockabilly or even traditional music. I'm definitely noticing a younger audience coming to my shows, and also an intellectual sort of college audience.'

British audiences had a chance to see her live – and marvel at her fluid guitar picking – when she toured in support to Shakin' Stevens, of all people, though both could be roughly put into the rockabilly box. A magnificent album like *Dance Hall Dreams* – recorded live at a San Antonio club – is self-consciously in the tradition of honky-tonk pioneers like Rose Maddox, but richer and more subtle.

Blood On The Saddle were the most extreme of all the cowpunk bands to emerge out of LA. Albums like *Poisoned Love* and *Fresh Blood* see punk speed used as a weapon, and country-music icons as their target. Annette Zakinska sings over stand-up bass and yodels, which made one reviewer describe their 1984 debut as 'a rodeo where even the horses are doing speed'. Guitar picker Greg Davis claims Doc Watson as an influence, but he would need a strong dose of amphetamines to fit in here. Annette keeps on gamely performing songs like '(I Wish I Was A) Single Girl (Again)', 'while her band, out of control, beat her to the finish'. They combine fervent covers of old chestnuts like 'Folsom Prison Blues' and 'Rawhide' with their own songs. Like most of their fellow travellers in the cowpunk scene, the band did not survive the '80s. Cowpunk was a great idea, but the music hasn't really lasted. It was a means to an end.

Over in Tennessee. Jason And The Nashville Scorchers, as they were first named, played the kind of fast country rock that originally attracted the 'cowpunk' label. Deeply religious Jason Rindenberg came south from Illinois for the downside of Music Row, where he met some Nashville locals, 'reared on country music but also infected by rock 'n' roll'. They played the local punk clubs, and guitarist Warner Hodges – whose parents had played with Johnny Cash – joined after he had heard about an incendiary gig the prototype Scorchers played with REM. As Jason now puts it, 'these fierce, ferocious rock 'n' rollers' run headlong into 'this kid off an Illinois hog farm that's never been south of the Mason-Dixon Line. You put all that together, and it was just an outrageous chemistry'.

In 1982, they recorded some tracks on four track that became their debut release, the *Reckless Country Soul* EP. It was a brand new sound, but one with deep roots, as the choice of songs by Hank Williams and Jimmie Rodgers showed. *Modern Twang*, always reliable, describes their music as 'an affectionate punch at Nashville's guts, raunchy but respectful'.

A mini album, 1983's *Fervor* has the band slouching moodily in semi-cowboy dress in front of original posters for Roy Acuff, Hank Williams and Bill Monroe, and the painted slogan 'Welcome Opry Boys'. It was a brave thing to do. Back then, as they told *No Depression*, 'literally you could go into certain places and do what we were doing with country music – forging it, melding it, slamming it together with punk rock and rock 'n' roll – and get beat up'. Listening to the disc now, though, 'Absolutely Sweet Marie' sounds a little amateurish next to Dylan's original, though they sound almost plangent on 'Harvest Moon'. Jason sings with spirit, and things end with a writing collaboration with Michael Stipe, and something happens. Hodges seems to have a nervous breakdown on electric guitar and Jason starts to lose his reserve, like a young Jerry Lee just before he goes beserk: the whole thing levitates, but with the drums keeping a beat going in the middle of a storm. Then it's back to boogie, but the threat remains, in that final chorus: 'The two steps out/and you're damned for all time/to walk both sides of the line'.

Listen too to the later take of 'Absolutely Sweet Marie' on *Wildfires & Misfits*, the version that 'got us 'The Deal' with EMI America', and it is far more urgent than on disc, with Warner Hodges blowing up a storm, like a young Richard Thompson, and some sweet harmonies that offset Jason's rough-hewn vocals. And a live take of Leon Payne's 'Lost Highway' for King Biscuit Hour – 'I'm not used to being up this early, you know' – bursts out of the speakers, with genuine punk energy, but respectful vocals. It is like two bands – and performances – in collision. The same retrospective shows the other side of The Scorchers, with their demo of 'Long Black Veil', with pedal steel and Jason singing with the wilderness in his voice. Suddenly it sounds like a revolution, and you could stick this on *Anodyne*, and hardly see the join.

On three albums released in the '80s, *Lost And Found* and the slightly stodgier *Still Standing* and *Thunder & Fire* they travelled the common ground between Eddie Arnold and The Rolling Stones, country and heavy metal and punk, before temporarily splitting up in 1990. *Essential – Jason And The Scorchers* adds rare tracks that show how burning a live band they were. Even better is a splenetic 1985 live show in Cologne, which has finally seen official release, as *Rock On Germany*.

Jason Rindenberg went solo for a series of duets with the likes of Steve Earle, BR549 and Lambchop. The Scorchers reformed in the mid '90s, and started where they had left off, putting out *Blazing Grace* – with George Jones and John Denver covers – and *Clear Impetuous Morning*, albums that made them heroes of the new alt-country scene, like proud godfathers. But this was a band that has always worked better on stage and, in 1997, they used Nashville's Exit/In club to record a live concert. The result was *Midnight Roads & Stages Seen*, released on double CD and video.

As to the band who shared that early gig at Cantrells, REM found a worldwide audience in a way that Jason And The Scorchers never did, with an upside-down sound where the bass player played the melodies and the guitarist provided colouring. You couldn't even hear what Stipe was singing about on the early albums. The band broke through by endless gigging, building their own alternative fan base, as Nirvana would do in their turn. Both bands paid a huge debt to early US punk, but REM then broke away to blaze their own trail deep into American folklore. It was one that would feed back into alt country, years down the line.

For *Fables Of The Reconstruction*, Michael Stipe surrounded himself with 'fables and nursery rhymes and Uncle Remus and old tales', entranced by the idea of stories – and songs – being passed down by word of mouth, then becoming 'as much a part of a way of living or a particular area as the religion or the trees or the weather. I like the connection between that and the South'. The year before, Stipe had spent a lot of his spare time listening intently to field recordings, 'cassettes recorded in Tennessee, in the mountains, Appalachian folk songs'. In his complex imagination, they resurrected a whole rural lifestyle, 'an old man with a fiddle, with a woman in the background with her hand on the stove'.

REM's debts to their adopted home of Athens, Georgia are legion, watching the trains go by in 'Carnival Of Sorts (Boxcars)', the graveyard in '1,000,000', even the man 'Gardening At Night' in suit and tie. According to Peter Buck, 'spooky gospel, that's what we wanted to be'. Stipe points out how important such local pride was in the rise of REM to national prominence – and they are words that will ring true for so many of the alt country bands that followed.

One band, the Beat Farmers were so fervent that drummer and singer Country Dick Montana ended up dying on stage, from sheer over-exertion. *Tales Of The New West* (1985) – which sees Sid Griffin and the Kinman bros along for the ride – starts with rockabilly, then goes on to cover songs by Lou Reed, Bruce Springsteen and even John Stewart, whose 'Never Going Back' replaces the voiceover at the end with a punky thrash. Later albums tell of everyday depravity, with titles like 'Are You Drinking With Me Jesus'. These intersect with songs by Tom Waits and Johnny Cash, Neil Young's 'Powderfinger' and – of all things – 'The Big Rock Candy Mountain'. The Beat Farmers' playing style is drawn equally from southern boogie and Creedence Clearwater Revival.

By 1990, this kind of stuff had lightened into a style statement. Colorblind James And The Death Valley Boys are the acoustic side of the Colorblind James Experience, and their album *Strange Sounds From The Basement* is studded with lines like 'I'm not a bible scholar, I'm just a hillbilly', with lots of mandolin – plus a brass section – but the whole thing is a kind of in-joke. Fine, in small doses, but the kind of artists covered in *South By Southwest* replant themselves in rural culture not as a kind of college jape, but to stop the nightmares.

The Meat Puppets are certainly the real thing, part of the first wave of US punk thrash, a thrash band from the Arizona desert led by Cris and Curt Kirkwood, who described his brother's later years as a 'suicide in progress'. Together with drummer Derrick Bostrom, the trio represent music on the edge of anarchy, at the place where punk meets psychedelia, but always found time for some country picking. Even their debut album (1983) included a cover of *Tumblin' Tumbleweeds*, painful on the ears, with wilfully out of tune vocals. Elements of bluegrass began to seep through from *Meat Puppets II* onwards, thankfully. *No Depression* argued that on such roots excursions, the band's sound is organic where the likes of X are merely visiting; 'it clearly recalls country, but no country that you've ever heard before'. Or again, though Ween later came close.

Back in LA, a number of bands emerged from the so called 'Paisley Underground', and traced psychedelia back to its roots. For older listeners, the Dream Syndicate, the Bangles and Rain Parade brought a certain nostalgia for the music of a decade gone by. Many were closer to the cowpunk sound than they might now like to admit – just listen to Green On Red's 1982 demo 'Gravity Talks': only the Farfisa-style organ played by Chris Cacavas sets it apart. Originally part of the Serfers, a band from Tucson, they moved to LA, and chose as a name the title of a song the Serfers used to play: for singer Dan Stuart, 'it was a direction we hadn't done, a sound that I liked'. The sound was country rock, but constrained, a precursor of lo-fi, and it reverberated through Green On Red's debut mini-album also released in 1982.

All that was missing was a lead guitarist, and when Chuck Prophet – 'he came from a different background, with a reverence for people like Merle Haggard' – joined for *Gas Food Lodging*, all the pieces of the jigsaw were all in place. The result is a great album, which combines fiery rock backings with real songs: as Stuart put it, 'we're pretty much into the Woody Guthrie/Hank Williams tradition. Every song we write you can play on acoustic guitar.' They sound better still here with Prophet's tough lead guitar, busy keyboards and 'Big Daddy' Dan gargling with gravel. The missing link between *Highway 61* and early Ryan Adams.

Recorded in a mere two weeks, this was yet another of those seminal albums with which this story is punctuated. For *Uncut*, the band had suddenly discovered a 'virulent cross-pollination of fierce country rock and writhing punk blues', developing 'contour, focus, and killer tunes'. Their lyrics now delved into age-old American traditions, and bemoan the loss of innocence, a 'road trip through terrain eroded by industrial avarice'. After songs about serial killers, madness and struggle, the album ends with Pete Seeger's folk anthem 'We Will Overcome', a plea for people to come together. As Prophet explains, 'this was at the height of Reagan's rising tide of fascism', so it is all the more heartfelt. And doomed.

The gigs the band played to publicise the 1985 mini album *No Free Lunch* – which includes a cover of Willie Nelson's 'Time Slips Away' are still talked about with awe, with encores sometimes longer than the set list. Even so, the tensions so memorably described on *Gas Food Lodging* started to tear the band apart.

For their dark masterpiece *Scapegoats*, they again appear on the same CD – 75 minutes of bloodied memories and self pity. *Too Much Fun* (1992), about the comedown, was recorded back home in Tucson. Next stop, 'alt country', of which Chuck Prophet is an honorary member.

Chuck Prophet is now a solo artist, and albums like *Brother Aldo* are always listenable, without plunging any great depths. More recently, *The Hurting Business* was a different kind of music, following in the footsteps of the likes of Beck or the John Spencer Blues Explosion: spiky guitars and what *No Depression* regards as cut 'n'paste electronica.

Dan Stuart seemed to take a long sabbatical. As for Chris Cacavas, he became a movie-set designer, and put out albums on the side, mainly in Europe. *Dwarf Star* is largely acoustic, and as one review puts it 'sparsely arranged, rough and ragged in patches' with his songs as 'grinningly gruesome' as any centuries-old murder ballad. Van Christian, the third member of the Serfers, stayed out in the desert and formed Naked Prey, with Cacavas guesting on *Forty Miles From Nowhere*.

Many have since characterised the sound that Green On Red helped evolve as 'Desert Rock', a style taken even further by fellow Arizona band Giant Sand, and which Dave Goodman identifies as blending 'rock and roots music with a Southwestern flavour. Giant Sand got together in Tucson, even if their mainman Howe Gelb was raised in Pennysylvania. 'The desert is unthinkable, words don't do it. It helped me open up.' It led Howe to write about an unease in America, glimpsed here in its heartland. 'There's a hole in the sky/it's as wide as this nation/it's as deep as a mountain/as big as your imagination'.

Punk thrash and haphazard playing remain integral to their sound – what made them so important was that they bolted this sound onto traditional themes and took it further into modern noise experimentation.

Howe Gelb was a close friend of fellow Tucson maverick, slide guitarist Rainer Ptacek, who joined him in the Giant Sandworms (an idea taken from Frank Herbert's *Dune* sf epic) and they made one obscure EP in 1980, *Will Wallow And Roam After The Ruins*, then mutated into Giant Sand – with a parallel line-up The Band Of Blacky Ranchette.

Giant Sand hit the public consciousness with the stark and spikey *Valley Of Rain*, issued in 1985 but still sounding ahead of the game. This is not comfortable listening, an aural equivalent of the stark monochrome cover, cacti under a dark sky, a featureless landscape and not a human being in sight. Musically, Gelb has long admired the 'sparseness' of Merle Haggard or Hank Williams. He gives cowboy tales a widescreen focus, learnt from the cinema. 'I like the idea of tracks being like they're small clips of film.'

Ballad Of A Thin Line Man sees the band stretch out more, with all kinds of strange noises coming from Gelb's electric guitar, using feedback – and a coke bottle. Backing singer Paula Jean Brown sours rather than sweetens, Gelb sings about graveyards and about how 'we all have voices deep inside of us/trying to surface somehow, someway', and the band cover Bob Dylan and Johnny Thunders, a unique combination.

Gelb set up a separate *nom-de-plume* The Band Of Rocky Blanchette, to make *Heartland*, with dobros and pedal steel, but the words contradict the surface charm. 'Let they try to save everyone/from the death squads/from the eye-gougers': Apocalypse, now. 'The songs were written a long time before we recorded them. Back then, there wasn't a lot of new Country music – we ended up making music that we couldn't buy.'

Giant Sand have been prolific, on just the kind of tasteful indie labels you would expect. *The Love Songs* is wilder and rockier than its title would suggest, with Chris Cacavas sweetening the sound. *Cover Magazine* shows all the expected influences – X, Neil Young, Marty Robbins, Johnny Cash – and others that make a kind of unexpected sense: Sonny and Cher, Black Sabbath, Nick Cave. *Core Of Enchantment* is the richest Giant Sand album of them all.

With his rhythm section increasingly busy with their own side project, Calexico, popularising the more approachable aspects of the parent band, Gelb himself retreated to his home studio for a clutch of solo, handmade projects. *The Listener* features Rennie Sparks from The Handsome Family, plus violins. 'The Nashville Sound' is about yet 'another sad leaving'. It is not so much a song, as a series of private observations. 'It would pale without me meaning to write the damned thing down.'

At the Barbican recently, Giant Sand was joined by long-term fan PJ Harvey, then cameo performances with Evan Dando, Kurt Wagner and Vic Chestnutt, and Mark Linkous (Sparklehouse) – 'If Giant Sand are an "alternative" to anything, it's cynicism and lack of imagination.'*

Ross Tolman's band True West came from Davis, California, and spanned the divide from Quicksilver Messenger Service to Television, twin lead guitars duelling at high noon, on psychedelic classics like 'Lucifer Sam' and 'Happening Ten Years Time Ago'. Their second album, *Drifters*, is masterful, with folk-rock elements, and featuring contributions from Chris Cavacas on keyboards and the Long Ryders on backing vocals. Even better is *The Big Boot* (1984), a live album taped at the Milestone – a Charlotte punk dive.

* Victoria Segal

More directly, in terms of the remit here, are Russ Tolman's brace of solo albums, *Down In Earthquake Town* and *Totem Poles And Glory*, considerably rawer and 'downhome' than the parent band.

Tolman had also produced a demo tape for another Davis band, Thin White Rope, and lured away their rhythm section for his own band. Ominous as a David Lynch soundtrack, Thin White Rope stake out their territory right from the start on the opening track of their debut album, *Exploring The Axis* (1985). 'Down In The Desert' combines chiming guitars and Jozef Becker's clattering drums, while Kyser's vocals have a strange, haunted quality. There is something claustrophobic about the band too, as if psychedelic guitar has been set to a metronome, accentuated by song titles like 'Lithium' and lines like 'everywhere nowhere at all'.

In the Spanish Cave sounds like a hoedown in hell. The *Red Sun* 12in was recorded after a tour of the Soviet Union. Maybe homesickness prompted these strange retellings of vintage Americana: a croaky rendition of Lee Hazlewood's 'Some Velvet Morning', the band switching rhythm masterfully, Gene Pitney's 'Town Without Pity' and Marty Robbins' 'They're Hanging Me Tonight'. *Sack Full Of Silver* (1990) has a cover version of Can's 'Yoo Doo Right', which explains where that taste for stern drum patterns comes from, and their own 'Americana/The Ghost': a sprightly instrumental intro with bluegrass elements.

On *Squatters' Rights*, Thin White Rope ooze twin guitar honey all over The Byrds' 'Everybody's Been Burned': Guy sings as sweetly as he can manage, and then things get heavy, bringing out the inherent menace in the original song. It ends with a guitar set on reverb. No '60s harmonies here. As to 'I Knew I'd Want You', Kyser almost sneers his contempt on the line 'and then we'll be happy'. No chance, in Ropeland.

A Thin White Rope gig in all its ragged glory is captured on *The One That Got Away*. Caren Myers recalls one night in a pub in Camden: the room is airless and 'this elemental noise, heavy and dreamy as the night' with Kyser's voice 'low and raspy, the edges fuzzy with a vinegar-sour vibrato'. One of the highlights of the live album is a re-interpretation of 'Wreck Of The Ol'97', with twangy guitars and a hillbilly vocal, while a sloppier yet far more appealing sound resulted when Steve Wynn and Green On Red's Dan Stuart took time out to play three shows and record a one-off album as *Danny And Dusty*. *The Lost Weekend* (1985) brought in Sid Griffin from the Long Ryders on dobro, and his band mate Stephen McCarthy on lap steel. The music is rough and woozy and there are lots of in-jokes: 'don't you know I'm in a music band, I know the word is out on me'. *No Depression* compared them to 'a young Willie and Waylon on a bender', but their musicians are more like the *Rolling Thunder Review*, crossed with Neil Young's *Tonight's The Night* tour band.

Meanwhile, in another part of America, Chicago's Eleventh Dream Day were working in much the same area as some of the LA bands who collaborated on *Danny And Dusty*. The band were like a chance collision between the Velvets, Neil Young and Television, but with all kinds of odd additions, from hillbilly to white noise, and albums like *Beet* are about as good as full-out rock music gets. Singer Janet Bean also dabbled in a quieter music backstreet, as half of Freakwater.

Steve Wynn's own band, the Dream Syndicate, started off as yet another Velvet Underground clone, but developed into a razor-sharp mix of good singing and explosive guitar breaks, then gradually evolved into a new-wave Crazy Horse on albums like *Ghost Stories*. Wynn is a natural storyteller, and his solo album *Kerosene Man* was a collection of urban folk tales, with shit-hot musicians in support, but even that did not prepare anyone for 2001's *Here Come The Miracles*, epic and sprawling and masterful. That someone should have made so much great music, and still be barely recognised outside the alt-country crowd is tragic.

Much the same could be said about Kentucky-born Sid Griffin. The Long Ryders were Byrds derivatives, but scuzzier round the edges. The band formed in LA from remnants of The Unclaimed, releasing a mini-album in 1983, and on *10-5-60*, the band's bar-room roots are sweetened by banjo, steel guitar and autoharp, though it is good natured in a way one could never say of Thin White Rope or Giant Sand.

The front cover of *Native Sons*, a full-length album released the following year, was a deliberate parody of *The Notorious Byrd Brothers* – but without the horse – but songs like 'Ivory Tower' and 'Tell It To The Judge On Sunday' are strong enough to back up the comparison. This is friendly music, a little out of time, but rough enough around the edges to make it more than simple music nostalgia.

As Sid Griffin told Peter Doggett, 'Punk fans liked the fact that we played with a punky energy, while the older guys liked the 12 strings, and the Clarence White-styled lead guitar. We had hippies from communes standing next to people with purple hair and shaved heads. It was a beautiful thing to see'. *Metallic BO* is a fascinating compilation with a double tribute to Johnny Rotten – 'Anarchy In The UK' and the *Public Image Limited* theme song – joining acoustic delights like the traditional 'Circle Round The Sun' and songs by The Cramps and the Velvet Underground. Simplistic country rock, this is not.

Sid moved to London and formed the Coal Porters, whose album titles like *Rebels Without Applause* were often better than the music. Griffin is now a respected writer on alt country and all points West, but he can never resist the lure of the road for long. 'I admire people like Ernest Tubbs who died waiting for the next tour to start.'

The Long Ryders were a world away from a raw and belligerent band like The Replacements, who walked the same razor edge between inspiration and mere noise as local rivals Husker Du. And yet it is The Replacements, a Minneapolis band, who proved to be a major influence on the alt rock scene a generation later. At the time they were spat on during punk club bookings by Black Flag fans for daring to wearing plaid shirts and not cut their hair short. Wild frontman Paul Westerberg would lead them into a clutch of dreadful country covers, 'Jolene' a speciality, just to further enflame the situation.

No wonder that Wilco dedicated 'The Lonely I' to Westerberg. The Replacements gradually mutated from the speed thrash of their 1981 debut, with its declaration that 'I hate music/It's got too many chords' and songs like 'Fuck School' to a rediscovery of melody, allied to a rhythmic thrust that the Long Ryders never quite managed.

Their 1991 swansong *All Shook Down* was an 'unnervingly bleak C&W jewel, lighting a torch for every new country act to follow'.* On the title track the textures are gorgeous, the pace slow and there's even a recorder break – admittedly a trifle out of tune. Originally intended to be a solo album, Westerberg later described it as 'the sound of someone having a nervous breakdown'. He told *Rolling Stone* that 'it was the end of many things. My band. My marriage. My excessive lifestyle'.

* *Uncut* magazine

The tour that followed was later referred to by the bass player as a 'travelling wake', and there was no resurrection, but The Replacements are now a thing of legend. Live bootlegs like *Shit, Shower And Shave*, from 1989 – 'The Rolling Stones are playing Philadelphia tonight but we're better, so fuck them' – show the band in their wild maturity, a rare combination of melody and sonic attack.

American Music Club were formed in San Francisco in 1983, and lasted until the mid '90s, when mainman Mark Eitzel took off on a solo career. Bruce Kapham's moody pedal steel has come centre stage on *Slider*, an album of ambient soundscapes 'part Americana, part exotica, part lounge, with a dash of massage parlour'.* He also joined other ex-members of AMC in Clodhopper.

The parent band have been a huge influence on the generation that followed. A gentler one, it is true, with 'post punk honky tonk'†. It links the quieter side of The Replacements to the lo-fi bands of the '90s, just as Eitzel's songwriting style is a bridge between 'serious' writers like Raymond Carver and a whole slew of modern troubadours with a university degree in the modern American novel.

American Music Club's 1985 debut, *The Restless Stranger*, draws equally on Joy Division's desperate joy and the introversion of Nick Drake. Subsequent records brought more than a hint of country to the mix, and the combination fully hit home on 1990's *Everclear*. The Australian band The Triffids used the same device on their album *Born Sandy Devotional*, using pedal steel to conjure up a sense of emptiness.

Such seeds often bear strange fruit. Ryan Adams told *Uncut* his aim in forming Whiskeytown was not to play 'country rock' but to emulate AMC. They 'would push the parameters. That's what I wanted to do'.

The Violent Femmes were an acoustic trio who came out of Milwaukee like a hurricane, blending folk and punk with an intensity never heard before or since. Singer Gordon Gano sang about extremely personal things with a violent passion. All-American boys, gone irreparably wrong.

Their second album, *Hallowed Ground*, is an aural chamber of horrors, from the glaring totem on its cover to the music. As to the subject matter here: 'Come gather round boys' Gordon sings, almost with glee before embarking on a tale of murder and self-harm. The aural sweetening

* *Mojo*
† *Rolling Stone*

of banjo, autoharp and a brass section, does not so much sweeten the sound as emphasise its starkness. 'Listen to me baby' Gano whispers with menace, 'and I will find you out/and I will cut you up'.

The album is a violent collision between the darker side of the folk tradition, old time religion – a fervent but sarcastic 'Jesus Walking On The Water' – and something malevolent. It ends with Noah waiting hopefully for the great flood – just try to stop yourself singing the chorus.

ii) New Wave Troubadours

'Now the hardness of this world slowly grinds your dreams away.'
– *Bruce Springsteen*

Bruce Springsteen has rightly been called the 'poet laureate of American music'. His work has a double focus. There is the very real America of urban New Jersey, where he grew up, but there is also the American Dream, a mythic America imagined by its founding fathers, and since re-imagined through popular culture.

In concert, Springsteen sometimes uses the spaces between songs to free-associate his deepest thoughts as an honest man thinking through his place in US society and history. Bruce is America as it would like to see itself: down to earth, sexy, thoughtful, friendly, optimistic. A dreamer.

As he once rapped in Newcastle: 'I started reading this book, *The History Of The United States*, and it seemed how the way that things were, weren't always the way they were meant to be. And it wasn't until I started listening to the radio, and I heard something in those old singers' voices that said there was more to life than what my old man was doing, and the life that I was living, and they held out a promise – and it was a promise that every man has a right to live his life with some decency and dignity'. This holds true for all the people we have looked at so far, from Dock Boggs to Johnny Cash, Gram Parsons to Jason Rindenberg.

There is something of the preacher in Bruce. And the gospel he proclaims is – as Badly Drawn Boy puts it – 'winning against all the odds, carving a path for yourself, making this crappy old world something good'. For Thea Gilmore, his songs 'hit you at an instinctual level. It's an amazing thing for a writer to do, to paint such a massive canvas with such simple – never simplistic – language that appeals to everybody'. Talking to Radio 2 recently, Bruce comments, 'Everyone has memories that live within you, an essential part of who you are, that reveal to you what it means to be alive – the writer creates and collects those moments'.

Bruce spent years scuffling on the Jersey shore, with a succession of loser bands, even if he passed his audition with John Hammond as a solo singer songwriter, having taken time off from playing rock music in bars to concentrate on songwriting. His 1973 *Greetings For Asbury Park* is packaged like a postcard from home with downtown Americana his besetting theme, 'that pure America brother, dull-eyed and empty-faced, races Sundays in Jersey in a Chevy stock super eight'.

Like the young Tom Waits, he is trying a little too hard to be the chronicler of his own subculture, but time will bring concision. That extraordinary ability to make the everyday mythic is already here in embryo, best of all in the key song, 'Growing Up': 'I swear I found the key to the universe in the engine of an old parked car.'

As to his backing musicians, they gradually coalesced into the E Street Band – early live tapes sound like a friendlier Van Morrison, with a soul combo. As one of the witnesses to the Radio 2 biography – *An American Story*, puts it, the band 'was made up of folk musicians, people played very personally and eccentrically. It's a little carney band, the influences are the boardwalk, the accordion.' They did a lot of acoustic work at this time and are captured wonderfully on a radio show from Houston in 1974, Denny Federici plays accordion, Garry Tallent tuba and Clarence Cellons sax, on early songs like 'Wild Billy's Circus Story'. They even give us a snatch of 'Roll Out The Barrel', to warm up.

On *The Wild, The Innocent And The E Street Shuffle*, Springsteen refined his storytelling to create a whole small-town world, even if fictionalised, and seen now as a place before disillusion set in. It is a vision given cinematic scope on the widescreen epic *Born To Run* (1975). The sound is smoothed out, and the world view almost a parody of the 'runaway American dream' of its title song, with fast cars and blue collar jobs and amusement parks and teen romance.

As he grew older, this appealing but somehow dreamlike world view began to give way to an encroaching darkness. 'I knew that I was going to be following my characters over a long period of time – I thought it would be interesting and fun for my audience to have a certain kind of continuity'. At a show bootlegged from Austin Coliseum (1975), he free-associates. 'I saw a friend of mine, he played organ in one of my bands, and we stopped and were talking, and he told me he was married and hadn't been playing too much and it set me thinking about all the guys I was in earlier bands with, that had settled down and got hitched up and stuff, hardly any of them still playing. And we're here still running around'. Then he goes into a slow and passionate version of 'I Guess It's Gonna Work Out Fine', with Clarence Clemens on backing vocal chorus.

A legal dispute that meant Springsteen was prevented from releasing any more records for two years worked hugely to his advantage. He played some of the greatest concerts ever seen. Nicholas Dawidoff quotes Bruce at this point as having just started to write a batch of 'south Jersey cowboy songs'. He has become an admirer of roots musicians like Hank Williams and the Louvin Brothers, because they grappled with the grown-up issues rock generally avoids. 'Country asked all the right questions about how you go on living after you reach adulthood. Everything after *Born To Run* was shot full with a lot of country music... The "Real Country" boom has recently tended to obscure the most arresting country music, but Johnny Cash, Merle Haggard, Ralph Stanley are still making it, and so too are gifted young singers'.

Then Bruce came back with *Darkness At The Edge Of Town*, an album released as he hit 30. 'Racing In The Street' recasts his earlier urban dreams as endlessly sad. He sings it as an elegy. For Billy Bragg, 'it's the first song that you get a message from Bruce that there is something deeply sad beneath the American dream, something quite hollow'. As Springsteen himself later put it, 'I began to think about who I was, where I came from. Initially you're in search of a certain sort of freedom, some sense of control of the arc that your life is going to take'. Bragg adds that 'he built on that subsequently, the famous line in *The River*, "Is a dream a lie if it doesn't come true?"' *The River* (1980) was a huge success, a double album with lots of hits, high energy rock 'n' roll, but also something dark and brooding at its heart. 'The Price You Pay' is about being barred from the Promised Land, like Moses, stuck on the wrong side of the river. As to *The River* itself, it ends with a car wreck song, which could have been written by Hank Williams, endlessly sad, but pitiless at its heart.

Next step, *Nebraska*. For Bruce, 'it was the early '80s and the sense of violence was in the air on a daily basis, sometimes. I was 30...just the way things were put to you, even if it was through television, it was much more aggressive and abusive, truly abusive.' One key to his mindset at this time was a live and acoustic version of 'This Land Is Your Land'. 'Why do I cover Woody Guthrie? Because it is what is needed right now. America just died emotionally. Nobody had any hope left. I sing that song to let people know that America belongs to everybody who lives there: the blacks, Chicaons, Indians, Chinese and the whites. It's time that someone took on the reality of the '80s. I'll do my best'.

It is yet another of those keystone albums that helped give birth to 'alt country'. Listen to Jesse Malin. 'I was into punk rock. My father gave me a copy of this album that was just done on a four track, and I thought 'this guy's a billionaire, yet there's something true about this record, it's stark and honest, so it got me thinking really different. I went back to his earlier stuff, and realised that everything I thought he was glorifying was the opposite, it was about getting out of New Jersey, or this small mainstream kind of town'.

Nebraska deals with mass killers, small town gangsters, a patrolman who lets his own brother escape over the Mexican border. Among those that did not make the album is an urgent, driven version of 'Born In The USA', with overdubbed electric guitar, and a '50s feel – it could be Hank Williams when he sings 'I'm a long gone daddy, a good rockin' daddy' and he ends with an unearthly howl, as if of pain.

As to the title song, it retells a true tale from the late '50s, also filmed as the 1973 movie *Badlands*. A young man seduces a young cheerleader but they go off into Wyoming on a killing spree, expressing no remorse. He is electrocuted by the state, with his sweetheart forced to watch. The song ends with a chilling motto: 'Sir, there's just a meanness in this world'. Bruce had reached the point in his life where 'I felt like I was teetering on this void, and I felt a deep sense of isolation. I think that led me to those characters, and those kinds of stories. When you get older, the price for not sorting through the issues that make your emotional life – and the choices you are making – gets higher all the time. I was at a place where I could start to really feel that price.'

You can feel it too when listening to his haunted tone here. It proved hugely influential on Steve Earle, another champion of the down and out, in particular those on murder row. The bone-chilling power of the original album is diluted to near zero on *Badlands, A Tribute To Bruce Springsteen's Nebraska*, with only Son Volt and Johnny Cash – on a song not even on the original album – capturing the real sense of hurt in Springsteen's voice. Except for Hank Williams III, who gives 'Atlantic City' a good country hoedown kicking, with a yodel to match, and even puts an optimistic spin on 'Everything dies, baby that's a fact, but everything that dies sometimes comes back'. Then even Hank III slows down, and his version ends uncertain and melancholy.

Born In The USA was being laid down in a New York recording studio at the same time as Bruce was laying down *Nebraska* at home. 'There was a period when I was going to put them out as a double album. I didn't know what to do.' The paean – or not – to Ronald Reagan's America self-consciously drew on previous styles, Jimmie Rodgers on 'Working On The Highway', Hank Williams and steam locos on 'Downbound Train'. Working-class models, as the sleeve photo suggests. The album ends back in small-town America, on 'My Home Town'.

Even if his career seemed to coast for the next 20 years, Springsteen remained an influence on the storytellers who followed. Dave Alvin, Maria McKee and Martin Zellar were among those contributing to *One Step Up, Two Steps Back, The Songs Of Bruce Springsteen* in 1997. He is crucial to *South By Southwest* because he is located at exactly the point in time when being American, and taking that fact as a guiding principle in one's own songwriting, suddenly became problematic.

But now let's backtrack to March 3rd 1940, Woody Guthrie played a benefit concert in New York for 'The John Steinbeck Committee for Agricultural Workers'. Shortly after, Alan Lomax persuaded Victor Records to produce an album of Guthrie's dust-bowl ballads. 'The Victor people want me to write a song about *The Grapes Of Wrath*' he told his friend Pete Seeger. The song that resulted, 'Tom Joad', was a 17-verse ballad that tracked the plot both of the book and the movie directed that same year by John Ford, starring Henry Fonda.

However stark its lyrics, *The Ghost Of Tom Joad* sounds wonderfully warm, with lots of harmonica and pedal steel and country fiddle, but the tales it tells deal with hard times, illegal immigrants and pointless violence. It is also ominously quiet: 'turn it up to 11, it's still quiet'.* *The Rising* is quite the opposite, with a reformed E Street Band, a producer who had previously worked with Pearl Jam and Rage Against The Machine, and a song sequence that centres around the events of 9/11 with people just doing their job 'somewhere up the stairs, into the fire'.

Steve Earle

There are many parallels, lifestyle apart, between Bruce Springsteen and Steve Earle. Both perform beautifully constructed live shows, both have a sympathy for the underdog and the working man, both responded to 9/11 from an unexpected angle, both could only be American.

Steve Earle once told *No Depression* that 'I think Hank Williams records have a lot more to do with The Sex Pistols than with Brooks & Dunn. His career trajectory is a simpler one than Springsteen's, from rebel to jailbird to hero. Steve dragged himself back from the pit to make the best music of his career, a truly American tale of reinventing yourself.

But it is the dark times that make for the most interesting music. Earle was born in Fort Monroe, Virginia, then moved to Houston, where, at the 17, he was playing a floor spot when a drunken Townes Van Zandt kept yelling 'Play the Wabash Cannonball', and they became friends. He then moved to Nashville, where he played bass with Guy Clark, sang backing vocals on *Old No 1*, and punted songs to the likes of Carl Perkins.

As Steve points out on *Train A Coming*, the album he made years later when he emerged from prison, 'this ain't my unplugged record! I made most of these songs up before I was plugged in the first place.

A 1982 EP, *Pink And Black*, is pure rockabilly, to catch a trend, but got nowhere. Earle had learnt to follow his own instincts by the time of his debut album *Guitar Town* (1986): 'I went back to trying to write how I'd always written, about things I'd ever cared about'. It was a return

* *Mojo*

to the Bakersfield sound, and the release the same day of Dwight Yoakam's *Guitars, Cadillacs Etc* saw the birth of 'new country' much heralded. The two singers are chalk and cheese. Steve described his sound as 'just '80s hillbilly music', and 'Hillbilly Highway' proves the point.

In her affectionate biography of Earle, Lauren St John suggests that the way Earle emotes 'My Old Friend The Blues', sung to a lonesome pedal steel, confirms how profoundly he has 'influenced alternative country's course until, in 2002, a whole new movement had sprung up from it and Ryan Adams, a scruffy, soul-bearing, hard-living incarnation of Steve at the same age, was on the world stage'. But then, surely so is Steve himself, now that his demons are finally behind him.

Back on the original album, there were nods to bluegrass and the Johnny Cash jog trot – a sophisticated response to his musical heritage. One critic noted 'hippie political rhetoric, Jimmy Rodgers humanism and Hank Williams debauchery' in there too. There is even a gloop of Music Row sentimentality on 'Little Rock 'n' Roller'. It is a rare blip on an album that showcases a writer who already has a gift for honing a telling line. Like Springsteen, he dreams of classic American cars and the restlessness of the endless highway: 'I got a 67 Chevy, she's low and sleek and black/sometime I'll put her on the interstate and never look back.'

Earle recorded *Exit O* the following year. It ranges from urgent rockers to an affecting, semi-acoustic ballad in the closing 'It's All Up To You'. 'No-one said it would be easy, but it doesn't have to be this hard' now sounds bitterly ironic, given what was to happen to him next.

Copperhead Road (1988) tested the boundaries of country music, recorded not in Nashville but in Ardent Studios, Memphis – and it sounds like the brakes are off, musically. 'We were starting to contrast twangy guitar sounds against crunchier guitar sounds; that was point of the record.' Lyric-wise, this is the troubadour tradition with a vengeance, tales of Vietnam vets in exile in their own country, snake-oil salesmen, and shootists. Even 'Nothing But A Child' skirts sentiment as it deals with the wonder of a newborn baby. Maria McKee sings backing vocals and a crack bluegrass band give this song the necessary restraint to make it affecting. Elsewhere, the Pogues lend a punky, acoustic thrash to 'Johnny Come Lately', about a GI getting drunk in wartime London. The sting in the tail is that the soldier's grandson is sent home crippled from Vietnam, and to a less than ecstatic welcome.

Much of *The Hard Way*, was straight down the line rock music (with unusually interesting words) that Earle was now purveying. There are oases of quiet, as on 'Billy Austin', a tale straight out of Woody Guthrie, told as if by a man on death row, 'quarter Cherokee, I'm told'. Elsewhere, there are cameos by a Baptist choir, and by Steve's sister Stacey.

The concurrent live album *Shut Up And Die Like An Aviator* captures the explosive and chaotic shows from this time, and made one Texan critic observe that 'Earle's once earnest, raspy vocals now sounded as if his voice box had been run through a tree shredder'. This album is not so much as 'new country' as the most intense roots rock. As if to further make the point, Earle and the Dukes – and Stacey – close with the Stones' 'Dead Flowers', and it sounds like a wake.

After a bust for possessing crack cocaine, Steve ended up in jail, but within ten weeks of his release in 1994, he had recorded the downhome, acoustic *Train A Coming*. 'It was a low pressure record in a point in my life when I needed a low pressure record'. Fellow songwriter Clive Gregson notes that there is 'no fat on Earle's songs here: it's all flesh and bone'.

Never more so than on *I Feel Alright*, a song cycle which just 'poured out of me in a six-month period'. Something happened to him during the wilderness years – now he has evolved a voice of his own, as passionate and fascinating as anyone in American music. And this is something new, with a vitality to the playing that you don't often find in Nashville. It takes up where *Copperhead Road* left off, 'mountain metal' with hard strummed mandolins colliding with chiming electric guitars and thundering drums. Alt country starts here, as much as anywhere.

I Feel Alright is another great album. A vibrant and life-affirming 40 minutes, with not a second wasted, and exuding a natural authority. The lyrics have natural sense of poetry, but never use 'poetic' language: 'I've been down a thousand trails I've never walked before/I found out that without fail they lead me to your door.' Steve's voice has years of pain etched on it, and it is by now a cracked purr, wrecked yet magnificent. Earle uses it to take the listener through betrayal, pain and redemption. Here are songs written as if in his own blood but lacking self pity, just a clear-eyed account of how low he sank. You don't need to have taken crack cocaine to recognise the truth of its effect.

But 'Valentine's Day' is as tender and needy a love song as you will ever hear, even if 'all the words just slip away'. After this trip through a modern inferno – 'I've been to hell and now I'm back again' – Lucinda Williams joins in for a final, joyful 'You're Still Standing There'.

As Earle told *No Depression*, his earlier argument with the Music Row hit machine was 'not about country or rock. It's about real. This record is probably closer to a pop record…but it's truer to what I think is the *spirit* of country music than most of the records that come out of Nashville. "Long Black Veil" wouldn't get recorded nowadays'.

Perhaps as a result, he set up E Squared Records, for which Steve and Twangtrust partner Ray Kennedy signed up fellow-minded performers, like the V-Roys, 6 String Drag, and Cheri Knight. *El Corazon* opens quietly, with a tribute to Woody Guthrie, accompanied by Steve himself on harmonium, like a church anthem. The album is dedicated to the memory of Townes Van Zandt, and shares his restless spirit.

This is an album that can touch the heart one minute, and give way to a gloriously dumb guitar record the next. Earle describes it as 'more of a rock record, even on the country songs'. Lauren St John claims, that this recording established Earle as 'perhaps alt country's most visible and popular performer'. It certainly pressed all the right buttons, climbing to the top of the *No Depression* Top 40, and of the Americana chart. *Exit O*, his online mailing list became the largest of any alt country performer, and he used his fame to give support to causes like Farm Aid, the Campaign for a Land Mine Free World and to argue against the death penalty and to take part in the Journey of Hope.

He also spent 1997 on the road, and through the magic of the bootlegger's art a great show in Bern, with Buddy Miller on lead guitar, has been captured under the appropriate title *Heavy Metal Bluegrass* – just listen to the way that 'Zen Mandolin' segues into 'Copperhead Road', and the ecstatic whoops of the Swiss crowd. Earle covers Jay Farrar's 'Windfall' and Gram Parsons' 'Sin City'. Earlier that same year, yet another double bootleg preserves his Copenhagen gig, with treats like the Steve Earle-Elvis Costello writing collaboration. 'Angry Young Man'.

Back in the studio, Steve followed up his collaboration with the Del McCoury band to record a whole album of bluegrass with the 'high risk, low tech' *The Mountain*. Warner Brothers withdrew their funding. As Steve told his audience at 'South By Southwest' that year 'It got down to Warners telling me that I couldn't make a bluegrass record. My attitude was "what part of fuck you do you not understand, fuck or you".'

Iris Dement took part in the sessions for *The Mountain*, as did the likes of Gillian Welch, John Hartford and Marty Stuart, and reckoned 'it was more of a family reunion than a studio session'. A large family, judging by the chorus of 'Pilgrim', which features just about everybody you have ever heard of.

The album opens with a jokey 'you want to be in the band, you've got to put your hat on'. The chuckling strings seem to release something in Steve's voice so that it sounds richer, more Kentucky. He has never before sounded so purely happy. Steve reminisces about Bill Monroe walking on stage at the Tennesse Performing Arts Centre on night, uninvited, and taking over his show. 'When I look back now, I believe this record was really born that night.' Del McCoury had been on the road with Monroe in the early '60s and is the perfect collaborator here, with his own sons on banjo and mandolin.

Live On Campus is yet another bootleg. It opens with Steve's solo set, just guitar and harmonica, extremely good humoured. When the band come in, they interweave around Earle with an easy perfection that is as close to heaven as any bluegrass fan could wish. Del fell out with Steve soon after, possibly because of what Del described as the 'vulgarity' that Earle had supposedly brought to bluegrass. If *The Mountain* is vulgar, then so is a Rolls Royce. On stage any animosity is channelled into the music and the concert ends with 'Hillbilly Heaven', which Earle introduces with a throwaway 'there are two sorts of songs, those about girls and those about roads'. His next album 'will be louder'.

Transcendental Blues was that disc, and it went straight to number one in the Americana charts. Which is great for an album that opens with a passage of Indian-style psych 'n' drone, just like The Beatles around 1966. The music here is Americana in the widest sense, a mix of rock and country and bluegrass and Irish folk, courtesy of Sharon Shannon.

Early copies of the CD came with a bonus four tracks recorded live at 'South By Southwest' in 2000, only three months before the album was released. 'The Galway Girl' is particularly joyful. *No Depression* saw the album itself as a patchwork of previous styles, but reflecting a new maturity. The emotional heart of the album is in the death row confession 'Over Yonder': 'I hope my goin' brings them peace'.

It is a theme taken up in the short story 'The Witness' in Earle's prose collection, *Doghouse Roses*, which transfers his stories about drifters and jailbirds and Vietnam vets into cold print, spare as his lyrics.

But the silence of the printed word is no substitute for that weathered yet hopeful voice. *Jerusalem* is based around Earle's response to September 11th. It is a short, but extremely powerful album, A sinister voice intones 'Ashes to ashes, dust to dust' – electronics give it a stutter – and then Earle starts singing, but he too sounds disembodied, with military drums and ominous electric guitar. It could be The The, as is the sense of civilisations crashing: 'every tower ever built tumbles'. Contemporary music, in every sense. A mile away from Dwight Yoakam, or Bakersfield. *Uncut* glories in how 'corrosive' Steve sounds, as he deals in other songs with 'the curdling of America's Great Dream' and the 'rampant perversity of the corporate Bush regime'.

'Amerika v 6.0' starts off like the long lost brother of 'Jumping Jack Flash', but Jagger never sounded this angry and despairing. Elsewhere, Earle adds harsh banjo to his prison saga 'The Truth'. His ability to get under someone else's skin, just like Woody, comes to the fore on the notorious 'John Walker's Blues', sung as if by an all-American boy who has converted to Islam, and declared war on his native land.

The album ends on a hopeful note, just like Steve Earle's career so far, and the best of his music. It is what makes him so vital. The hymn-like 'Jerusalem' is a vision of peace in the Holy Land. It is also the least convincing song here: Steve just does the dark better than the light, lions better than lambs. 'My only responsibility is not to *not* say something.'

Meanwhile, while not hosting 'South By Southwest', Austin was becoming a seedbed of laconic troubadours. Their work provides a low energy contrast to the passion of Earle. Steve himself advised Robert Earl Keen Jr to try out his luck in Nashville. Nothing happened, and Keen moved back to Texas. He found an audience with wry albums like *Picnic*, its title referring to a disastrous day in Austin when Robert went over for Willie Nelson's 4th of July concert, and lost both his girlfriend and his car, which caught fire. The music was OK, though. Keen studied English at the University of Texas at Austin with Lyle Lovett, the master of low-key irony, who namechecks him on 'Record Lady'.

You could encapsulate Lyle's whole style in the (apparently) throwaway lines from the same album, 'and he's really not that ugly dear/she could have done much worse'. This plays off his relationship with screen goddess Julia Roberts around the time he recorded the acoustic *I Love Everybody*. This is a mile away from Steve Earle. Lyle plugs into the spirit of western swing, and is the honourable tradition of the cool and witty dude, from Bob Wills to Dan Hicks.

This Texan farm boy found out about the local music scene from reading *The Improbable Rise of Redneck Rock*, and began singing in Houston coffee houses. Robert Earl Keen shares songwriting credits on Lyle Lovett's self-titled debut and its follow up *Pontiac*, described by Dave Goodman as 'two outstanding alt country albums of the '80s. They are certainly excellent, but hardly 'alt country' as anyone now knows it.

Lyle Lovett And His Large Band adds big band swing, but you feel that Lovett is greatest out on the margins of his own career. Just Lyle and a cello is heaven enough. *Step Inside This House* is a personal tribute to ten of the best from the Texas singer songwriter tradition. Lone Star troubadours highlighted here include not just Townes Van Zandt and Guy Clark, but lesser-known names like Steve Fromholz, with a wonderul off-kilter song about bears, and Eric Taylor, whose career somehow got lost. His 'Memphis Midnight/Memphis Morning' is as good an evocation of a time and a place and a love affair gone wrong as you will find: like everything here it says what it needs to in as few words as possible.

The hefty CD booklet is an anthology/photograph album, in its own right, but one man missing is Darden Smith, another alumnus of the University of Texas at Austin from the early '80s. Both Lyle and Nanci Griffith provide guest vocals on his early albums, and the self-titled *Darden Smith* from 1988 is the kind of album I would play anyone as representative of Texan music at its best.

As Lauren St John puts it, 'everything changed in 1985', at least in the country music universe. At MCA, Tony Brown added Nanci Griffith and Lyle Lovett to his roster, just months after signing Steve Earle. True, she is peripheral to 'alt country'. But even her first, and folkiest, offering, *There's A Light Beyond These Woods* – laid down in a small Austin studio in the late '70s – has songs about Alabama, Montana and West Texas. Griffiths is American as apple pie, and it shows in every song.

Nanci's voice is clear as spring water and radiates optimism, as do her songs, though it can be sly and sexy when you least expect it. As time went by, she surrounded herself with musicians of the calibre of Bela Fleck and Mark O'Connor and bluegrass-flecked arrangements to match. *The Last Of The True Believers* is particularly subtle. Tom Waits, Phil Ochs, Tom Russell and Jimmie Dale Gilmore are among the songwriters whose work she has covered, quite apart from side projects like *Other Voices,* which show a becoming modesty.

One Fair Summer Evening presents Nanci at her best, live and acoustic: 'I learnt my trade watching the hands of Eric Taylor, Bill Staines and Townes Van Zandt fly across acoustic guitars and listening to their melodies of short storied splendour.... And I was not the only juvenile learning with cheek to glass, Lyle Lovett, Robert Earl Keen and Darden Smith were among the many of us who had their respective corners.'

Dust Bowl Symphony is at the other end of the musical spectrum, a layered creation close in spirit to Joni Mitchell's recent offerings. Nanci has never sung better. Joined in the studio by the London Symphony Orchestra and vocal harmonists like Darius Rucker – from Hootie And The Blowfish – and Beth Neilson Chapman, this is far indeed from the ornery spirit of Woody Guthrie.

But there are tougher female voices around. Rosanne Cash is Johnny's daughter, and was tutored by Maybelle Carter in how to play guitar. How odd that she now should exemplify not exactly alt country, but the alternative to country. As early as 1980's 'Seven Year Ache', recorded in Hollywood by her then husband Rodney Crowell, Rosanne's fresh voice and world-weary lyrics could have been airlifted in from today.

Rosanne went on to make music as revolutionary in its era as her adopted grandmother's back in the '30s. Influenced by concept albums by her father, like *Stop This Train* – 'I liked listening to my dad in character' – she released an emotionally brutal sequence of song cycles about being a woman in post-feminist America. None was more naked than *Interiors*, about her marriage break up 'we crawled night and day through the tears and debris'. This is closer in spirit to Virginia Woolf than Shania Twain, and Rosanne later published a collection of short stories, capturing the same cool tone and careful self-probing: 'And when the children awake – should they need me – I will stand ready to navigate all the countless and strange bodies of water they might be required to cross.'

Producer and second husband John Leventhal puts together a rich, electric tapestry for *The Wheel*, over which Rosanne sings quietly but with a reined-in passion and total verbal control, 'I am a river with a voice/I came into your life by choice'. No wonder that Mark Cooper describes Cash as the 'queen of a new kind of country in which the genre's traditional straight talking was psychologised and turned steadily inward'.

Despite Rosanne having as many country number ones as her father, Nashville never quite knew what to do with her, though it was a brave thing even in 1996 to issue *10 Song Demo* as it came: even the packaging is deliberately basic. The stripped-back sound makes Rosanne sound naked, though never vulnerable. Then a rare throat condition robbed her of her voice, and Cash had to learn how to sing all over again. A free show six years later in Manhattan was a rare sighting.

The outdoor setting was particularly resonant. Castle Clinton was the original entry point for immigrants to the US, and lies only a few hundred yards from Ground Zero. Rosanne's song 'September When It Comes' had first appeared on *Transatlantic Sessions* in 1997: now it became almost unbearably poignant, a song about the loss of faith, and growing older, and encroaching death: 'When the shadows lengthen and burn away the past/They will fly me like an angel to a place where I can rest'. When her father joins in on the recorded version on *Rules Of Travel*, it enters another dimension. Mark Cooper puts it best: 'Johnny's voice is weakening now but one of the beauties of the song is the father's admission of fraility'. Apparently, hearing her own dad singing 'I cannot move mountains for you, I can no longer run,' with a weary magnificence of which only he is capable, reduced Rosanne to tears.

Elsewhere, Steve Earle does not so much duet as interject on 'I'll Change For You'. Both the writing and the way the song is performed carries out the difficult feat of being totally believable while letting you know that every word is false. If all 'new country' sounded like this, it would rule the world. If anyone exemplifies the meeting point of the best of Nashville and the new wave, she does.

Aside from being Rosanne's first husband, Rodney Crowell is still best known for the time he spent with Emmylou Harris's Hot Band, and nowadays for being omnipresent as a session player. But his 2001 album *The Houston Kid* is almost worthy of his ex-wife, so careful is it as an evocation of growing up in Texas. This is far more than the usual exercise in nostalgia – 'I Wish It Would Rain' is about a male teenage prostitute, and other songs deal with homophobia and murderous thoughts. 'Topsy Turvy', with its violent father, sounds more autobiographical than mere fiction should. More positively, there is a rewrite of the song that started it all off for him, dedicated to his one-time father in law. 'I've seen the Mona Lisa, I've heard Shakespeare read, real fine/It's just like hearing Johnny Cash sing "I Walk the Line".'

Folk Roots reckons that Iris Dement's voice 'cuts like a knife, takes you apart, then kisses it better'. It is hardly surprising, given her childhood. One of 14 children, she was born on a poor Arkansas farm, then migrated with her family to California, and hard times. During a brief move to Nashville, Nanci Griffith took Iris under her wing, while John Prine endorsed her debut album, *Infamous Angel* (1992). It was an amazingly self-assured debut, though radio stations have never quite known where to place her – under folk or country, or dangerously political? Outspoken in her views on the exploitation of the workers – Woody would have been proud – Dement also blazed a path back into the music's past, which soon became a well-worn trail. She paid tribute to the realism of Loretta Lynn, and in turn provided a role model for the likes of Gillian Welch.

What first hits you is her voice, perky and warbly and even harsh at times, very much of the South. The whole album is folk art at its best, with hidden depths to simple songs. It is a series of observations about lives being played out in a small town, though leaving it can be even worse – note the subtle change from 'our' to 'my' in 'Our Town', with dobro and fiddle like a second voice. 'Mama's Opry' is about a mother failing to make the Ryman, so she recreates it at home. The album ends with the traditional 'Higher Ground', with its spoken intro and which does indeed feature her mother on wavering vocals.

My Life cuts even deeper, and Dement looks back on a childhood that has been stolen from her by the strict Pentecostal faith of her parents. It is dedicated to the memory of her father, and Iris reminisces about once finding his fiddle, where it was hidden once he got 'saved', 'high upon a shelf, next to a stack of quilts. At the album's heart is 'No Time To Cry', about not giving way to emotion, even if your heart is broken. She sings it as half lament, half lullaby, and as if to herself.

On 1996's *The Way I Should*, Dement takes this kind of personal hurt into the public arena: 'we kill for oil and throw a party when we win/some guy refuses to fight and we call that the sin'. Singing in front of a full electric band, her voice like a blowtorch, the results are scary. And since then, silence.

To quote Emmylou Harris, 'just when you thought there no more truths to be unearthed in the human heart, along comes Lucinda Williams who ploughs up a whole new field'. Her real gift as a songwriter is her detail: 'I want to paint a picture, and I want the listeners to know what I'm going through. And the only way they can is if I really get detailed.'

She grew up in Louisiana, and whereas Iris Dement could wake the dead with her fierceness, Lucinda could sing them straight back to sleep. Having grown up on traditional folk songs, 'all those terribly dark murder and incest ballads', she fell in love with Delta blues, and the southern boogie of ZZ Top and the Allman Brothers. Then Lucinda moved, this time to Houston where she became part of the same clique as Lyle Lovett and Nanci Griffith, but with wider tastes than either: 'I drew on everything from Robert Johnson to Cream'. For her debut, recorded in an afternoon for Smithsonian Folkways, Lucinda dropped anything modern from the set list, so *Ramblin'* is a mix of Robert Johnson and Carter Family covers.

By the time of *Happy Woman Blues*, she was writing all her own material, but her real breakthrough came with a self-titled album in 1988, issued by Rough Trade, and later reissued with lots of bonus tracks. With a rootsy band featuring lead guitarist Gurf Morlix giving her songs just the thump they need, the result was 'one of *the* best alternative country albums'.* It is something new, a statement of female demands to have it all: 'I want a full house/and a rock and roll band'. Lucinda had just divorced drummer Greg Sowders – though never part of the 'cowpunk' scene musically, she would often open for the likes of Rank And File, and once sang lead vocals with Greg's band, the Long Ryders.

She moved to Austin, and spaced out the time between albums, so that each one was an event when it appeared. *Sweet Old World* was a dream combination of country, R&B, careful words and wild singing.

Things did not go well on the next album, originally commissioned for Rick Rubin's hip hop label, with Steve Earle brought in as producer and then dropped, swearing that 'I'll never work with a woman again.' Just when everyone had given up on the project, *Car Wheels On A Gravel Road* came out to worldwide acclaim, a rich soup of memory and death and desire. *Time Out* called it 'contemporary American songcraft at its very best', and who could disagree. Just listen to the way she sings 'I take off my watch and my earrings/my bracelet and everything' and try not to shiver.

Lucinda opened up to Charlotte Grieg. 'We all have demons inside. I've witnessed a lot of self-destruction in the world I'm in, and writing about it is my way of dealing with it. I've also started writing about my childhood.' Having a famous poet as a father – Miller Williams was also a rabid Hank Williams fan – must help. *Essence* went in still deeper, a sad and scary album right from its opening moan of 'lonely girls' and which, for *Mojo,* inhabits a space 'where the directions are muddled and the heartbreak is total'. At times, her vibrato carries her and the song away: 'you can virtually hear the sound move across the open landscape'. *Uncut* too found the album 'panoramic' as America, and much of this was unveiled at a 'South By Southwest' showcase. Each song is a 'slow burn', as tactile as music can get. 'I feel this is kind of a woman's record. Love songs *and* lust songs', she later said.

One puzzled as to where she could go next. People in Nashville are 'frightened of Lucinda'. Reviewing 2003's *World Without Tears*, Grant Alden found it impossible to imagine her ever being joyful: 'hers remains the quintessential voice of loss, and longing. And lust.' That word again,

* *Modern Twang*

and it infuses the new album, recorded virtually live in an old mansion in Silverlake. The opening track comes as close to the joys of feeling half-drugged with sex as anyone could ever manage in song, slowed almost to a halt and slurred and with new guitarist Doug Pettibone's soul licks. But Alden is right when he reckons 'nobody should hurt this much, this often, and with such vitality. And in public'.

For *Uncut*, it is a more outgoing album than what has gone before, 'there's less small-town blues here, more grappling with the bigger picture today', a country of 'forgotten people', where 'everything is wrong'. And her voice is now a rock 'n' roll instrument par excellence, 'with all manner of drawl, slur and snarl'.*

She is certainly being noticed by the highbrow press, a world away from alt-country fanzines. Hailed by *Time* as 'America's greatest living songwriter', Bill Buford, the literary editor of *The New Yorker*, described her as the great new muse of the South, possessed of a 'vision in which Jack Kerouac meets Robert Johnson and General Robert E Lee and they form a blues band, singing lyrics dashed off by Eudora Welty'.

Hardly surprising, given that when she was still a child visitors to the family home included Allen Ginsberg and Charles Bukowski, and her own work is influenced by 'the beat poets and Southern writers like William Faulkner and Flannery O'Connor'.

A live show at the House of Blues in West Hollywood in the summer of 2001 is introduced thus: 'and now to show us the true essence of her work, Lucinda Williams'. For once it is true. Lucinda and a crack band take us through her greatest songs, and she sings with that disconcertingly laid-back, almost lazy delivery of words that cut to the bone. 'Car Wheels On A Gravel Road' sets chiming guitar and mandolin against her sinister purr, and the last thing you would want to do is take a ride.

The fan-made double CD that captures this concert, so perfect that it must have originally have been a radio broadcast, adds some acoustic home demos. 'Essence' is disarmingly intimate. 'Blue' sounds naked and as lonely. As to a rare cover version of Dylan's 'Positively Fourth Street', Williams sings with unusual sweetness, and a touch of Joan Baez in the vibrato department. She has never sounded so loving as when she sings the lines about being 'paralysed'.

* *Mojo*

Some reviewers thought that Lucinda and Victoria Williams were sisters – they are both from Louisiana, but there the similarity ends. Victoria is just as unique a singer as Lucinda, but early albums like 1987's *Happy Come Home* sound like Tiny Tim with strings, arranged by Van Dyke Parks as it happens. The only thing 'country' about it is her warbly voice, which sounds speeded up.

After Victoria was diagnosed with multiple sclerosis, friends and admirers like Maria McKee, Lucinda Williams, The Jayhawks and Giant Sand clubbed together to record a cross-section of her songs as *Sweet Relief*. Williams herself recorded *Loose*, an album 'as direct and honest as anything The Carter Family mined from their hills'.*

Victoria formed the Original Harmony Ridge Creek Dippers with her boyfriend Mark Olson, once of The Jayhawks, and they moved to Joshua Creek. Her 1998 album *Musings Of A Creek Dipper* is darker around the edges, with lots of cellos and electronic effects, Buddy and Julie Miller adding their own indefinable magic, and Victoria on banjo. Even Williams admits that it looks at 'a lot of life-death issues', and it doubles as an album of classic Americana.

The early, purest albums by 10,000 Maniacs – in particular 1985's *Wishing Chair* – sketched out this same territory. Kate Jacobs comes from Hoboken, New Jersey, but her debut, 1993's *The Calm Comes After* takes a wider focus: 'the songs in my head: the hymns and show tunes and folk songs and operettas and country radio and dreamy ballet music': she is part Russian, with a great grandfather who knew Tolstoy. She has that same little girl voice as Victoria Williams or Natalie Merchant.

Hydrangea uses 200-year-old journals she found in her parents' attic, and an uncle's memories of studying painting with Thomas Hart Benson in the '30s. These are songs about hope, 'something between the sadness and truth of old stories'. Musicians include Vicki Peterson from the Bangles and guitarist Dave Schramm: the solo female voice is played out against textured and fully electric backings. Rock music for grown ups.

The biggest surprise recently was the emergence of Steve Earle's kid sister Stacey as a solo artist in her own right. Her debut CD *Simple Gearle* is full of sweet and lilting vocalising and homespun lyrics – 'daddy spent a fortune on my wedding gown' – which are more sly than they first

---

* *No Depression*

sound. The disc has a deliberately old-fashioned sound: it even starts with the sound of a needle hitting vinyl. *Dancin' With Them Brung Me Proper* is even better. It is a fuller sound than her debut, with both her husband and son in the family band. *No Depression* identifies 'an undisguised twitter and twang that recalls Nanci Griffith and Iris Dement'.

Stacey toured the UK as an acoustic duo with her husband Mark Stuart, following a year in the States when they played over 280 shows, touring small coffee houses, bars, honky tonks and even sidewalks, to publicise their music. The double-CD *Must Be Live* is full of chatty asides – 'they liked my stuff, they just didn't know what to do with it' – clever picking and intimate songs. All her albums are released by Stacey's own back porch record label, Gearle Records, through her website.

This the face of the new revolution in marketing. Do it yourself, and find yourself a niche, and the audience will follow, especially if you tour a lot, and can sell records at your gigs, and rely on enthusiasts to spread the word. Another sign of her rising stature is the appearance of *Must Be Love*, a double-CD bootleg recorded at The Secret Chord Club, Ireland in 1999. It's the perfect complement to the aforementioned *Must Be Live*.

Magazines like *No Depression* gave exposure to new artists like Kate Jacobs, late-starters like Stacey Earle, and mavericks like Chip Taylor. The controlled wildness of his *London Sessions Bootleg*, with vocal support from Lucinda Williams, captures a new spirit coursing through the common ground where country meets rock. Some people even give it a name. They call it 'alt country'.

iii) A Tour Of The Garden

'Another treasure found/another tumbling down' – *Son Volt*

Kevin Russell reckons that 'If Bob Wills was around today, he'd be alternative country. Willie and Merle, they're both alternative country now, aren't they'. Music Row, with its hat acts and Shania Twains and Faith Hills and Garth Brooks and 'Achy Breaky Hearts', is the mainstream against which 'alt country' rebels. There are other terms to describe this music, like twangcore, or 'insurgent country' or 'no depression'. This last is named after a magazine, whose importance far outstrips its circulation figures.

No Depression, the new favourite Alt Country (Whatever That Is) bimonthly emerged from a website run by Grant Alden (from Nashville) and Peter Blackstock (from Seattle). They later wrote about the 'gentle sarcasm 'with which they first used the 'alt country' term, but virtually everyone since has ignored this nuance, and taken the two words as gospel. Grant first heard the phrase from Bev Chinn, then managing the San Francisco band Tarnation.

As to 'No Depression', it is the name of a song recorded in 1990 by the ground-breaking Uncle Tupelo as the title track of their first album. This is itself a statement of intent, a respectful nod back to The Carter Family, whose leader AP first copyrighted the song, as an antidote to economic uncertainty. The full title is 'No Depression In Heaven'.

It is ironic that the magazine, and the acts it celebrates, should hit its commercial zenith at a time when depression – and wealth beyond the wildest dreams of mountain farmers – is the latest growth industry. Further ironies accrue when Grant Alden now states that he had published 'five or six issues before I bought Uncle Tupelo's first three discs from a Santa Monica used record store', and found the band 'disappointing'. He was far more fond of a song like Robbie Fulks' 'She Took A Lot Of Pills And Died': '*That* I understood as a country punk fusion'.

Stranger still, the original Carter Family version of 'No Depression' is absent even from the recent, near-definitive Rounder release programme. The song is only available on cassette – the vinyl has long sold out, and there is no CD version – from a 1936 radio transcript, issued by a Carter Family museum in Southern Virginia.

It is the proud claim of its editors that *No Depression* features 'an assortment of artists who are either too old, too loud or too eccentric for country radio'. The magazine remains the best place to find reviews and interviews with such artists, conducted with respect rather than the cynical cutting down to size of so much of the music press , or the equally absurd idolatry of mass market newsprint. It is now far more than a magazine. In 1997, the magazine organised a *No Depression* Tour featuring the Old 97s, The Picketts, Whiskeytown and Hazeldine: it is also involved in the Americana Music Association, formed to promote and celebrate real, honest music, whatever label you wish to put on it.

I shall use 'alt country' as a term of convenience, to differentiate the music in general from even more specialist terms, many coined by Dave Goodman whose home-produced encyclopedia *Modern Twang* is equally authoritative, terms like 'lo-fi', or 'gothic country'. Other coinages, like 'woodchuck nation' or 'melan country', are useful but demeaning. Then there is 'old time', which I will restrict to mountain music.

'Alt country' – by its very title – is often seen as an anti-Nashville movement. Which it certainly is, if you restrict Nashville, Tennessee to 'Music Row', the part of town that dominates the country music industry, through its choice of whom to record, or put out on commercial radio, or feature at the Country Music Assocation Awards. Even here, the likes of Dolly Parton or Alison Krauss can sneak in through the back door. Since that last brief flowering of MCA in the mid 1980s, the Music Row establishment has tended to exile music that is too real, or cannot be easily mass-marketed to the margins. Where it is doing just fine.

And, as if in revenge, bands like Lambchop, who create strange musical hybrids, actually live in Nashville. And they are the true inhabitants. As Mac Gayden once explained, 'Country music was actually imported to Nashville. The native Nashville musicians have always favoured R&B or alternative styles. Nashville is a river town and, much like Memphis, the dominant influences are blues and soul'.

Even the mainstream country-music industry was once far more receptive to a variety of styles, so that a recent obituary in *The Guardian* of '30s star Bill Carlisle attested that he drew from the 'vast and variegated songbag that then bore the label of country music – cowboy songs, inspirational gospel numbers, "heart" songs and out and out nonsense'.

'Alt country' has developed its own style and constraints, though, as best experienced in the UK on the *Captain America* show on Virgin Radio and *Uncut* magazine. Its godfathers are Gram Parsons and Neil Young, rather than Hank Williams or Dock Boggs. There are lots of electric guitars and drums, and not too many banjos. The really inventive thing tends to be the lyrics, world-weary and quirky. *NME* recently argued that alt country is 'the final resting place for all those rabid kids who used to go to gigs, but have now settled down'.

It is an odd phenomenon that music that is just as popular in Europe as it is back home in the United States has many of the best records coming from obscure labels in Germany and Scotland, while some US-released CDs are extremely hard to track down outside the States.

This is also very localised music, at least in origin. The best way to approach alt country is to circle North America, starting with rural Illinois – which spawned Uncle Tupelo. Then go counter-clockwise, west, south and then back to the northeast, before stop-offs in Canada, and then across the Atlantic. All kinds of strange conjunctions are then brought to light, even if this is, by necessity, a whistle stop tour.

North By Northeast

The most influential alt country group of all were Uncle Tupelo, three friends from smalltown America, one-time punks who formed a band in 1983 when they were still in high school, and split early in 1994 without ever really breaking through to a wider audience. Their albums have never been easy to get hold of, though they are at last the subject of a proper reissue programme.

At the start, Uncle Tupelo comprised Jay Farrar on guitar and banjo, Jeff Tweedy on bass, and Mike Heidorn on drums. They came together in Belleville, Illinois, a tiny Midwestern town near St Louis, and had evolved from The Primitives, a punk cover band who wouldn't talk to anyone who didn't like Black Flag. In his early teens, Farrar had seen a double bill of X and The Replacements, which left a deep impression. 'Paul Westerberg fell off the stage on the first note of the first song, Bob Stinson played a nude guitar solo and Exene Cervenka jumped into the under-age corral to inspire a Midwestern mash.'

Uncle Tupelo scuffled for small-time gigs, virtually unregarded except by fellow musicians like the Bottle Rockets and Gary Louris, later of The Jayhawks, drawn as if by instinct. Roy Kasten remembers seeing Farrar and Tweedy busking for small change near the university campus in St Louis. He saw them later that same night in 1989 at Cicero's, a local bar with a club downstairs, 'as spacious and inviting as a meat locker'.

Gram Parsons, the 'godfather of alt country', who lived hard and died young

Buddy and Julie Miller, unsung heroes of modern alt country who record great music in their home studio in Nashville

Beck, a man of 1,000 musical disguises

The Carter Family influenced
everyone from Johnny Cash
to Rodney Crowell (both of
whom became family members)
and the Nitty Gritty Dirt Band
to Gillian Welch

Hank Williams Jr, keeping his father's
heritage alive and paving the way for
Southern boogie

Jason And
The Scorchers,
who brought
the energy
of punk rock
to Nashville

The Singing Brakeman.

Jimmie Rodgers, the first man to bring together country music and the blues

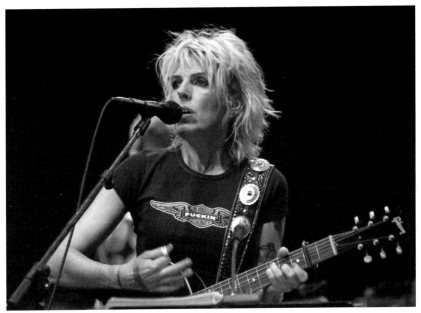
Lucinda Williams, a singer/songwriter of frightening power

Lynyrd Skynyrd, a huge influence on alt country and themselves now figures of myth

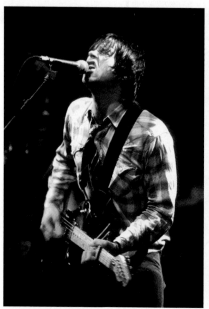

Ryan Adams, branded a brat by some, a genius by others, but he sure can sing

Steve Earle, who went to hell and back yet never betrayed his inner truth

The Borderline, UK home of alt country, where the media gather to watch the latest acts

The Handsome Family – genuinely weird, genuinely funny, genuinely scary

The Jayhawks, as tuneful a band as you will ever find

Wilco. Jeff Tweedy (LEFT) rocks as hard as anyone but can also stir the deepest emotions

Will Oldham, whose music is
the most terrifying of all
contemporary Americana

As he recalled 'they were loud, the sound excruciating, the songs indecipherable'.* They had energy to burn, but not much else.

'It wasn't like we were ever intentionally trying to merge punk and country, that's just what came out', according to Jeff Tweedy. Uncle Tupelo released their debut album, *No Depression* (1990), on a small independent label, Rockville Records in New York. It doesn't look much, the photo inside is of the band playing in a small club, all floppy hair and concentrations. They thank everybody 'who ever bought us beer, let us sleep on their floor or came to see us play', and produce a sound that is a bit like slowed-down heavy metal. Peter Doggett hears the 'sonic propulsion' of Husker Du mixed with 'rockabilly restlessness', so that on 'Whiskey Bottle' Farrar uses 'hard rock guitar riffs to drive home his desolation, then a gentle pedal steel to breath in some humanity'.

The first track, 'Graveyard Shift' opens with pulverising lead guitar playing a tricky riff, with bass and drums tightly in support, and Farrar's urgent but clipped voice shouting his disaffection. 'Old town, same town blues/same old walls closing in'. The feeling is much like Patti Smith's 'Piss Factory', but without the yowl of triumph at the end. There's also a namecheck to Roger McGuinn, and The Byrds singing 'Turn, Turn, Turn'. The mix of guitar attack and urgent singing is like a howl of pain.

There is more going on here than just another Minutemen clone. Both singers have a pronounced twang to their voices, and a country breeze blows through the hard core. 'That Year' almost breaks into a square dance. Humanity courses through 'Life Worth Living', sung to an acoustic guitar. 'This song is for the broken-spirited man'. The stress of modern life is why 'we drink ourselves asleep'. Electric fuzz guitar comes in towards the end, like an omen, plus the odd chink of mandolin.

There are two unexpected cover versions, a rapid 'John Hardy', with Tweedy's bass taking up the melody line, and the title track. 'No Depression' is taken straight, to an acoustic guitar strum and electric bass, and at a fair lick. Here, in a lightning bolt of sheer genius, old time country music is reborn, not as a curio or merely out of respect, but as a cry for help, almost lost amidst the loud guitars elsewhere on the album.

Uncle Tupelo came close to playing sheer noise at times, and their sophomore album *Still Feel Gone* took the band's sound to extremes,

* *No Depression*

with massive drums and the messy feel of a live gig. The opening song is appropriately titled 'Gun'. A touch of banjo from Farrar is just about the only concession to country here. Except the pervasive feeling of lives going nowhere: 'I sold my guitar to the girl next door.' One outtake later collected on *89/93: An Anthology* is the Stooges' 'I Wanna Be Your Dog'.

Roy Kasten remembers seeing the band regularly at the Blue Note in Columbia, Missouri around 1991, and hearing 'some of the most overwhelming rock shows I've ever experienced'. Uncle Tupelo could 'hit like a piledriver' then collapse during an encore through excessive drink. 'When they covered Black Flag, they slowed it down and countrified it. When they covered 'Cocaine Blues', they punked it into oblivion.' But what lived on after these gigs in the memory was the strength of the songwriting, and the vocal harmonies between Farrar and Tweedy.

The real masterpiece came third, quiet and ominous and with its own strange beauty. *March 16–20, 1992* was produced in Georgia by Peter Buck from REM, who had similarly added melody and mystery to their punk roots. 'Grindstone' starts raucous, but suddenly slows right down and John Keane comes in on pedal steel. There are traditional songs like 'Satan Our Kingdom Must Come Down', 'Great Atomic Power' by the Louvin Brothers, and new songs about social desolation. The clenched-teeth anger with which Farrar sings is daunting, while Tweedy shows sweetness and more melancholy on songs like 'Black Eye'. The feeling is of hope in the midst of emotional desolation, and of a band who are singing and playing for their very lives.

People way outside Illinois were taking note by now. Steve Sutherland argued that 'you'll not hear a more honest, look-you-straight-in-the-eye record this side of Armageddon'. The only comparison Steve can make with songs like 'I Wish My Baby Was Born' – in which the singer is torn between love of an unborn child and his desire to kill its mother – is with Violent Femmes, acoustic punksters from Milwaukee, 'at their most diseased, around the time of *Hallowed Ground*'.

Heavy stuff. Others were taking note. *Melody Maker*'s David Bennum interviews the band's two mainmen in London, but it's a struggle. Finally, they admit 'it took us a long time to overcome the negative connotations that country music has on radio in America. We had to dig in record stores to find the right stuff'. This includes bluegrass, white gospel, gritty folk ballads, the twang of Hank Williams, and the harder side of '60s West Coast country rock.

A couple of months later, Allan Jones sees them play the Borderline. The acoustic sound – or any of the songs – of the latest record is notable by its absence. This is a sonic attack, which reminds Jones of cowpunk bands like Blood On The Saddle, and more recently Thin White Rope'. They end with a ZZ Top song.

Anodyne was their debut album with a major label, and added Max Johnston – Michelle Shocked's brother – on fiddle and banjo, John Stirratt on bass and Lloyd Maines on pedal steel. The band had plugged back in, but the primal melancholy of the previous album has entered their bloodstream. Jay's singing is majestic in its intensity. The songs are self written, and still jointly credited to Tweedy and Farrar, while Doug Sahm makes a guest appearance, singing a verse of his own song 'Give Back The Key To My Heart'. This is not so surprising, as the album was recorded, virtually live, in a small studio in Austin. *South By Southwest*, with a vengeance.

Posters for the band's final tour were ironically labelled 'St Louis's 4th Best Country Band'. A gig at the Blue Note, Columbia, was reviewed for posterity by David Bennum. In a world that boxes up 60 years of guitar Americana and puts it in dusty aisles labelled folk, or bluegrass, Uncle Tupelo 'make you remember that people first played and heard this stuff because it was their idea of a good time'.

In the words of 'Anodyne', 'not a word, you're out the door'. Inner tensions blew the band apart. For Jeff Tweedy, Uncle Tupelo had become 'more and more repressed, to fit into Jay's world, which is a hard world to fit into, for anybody'. He came to reject their 'lack of showmanship' and even the idea that they were anything special, just a young band 'trying to decide whether or not it wants to be Dinosaur Jr or Husker Du'. Not that either those played Carter Family songs.

The final gig was back in St Louis on May Day 1994, with new drummer Ken Coomer. They open with a singalong, jaunty 'No Depression', play a cross section of their greatest songs with splenetic playing and soaring harmonies, then close with cover versions of songs by Neil Young – 'Everyone Knows This Is Nowhere' – and 'Take Three Steps' by Lynyrd Skynyrd. 'Alt country', in a nutshell.

Surly people, mysterious music, ornery and talented oddballs destined to trip over each other's egos: it could be the Velvet Underground all over again, and Uncle Tupelo's influence has been just as cataclysmic. It was 'the foundation of a new generation of bands. They were the galvanising influence, of the few taking a more countrified approach to rock music, and it was the quality of the songs they were writing.'* That, and the wide range of country and rock 'n' roll classics that they would play live. There are even bootlegs on sale now of high-speed cover versions, ranging across the spectrum, from Woody Guthrie to Buck Owens, 'Maggie's Farm' to 'Dead Flowers', 'Mr Soul' to 'Good Year For The Roses'.

Once Uncle Tupelo were gone, a whole gamut of bands tried to fill the gap – of Blue Mountain, Richmond Fontaine and Whiskeytown. At the time, though, Jay Farrar bemoaned the decline of 'real' country music, a style that was 'definitely not the contemporary Nashville sound'.

Farrar formed Son Volt, with Mike Heidorn back on drums. They debuted with *Trace* in 1995, with Dave Boquist on lap steel, dobro and fiddle and his brother Jim on bass. The sound is moody and alternates between acoustic and electric just like Neil Young, to whom these sombre songs bear comparison. Jay's voice is more countrified than Jeff Tweedy's and now that he has sole control of a band the sound is smoother than Uncle Tupelo, and somehow more generic.

For Grant Alden, 'Jay Farrar's voice hits like raw coffee on an empty stomach'. Sid Griffin reckons that Dave Boquist gives the band 'that Southwestern Green On Red cactus feel'. Nashville star Kim Richey puts comments 'The guys in Son Volt, when they do country stuff, they sound like a rock band playing country because they really *like* it.'

Straightaway (1997) winds down from a roar to a whisper, with just Farrar's acoustic guitar and harmonica backing his lonesome voice on 'Way Down Watson'. 'Through my teenage years, I began pulling records out of my mom's collection – Leadbelly, Woody Guthrie, The Dillards – and I gradually assimilated all of it. I got into X and the Meat Puppets, and started putting some of the common influences together. It all started to make sense over time'.

* Peter Blackstock

The third Son Volt album *Wide Swing Tremelo* was recorded semi-live in an old factory. Like early REM, Jay builds a little inner universe, all by himself. Then, Farrar went solo. *Sebastapol* features Gillian Welch on backing vocals on 'Barstow', named after a town on Route 66. *No Depression* found it Farrar's most varied album yet, 'planting traditional-style folk ballads next to off-kilter rhythmic rockers, gorgeous pop melodies next to spacey instrumental sketches.'

Jay is a notoriously taciturn interviewee, but opens up about his famously obscure lyrics: 'sometimes the sound of the words is as important as the literal meaning'. He cherishes each one, and among the words to surface here are 'parabolic louver lighting' and 'sanguinary vitamins'. But what saves all this from preciousness is the resonant way he sings them; 'he opens his mouth and it's just pure fucking tone', to quote the album's co-producer.

On *Terroir Blues* (2003), Jay's rustic, insistent voice has never sounded so close. He strips the sound right back, to bare acoustics, while the songs are becoming even more abstract and austere. Given his love of wordplay, *terroir* is the French word for soil, sort of, and native land, but is pronounced like a cross between 'terror' and 'war', which has all kinds of resonances post 9/11. The mixture of primitive textures and experimentation makes it 'a work that is both timely and timeless.'*

Brian Henneman remembered St Louis as having 'the worst music scene in the world': as leader of the Bottle Rockets, 'we always played on the same bills with Uncle Tupelo because we were the only two bands that they could figure out to put together'. Their debut, from 1995, alternates between quiet old-time and straight down the line rock music Their major-league debut album, *24 Hours A Day*, was 'hard-hitting songs about hard hit people'†. *Brand New Year* is more of the same. There's a tribute to Nancy Sinatra, inspired by 'swinging sounds of the '60s on late-night TV. Their tribute album *Songs of Sahm* is in much the same spirit, breaking down any mutual suspicion between career hippies like Doug and the alt rockers of 30 years later.

Still under contract to Sire, Tweedy continued with the remnants of Uncle Tupelo – Ken Coomer, Max Johnston and John Stirratt. He renamed the band Wilco, then steered them towards pure pop on their 1995 debut

---

* *No Depression*

† *Modern Twang*

AM. Having created alt country in the first place, it is as if the self-willed Jeff Tweedy has spent the rest of his career trying to escape it, or at least transcend the horde of Uncle Tupelo imitators. This is an album full of tuneful songs and ringing electric guitars – early '70s country rock, crossed with the quieter side of the Stones rather than frenetic punk. The whole thing sounds like a release. As Jeff said, 'I never dug that whole sombre approach to making music. Music is entertainment. It can be serious, it can be sad, but for the most part I want to feel better.'*

Just as Jay Farrar has further honed his style down to one note, Tweedy went on with Wilco to explore a whole new spectrum of sound. Whether or not the band are still alt country is almost beside the point. The following year saw the release of *Being There*. Named after Tweedy's favourite movie, in which Peter Sellers played a naïve gardener who is taken as a mystic, it was marketed as two albums for the price of one, with the band waiving their royalties.

The big plus here is multi-instrumentalist Jay Bennett – on guitar, keyboards, lap steel and accordion – who overlaps with Max Johnston, and had already replaced him in the touring band. He sweetens the sound, though things couldn't get much darker than the opening song, 'Misunderstood', a tribute to the doomed Peter Laughner of Pere Ubu, a man killed by his love of rock 'n' roll and its lifestyle.

Jeff further opens up to new country. Those lines, like much here, were ad-libbed, but the man who was once seen as having to play music or he would have killed someone has now discovered, 'there's a lot more to life than just music, and I'm healthier and I feel better about music when I am at peace with the other 90 per cent of the world'. This resounds in the country shuffle of 'Forget The Flowers', or a playful update on The Eagles in 'Hotel Arizona', about the rock-star lifestyle, which Wilco hardly exemplify. 'It's not something I'm going to get used to.'

Barry Miles once described The Beatles' *White Album* as a series of parodies and musical tributes. This seems true too of *Being There*. At times, Tweedy seems to be imitating his hero Paul Westerberg. 'I wanted it to be really obvious that our influences are there and acknowledged'.

Many of the tracks pay homage in style to '60s pop, and have a strange, echoey sound, as if not quite in focus. The band played live in

* No Depression

a Chicago studio without monitors or headphones, 'just trying really hard to hear each other'. Tweedy is amazed that some people still regard Wilco as a country-rock band. 'The instrumentation is very different. We managed to get some of the songs into an orchestrated pop realm'.

Wilco came spectacularly undone at an early London gig, which ended with Jeff trashing his gear onstage, as a roadie picked out 'Ziggy Stardust' on a spare guitar. A live broadcast from the West Coast in May 1997 finds them relaxed and countrified, playing highlights from their first two albums, plus 'New Madrid' (*Anodyne)*. They vary the tone and pace in a way that live CDs by Son Volt at this time do not.

Wilco did a tour support with Sheryl Crow, and developed a 'serious prescription drug habit' as a result. It certainly didn't harm them for a prestige gig at the Fillmore West, and songs from *Being There* blossom on stage, like rare orchids. On the evidence of the Deep Six release *Why Would You Wanna Live*, Wilco are by now one of the most awesome rock bands in the world. Pedal steel and banjo are notable by their absence – this is a guitar band, with keyboards for relief. They even give a snatch of Led Zeppelin's 'Immigrant Song', before launching into 'Someday Soon' instead, with a cheery vocal chorus and playful fretwork. Jeff has to teach Jay the chords to 'New Madrid' onstage, but by the time of the radio in-house section he had it down pat.

Tweedy had also begun to work with Golden Smog and Wilco seemed to have left the rough-and-ready aesthetic of Uncle Tupelo behind, but it resurfaced when they collaborated with Billy Bragg on *Mermaid Avenue*. As Tweedy said during a June 1998 set at the Fleadh Festival on Randall's Island, which contained some of the 'new' Woody Guthrie material, and features Bragg guesting on 'Hoodoo Voodoo', 'we're going to make this sound as if it has a few more balls'. The spirit seems to spread to their own songs, most of them from the forthcoming album.

And so to the masterpiece that was *Summerteeth*. The title is a pun on the dental problems they experienced on tour, hence the reference to prescription drugs. For all that, this is a dark pop record that journeys into the light. As one website put it, '*Summerteeth* doesn't twang – but who said it had to.' It is as if the 'alt country' of Uncle Tupelo has become internalised, and the music then is free to jump off in all kinds of interesting directions. Let's just call it Americana, albeit with a strong dose of late-'60s Beatles. Even so, Jeff's 'Hey Ho' on the opening track is resigned but hopeful even if things 'get so low' and 'your prayers will never get answered', with an echo of Walt Disney's seven dwarves, off to work.

The band have become something else, a rich soup of sound with ancient keyboards and state-of-the-art production. Jeff Tweedy's throaty vocals are a 'blend of understated menace and quiet regret, rising to a peak of parched exasperation.'* It is an album that deals with pain, and its aftermath. 'She's A Jar' sounds like McCartney fluff, a love song to a treasured partner, until Tweedy oozes out the last line with menace, 'she begs me not to hit her'. The string sound here is straight out of 'Strawberry Fields Forever', not a song readily associated with The Carter Family, and the album also resounds with 'washed out woodwind quartets'.* But then a Dixie marching band turns up at the end of the 'exalted riverboat dream voyage' that is 'Pierholden Suite'. 'Via Chicago' encapsulates the Appalachian mindset: 'I dreamed about killing you again last night, and it felt alright to me'. He buries her alive during a fireworks display – you can't get much more Americana than that.

I am reminded of the bird with the worm in its mouth at the end of *Blue Velvet*. Tweedy's lyrics are like David Lynch's movies, they take the outward signs of Americana – the 'plastic Jesuses and US flags on every mailbox' described by Holly Pedlovsky – and then show the horrible and scary things crawling underneath. But it doesn't end there, that's David Cronenberg territory. What makes Lynch and Tweedy such important oddballs is that both – in film and on CD – celebrate a rich cast of ornery characters, mostly based on different aspects of themselves, who triumph over evil. 'You fell in love, to the key of C.' Dreams of murder stay just that, dreams. Daybreak will come, even to an everyday world of 'barking dogs/in fenced-in yards.'* With 'stumblebum synths, tearful piano and country banjo', Wilco's stroll down 'arcane musical byways has produced The Last Great American Album of the 20th century'.

There is a fascinating CD of the band playing live 'in an American bar – spring 1999' and giving songs from the new album light and air, in necessarily stripped-down arrangements. And yes, indeed, it does sound like alt country, with lots of harmonica and electric guitar. Talking

* *Uncut* magazine

to *Uncut* at much the same time, Tweedy rejects any comparisons between *Summerteeth* and Mercury Rev's *Deserter's Songs* – though both share the same antique sound. 'Our record is more atmospheric, more varied. They wanted those textures, and washed them over the whole album.' When Nigel Williamson points out, sensibly enough, that hearing the new album after what came before is like moving from black and white to technicolour, Tweedy concurs that 'it's certainly a denser canvas. We were perceived as a specialised band. No Depression, alternative country. All those tags. And I know people still call this a country-rock record, which is weird.'

When *Yankee Hotel Foxtrot* was released in 2002, *Uncut* reckoned 'Jeff Tweedy invented alt country. Now, with Jim O'Rourke's help, he returns to destroy it.' O'Rourke is an 'underground polymath', connected to Sonic Youth. He, Tweedy and Glenn Kotche briefly convened as Loose Fur, and an eponymous album sees them play 'a rolling, hazy style'.

As to Wilco's own new album, it is a 'blasted deconstruction of the old music'. Even Bennett now admits that it was perhaps a mistake to drop all the 'catchy, uptempo numbers'. Influences include *The Cornet Project*, a collection of secret-service call signs, and radio static surrounds Tweedy's voice on 'Radio Cure'. The lyrics are strange, yet also typically 'Yankee – 'I am an American aquarium drinker.' The whole thing is a universe away from the rough-and-ready Uncle Tupelo. The album was originally to have been called *Here Comes Everybody*, taken from James Joyce's final 'novel' *Finnegan's Wake*, which mixes together all language and all history to race an endless circle. 'Unbroken', for sure.

Mojo found Tweedy has 'left his alt country contemporaries eating dust in the middle of the road'. Here is 'modern punk rock soul music', as indebted to John Fahey and Neil Young as to Aphex Twin and The Clash. Tweedy sings like a man dreaming in slow motion. But this is still country music, in its truest form, even if stripped right back to the bone.

'Ashes Of American Flags' was written before September 11th, but this 'giant purple bruise of a song'* is agonising enough to have been composed in retrospect. Its final lines always get a reaction in concert, 'I would like to salute the ashes of American flags/and all the fallen leaves

* *The Guardian*

filling up shopping bags'. This from an album due at one point to be released on September 11th, and with other, oddly prescient lines, like 'Tall buildings shake/voices escape singing sad, sad songs'.

The album certainly passes the 'Americana' test – learning to deal responsibly with what that ice-blue morning did to a nation's sense of itself. But Warners found it all too experimental – Tweedy bought the masters, and the album came out on Nonesuch. There were inner ructions, though, that led to drummer Ken Coomber being sacked. Jay Bennett now says 'Ken Coomber was the heart of Wilco, and we kicked him out. And we were fucking idiots...I don't think we saw the emotional side of what we were doing.' And 'heart' is what's missing from the album.

Bennett also left, to be replaced by Leroy Bach. He went on to release, *The Palace At 4am*, 'full of sweet melody, heartfelt lyrics and classic pop rock stylings'. Everything shed by *Yankee Hotel Foxtrot*, in fact.

The dropping of the band by Warners, and the building of this new sound and vision in the studio are captured by filmmaker Sam Jones on *I Am Trying To Break Your Heart*, a two-disc DVD filmed on hand-held cameras and in monochrome. You come back to the album with new eyes, having seen the intensity and argument that led to its creation.

Tweedy played some solo gigs to promote the album. Live, 'the songs had more space to breathe'*: the 'yearning quality of the melodies' shine brighter when shorn of studio trickery. Tweedy apologises for the songs being so 'down', and even if he has now left alt country far behind, he drops in old highlights like 'Sunken Treasure' and 'She's A Jar'.

The new Wilco line up toured in May 2002 – full-on rock music powered by Glenn Kotche's thunderous drums, Tweedy's urgent vocals, and angular guitar breaks that circle around themselves, at speed. A bootleg of their gig at the Cajun House, Phoenix, finds Wilco playing with venom and mystery – more approachable than the sometimes airless feel of *Yankee Hotel Foxtrot*. There are strange sound effects, but here they seem part of a great band playing with spice and danger, not simply laid over the top. Tweedy's voice binds it all together, wry and haunted.

Tweedy looks 'oddly demure' for the country songs, grins at his bassist 'when things take a summery turn', and then 'glowers when the sound fractures'. On 'Misunderstood', his agonised vocal and Kotche's drums

* *Uncut* magazine

'could cleave the ground apart'. But, throughout, Jeff looks 'coolly distanced' from his audience, and even from the bleakest of his lyrics.

By September, the new line up had bonded further. *No Depression* regrets their stylistic shift, 'goodbye fiddle and banjo, hello tinkly-tack piano, dissonant vibraphone and throbbing feedback'. Again it is only during the encores that Wilco gives way to 'contagious warmth'.

But Tweedy is set, once again, on breaking out of a musical consensus. 'I'm used to traditional song structures, although I'm very bored with them. I'm really happy with the way these (new) recordings shift and blur. If you can get actively involved in listening to them, they disappear.' But Jeff himself is unlikely to disappear, and one feels that he still has many surprises in store for those who care to follow his musical career.

Back in St Louis, more down-to-earth bands were following in his earlier footsteps. Wagon tended towards the mellower end of alt country, with acoustic colourings from Steve Raunder on accordion and much else, and Chris Peterson on fiddle. *Anniversary* (1998) was recorded in a barn in Illinois but released in Europe, by the German label, Glitterhouse.

Meanwhile, in another part of Illinois, 'Insurgent Country' was a phrase that originated in the Chicago area, and was used to publicise alt-country acts who played hard-core country with a punk attitude. Under the guidance of Jon Langford, who had moved here from Leeds, local label Bloodshot Records led the way with *For A Life Of Sin* – the first of its series of landmark 'Insurgent Country' compilations.

Longford issued an EP, *Gravestone*, which matched the sculptures (created for an exhibition, *The Death of Country Music* – 13 huge granite headstones, each one carved with an iconoclastic portrait of a country star): it includes 'Nashville Radio', a savage but fully justified indictment of the current state of mainstream country music. Radio DJs would rather blow themselves up than play a Waco Brothers record. Humour this disturbing is rare, even on Americana stations.

The Waco Brothers – 'five blokes pretending to be Hank Williams fronting The Clash'* – grew out of a one-off track by Hillbilly Lovechild, and as a US branch of Leeds punks the Mekons. Three of the British contingent came to Chicago because they married local women, the fourth, Tracey Dear, 'to escape a woman'. Led by the saturnine Langford,

* *Uncut* magazine

the Waco Brothers are named after David Koresh and his millennial cult, whose fortified compound was stormed by the FBI. And their particular twist is to take heroes like Johnny Cash and Buck Owens as 'white man's urban blues. Merle Haggard never was on a horse'.

The *Chicago Sun-Times* reported in late 1994 that 'on the boot heels of the city's cutting edge rock movement comes a hybrid of alternative country that is passionate, powerful and honest'. The Wacos are the 'godfathers' of this scene, and play 'to standing-room-only crowds every other Wednesday at Augenblick on the North Side'.

The Waco Brothers' 1995 debut *To The Last Dead Cowboy*, opens with whistling, then a punky thrash, twangy guitar and a male choir. The music is rough, played with spirit rather than grace. 'Bad times are coming round again,' they sing almost cheerfully. The band use country stylings as a mask for real anger and self-loathing. Americana becomes a code for British concerns, with mentions of the King and leaving Leeds with stolen booty. They do not so much parody C&W as raid it. Here are songs about incest, a sleazy new President – 'Bill The Cowboy' – and a remorseful drunk swimming in a 'lake of vinegar'. The title song is about a world perverted by 'bankers and lawyers' and where a dollar burger is the 'final cattle call'.

The most savage and jaw-dropping song on *Cowboy In Flames* (1997) is 'The Death Of Country Music', sung by another Bloodshot artist, Iggy Yoachum. Over a bouncy beat, they rescue the bones of true country from 'beneath the towers of Nashville in a black pool of neglect', grind them up and snort them like cocaine. Next, they drizzle some of their own blood onto the corpses of George Jones and Johnny Cash, to resurrect them, as 'skulls in false eyelashes'. 'Take Me To The Fires' turns the revelation that fired Hank Williams 'I've Seen The Light' into the flames of hell. Johnny Cash's 'Big River' is another song to be wilfully distorted. This is very knowing music, even if 'when it started the whole purpose of this band was to get beer and money'. The 1999 *Waco World* has more great one-liners like 'that's why they're called bars, 'cos they keep me inside', and a sound totally of its own. It also has far more musicianship than earlier efforts, largely due to Mark Durante on pedal steel. This is real country, 'with the kind of fire missing in too much music these days'.*

* *Folk Roots*

It no longer sounds like a mere side project. Bassist Alan Doughty and ex-Graham Parker drummer Goulding are a world-class rhythm section.

The Wacos continue to release albums sporadically. *Electric Waco Chair* is more internalised, less obviously angry. The 2002 *New Deal* packs the usual punch, with 'Johnny Landfrog' on ranting vocals and lyrics like 'it's your party, I don't want to go', and 'a one party state of mind'. It becomes rapidly obvious that the band are not the greatest natural fans of George Bush Jr – now there's a surprise.

Langford went on lend his 'throaty gallop' to *Mayors Of The Moon* with Toronto band the Sadies. 'His tunefulness is credibly frayed, by pure emotion. It's an asset lost in the raging barrage of the Waco Brothers.'*

Another Langford project is the Pine Valley Cosmonauts. They provide the backing music on *The Neal Pollack Anthology Of American Literature*, a spoken-word spoof of American literature with diatribes like 'I Wipe My Ass On Your Novel'. The album is packaged like the *Harry Smith Anthology*, and the Pine Valley boys add their own parodies of old-time music, accordion led sea shanties, and Latin rhythms.

Far less funny are two volumes – so far – of *The Executioner's Last Songs*, the latter a double-CD, in which the Cosmonauts act as the link between a series of reinterpretations of songs about death, from 'I'll Never Get Out Of This World Alive' – sung by Rosie Flores – to The Adverts, the Louvin Brothers to Roger Miller. Murder as part of the all-American way. The results are often surprisingly cheerful, and this is about the best portmanteau of alt country singers you could ever find.

Here is Steve Earle putting the blood back into 'Tom Dooley', Kurt Wagner on Tom Waits' sombre 'The Fall Of Troy', and Dave Alvin singing 'The Green Green Grass Of Home' with gruff-voiced solemnity. Brett Sparks revives the savagery of 'The Knoxville Girl', Johnny Dowd duets with Langford on his own 'Judgement Day' and Paul Burch reinterprets Peter Rowan's 'Walls Of Time'.

All proceeds go to the Illinois Death Penalty Moratorium Project, but so cold blooded are some of the murders described here that is difficult to justify keeping their perpetrators alive – which is exactly the point. Various guests turned up for a gig at Chicago's Double Door. Sally Timms started things off with 'Long Black Veil', via The Band, and an early

* *No Depression*

highlight was Lonesome Bob's fearsome retread of Johnny Paycheck's 'Pardon Me (I've Got Someone To Kill)'. Jenny Toomey showed another side of Americana with Cole Porter's 'Miss Otis Regrets', in which murder and a lynching are made polite. Paul Burch and his band transform 'Walls Of Time' yet again, in to 'hurtling honky tonk'. Then the Wacos made a rare appearance, dressed in black, and playing all their greatest songs.

The Mekons operated from the start as a collective, resolved to explode the myth of the individual artist, hence the looseness of their line ups. But conversely, you could not get more original than Jonboy Langford, who puts his own uneasy stamp on everything he touches, or the honeyed, English tones of Sally Timms. On *Cowboy Sally's Twilight Laments For Lost Buckaroos*, her voice floats over fiddle and pedal steel. Sally herself always thinks her own work sounds languid 'everything's very drawn-out, it's poignant and sad, also a little arch and campy'. The writing credits here include The Handsome Family and Robbie Fulks, but also a cool rendition of Johnny Cash's 'Cry, Cry, Cry' and the traditional 'When The Roses Bloom Again'. Who just mentioned Laura Cantrell?

This is an entrancing album, right from 'Dreaming Cowboy', a tale of a man on his barstool, sitting 'in the saddle of his make-believe horse', and riding the range until they bring up the bar lights. Sally sings without spite or pity, and the whole lope of the music is western swing brought into the digital age. 'In Bristol Town One Bright Day' sounds like a Harry Smith trad ballad, but, in fact, it is a new song by Robbie Fulks.

As to the parent band, the Mekons' mid-'80s live album, *New York*, originally available only on cassette, was re-released. The 'seeds they planted have born fruit'* in the likes of Lambchop, Will Oldham and The Handsome Family. *Out Of Our Heads* (2002) sees them moving on again, interpreting their own new songs with a ten-piece vocal chorus. They have taken 'the sounds of church music and respectfully pushed them through the art-punk filter'.† Timms observes, 'it's all very discordant…it's the ideal community singing. Trying to get the dissonance that white gospel singers had in their choral singing.'

Bands already active in Chicago got sucked up into the 'insurgent country' thing. Moonshine Willy featured the sweet voice of Kim Docter, who belted out twisted new songs over a punkbilly beat. The Texas

---

* *Uncut* magazine
† *No Depression*

Rubies worked on an album of 'Jesus songs'. The Riptones added humour to their trad roots on *Extra Sauce*. But two solo artists were far closer to the Bloodshot ethos. Neko Case had drummed with the punk band MAOW, but on 1997's *The Virginian* she covers songs by Loretta Lynn and Ernest Tubbs, with an edge. Her dreamlike version of 'Poor Ellie Smith' is a highlight of The Executioner's Last Songs, and recent albums like *Blacklisted* have kept her in the alt-country limelight.

Robbie Fulks once said of his music that 'the theme is fun, yours and mine'. Robbie exemplifies the spirit of 'insurgent country', and has every right to, having grown up with the music – his father handed him a banjo at the age of seven. After a spell in New York, where he attended Columbia University and played with early alt-country band 5 Chinese Brothers, Fulks moved to Chicago. Infatuated with Elvis Costello's *Almost Blue*, he formed a parody band, the Trailer Trash Review, complete with girls in bikinis but also played wild bluegrass with Special Consensus.

On his 1996 debut, *Country Love Songs*, he sings stuff like 'She Took A Lot Of Pills And Died', a young brat trashing his heritage. He is backed by the Skeletons, who also supported the equally odd Jonathan Richman on his *Goes Country* CD. Fulks is suitably succinct about what he thinks of Nashville's Music Row in 'Fuck This Town'. He later moved closer to the rock mainstream, and made *Let's Kill Saturday Night* for Geffen, which sounds like the best bar band ever.

His return to Bloodshot, *Very Best Of*, is anything but. This collection of scraps and outtakes contains a love song to Susanna Hoffs, about making love to a woman so bored she falls asleep and 'Roots Rock Weirdoes', 'dressed in black since 1971'. He reaches true depths on 'White Man's Bourbon', supposedly from a Bloodshot compilation, which graphically describes trans-racial seduction in the bushes.

Much in the same vein, but less sophisticated were The Blacks, who play what they describe as 'bastardised punk-inflected cowboy blues'. Something reflected in the title of their 1998 album *Dolly Horrorshow*. *Modern Twang* describe an ominous sound, made up of loud fuzzy guitar, drunken trumpet and angry vocals, and songs like 'Tortured Holiday'.

Even more disturbing are Slobberbone, who began life in the back room of a liquor store and home in on songs about booze, heartache, and murder. *Barrel Chested* is 'flat out nose bleeding, ear ringing "twang thrash".' Hazledene are gentler on the ear, but just as obsessed. Shawn Barton, one of their two girl singers, admits to a death fixation, as reflected on their debut album *Digging You Up*.

Utah Carol are a Chicago duo, named after a Marty Robbins cowboy hero. Their home-produced *Wonderwheel* is bittersweet Americana, like a 'hillbilly fairground taken over by a couple of kids on mushrooms'. *Comfort For The Traveller* emerged two years later, with songs like 'Misfits' evoking 'cowboys on a carousel horse'.*

Although they too started with a home-produced CD, 1995's *Mouthful Of Lies*, Dolly Varden (named after a species of trout) is a far more commercial proposition. Having found local fame in Chicago bar band Stump the Host, and then taken a sideswerve into PJ Harvey-style angst with loud guitars, Steve Dawson moved to Nashville to work as a commercial songwriter, and got nowhere. Frustrated as hell, he wrote 'the most absolutely, abysmally, depressing country song' he could conjure up. 'All I Deserve', as sung by his wife Diane Christiansen, proved to be a highlight of the band's second album, *The Thrill Of Gravity*. The album was remixed by Bundy K Brown, best known for his work with New York cult band Yo La Tengo. The later album *The Dumbest Magnets* was compared with Whiskeytown, while *Forgiven Now* drew comparisons with Lucinda Williams, for the precision and mystery of its lyrics: 'So Jesus came without warning/Right over your bed and hovered like a flower/in the coldest hour of the morning/wiping your lips clean'.

Another Chicago artist to attract the *cognoscenti* is Chris Mills, whose lyrics resemble Uncle Tupelo, 'sometimes whispered, sometimes growled'[†], though his second album *Every Night Fight For Your Life* is more electric, in every sense. Other interesting music from Illinois comes from the avante-garde Pinetop Seven, the lo-fi of Souled American, old-time enthusiasts Volo Underground and the modern gothic Handsome Family.

Back with Uncle Tupelo, Jeff Tweedy reunited with Jay Farrar, plus Roger McGuinn, on three songs at a Harry Smith tribute show. His most fruitful sideshow, however, was Golden Smog, named after a cartoon band in an episode of *The Flintstones*. He joined after a trio of jokers from Minneapolis had already released the five-track EP *On Golden*

* Sylvia Simmonds
† *Modern Twang*

Smog, issued in 1992 by Crackpot, a small Minneapolis label, and featuring cover versions of Thin Lizzy's 'Cowboy Song' and the Stones' 'Backstreet Girl'. But there was something more here than just a spoof – the melodic sense and tight playing here looks back to the '60s, ironically a direction that bands like The Jayhawks would later pursue.

Those responsible were Gary Louris and Marc Perlman (The Jayhawks), and Dan Murphy (Soul Asylum), though they adopted pseudonyms Michael Macklyn-Drive and Raymond Virginia-Circle, based on the streets where they were born. The roots of Golden Smog were in a pick-up band consisting of Minneapolis mainstays like Martin Zellar of the Gear Daddies, and future Son Volt bassist Jim Boquist, who called themselves Take It To The Limit. As Murphy told *No Depression,* 'Everybody was really big on punk rock and hardcore. We went to this place and bought driftwood lamps, and wore ponchos and we did these Eagles covers, real quietly…people just flipped.' They played fun versions of songs from their childhood. Another night would be devoted to Rolling Stones covers, under the title 'Her Satanic Majesty's Paycheck'. This rough band gradually became Golden Smog, a collective like the Mekons never quite were, despite all their theorising, and with members of The Replacements and even Soul Asylum's road manager.

Jeff Tweedy joined Golden Smog for 1995's ironically titled *Down By The Old Mainstream,* a highlight of which is their version of 'Glad And Sorry', written by Ronnie Lane for the Faces. Packed with good tunes and inventive guitar work, its lasting importance is the link between Wilco and The Jayhawks, which makes this an alt-country summit.

Kraig Johnson from Run Westy Run had been involved at the start – now he and drummer Jody Stephens joined for *Weird Tales,* packaged like the old fantasy magazine. Lyrics are disguised as ads, but by now the music has far outdistanced simple parodies. 'Until You Came Along' sounds more like Gene Clark than he himself did towards the end, with lovely harmonies, chiming guitars and sadness coursing through. Band members are finally credited under their own names.

The band's *Lounge AX, Chicago* bootleg is a continuation of the pop leyline that links The Byrds, Teenage Fanclub and The Eels. In an age where the American underground is struggling to break free from the shackles of its history with the genre-breaking works of Beck, Sparklehorse and the myriad sub-sections of Tortoise, Golden Smog's plaintive ballads and pop-ist frenzies offered a return to backwoods basics.

North By Northwest

The same could be said of The Jayhawks. Though they adapt the colouring of country rock, they are really a tuneful and guitar-friendly American band, with an edge of sweet sadness, which ties them back to the Appalachians. Minneapolis is a long way from Georgia, but even so, they have been referred to as 'the only country rock band that matters'.* Bassist Marc Perlman comments 'If there was a common denominator, it was country and folk music… We were from a city that had produced Husker Du, Prince and Soul Asylum.' Not to mention The Replacements. 'Everybody had their own niche, and this was ours'. They were also fully in tune with the punk ethos: 'We would go onstage and thrash through songs we didn't know.' As Marc grew up, he reacted against the blandness of MTV by going back to Fairport Convention, the Stones, Patti Smith and the like. 'Television is still a huge influence on The Jayhawks'.

Another future Jayhawk, Gary Louris, did not pick up an electric guitar until the age of 22, and then played '60s English guitar pop.

Perlman and singer Mark Olson began by playing around local bars, then they grabbed Gary Louris and drummer Ken Callahan. They drew comparisons with early country rock, then, when their 1986 album came out, the Flying Burrito Brothers. Hence songs like 'The Liquor Store Came First' and 'Six Pack On The Dashboard'.

Their second album *Blue Earth* took three years to appear and only sold around 5,000 copies, but it left observers like Dave Goodman in no doubt that 'they, not The Eagles, were the true successors to *Sweetheart Of The Rodeo*'. It enabled the band to play industry showcases like 'South By Southwest', and win a contract with Def American.

The resulting album, 1992's *Hollywood Town Hall* has been described as 'alt country's totem'. It is a very American album with songs like 'Wichita' and 'Nevada, California'. But no fiddle or pedal steel or banjo. A sly reference to their position, perhaps, is the band photo in the CD booklet, sitting comfortably on a sofa, bang in the middle of the road.

* *Village Voice*

When Mark Olson left to spend more time with Victoria Williams, in 1995, the band briefly broke up, but Gary and Marc decided to give it another go, with Louris stating that this time round he would 'rather risk being silly instead of this safe, pure, timeless Midwestern prairie band'. A bootleg from New York that year adds keyboards to the stellar harmonies. The band sound fresh, and ready to take on the world, *Poised For Stardom*, as the CD title has it.

Sound Of Lies (1997) adds fiddle player Jessy Greene from the Geraldine Fibbers on fiddle and guitarist Kraig Johnson, from Run Westy Run, via Golden Smog. They develop a whole new sound palette. As Louris puts it, 'I tend to write real pretty stuff, so I like to get people involved who will kind of fuck it up a little bit, because if it's too pretty, then it's sugary sweet.' Even so, this is supremely warm music, inviting the listener in, but then the lyrics lay bare the break-up of a love affair with forensic skill: 'Hurry up, it's late and I'm dying in the shadows.' Marc Weingarten reckons this the most harrowing break-up album since Richard and Linda Thompson's *Shoot Out The Lights*, and that Louris 'can't decide whether he is the victim or the victimiser'.

The new 'more majestic and emotional'* sound caused an 'outright split in the alt country community'†. Joss Hutton reckoned the album 'takes the band away from the 'no depression/alt country' end of things with great aplomb'. It's not quite so easy. Producer Brian Paulson had also worked with Son Volt and Wilco, and *Mojo* describes how he has 'rubbed away the burnished veneer leaving only exposed drums, wires, and fulsome voices'. This is actually truer to 'real' alt country even if it is a sound that will 'hardly endear the band to BR5-49 fans'.

No Depression sub-titled an article: 'The Jayhawks glide beyond Americana in relentless pursuit of a great pop record'. Just like Wilco once freed from the shackles of Jay Farrar, without Mark Olson, the new sound is 'remarkably, refreshingly different'. 'I'm going to be a big star, someday' as Gary Louris sings over big guitars and tinkly piano. He told *Mojo* that 'when we first started playing these songs, we played them in the standard country-rock way, and it worked fine, but then we played them acoustically, and interesting things began happening. This record goes back to my real roots, which are pop'. He took roots rock as far as

* *No Depression*
† *Modern Twang*

it would go, 'and wound up becoming the torch bearer for Gram Parsons, and that's not the way I want to live my life'.

The band now appointed Bob Ezrin as their new producer, a man who had worked on albums like Lou Reed's graphic pain-fest *Berlin*. Ezrin worked on the 'boy-girl' dynamic between Louris and keyboard player Karen Grotberg. 'I loved the fact that here was a band that could sing about life and pain from both points of view. Gary created little mini-dramas. Karen gets best supporting actress for my money.' She left shortly after the recordings, to concentrate on her baby. Ezrin knew the band's 'Americana-ish past' and was amazed by their lush new sound.

If there is a point where The Jayhawks part completely from alt country, it is here, despite Ezrin's claim that it is still 'essentially great folk music, but if you framed great folk music in a more modern presentation package, and opened up the spectrum sonically', not to mention with the use of drum loops and the like.

Smile is more akin to soul music, hence Perlman's claim that 'even when we were supposed to be alt country, to us it was the soul aspect of country music. If you look at Gram Parsons, the best stuff was "Dark End of the Street".' Well actually no, it was Parsons' own songwriting and the spirit he encapsulated. And what a DJ described as the 'cinerama sound' here would have been anathema to Gram. Frank Rabey put it best on his website: this is a 'Tinkertoys approach to production, embellishing *ad nauseum*'. The folkiest numbers, like the plaintive 'Broken Harpoon', worked best. The rest was 'strained, often strident'.

A tape of the band live on WPXN radio, where they play 'stripped-down versions of these pumped-up sounds', and that country sadness oozes through, just like before, shows that it's not the songs or the playing, it's the production.

The winter of 2001 saw The Jayhawks stripped right down to an acoustic line up of just Louris, Perlman and Tim O'Reagan on percussion. 'And then there were three' as Gary announces to a rowdy crowd at Schuba's in Chicago. Some gigs saw ex-Long Ryder Stephen McCarthy add guitar and dobro, while at the Bowery Ballroom in New York, James Mastro of *The Health And Happiness Show* guested on mandolin and accordion. Barry Mazor noticed a 'Latin tinge' to the sound, but things went back to country basics when support act the Cash Brothers added their close harmonies to the encores.

Rainy Day Music (2003) was a double album, if you were quick, and an instant classic. The ever-reliable Nigel Williamson heard 'not so much alt country as classic late '60s Byrds/Burritos-style country rock', and the expected conjunction of jangling melodies and heavenly harmonies, plus lots of acoustic instruments laid over the electric band. And that's just the opening song, 'Stumbling Through The Dark', which tops and tails the album, plugged and then unplugged. Stephen McCarthy provides lap steel, and former Eagle Bernie Leadon plays banjo. Ethan Johns produces and Rick Rubin supervises the sparkling sound. We're back to a great American band, singing and playing as if for pure joy.

Gary Louris admits that he is reacting against *Smile*: 'We just wanted to have a more simple approach.'* The last album had been both 'liberating' and 'confusing' for the band, but it helped to clear the decks.

In a world that was fair, The Jayhawks would be a household name. A recent show back home, at the Guthrie Theatre, Minneapolis, sees a sell-out auditorium that feels like a coffee-house gig from their early days in this town. Everyone in the audience feels like a friend. Louris tells them that 'we're here to take your mind off the world for a while', and Bill Snyder reports that Gary 'seems to have found new strength and warmth in his voice, bringing a new sincerity to the band's older material'. For the encore, old friends Dan Murphy and Jim Boquist join him for a Golden Smog golden oldie, 'Until You Came Along'. As Snyder puts it, 'On a day when people were walking around dazed by reports from the (Iraq) war, they brought a community together to share music and take comfort.' Which is worth more than all the platinum records in the world.

Joe Henry is an extremely literate singer songwriter, who combines a respect for Doc Watson with a teenage passion for Iggy Pop. His songs have a 'healthy respect for mystery', and were first heard to advantage on 1990's *Shuffletown*, produced by T-Bone Burnett, with jazz legend Don Cherry on trumpet. The Jayhawks helped out on *Short Man's Room*, and Joe was seen as part of the alt-country crew, but then decided to 'jump off the bandwagon just as it gained corporate sponsorship'. *Trampolene* is a superb collection of Americana, with songs like 'Ohio

* *No Depression*

Air Show Plane Crash', but it adds drum loops, treated pedal steel and noise guitar from Helmet's Page Hamilton.

Minneapolis roots rockers the Gear Daddies were a superb live band, and played 'great rambling sets' in the late '80s, 'filled with alternatively delicate and raging rock 'n' roll',* with plenty of 'big, sincere emotions'. Martin Zellar's 'raspy vocals' made his songs about small-time America all the more poignant, as did Randy Broughton's pedal steel. Zellar later moved closer to the mainstream, but as he told David Cantwell 'I loved that band as much as anybody. We were young then and they were songs that hit home when you're younger. I'm not young anymore.' His album *The Many Moods Of Martin Zellar* is built around people trying to communicate with those around them, 'and usually failing'.

Another local Minneapolis band to note was the Honeydogs. Brothers Adam and Noah Levy had previously worked with Martin Zellar, and after appearing at 'South By Southwest' in 1997, they made *Seen A Ghost*, full of vim and vigour. Accident Clearing House were a young band from Champlin, Minnesota, who played banjo, accordion, even spoons, but with a sly twist, with darker elements intruding on songs like 'The Night Daddy Got His Gun'.

To fill in the musical jigsaw between Minnesota and Illinois, EIEIO came from Wisconsin, and made the great but now hard-to-find album *Land Of Opportunity* (1986), which gathers all the styles, from country rock through cowpunk to alt country, on one piece of vinyl. Co-producer Steve Berlin had also worked with the Blasters, and they are the main pattern here, with extra twang and two lead guitars. Over the border in Iowa, High And Lonesome were a solid rock band with country elements, and singer David Zollo was often compared to Jay Farrar, especially when he made solo albums like *Uneasy Street*, a perfect alt-country title.

Greg Brown is another native Iowan, who, having failed to make it in New York, came home and has released many albums on his own label. He is 'part poet and part philosopher'†, with a special talent for 'fleshing out the essence of the landscape, or nature, or cultural icons, or disillusionment'. *One Big Town* (1989), added Kelly Joe Phelps on slide, and later albums like *The Poet Game* put Greg high up the Americana chart, without bringing him any kind of crossover success.

* *No Depression*
† *Modern Twang*

Midwest

So far in this grand tour of the States, we have looked at three clusters of musicians, in Belleville, Chicago and Minneapolis, mutually supportive and swapping band members and influences. As we plunge further into the American heartlands, music gets stranger, lonelier, more eccentric. If you are mystically inclined, you could claim that it picks up vibrations from the landscape: otherwise it might just be that the artists are forced to spend more time on their own with their record collections.

As we plunge into the centre of the continent, we find the weird gothic rock of Sixteen Horsepower, from Colorado, or the lo-fi Lullabye For The Working Class, from Lincoln, Nebraska. Although Josh Rouse now lives in Nashville, he is almost a case study for the beneficial power to one's music of disruption – geographical or personal. Nebraska was just one of seven states that Rouse called home before going off to college, living in turn with his dad, mum, stepdad, stepdad's best friend... What he remembers most is 'starting off over again in yet another small town'.

Here, in Nowheresville, he formed a punk band, The Victims Of Society, and, more to the point, developed his writing style, hot wired to his unconscious, in which he sings whatever comes to mind to a pre-arranged melody. The results first surfaced on 1998's *Dressed Up Like Nebraska*, and are a gorgeous blend of dreamy vocals and cello and trance rock, with song titles like 'The White Trash Period Of My Life'. You can hear the influence of English post-punk bands like The Smiths or The Cure, but with an alt-country twist. Not that Rouse himself sees why: 'it was recorded in my living room, is that why it's considered roots rock?' Well no, it's in his Midwest whine, or the half-caught words. It's something in the atmosphere he recreates.

Rouse went on to record the EP *Chester* with Kurt Wagner, a second solo album *Home* 'with the muted colours of an autumn weekend', and then his masterpiece so far. *Under Cold Blue Skies* conjures up the strangeness of the landscapes of his childhood, viewed from somewhere far off Music Row. It starts with pump organ and trumpet, then firm drumming and Josh sounding quiet and ominous – 'home is where I always want to be'. 'Feeling No Pain' is a title that could come right out of the Lucinda Williams songbook, but here it is joyous. Josh slurs the lyrics as if in ecstasy, and captures an endless highway in the wordless, whooping chorus and the ringing guitars. The places evoked here lie far outside any known tourist trail.

Interviewed recently on the *Captain America* show, Rouse sounded a little disconnected, far from the usual Nashville bonhomie. He has moved on, and unveiled his latest project, *1972*, a recreation of the sound and tone of the Laurel Canyon school of country rockers. It is a place and time Josh only knows from the albums that now form its relics.

But things get stranger. Scroat Belly come from Wichita, Kansas – made mythical by Jim Webb's famous song, with its linesman somewhere out in an endless landscape, strung up high in the air. They pushed 'insurgent country' to its limit, being 'closer to a breakneck metal band than an alternative country outfit'.* More accurately, they are part of the 'can't slow down on the old hoe down'† school of cowpunk and 'the roughest, toughest band of hard hittin', fast pickin', hellbound hayseeds to spew forth from the fiery bowls of the Midwest yet. Their 1996 debut *Daddy's Farm* will rock you up one side and hillbilly down the other.'**

It is a concept album about drunkenness, sample titles being 'The Booze Won't Let Me Down' and 'Whiskey Drinkin' SOB' and as downhome as you can get. Cowpunk on speed, with each 'song' trying to get to the end as fast as possible. The stand-out track is 'Honda'. A severely hung-over man catalogues the things he has lost in his inebriation: keys, shoes, his 'soul, strength and will'. It starts slow and twangy (for Scroat Belly), but gets faster until Kirk Rundstrom and Roy Gottstine howl 'where's my blood?' in unison, over and over. Jim Reeves, this is not, even if it slows down again at the end, in a most disconcerting way.

Over in Kansas City, Canyon evolved from the local punk scene, then singer Brandon Butler and guitarist Joe Winkle moved to Washington DC, but took the prairies with them, locked deep inside. On 2003's *Empty Rooms*, it is Kansas that continues to inspire their vast, melancholic landscapes. A song like 'Sleepwalker' is full of grandeur, almost U2-like, with heartfelt vocals, strange textures, and yearning lead guitar.

The effect is almost psychedelic, and bears comparison with some of the quieter passages of Oklahoma's deranged Flaming Lips. It is 'a new kind of traditional American music, not rootsy, but rootless'.††

* *No Depression*   ** *Music Wichita*
† *Modern Twang*   †† *Uncut* magazine

For all its studio trickery and speeded-up voices, a later track 'Do You Realise' rightly turns up on *Both Sides Now; The Spirit Of Americana*, with lead signer Wayne Coyne musing tenderly that we are all floating in space and that 'happiness makes you cry' and that 'everyone you know someday will die'. That, at least, is a staple theme of alt country.

In Missouri, the Starkweathers were a down-to-earth band whose hard-driving country rock took on local yet universal themes like religious bigotry, sex and small-town claustrophia. Inner tensions drove them asunder in 1995, but a compilation cassette *Learning The Hard Way* gathers together the remnants. Lead singer Mike Ireland and former Holler, gave us more of the same, and *Learning How To Live* ranges from the murder ballad 'Banks of the Ohio' to the sombre 'Graveyard Song' and the morose and bitter 'House Of Secrets'.

Over in Kansas City's Hurricane club, the country-roots band Big Iron got a big local following, then changed their name to Hadacol, after the alcohol-based patent medicine that cheered up dry days in the South. Led by brothers Fred and Greg Wickham, *Better Than This* is straight-down-the-line cowpunk. The drumming is almost military, always on the beat. But there are subtler touches, lyrics like bar-room smoke that 'feels like a girlfriend's arms', plus the pedal steel and mandolin. You really couldn't get a better example of basic, honest alt country.

Over in St Louis, Missouri, Wagon were a mellower variant of this generic sound, with Steve Rauner adding accordion, mandola and organ to the basic sound on albums like *No Kinder Room*. He later joined Nadine, whose *Back To My Senses* was a US EP that Germany's Glitterhouse augmented to a full CD, and a fine one too.

Its follow up, *Downtown Saturday*, was described as 'peopled with losers and dreamers, gentle reflections and lonesome wanderlust'.* Neil Young presides, and, like him, the band are not afraid to think outside the country envelope, with trip-hop beats and the like. The opening song, 'Closer', is praised for pitching the 'melancholy sweetness'[†] of Reichmann's vocals against a hypnotic pastiche built up from drum loops and 'unidentifiable snippets from old records'. A touch here of the sound collages spliced together by Flaming Lips and their like. Just because you come from Missouri, it doesn't mean that you need to be stuck in the past.

---

* *Uncut* magazine
† *No Depression*

Northwest

So much for the Midwest, and lands set as far from the ocean as you can get. Up on the western seaboard, bands like The Pickets, The Walkabouts and Ranch Romance set the scene for 'Grange Rock',* a wordplay on 'grunge', the music style with which Seattle is most popularly associated.

No coincidence, then that The Walkabouts surfaced on Germany's Sub Pop, a grunge home from home, and came good on 1996's *New West Motel*. Their leader was Chris Eckman on vocals, guitar and 'lyrics', which are abstract, yet somehow make sense. On 'Glad Nation's Death Song', which could either be about 'us' or the 'US', 'these are the ghosts that I half believed/guns and liquor and the carnival freak'. Out in the New West, the long arm of the law turns out to be a 'one-armed acrobat'. Carla Torgerson adds harmony vocals to sweeten the sound, and the others add a rich soup of sound, with organ, lap steel, mandolin, accordion and 'noises'. Earlier albums feature Brian Eno and Natalie Merchant.

The real heart of *New West Motel* is 'Findlay's Hotel', with ominous strings, and Chris and Carla singing quietly but intently, about an armed robbery with a woman holding the gun. The Walkabouts went on to make a series of peerless albums, rightly described as 'mining a richly shadowy strain of Americana'[†]. Beautifully written, played and packaged, even the odds and sods double CD collection *Drunken Soundtracks* – arranged back to front, chronologically – is interesting from start to finish. Their 'best of', *Watermarks*, was given a US release on Ross Tolman's Interstate label, and presents 'this absolutely magnificent band at their absolute best', to quote one review, so, of course, sold zilch.

Satisfied Mind came out in 1996, and features low-key covers of songs by Gene Clark and The Carter Family, but also edgy Australians like Nick Cave and Robert Forster of the Go Betweens, Patti Smith's 'Free Money' and the traditional 'Will You Miss Me When I'm Gone'. Taken at a slow pace, with lots of acoustic playing from the likes of Peter Buck and Larry Barrett, it is all of a piece.

Setting The Woods On Fire might quote an old Hank Williams song, but this is an album of new songs, plus a full electric sound, plus a horn section on 'Hole In The Mountain', so that the album exudes a 'spikey, full-bodied grace'[†]. It is also unsettling, like a soundtrack to *Twin Peaks*.

* *Modern Twang*
† *Music Wichita*

One reason for this strange band not getting more notice in the US is The Walkabouts' refusal to push their personality on the listener, either on their CD sleeves or in their music, where they seem in thrall to a higher force. Just listen to 'Firetrap', with rolling and rich organ chords, and odd words about having Jesus 'in my pocket, and matches in my coat', as if rasped by a pyromaniac. But is this fire divine or real?

It could easily become a parody of itself, so that you just knew they would release an album called *Devil's Road*. But it's another great album of Americana, about corporate murder, staging one's own death, mysterious woods, 'Fairground Blues' and a child murder. In which the child was the murderer. With lyrics like 'city of crows' and 'I came from nowhere/I was nowhere bound' this is like an orchestrated *Nebraska*, and no happy endings. Not exactly the formula for pop success.

As usual, Dave Goodman gets them into context, working hard to find the 'commonalities between folk and country and modern rock, with Eckman's gruff, whispered vocals providing counterpoint to Torgerson's lush soprano'. *Nighttown* (1997), saw The Walkabouts change direction towards a more urban sound, with synthesisers replacing the pedal steel. More recently, they completed another side project, *Train Leaves At Eight*, but, despite the presence of Steve Berlin from Los Lobos and Peter Buck, this abandons America as a subject for old-world songcraft, from Jacques Brel to Deus. Even if a banjo 'chews over the bones of a dark waltz' and a 'bruised melancholia'* makes the music easy to admire but hard to love. Even so, the spirit of this troubled band lives on in Chris and Carla, basically the two lead singers with different players, and again they found their most receptive audiences in Europe.

Maybe it is because Seattle is so isolated from the rest of the States that all of its greatest exports, from Jimi Hendrix to Nirvana, needed to get away to find fame. The Green Pyjamas are even less well known in their city – or country – of origin than The Walkabouts, with albums in Australia, Walthamstow and Pittsburg, and a well-kept secret to a close conspiracy of fans. Which is a shame, as, though Jeff Kelly and his cohorts steered closer to the gentler side of psychedelia than to country, backwards guitar than lap steel, albums like *Ghosts Of Love* blend careful words – 'that werewolf moon, that driftwood smoke' – precise playing and

* *Uncut magazine*

intimate vocals. It taps into a specific tradition of American songwriting back through '60s mavericks like Tom Rapp and his band Pearls Before Swine to writers like Edgar Allan Poe. Disturbing tales, told softly.

The recent Northern Gothic took on a strong country flavour, plus lots of electric guitar, and started as it meant to go on, with a song called 'In The Darkness'. *Ptolemaic Terrascope* magazine, which has consistently championed the band, describes the atmosphere they create as 'a mournful autumn that lasts all year, haunted twilight of nocturnal landscapes'. Maybe it's something to do with coming from Seattle. The songs seem to come from 'a mythical American west'. 'First Love' is a new but ancient murder ballad, which then 'explodes into thick walls of electric guitar terror'. Check out too the live official bootleg *Lust Never Sleeps*, with Kelly's extended lead breaks 'recalling equally Richard Thompson and Neil Young', which sounds like heaven to me.

Seattle boasted other bands who sought connections between alt country and grunge. The Picketts featured Christy McWilson on lead vocals and, after appearing at 'South By Southwest' in 1994, made their album debut *The Wicked Picketts*, featuring Yoko Ono's 'Walking On Thin Ice' as rockabilly. Their next album has The Who's 'Baba O'Riley' as country rock, and 'Should I Stay Or Should I Go?' as a two step.

The Supersuckers were a punk band from Tucson who relocated to Seattle. Their 1992 debut album *The Songs All Sound The Same* (true in their case, because they all sound crap) contained cover versions of Madonna and the Dead Boys, and the band would dress up in 'flannel cowboy schtick' on stage. Singer Edward Carlyle Daly III, better known as Eddie Spaghetti, shouts a lyric rather than caressing it 'making enough slovenly noise to ensure that nothing else much matters'.*

The band also got into the habit of giving Willie Nelson songs a good kicking, and this led to Steve Earle recording them, and Willie himself joining them on stage, and some of the more adventurous country players appearing on *Must've Been High* in 1997, recorded in a small Seattle studio. Eddie Spaghetti jokes to *No Depression* that he and his band have been ahead of the game every time, moving to Seattle, doing heroin, stopping doing heroin. 'And then the country thing. What is it called, Incipient country or something?', and the whole room rocks with laughter.

* *Trouser Press*

No less than Grant Alden, the Pope of Americana, gives the band his seal of approval, and describes himself, like the Supersuckers, as 'a Seattle grunge survivor who still wears flannel'.

Talking of style, Ranch Romance was an 'all star cowgirl revue' with vintage costumes to match. They put out *Blue Blazes* in 1991, a 'sparkling blend of Western swing, honky tonk and sultry ballads',* plus the odd yodel. The four Seattle girls responsible chose to call their music 'regressive country', in a tongue-in-cheek way, but *Sing Bluegrass* and *Old-Time Music* (1996) shows that they know their history, with songs by Jimmie Rodgers, Patsy Montana and Bill Monroe.

Larry Barrett was born in Idaho, but moved to Seattle after serving with the US Army Ski Patrol in Germany. Ironically, some years later, it was the German label Glitterhouse that picked up *Flowers* as a home cassette, and put it out on CD. They describe Barrett's music as 'Dylan meets Merle'. He prefers 'front-porch swing'. The blend of harmonica, accordion, fiddle and pedal steel here sounds self assured and comfortable, as does Larry's smoky voice. The album has a lovely downhome ambience. He pays thanks to The Walkabouts, and writes songs about murder and faithful hounds and 'one afternoon while Wall Street was crashing', with Carolyn Wennblom blending her voice to his. Lovely stuff.

Beyond The Mississippi doesn't have quite the same magic blend as the debut, even if it was taped live in the studio, and contains oddball songs like 'Czechoslovakian Coal Miner's Daughter Disaster of 1992', in waltz time. 'The trees are all dead, or they're dying at best/The fish are all gone, north south and west' he sings cheerfully. Larry is best known, however, as the glue that binds together local bands like The Walkabouts, The Picketts and the Wigglin' Taters, sweetening their studio sessions with lap steel and mandolin.

In the late 1990s, Portland, Oregon was second only to Seattle as a breeding ground for alt country in the Northwest. Bands like Richmond Fontaine and Little Sue were crucial. The latter were formed when Susannah Weaver joined The Crackpots and – taking a new name – they combined various styles, from honky tonk to lo-fi. *Chimneys And Fishes* (1997) is a 'friendly collection that twangs in all the right places'* with local old-time band Golden Delicious adding musical colouring.

* *Modern Twang*

Other Portland bands of note were lo-fi specialists Birddog And The Shivers who had moved up from Austin in their campervan (plus drummer and children). Pete Droge was born in Atlanta, then moved to Seattle, where he played punk with March Of Crimes, but relocated to Portland, and reinvented himself as a singer songwriter. *Necktie Second* (1994) is full of melody and humour and rich organ chords and songs like 'If You Don't Love Me (I'll Kill Myself)'. Sunspot Stopwatch is an update of Dylan's 'Positively Fourth Street', addressed to an ex-lover, and predicting 'when your mini skirt'll hit the dirt/and baby you'll be crying and bleeding'.

Droge later went all the way to harmony heaven with The Thorns, a singing trio that connected him to two other fine singer songwriters, Matthew Sweet and Shawn Mullins. Sweet as honey and 'a glorious soothing summer soundtrack', it drew all the expected comparisons with Crosby Stills And Nash.

Heatmiser were a Portland punk quartet, but singer Elliott Smith started branching out on his own, playing acoustic shows and issuing a dark and disquieting, self-titled album in 1995. *Either/Or* is the real McCoy though, with mysterious words fused to pretty tunes, and fulfilling his stated desire to be 'both John Lennon and Paul McCartney at once', while wearing an omnipresent Hank Williams T-shirt. Subsequent albums have mined the same quiet, jazzy territory, a Nick Drake for the lost generation, plus a good dose of Americana: 'Clementine', 'Southern Belle' and 'LA' are later song titles. It's all very pleasant, but somehow inessential.

More recently, and heavily hyped in the UK press was Portland's M Ward, backed on his second album *Transfiguration Of Vincent* by the Old Joe Clarks. The record starts with insect noises, and a melody line passed from guitar straight out of the Bert Weedon songbook to slightly out-of-tune piano. Then Ward starts singing, and the band get really stuck in. There's some good ragtime guitar, but his lyrics are either meaningful, or gibberish. 'A Voice At The End Of The Line': 'the sky goes on forever in a symphony of song', and 'Better call the undertaker, take me under, undertaker, take me home'. All sung in a holy whisper. Either this man is a mystic, or he is possibly on mind-altering drugs.

The one thing known about Matt Ward is the early patronage of Howe Gelb, and a previous, highly praised CD, *End Of Amnesia*. *Uncut* describes the follow up as a masterclass in 'deft guitar picking and a voice like honey drizzled onto a dry creekbed'. The strangely muted production adds to the effect. Time alone will tell whether this is genius or bathos: it certainly contains the unlikeliest cover of David Bowie's 'Let's Dance' ever, bossa style and sung in a graveyard croak. The harmonica and piano breaks seem to have been recorded in a different key, then spliced in.

One fanzine reckons the CD is a corrective to commercial country, but personally I wouldn't give up one Dixie Chick for this, let alone all three. It also supposedly showcases songs 'alive in metaphor and imagery in the spirit of Tom Waits and the late John Fahey'. Who I reckon would be turning in his grave at the comparison. Time to press on down the coast, to the Golden State of California.

Southwest

It comes as a considerable relief to surrender the CD tray to LA's Geraldine Fibbers, with its blend of thrash and a female voice on the edge – and even more disturbingly melodic when quiet – plus genuinely strange lyrics: 'you're in my blood, box and blanket and broken rosebud'. A lot of them deal with female needs and revenge, as in 'A Song About Walls', where a woman sticks a needle in her boyfriend's eye. The Geraldine Fibbers also cover songs by Bobby Gentry and Dolly Parton, but not as you have ever heard them before.

Jessy Green's violin give the whole thing an edge, and the results went down well with the LA punk scene, leading to the release of the 10in album *Get Thee Gone*, in 1994. Well-received gigs at the likes of 'South By Southwest' led to the release of the magnificent, but terrifying full-length album *Lost Somewhere Between The Earth And My Home* in 1995. It lies somewhere between self-therapy and storytelling, with Carla alternately screaming and purring, over sawing fiddle and electric guitar, together with a flexible rhythm section, with sonic peaks and troughs just when you least expect them.

By its very nature, this was not a musical collective destined to last too long. Anger is great for a while, but it doesn't sustain. Jessy Green went off to the quieter pastures of The Jayhawks, and after a collection of early and live tracks, *What Part Of Get Thee Gone Don't You*

Understand?, and Virgin dropped the band after releasing *Butch* in 1997. It was another totally unique concoction, uniting the punk aggression of 'Trashman In Furs' with country waltzes and 'backwoods twang'.

Even so, at first glance, California hardly seems to be a natural home for alt country, not unless you go out to the desert wilderness, or take a trip back in time by driving out to its ghost towns and 19th-century mining encampments. As the Geraldine Fibbers proved, even in the big conurbations one can find adventurous and interesting music, if you look in all the wrong places. After all, Los Angeles was previously home to the Laurel Canyon brand of country rock, and then to much of cowpunk.

Very much in their wake, the early '90s saw informal jam sessions at LA nightspot Raji's with the likes of Peter Holsapple from the DBs, Bangle Vicki Peterson and Mark Walton from Dream Syndicate, a band who had recorded a live album in the same place some years earlier. Eventually they coalesced into a more formal unit, the Continental Drifters, and made a memorable appearance at 'South By Southwest' in 1994. *Vermilion* was recorded in Louisiana, and still sounds fun. Lo-fi specialists Acetone were also resident at Raji's, and LA has produced such maverick talents as Beck and Gillian Welch. But, given its importance to the recording industry, alt-country elements can be found, mostly disguised, in the work of some contemporary bands marketed as anything but.

Americana crops up in the strangest places. The Eels were two white boys from LA who used samples and sonic distortion learnt from hip hop, just like Beck. *Electro-shock Blues* (1998) is their masterpiece. The whole thing is about dying in small town America – in every sense – though it does end happily enough with a love song and the thought that 'maybe it's time to live'.

Daisies Of The Galaxy was a more cheerful affair, even if recorded back to back with an as yet unreleased album that is 'loud and dark and scary'. It starts with the sound of a New Orleans funeral band, but is slyly humorous and easy on the ear: E 'needed to make something in love with life for my own sanity, it became most important that I make simple, sweet, pure music'. Peter Buck and Grant-Lee Phillips help out.

Counting Crows are a more traditional band, in every sense, though Robbie Robertson got it right when he urged his daughter to see them, then called them 'a bit derivative perhaps'. Which made their debut album such a huge seller: *August And Everything After*, produced by T-Bone Burnett, sounds familiar even on first hearing, and is topped with Adam Durlitz's seemingly casual storytelling, and passion for the minutiae of Californian life. Except that if you listen carefully, like E, he seems to regard everyday existence in the US as a death sentence. 'Time And Time Again' ends with deep sarcasm 'some day I'm gonna walk on water'.

Adam explains the song thus, 'the driving he does at the end of that song is a different kind of driving than Springsteen's. He wants to set fire to his city. He's moving on and destroying it. It's a horrible cycle.' Later albums got more melancholic, but at a recent open-air festival, after loads of teenage bands making a din, Counting Crows came on and suddenly there was a human being singing to the crowd, a real storyteller, with aural colouring from organ, string bass, pedal steel and the like.

During the '90s, Grant Lee Buffalo produced four albums of beautifully arranged and produced 'uncategorisable Americana', on which Grant-Lee Phillips, when not playing a mix of acoustic strums and intricate electric lead guitar, was singing about the Lone Ranger, and the closing of the American dream. This was at heart a rock band, with The Doors and REM also strong influences. *Copperopolis* (1996) is named after a small town in the Sierra Nevada, and this sombre song cycle deals with dust-bowl life right up to the Oklahoma bombing, bringing the musical temperature right down, with pump organ and pedal steel. The highlights of the band's career were gathered together on the double CD *Storm Hymnal: Gems From The Vault Of Grant Lee Buffalo* – which includes some interesting acoustic versions of the likes of 'The Shining Hour', a secret history of America in one song. The music certainly is, always melodic, electric but not overbearing, with Grant-Lee singing with power but also tunefully, and with words that usually transcend the mundane. For a band discovered by Bob Mould, this is remarkably pretty music.

The opening track on Grant-Lee Phillips' *Mobilize* starts with a sleepy look at modern America. Phillips sounds doubtful, at first: 'and the point of my life is/what if it doesn't add up'. But he ends up on a lake in April, counting the seconds between each lightning strike, but harmony is all, and his ship is – literally – coming in. This is an album that voices America through a cast of characters, and meaning is found in the past, 'to trace the paces backwards'. Rounder Records claim that the 'sweeping rural gestures' and 'haunting Americana' of his early albums have now given way to 'an inner landscape alien, digital, but strangely inviting', but I really can't see the join. Maybe somebody should make Grant-Lee Phillips America's laureate.

California, and in particular San Francisco, is well stocked with musicians revisiting the quieter side of Americana, bands like the Old Joe Clarks, Granfallon Bus and Richard Buckner, plus the old-time delights of the Hillbillies From Mars. Tarnation are far closer to the avante-garde, even if *Mirador* does relate to Ennio Morricone's sound-tracks (the Wild West, via Italy), and while they have a lap steel, they have yet to 'get it together' to learn how to play it. What does come through on this strangely textured album is the landscape of northern California as it does in Paula Fraser's solemn voice and the wordless female vocals behind her – a sense of a land stretching away into infinity. 'Out there stands a *manzanita*. Underneath there lies a stone, without a name or a symbol, fading in the waiting light alone'.

Just as respectful, but oddly skewed into a sonic landscape all of its own, is the ghostly music of the Beachwood Sparks. At under 30 minutes, *Make The Robot Cowboys Cry* certainly does not outstay its welcome, but for a band already praised as the natural heirs to Gram Parsons, this 'wistful, serendipitous ride' uses glockenspiel, mellotron, banjo and the rest, with the kind of male vocals beloved of fellow soundscapers Mercury Rev, all ethereal and high toned and sexless. 'Eunuch country', maybe. Lyrically, the Beachwood Sparks are Steely Dan with a doctorate, with a song about Charles Darwin on the Galapagos Islands and 'Ponce De Leon Blues' dedicated to an associate of Christopher Columbus. Pre-Americana, anyone. Chris Gunst and his musical colleagues 'take their genre and proceed to bend, twist, enhance and modify it to fit their own bizarre but beautiful visions'.*

Beachwood Sparks emerged out of Californian '60s obsessives the Lilys, so that they can make a Sade song – 'By Your Side' – sound like something by Gene Clark. Their previous albums are closer still to The Byrds of *Sweetheart Of The Rodeo*, even if the second, *Once We Were*

* *The Guardian*

Trees, was recorded at the studio of J Mascis of Dinosaur Jr. It could not have been archetypal, though, 'there was seven feet of snow. J has this beautiful cabin and we were playing with the snowdrifts.' As to the claim that they are the inheritors of Gram's Cosmic American Music, 'it's a high compliment, but when you're playing, you don't think. We just try to be positive, especially in our lyrics. It's very important to spread light'.

Tell that to San Diego's Mojo Nixon, whose chosen path is to spread dissent and anarchy. No one could ever accuse his singing style of lack of balls, and he tramps on any delicate sensibility he can find, like early Elvis with a twisted mind, and yet a love for the roots of the music. This is the man who once sang 'Don Henley Must Die' from the back of a flatbed truck, outside the offices of David Geffen, on Sunset Boulevard. Then had Don join him onstage to duet the same song.

Honky tonk delights like 'I Don't Want No Cybersex' – 'baby let's forget the internet, let's just go park and pet' – and 'Redneck Rampage' appear on *Sock Ray Blue*, recorded in Austin and supposedly volume three of 'Texas Prison Field Recordings'. There's an affectionate but graphic obituary of Country Dick Montana; 'he had three wives, he told 'em bald face lies/but that evil rotten turd/Mister Mike Perv' laid Country Dick in his grave'. Every word is a delight – this is a man who can rhyme 'there was blood in my urine' with 'the holy shroud of Turin'. Mojo growls and moans, rather than singing in any accepted sense, but the Toadliquors whip up a storm behind him.

Kirby McMillan Jr started off singing Woody Guthrie songs in soup kitchens where his paid employment was 'organising winos'. He joined a punk band, 123, then heading back home had the 'The Mojo Nixon revelation', 'in which he performed front-porch boogie woogie to make your grandma buck dance, blush and hit you in the head with her purse'. MTV refused to broadcast the video of 'Debbie Gibson Is Pregnant With My Two-headed Love Child', but he recorded his 1991 album *Otis* with John Doe, Eric Amble and the soon-to-be-deceased Country Dick Montana. He also indulged in a project with Jello Biafra. *Prairie Home Invasion* has songs like 'Are You Drinking With Me Jesus' and an exultant 'Let's Burn Old Nashville Down'. It's the kind of album where 'Will The Circle' becomes 'Will The Foetus Be Aborted'.

A smoother sound to emerge from San Diego, but equally in touch with country's roots, was the Hot Club Of Cowtown, whose re-jigged western swing brings together Bob Wills and Stefan Grapelli, with lots of slap bass, nimble guitar picking, winsome fiddles and sweet female voices. Hot guitarist Whit Smith came from New York, where the band he fronted, Western Caravan, seemed like fish out of water. Along with the sweetest of fiddle players Elana Fremerman, he switched coasts and formed the Hot Club with a changing cast of bassists. No drums, the slap bass has to carry the rhythm too.

Needless to say, they were signed up after a show at 'South By Southwest', and 1998's Swingin' Stampede turned them into a concert favourite, worldwide. *Ghost Train* is more of the same, less cheerful than it sounds, with lines like 'the wheels are coming off this ride'. Even so, musically, this is sugar sweet. The band have relocated to Austin.

Much in the same vein, California saw an alt-country movement in the late '80s that self-consciously revived the Bakersfield sound, and produced three influential compilations, *A Town South Of Bakersfield Vols 1–3*, from 1985 onwards. Its most celebrated exponent was Dwight Yoakam, rejected by Nashville but welcomed in LA like a Messiah. There's a rebel feel to Dwight's music and stage persona. In south California, he founded the Babylonian Cowboys with lead guitarist Pete Andersen, also well known as a session man and record producer. *Guitars, Cadillacs Etc Etc* (1986) was an energetic debut, though, to be honest, everything since has sounded much the same.

Out of the same scene came Big Sandy And The Fly Rite Boys, LA-based rockabillies who on *Swingin' West* developed their style into an exact copy of the classic pre-war Bakersfield sound, as pioneered by the likes of Rose Maddox. The Lonesome Strangers appeared on volume one of *A Town South Of Bakersfield*. Their own debut came in 1986, with *Lonesome Pine*, then, 11 years later, they burst back on the scene with *Land Of Opportunity*.

Dale Watson is now based in Austin. His croon has been described as sounding like 'Willie Nelson after swilling some of Ozzie's gin', and his looks are straight out of the Wilburn Brothers. Despite a brief move to Nashville, neither endeared him to Music Row. Frenetic live shows put him in the same league as Yoakam, Don Walser and the Derailers. Watson won a songwriter of the year award for *I Hate These Songs*, which pays tribute to the likes of Buck Owens and Johnny Paycheck. Dale also took part with Kelly Willis and his great supporter Rosie Flores on *Songs Of Forbidden Love*, a classic anthology of yet more cheatin' songs, under the collective name the *Wandering Eyes*.

In the mid to late '80s, Camper Van Beethoven were right out at the other extreme, alt rockers with a college education and a psychedelic record collection. And songs like '(We're A) Bad Trip' and their celebrated 'Take the Skinheads Bowling'. The music on those early albums released on Pitch A Tent is '60s drug music, speeded up, but with all kinds of other influences: eastern scales, beat poetry and the wilder side of country rock. As bassist Victor Krummenacher comments, 'a lot of people who were into Camper then are into alternative country now'.* 'We kept that folk and country element alive in modern rock when most bands wanted nothing to do with it.'

The story begins in Redlands, California, which, in singer David Lowery's words, is 'not so much a suburb as the last town before the desert'. Redlands was close enough to LA that they could check out the burgeoning punk scene in the late '70s, catching acts such as X, Black Flag and The Circle Jerks. 'They were part of an urban lowlife scene – they were big-city types and we were hicks.' The band took the classic rock they heard during their childhoods, added a punk rock 'anything goes' attitude, 'and mixed that with country and weird ethno stuff, borrowed from bad television. After their debut album *Telephone Free Landslide Victory* (1985) someone made them a tape of Kaleidoscope, a band playing much this kind of music in California, 20 years before. It led them to explore more 'hippie folk-rock stuff', from Syd Barrett to Richard and Linda Thompson, and in particular David Lindley's strange collective. Everything coalesced on 1988's *Our Beloved Revolutionary Sweetheart*. The band play with a new confidence and weirder words than even before.

Camper Van Beethoven also worked with fellow maverick Eugene Chadbourne, as Camper Van Chadbourne. After the parent band split in 1990, Jonathan Segal produced the debut of Bay Area alt-country

* *No Depression*

group Granfaloon Bus, and David Lowery started Cracker – who dropped all the elements that made Camper Van Beethoven so interesting – but also worked with Mark Linkous, who is in much the same madcap spirit.

Next stop the desert. Over in Joshua Tree, the scene of Gram Parsons' death and immolation, Victoria Williams formed a trio, the Original Harmony Ridge Creek Dippers, with boyfriend Mark Olson from The Jayhawks and Mike Russell on fiddle. They recorded themselves playing in their wood-panelled living room, and Mark's first impulse was to simply hand out tapes to friends. The music sounds like the direction The Jayhawks might have taken if they had unplugged, then plunged further into country music, rather than taken a sharp left turn into pop. Olson is like 'an old backwoods crooner singing traditionals on his porch,'* while Victoria Williams provides the counterpoint, 'her unmistakeable midrange warble grounding the skyward harmonies'. But you must add the words in too, oozing fulfilment and a love affair that deepens with the years: 'If you look now, you'll see I'm on your side/each cloud that passes us by/trying to find the rainbows of your heart.'

Their debut self-titled album was at first only for sale through a PO Box address in Joshua Tree, but music this pacific was bound to leak out to a wider public, seeking rural solace. Music without shadows. You know exactly what to expect from the song titles: 'Flowering Trees' or 'Run With The Ponies', a vision of rural peace and beauty. Victoria Williams also runs the Sweet Relief Foundation, which raises money to pay medical bills for uninsured musicians.

As to the name of their new band, Victoria says 'I was out opening for The Jayhawks years ago. Mark left the tour bus and we'd go creek dipping every day. We came to this one place, it was called Harmony Ridge.' They also adopted the name Rollin' Creek Dippers for a European tour with Buddy and Julie Miller.

Not that the sound stays the same. The Harmony Ridge Creek Dippers later featured drums, clarinets and mandolins, and evoked the sound of The Band, around *Big Pink*. Their fourth album, *My Own Jo Ellen*, is every bit as affecting as the others. Olsons' songs, as ever, seem to have fallen together, as if he's determined not to let them get too polished for their own good.

* *No Depression*

As to Victoria, her album *Loose* made use of desert rockers Calexico, and 'Train Song (Demise Of The Caboose)' – you can't escape railways for too long, even in the desert – sees her using drum loops. Another Joshua Tree resident is Kristen Hersh, and her unsettling music fits the landscape like a glove: Olson and Williams seem wilfully to ignore the darker shadows that gather around them, but given Victoria's bravery in adversity this is all part of their charm.

Plunging eastward through Arizona, we reach New Mexico, and Marty Robbins territory – El Paso nestles on the border. It was here, in Alburquerque, that three girls and a drummer made their debut at a Dia de Los Muertos (Day of the Dead) party in 1994. Hazledene later appeared at 'South By Southwest' – celebrating those who are still here on earth – and took part in the 1997 *Bloodshot/No Depression* tour. It was the same story as so often before, one-time punks who had grown up on country, and now turned back to it, with an attitude.

At their quietest, Hazledene almost sound like the Original Harmony Ridge Creek Dippers, with an edge – 'there's blackness all around, but lights too and elegy' – and a more insistent guitar sound. But they can also rock with a vengeance. One of the two lead singers, Shawn Barton, said of their 1997 debut, *How Bees Fly*, that 'Gram and Emmylou built the house of Hazledene'.

The band briefly signed to a major label for *Digging You Up*, and Allan Jones summed it up perfectly. 'Shawn and Tonya have the kind of voices you could listen to forever and not get tired of. They can be sweet, mournful, sexy, desolate and there's gravel in there too when it's needed.' They certainly carry on the death obsession of their debut with Shawn singing 'Let me be one of the names upon your grave,' and Tonya demanding 'Let them know that I died for love,' both in the very sweetest way. For Jones, this is 'music from the other side of midnight. Even by the standards of other alt-country stalwarts this record scours some of the darkest edges of New Country.' Which is why it is so great.

Digging You Up employed producer Jim Scott (who also worked with Whiskeytown), it revisited some of the songs from their debut, and made them even more intense. Hazledene were themselves given a death sentence, in a series of corporate murders. Nigel Williamson raged at whoever took such a stupid decision: 'Hazledene ought to be highly marketable as a kind of alt-country version of the Dixie Chicks. Instead, they're back where they started on the German based Glitterhouse.'

Which actually suited them fine, if *Orphans* is anything to go by. Later re-released in the States by E Squared, this is a mini album of cover versions, by the expected – Gram Parsons and Mark Linkous – and the unexpected – Peter Gabriel and Radiohead. They open with the traditional 'Mining Camp Blues', with banjo and yodels. But, of course, it is a murder ballad that cuts the deepest. Sparklehorse's 'Heart Of Darkness' starts like a love song, spoken by the man and set in a parking lot, and in just over two minutes covers the emotional waterfront. They follow up with 'Whiskey In The Jar', with crunchy lead guitar and fine picked mandolin, then close with an acoustic version of Gram's 'A Song For You'.

Elsewhere in the region, Dan Bern – originally from Iowa – now lives in Truth or Consequences, New Mexico, and his songs are quirky to match. *Smart Mine* contains his 'raucously self-referential' 'Talkin' Woody, Bob, Bruce & Dan Bern Blues'.

Hope Sandaval first found fame as the witchy singer in Mazzy Star, in which her partner was David Roback, who put together Rain Parade in the early '80s. With her own band the Warm Inventions, Hope recorded *Bavarian Bread Fruit*, and it brings to the fore her own special brand of remoteness, almost sullen at times, 'full of stark Americana, wasted beauty with minimal accompaniment'.* For *Uncut*, playing the disc is like 'treading softly into a room full of candles and ghosts'.

Camper Van Beethoven mutated into Cracker, who for six months in 2002 toured 'redneck and biker bars' as Ironic Mullet, named after the much-derided '70s hairstyle, short on the top and long at the sides. Somehow they survived the process, and recreated this rough, masculine music in the studio as *Countrysides*, which includes a cover of 'Up Against The Wall, Redneck Mothers'. The sound is closer to 'garage country' than alt country, and reflects a time of 'coming war, resurgent American imperialism and a far-right Christian fundamentalist regime in Washington DC'. 'Ain't Gonna Suck Itself' is a kiss-off to the band's former label.

But we must press on, anything but softly, across the border to Texas, and on to Austin, where *South By Southwest* started off.

* *Mojo*

iv) Desert Rock

'Living here is a time to get in touch with your reptilian spirit.
You go out at night, avoid the sun and crawl under a rock'
– Calexico

'Desert Rock' is a branch of alt country that first evolved out of cowpunk in the Phoenix, Arizona/Tucson area in the mid '80s by bands like Giant Sand and Green On Red who joined the dots between country, roots rock and indigenous Southwestern musical styles. A decade on, the rhythm section of Giant Sand, bass player Joey Burns and drummer John Convertino, came to exemplify this new sound, first under the name Spoke, and then as Calexico, guesting on albums by fellow desert dweller Victoria Williams, and Michael Hurley and Vic Chestnutt.

They themselves operate from 'Our Soil, Our Strength' in the heart of Tucson. But both have chosen to come to Arizona. Burns was born in Montreal, and then got involved in the LA punk scene, based around SST Records. Convertino was born in New York, but grew up in Oklahoma, where he played in a gospel group with his family.

Calexico make a lusher sound than Howe Gelb would ever have done, with odd things happening in the margins. Dave Goodman describes their 1997 debut *Spoke* as 'Southwestern Americana'. The band themselves reckon their debut album 'very acoustic and front porch, with a dusty feel. Latin-influenced, Spaghetti Western, Californian desert noir'. It is an odd collection of musical fragments and half-songs about chance encounters at service stations and the like. The edgy sound is dominated by heavy drum patterns and loud electric guitar, plus dabs of accordion, vibes, marimba, mandolin and cello, recorded on an eight track in Tucson. Additional musicians include a female drummer and a fiddle player.

They take their name from a town on the cusp between California and Mexico, and look 'south by southwest and over the border'. Their music takes on local sounds, on secondhand instruments, 'mariachi trumpets, clicking castanets and accordions. Not so much alt country as adobe country'. Having worked as a duo in LA, it was when they moved to Tucson that they began experimenting with local sounds, using old instruments bought. 'You hear the neighbours blasting out mariachi stuff on the AM radio. There are all these stations coming up from Mexico.'

They honed their sound at the Hotel Congress: 'John Dillinger's gang hid out there. People check in for 20 dollars and commit suicide. It's got that haunted feel.' As a two piece, with John on drums and Joey on everything else, it 'allowed us to explore a kind of improvisational jazz approach. But you can only do so much as a two piece, so we started to pick up local players everywhere we went.' At 'South By Southwest' they play a different bar on each of the five nights, with a pedal-steel player they borrow from Sally Timms, and a stray trumpeter.

Black Light was the second of a planned trilogy, a 'gorgeously textured, slow burn of an album, full of magical turns and soulful twists'.* The duo had planned to sample sounds from Bundy's huge collection of salsa, Cuban and Latin jazz sounds, but in the end played their own versions instead, creating a 'natural, organic brew that took the sound in a totally different direction'. Then they added lyrics to match. The words were written as a complete unit, not just as separate songs. It is the story of one man's journey 'into the desert, and out over the border and into the unknown'. Like life, really. As Joey explains, 'I wanted a modern-day version of Cormac McCarthy's *Border Trilogy*. The blood and the guts.'

Hot Rail completes this trilogy. As John puts it 'it carries on with the mariarchi influence and combines it with a country vibe and a jazz tinge'. They have even more ambitious plans, though. 'We'd like to arrange for an entire orchestra.' Meanwhile, they play a set of cover versions of Minutemen songs at the Congress and show in passing how the late D Boone's music was influenced by his own awareness of Mexican music, and lyrics like 'the dirt, scarcity and emptiness of our South'.

Burns agrees with John Mulvey that Calexico spin the 'alt country' spotlight onto the Southwest and its culture, taking in Gil Evans, the 'dust-caked twang of Duane Eddy and Lee Hazlewood', Ennio Morricone's widescreen passion, and even Californian punk. 'I like bringing all those aspects to this location, the greater Southwest'. On 2003's *Feast Of Wire*, he takes his main inspiration from the writings of Luis Alberto Urrea, who spent half a lifetime interviewing the inhabitants of Tijuana's garbage dumps.

* *Uncut* magazine

Feast Of Wire clarifies Calexico's 'complex vision of the Southwest as an area both stimulating and problematic, where economic realities play as critical a role as tumbleweed fantasies'. The voices are mixed higher this time, but it just makes weird lyrics about a 'head like a vulture's/ and heart full of hornets/he drives off the cliff, into the blue' in a song about a man's last moments listening to Stevie Nicks odder still.

They have played down the Mexican elements this time, giving a border song like 'Across The Wire' all the more impact with its trumpets and Tijuana swing. As a result, what one reviewer describes as 'music that can double you up with its beauty' shines through all the clearer. One track reminds you of Portishead, another pays tribute to Charles Mingus and Theolonious Monk. 'It makes us feel more connected to the whole, as opposed to just being associated with part of American music.'

Captain Beefheart (Don Van Vliet) is – or was – another man mixing up strange medicines in the desert, on the fault line where avante-garde jazz meets the old-country blues and campfire storytelling.

Don came from the town of Lancaster, deep in California's Mojave Desert. Long time drummer Don French grew up there too, in the 1950s. 'The freeway hadn't reached us and that affected the music. Don had no cultural input, no way of categorising or restricting things'. Ry Cooder plays slide on his debut *Safe As Milk*, a mixture of white blues and visionary fragments. Beefheart called 1969's *Trout Mask Replica*, his greatest creation, 'bush music'. To achieve it, he dismembered the 'fascist' rhythm of rock music, as well as afterthoughts like harmony and static time signatures, then put them back together again, like the avante-garde painter that he now is.

Any account of Americana can hardly ignore this album. Lester Bangs: *Trout Mask Replica* was a 'catarrh spew of images at once careeningly abstract and as basic and bawdy as the last 200 years of American folklore. This came closer to a living, pulsating, slithering organism than any other record I'd ever heard.' And nothing since has touched it.

In a recent biography, Mike Barnes has looked further into how a 'wide timespan of American culture is recontextualised, (as) demonstrated by the obvious quote from "Old Time Religion"'. 'Orange Claw Hammer' takes off from an album of sea shanties given to Van Vliet by his teenage best friend, Frank Zappa, and which, as late as 1980, he still claimed was his favourite record. Beefheart himself described the work in progress on this album as 'field recordings' done at the group's house, and with brief snatches of conversation between songs. 'The Dust Blows Forward 'n' The Dust Blows Back' was created with the tape pause button audibly pressed down after each line. It now sounds as if recorded on a field trip by Cecil Sharp in different universe. But this is also an aural canvas that can encompass Dachau and riding freight trains and talking to the bears and the sad realisation that 'man's lived a million years and still he kills'.

Which brings us to Charles Manson, the ultimate purveyor of 'desert rock'. Manson's own music, either the demo tapes financed by various ex-Beach Boys or more recent in-cell recordings smuggled out from maximum security, is close to traditional country. 'Put him in a plaid shirt and a stetson and he could be the truck-driver's favourite.' He sounds a lot like David Allen Coe.

The odder side of Manson's 'music' consists of strange monologues in which he seems to free associate, and you almost see his mind, a genuinely disturbing mixture of expletives, threats and echoes of his own particular favourite, Hank Williams. Needless to say, the governing metaphor of one of the strangest, 'Dream Train', is our old favourite, the locomotive powering down its long, straight track.

'And I board my dream train back home to you
back to you Luke the Drifter, Hank Williams…

Now Elvis, the epitome of fake phoney jive on freak
you made a laughing stock of country music,
you took away my cowboy feet
you thought you had someone's heartbeat
but Lefty Frizell and Hank Williams was riding that train
and then there was Woody Guthrie, he used to sing
he'd sing them folks right to insane
listening to the radio
My Oklahoma angel'.

v) Avant Garde

'Surrural' – *Tom Waits*

Tom Waits started off sounding like Charles Bukowski playing piano in a late-night bar, and singing everything that Bruce Springsteen left out, and in the voice of a dime-store Sinatra, with some horrible throat disease. Romanticising the intractably unromantic. The stuff he laid down on *Asylum*, largely recorded live in the studio, was supremely urban music, and extremely theatrical at that. A song like 'Ol' 55' from his 1973 debut *Closing Time* is about a scuzzy car, not a steam train.

You couldn't get much further away from country music than Tom Waits. Dirty saxophones and diseased lowlife, rather than pedal steel and hickory winds, New York dives, not mountain hollers or life on the range. Yet, just like the best country music, he scraped off the glossy surface of his chosen location – in this case the decadence of LA – to show what crawled underneath, stories of messy failure and dreams gone sour.

After 30 years, his life's work can be seen as the impurest essence of Americana. A rare live appearance at 'South By Southwest' is still talked about in hushed voices. The turning point was a move to Island records, and the 1983 album *Swordfishtrombones*. Tom had chopped up his piano for firewood, and he set out his new agenda on the opening track, to stomping percussion and a distorted brass band, 'there's a world going underground'. It was an antidote to the '80s, and its pursuit of smart living: a 'gothic' mirror image of what was going on.

The influences were easy to spot: Beefheart, Charly Patton, the avante garde composer Harry Partch. But Waits derived a delirious new sound, 'teeming with life and vitality', using calliopes, tubas, glass harmonicas, marimbas, trombones, squeeze drums, Balinese percussion, plus found sounds – 'chains dragged across the studio floor, meal lockers beaten with a two-by-four, bells were pealed and police bullhorns squawked'. A little-seen video of the emotive, joyful, transgressive 'In The Neighbourhood' saw Waits lead a procession of lowlifes, dwarfs and the like along a suburban street, like The Doors *Strange Times* album cover come to life. Except that this time the artist looked like part of the carnival.

Swordfishtrombones was like a cry of resistance, as much a jolt to middlebrow complacency as the *Harry Smith Anthology*, 'a vibrant and instructive aesthetic'* created out of scraps and secondhand instruments (just like Calexico), 'a bricolage of broken dreams and dismantled music'. Time has made it sound timeless, albeit with 'a strange, angry, ghostlike quality'. Along with two further instalments of the same urban myths, *Rain Dogs* and *Frank's Wild Years*, drawn from a stage show, the spirit celebrated here is all too human, clinging to existence with the blind determination of a weed seeking a crack in the pavement, and influenced a whole generation of lo-fi cowboys, from Wilco to Mercury Rev.

But Waits' 'wracked and horrified peak'† on 1993's *Bone Machine* is a true horror show for the ears, with a rough, despairing humour worthy of Samuel Beckett; a world of pimps and poison and updated murder ballads in the red barn. But the most graphic song of all is 'Dirt In The Ground', each word rasped out by Waits over funereal New Orleans brass. Even Ralph Stanley doesn't look at death any closer.

With the *Mule Variations*, Waits himself noted a shift in his subject material to something 'more rural – what I like to call somewhere between surreal and rural, or surrural'. When he released two albums at once in 2002, both based on stage shows, *Wire* found him 'sitting comfortably outside Americana's pseudo genre' – how dare he – 'and effortlessly linking American and European traditions'. Alice is based on the sinister childscape of Lewis Carroll, but Waits adds his own black humour: 'let the crows pick me clean but for my hat'. *Blood Money* evolves from Georg Buchner's play *Woyzek*, performed in a style 'where a barker from a medicine show is mysteriously transported to the Weimar Republic, via Tin Pan Alley'. Waits himself describes it – completely inaccurately – as 'bad news out of a pretty mouth', and there is a rough humour here to balance the doominess.

At the Beacon in autumn 1999, his first live concert in 13 years, he suddenly stands 'twice as tall', with guitar in hand like a new Woody Guthrie, offering up the affecting 'Jersey Girl'. Musically, he builds on 'every thread of Americana imaginable'**: carnival barker, minstrel showman, lots of country ('but subtly'), Beefheart, show tunes, even the imaginary South of Brecht and Weill's *Happy End*.

* Gavin Martin   ** Barry Mazor, *Uncut* magazine
† *Uncut* magazine

Waits has long acknowledged the influence of Harry Smith, 'digested early when he was a folk-club doorman', and here his interest is in the new weird America. He keeps country music's lyricism, but discards its usual sound. No wonder that the Violent Femmes and Dave Alvin are among those who have recorded his songs, with their own old-time twist. And yet, at the end of this performance, the hard-bitten New York audience are singing along like a hootenanny crowd, or a tent show. 'It's his last and greatest trick. Like a great country singer. No trick at all.'

Pere Ubu's lead singer David Thomas is a man of weird obsessions, and an ability to evoke the backroads and back alleys of modern America, without sentiment. Pere Ubu's early music is a clanging requiem for the industrial wastelands of Cleveland. *St Arkansas* is their 18th album, not bad for a band that planned to break up after releasing one single. This is America, viewed from inside a car – 'I love that highway US 322.' But by the end, Thomas claims to have 'lost my will by the side of the road'.

The *Mirror Man* stage show, a 'Road Opera', was an attempt to recapture the spirit of small-town America, before they 'took that smallness and made it big'. It was first performed in April 1998, at Queen Elizabeth Hall, London, and the first half was later released as *Mirror Man: Act 1: Jack And The General*. Jack is Kerouac, forever on the road, and the General is Eisenhower, who as President developed the network of Interstate Highways, 'nothing to do with getting somewhere and everything to do with time and space and the hieroglyphics of the mind'.

It has since solidified into a bargain-basement Broadway musical with spoken passages and an array of great singers. The narrator (Bob Holman) speaks tonelessly into a '30s radio mic. The first singing voice is Jack Kidney from the Numbers band in punk Cleveland, howling into another microphone. Then David Thomas opens his mouth and out comes that patented bleat, and we're off. We also have Linda Thompson – re-emerging from a long musical retirement – and her fellow Scot Jackie Leven, whose duet with Thomas on a desolate 'Surf's Up' is one of the stage highlights. Players and singers are arranged in a broad semi-circle, like an updated minstrel show. The settings are a truck stop and a bus stop. Act One 'happens in the space where you are and where you want to be, where the county seat is Nowheresville'. So does Act Two.

There's accordion from Thomas, plus distorted trumpet, electronic percussion and maestro harmonica from Jack Kidney, so that the music sounds at once from the past and the future. The overriding literary influence is beat poetry, mixed in with Edgar Lee Masters' *Spoon River Anthology* – a series of graveyard tales from a smalltown cemetery – and a strong dose of Woody Guthrie. 'Native folk culture in 21st Century is a driven and heroic scrabbling together of...pop songs, handcrafted iconographies, and the odd issue of *Practical Mechanics* magazine.'

A press release talks of how *Mirror Man* aims to show how places absorb sound, and then 'underwrite different sensibilities...of "home"'. And here, nowhere is an America of the mass unconscious, home and abroad, and it is evoked in a whole tapestry of folk tales.

David Thomas has not lived in the States since 1984, which gives him the 'heightened perception of the exile'.* Here is a landscape of 'forlorn, hand-crafted theme-parks', with electronically mutated music to match, drawn from sci-fi movies and spaghetti westerns, and evoking images of 'weird Midwest weather whistling down Lost Nation Road'.

Act Two has yet to appear on disc, but 'Surf's Up' is on the album of that name, with more of David's own songs, located among the 'dried rivers, broken bridges, lost highways and ghost towns of Thomasville'.

Eugene Chadbourne fled New York to avoid the draft. When he returned from Canada, in 1977, he was a genuinely wild free-form guitarist. Nevertheless, he has forged a strange synthesis of avante-garde jazz and what seems like a genuine love for bluegrass and old-time country. Outside of *Shockabilly*, most of his solo stuff is very rare and usually released by Eugene himself, and mostly on vinyl or cassette.

Terror Has Some Strange Kinfolk (1993) is a series of duets with Evan Johns, two hot pickers for the price of one, plus a rhythm section, and it sounds like western swing through a distorting mirror. And yet, unlike the debut album by Chicago's Pinetop Seven, the kind of band who seem to play deliberately a little out of tune, there is something winning in the dischords here. Even the *Wire*, the most tolerant music magazine going, finds Eugene sometimes so 'wilfully contradictory' as to be perverse. His album covers are deliberately messy, to give that scuzzy 'hobo' feel, and sometimes his angular guitar lines are to match. He meets his match on

* *Mojo*

Camper Van Chadbourne, where Camper Van Beethoven add real musicianship to his toneless versions of the likes of 'Ballad Of Easy Rider'. And yet there are passages of real beauty on that album, admittedly usually when Chadbourne isn't singing.

Perhaps albums like *There'll Be No Tears Tonight* (1980) with their 'free improvised country and western bebop' or *LSD C&W* – which includes a Roger Miller medley – or the now surely banned *Country Music In The World Of Islam* are better imagined than actually heard. That really is the Red Clay Ramblers playing on *Country Protest*, while *Strings* is dedicated to 'one of the true giants of bluegrass, John Coltrane.'

In 1996, Chadbourne recorded *Jesse Helms Busted* with *Pornography: A C&W Opera*, which sees the long overdue return of the Legendary Stardust Cowboy, alongside Jimmy Carl Black working their way through some country covers. The most significant item in his catalogue is *Texas Sessions: Chapter Two (To Doug)*, mostly retreads of Doug Sahm songs with Doug's own favourite bassist , drummer, and steel guitarist, and it works a treat.

As compared to The Residents who ponder everything first, and control every last 'random' note. These anonymous Californians benefited from the occasional slide-guitar interjections of Snakefinger, aka Phil Lithman, once of London pub rockers Chilli Willi. They paid a twisted tribute to Hank Willliams, alongside John Philip Sousa on volume two of their 'The American Composer Series', 1986's *Stars* and *Hank Forever*, with songs like 'Jambalaya' treated to a disco beat. The band got out from behind their computers and toured Europe 'live' with *Cube-E*, their history of American music in '3 E-z Pieces'. The show opened with dancers silhouetted against the moon, with '100-gallon hats on their heads, and an electric campfire at their feet'. The resulting album devotes one whole, seemingly interminable vinyl side to *Buckaroo Blues*, with traditional cowboy material like 'Oh Bury Me Not On The Wild Prairie' sung without any noticeable emotion, and to the sound of coyotes and clopping hooves. The whole thing sounds curiously, and deliberately, dead.

But the real impetus for what alt country has largely turned into has been that of 'lo-fi' and its bedfellows. The Pinetop Seven redeemed themselves – to me, at least – for their near unlistenable debut, with what followed. Two former psychology students, Charles Kim and Darren Richard subsumed the avante-garde influences of everyone from Charles Ives to Tom Waits to form an other-worldly sound on albums like *Bringing Home The Last Great Strike*.

It is a rich mix of distant voices, banjo, clarinet and violins, and with words to match, making no overt sense. On 'A Black Eye To Be Proud Of' 'the rails go on for good/and the crazy lights and sounds'. After all that twang, the way forward is what even so conservative a magazine as the *Country Music Journal* describes as 'gentle, unsettling compositions of subtle beauty'.That is exactly where we are going next.

vi) Lo-Fi

'If Michael Jackson wants all the money we've made from this record, he's welcome to the whole fifty bucks.'

– Lambchop

'Lo-fi' is a term invented by Dave Goodman to describe the brand of alt country that is 'played and sung at a snail-on-quaaludes pace, setting a mood ranging from dreary to downright menacing.' Melan Country is another description. *Trouser Press* calls it 'country 'n' strychnine'.

A less elegant phrase is 'Woodchuck Nation', coined by Lambchop, from the sleeve note on *I Hope You're Sitting Down*. Ben Thompson argues that some of the most 'bewitching' sounds of the '90s have been made by 'quiet Americans singing the body acoustic'.

One of the first bands to play in this style and at an increasingly funereal pace, years before it became fashionable, was Chicago's Souled American. They were formed in 1983, well before alt country was even thought of, by guitarist Chris Grigoroff and bass player Joe Adducci – whose instrument often takes lead role. With a second guitarist and drummer, they created a strong impression at 'South By Southwest' in 1988. The same year saw their debut *Fe*, and the next year *Flubber*, their two most accessible albums, with hillbilly vocals and honky-tonk playing, and 'a rowdy, drunken landscape of the Deep South',* straight out of a

* Peter Doggett

Harry Crews' novel. 'Marleyphone Hank' fuses Bob Marley and Hank
Williams, to a reggae rhythm.

Their 1992 album *Sonny* was a collection of covers of the Louvin
Brothers and Merle Travis and the like, taken at a snail's pace. 'Haunting
and hypnotising stuff.'* Later albums like *Notes Campfire* seemed to
enter the realm of parody, scaling old-time music down to 'single tones,
long guitar chords, intermittent drumdots and mournful singing'†. Their
track 'Suitors Bridge' on the compilation *Howl* is like punk music in
reverse – their music has slowed down to a drone, a universe in stasis.

The real pioneers of lo-fi were The Cowboy Junkies, once memorably
described as 'country music on valium'. They were outsiders from the
start, due to their being based in Toronto – with a short spell in New
York in 1980 – and having their roots in Hunger Project, a band heavily
influenced by The Cure and Gang of Four. Under their new name The
Cowboy Junkies, itself an assault on truth and decency, their 1986 debut
Whites Off Earth Now! is an album of intense versions of blues and
psychedelic rock, plus Springsteen's 'State Trooper', with something
stranger lurking just under the surface. To promote it, the band toured
the Southwest, and recognised a deep kinship between their sultry passion
and country music. The spectacular result was *The Trinity Sessions*,
recorded live in 1987 at the Church of the Holy Trinity in Toronto, using
one microphone and a digital two-track recorder.

The album opens with Margot Timmins' solo rendition of the
traditional song 'Mining For Gold', then a muted electric band gently
embroiders the rest. Three of them are her brothers, with Michael
Timmins on clipped lead guitar, plus friends adding fiddle, mandolin,
pedal steel, harmonica and accordion, all finessed by Margot's gentle
but insistent lead vocals. The set list stretches from Hank Williams' 'I'm
So Lonesome I Could Cry' to 'Sweet Jane', genuinely regretful and with
much more heart than Lou Reed's original, plus loads of original songs.

This album lit the blue touch paper for a revival of quiet music,
far beyond 'lo-fi'. When the band started playing live in bars, often
the pinball machine was louder than them, and with the band seated
and completely silent 'in the passages when they weren't being
extremely quiet'.**

* *The Rough Guide*   ** Peter Doggett
† *Modern Twang*

Looking back years later, *Uncut* described *The Trinity Sessions* as having 'dragged the forlorn mannerisms of country into a new era, ditching the trad in favour of shell-shocked, transcendent eeriness'. Except that what they are doing is relocating the eeriness that was already there in early country. Live, The Cowboy Junkies could be far more in line with their true predecessors the Velvet Underground, 'often laid-back to the verge of inertia, sometimes diving startlingly into white thrash'.

This side of the band would occasionally surface on later albums, to thrilling effect. Their back catalogue, including the obligatory live album, *200 Miles*, and a more than usually interesting collection of outtakes, *Rarities, B-Sides And Slow, Sad Waltzes*. The latter, *Record Collector* found a great album in its own right, 'which can stand proudly alongside Wilco, Whiskeytown and Blue Mountain'.

But the ace in the pack is 2001's *Open*, described by the band themselves as 'menacingly beautiful'. Critics sometimes accuse the band of being depressing, and Margot always counters that 'the characters we sing about fight against the depression and try to get somewhere better', On a later album, they perform 'Blue Guitar', a tribute to their friend Townes Van Zandt that includes lyrics from his unfinished and suitably grim song 'Screams From The Kitchen'.

At much the same time as The Cowboy Junkies were discovering the new quiet, over in Perth, another colonial outback, The Triffids were coming to much the same conclusion. Country stylings on albums like *In The Pines*, recorded in a sheep-shearing shed in 1986, and the following year's *Calenture* – an album about dislocation – were provided courtesy of 'Evil' Graham Lee on lap steel. He and The Triffids' lead singer David McComb later went on to form one of Australia's few alt-country bands the Blackeyed Susans, before David was killed in a car crash.

Another much-touted influence on lo-fi (which he denies – 'it means nothing to me') is Smog, aka Bill Callaghan with a rotating line-up of sidemen, of whom it was once said that 'with his mournful, deadpan voice, he is 33 going on 70'. Ben Thompson describes him as 'a less trustworthy Kris Kristofferson' or a 'post-punk Leonard Cohen'. Bill himself says that he writes mainly for 'jilted men'. It is a shock to then see how young he still looks.

His music was never really 'country' as such, more experimental and sheerly miserable, but with a pleasant singing voice. Bill's 1995 debut *Wild Love* is rich in moody cellos and bedsit angst, but an EP of the same year, produced by Steve Albini, stripped things down 'to the point of nothingness', apart from 'some skeletal strumming and the gentlest tapping of a tambourine, almost *a cappella*'.* Then, in 1997, came his masterpiece, *Red Apple Falls*, with hurdy gurdys and pedal steel.

His lyrics are extremely unsettling, about girls on mortuary slabs and making a doll out of a lover's discarded clothes, and then making love to it. As to his music, it is so slow and introverted that it sounds like the universe running down.

Knock Knock (1999) was written in a remote South Carolina farmhouse, and is full of images like 'I lay back in the tall grass/and let the ants cover me'. But it also has a chorus of children from a Chicago city choir, who seem to be laughing at him. A later song is titled 'Dress Sexy At My Funeral'. As compared to the truly glacial nature of latter day Souled American, and the hypnotism of The Cowboy Junkies, this later lo-fier is really quite a joker, even if he now seems to be developing an unnatural affection for cathedrals and high altars.

Live with a band including Jim White on drums at the Old Vic, he is mesmeric and shows a 'refreshing streak of cruelty, while his ensemble sound like the Velvets playing Afrobeat, 'utterly implausible but oddly beguiling'. *Mojo* described his recent album *Supper* as equally ground breaking, with freeform drums and banjo fills forging 'previously unimagined links between The Carter Family and Pharoah Sanders.

Will Oldham inspires devotion and derision in roughly equal measure. He changes his name from Palace to Palace Brothers to Palace Music to Palace Songs to Bonnie 'Prince' Billie, and sometimes even uses his own, but always sounds much the same, kind of amateurish. He told *Mojo* that 'I like old music, but it doesn't seem different to me from new music. As for Greil Marcus's vision of America, well fuck him.'

Will was raised in small-town Kentucky, then briefly moved to New York to make his name as an actor, notably as the Depression-era child preacher in John Sayles' 1987 movie *Matalan*. Instant wealth followed, then something probably close to a nervous breakdown. He became his

* *Uncut* magazine

most famous part. He gave up acting, and moved back to live with his older brother, Paul. While out sailing, he had a 'catatonic episode'. 'I knew there was something wrong and that I didn't know how to fix it. My brother said 'Why don't you put a band together and play some of those Virginia songs.' He began playing around Louisville.

Oldham formed Palace and its offshoots with friends, family members and even some college professors: the first line-up of all was called Palace Flophouse, a duo with his elder brother. 'When we coined the name Palace Brothers, we were specifically thinking of the Everlies and the Louvins. But we had it easier than they did, we weren't thrust together at the age of four, like the Everlies. I think their music is my longest-standing favourite music.' He subsequently recorded with two of his own brothers, Ned and Paul.

The Palace collective was set up with a game plan of letting things flow in the studio, without undue preparation. What resulted was a scratchy, melancholic, death-obsessed reverie, sometimes barely in tune, and the closest that anyone now alive has ever come to recreating the inner world of Dock Boggs. 'Behind you, I have warned you, there are awful things.'

What actually turned him onto the music was a Mekons tour of the States, as he told Gavin Martin. 'They were making all sorts of weird music and got called country by the same stupid press that I get called country by.' It was through the Leeds band that he first heard Gram Parsons – 'I went to see them in New Orleans, and they did 'Sin City'. Sally Timms sang it *a capella*, and it was like 'Awesome song, who wrote it?' As to the band Gram so briefly joined, though, 'I hate The Byrds, I've always loathed The Byrds. I can't stand them.' And wrath and hatred seem to be among Will's most powerful emotions.

Let's look at his 1993 debut as the Palace Brothers. From its deliberately ungrammatical title, *There Is No One What Will Take Care Of You*, to its equally deliberate out-of-tune vocals, this is a collective of young men – principally from alt rock legends Slint, and doubtless influenced by the Mekon's anti-stardom – playing guitars and banjo extremely slowly. The songs seem to go nowhere, just hang in the air, with titles like '(I Was Drunk) At The Pulpit' and 'Idle Hands Are The

Devil's Playthings', and lyrics that you at first don't believe you are hearing, like 'his head buried within the breasts of a lunatic'. It is all oddly hypnotic, like a private treasure hoard.

Even so, you do wonder how this got released. There is no sense here of kids mucking about, or taking liberties. Rather, this is all played and sung with a weird, steely kind of determination. One song, 'Riding', is about a boy's unnatural love for his sister Lisa, and suddenly Will is singing almost beautifully, and the instruments coalesce into a slow blues. The verses take on the question/response pattern of traditional murder ballads. Both the song and Oldham's voice rise to a terrifying, triumphant climax: 'I'm long since dead and I live in hell/she's the only girl that I love well/we were raised together and together we fell'.

Peter Doggett hears music with 'the strangeness of a serial killer secluded in rural desolation', even though it owes no more to Hank Williams than it does to Charles Manson. *Uncut* finds a man 'consciously disappearing into the world of an Appalachian farmer'. *Trouser Press* goes as far as to compare Will's voice to Ira Louvin's, and the whole thing to Depression-era country.

Will next covered the Mekons' 'Horses' on a subsequent EP, and on his (barely length) album *Palace Brothers* – a totally solo recording, of course – he actually sees himself as equine, 'I am a racing horse, I am a grazing horse, I am your favourite horse.' Maybe this is why Ben Thompson reckons that his voice 'strains and cracks like an old saddle'. The recording quality is far better than the debut, and everything is in tune, which only serves to make the songs more terrifying. 'Will you miss me when I burn/and will you close the others' eyes/it would be a such a favour if you were blind, now.' Another song is about Pushkin, though it might be the name of a thoroughbred.

In interviews, Oldham is infuriating (and probably deliberately) inarticulate. Remember, he is an actor. He once described *No Depression*, and the music it so bravely champions in *Time Out New York* as being a 'culturalist, racist magazine' writing about a 'certain kind of white music'. This from a man who sings about 'half breeds and lesbians'.

It all rebounded, with one reader, who teaches Afro-American literature but also loves alt country, describing Will as a 'jackass'. Another reckoned that Oldham could hardly throw the first stone, when his own market comprised 'more "whites only" than you could find at a drinking fountain in the deep South in the early '60s. And this from a musician with 'ludicrous vocal stylings and obscure, seemingly meaningless lyrics'. Even Ed Ward, doyen of rock critics, had once seen the Palace Brothers, and hated them. People who loved alt country would probably love alt soul too. Most of them would have racially integrated record collections, and maybe Oldham would one day be represented in his own, amongst the Stanley Brothers, Don Covay, Henry Purcell and Ray Davies. Somehow, you doubted it.

Sean O'Hagan from the High Llamas joined Will's band for the mini-album *Hope*, which is something closer to conventional rock music – slowed down, true – with Hammond organ. *Viva Last Blues*, was even more so – loud and cacophonous. But 1996's *Arise Therefore* was back to acoustics, a 'backporch recording',* except that it is so primitive that you doubt if there is even a porch. Banjo and cardboard box percussion are strictly subordinate to 'cracked-voice renderings of Pentecostal fury and sordid behaviour'. The roughly typed lyrics are there for all to see, about angry sex and hatred and something close to a lynching.

Yet Oldham can also record something as ethereal as *Blue Lotus Feet*, five 'devotional songs', just him, his guitar and his God. This is Will in tabernacle-going mode. 'When Thy Song Flows Through Me' sounds truly ecstatic as he repeats over and over phrases like "life is sweet and death is a dream", with something close to religious abandon.

This is followed immediately with the x-rayed skull decorating the front cover of *I See A Darkness* (1999), under the name *Bonnie Prince Billy*. The new moniker is presumably a reference both to Billy the Kid and William of Orange, close to the heart of the provocatively Protestant beliefs of the Scots Irish emigrees from Ulster to the Appalachians.

The haunted beauty of *I See A Darkness* inhabits a world all of its own, with one chorus, sung over and over again, 'Death to everyone is gonna come/it makes hosing much more fun'. The sound is electric, in more senses than one. His songs have gradually revealed more of a 'latent spirituality', and an emphatically Southern brand, at that. The title track is both hymn-like and 'oddly ominous'[†]. No wonder, as it balances his

* *Trouser Press*
† Sean O'Hagan

'love for everyone I know' with something else deep inside him, which comes 'blacking in my mind'. Oldham is 'both a product of the American South and an extreme reaction against it'.* And totally unique.

Allan Jones finds a man beginning to locate some kind of inner peace, just as 'the scars of last year's storm rest like maggots on my arm'. The result is an album of 'immense and fragile beauty, full of trembling emotional meditations'.

Will's good mood continues into 'Ease Down The River', even if he is just 'making records and writing songs, it's not like I'm publishing diaries. The title was maybe an attempt to convince myself that things were getting easier'. The closing track is 'Rich Wife Full Of Happiness', with banjo accompaniment, 'an earthy declaration of love and laughter'†.

Master And Servant (2003), and was another new departure, with careful production by Mark Nevers, who had also smoothed up Lambchop on Nixon, and with Nashville-type duets. This is the first Oldham album that you could call professionally recorded, even if details like his fingers sliding down the guitar strings, could still be heard.

Oldham has also had singing lessons, maybe, but there is still that same old mix of sin and salvation: 'let your unloved parts get loved'. As he sleepily duets with Marty Slayton, 'there's no pain to the night/and no dream undreamt'. But, being Oldham, the final song ends with Will saying hello to his 'demons' again, and moaning for release. 'Let me go/where you don't know,' he quietly howls, like a wolf with its paw stuck in a trap – there's something feral and untamed about Oldham, and the quieter he gets, the more closely you listen.

Even Grant Alden finds forgiveness in his soul, describing this album as a 'beautiful piece of work', of finished songs – 'polished, even' – amid well-played music. But there are various stings in the tail. 'He sings of life, love, solitude and faith, and quite possibly has a few worthwhile things to say on those subjects. He may even mean what he says'.

For *The Guardian*, it is an album of 'whispers and echoes', and if country music at all, it is 'country heavy and glittering with frost'. There was only one dissenting voice. Ian Penman moaned that 'all I previously loved about Oldham is gone, all the messy jouissance scoured, all mood swings erased, and it just sounds to me as so-what tasteful as 50 other

* Sean O'Hagan
† *Uncut* magazine

"Roots Album Of The Year"-type artefacts'. Spectacularly wrong, as usual, mistaking a smoother sound for a less troubled soul, Penman does identify a key problem in alt country – how do you make your sound palatable for a wider audience without watering it down?

Nobody is ever going to tidy up Will Oldham for long, and *Guarapero: Lost Blues 2*, released under his own name, fails to cohere into anything more than a gathering together of loose ends. Two tracks come from the original *Guarapero*, an abandoned project with Steve Albini, and others include a Lynyrd Skynyrd cover and a live tribute to the Mekons.

Playing at 'Further Beyond Nashville' at the Barbican, Will skips on stage playing a child-sized guitar, then sings about 'that grand, dark feeling of emptiness': the most affecting thing all night is a couple of 'spare' songs performed just with his brothers, including a 'goosebump-raising "Weaker Soldier"'. Somehow, Oldham seems to have survived his own inner battles. No wonder that Johnny Cash chose to re-record 'I See A Darkness' as part of his *American Recordings* series.

There are many other one-man bands putting out uneasy listening, and we have time and space only for the briefest of trawls. *Songs: Ohia For Cleveland* is 99 per cent Jason Molina, and he has been much compared with Oldham. Here was yet another moody backwoodsman, with a whiny voice to match, and an obsession with the more savage passages from the Old Testament, chewed over in songs like 'Sin And Death'. But unlike his mentor, Molina could sometimes even be playful, and a later album like The Magnolia Electric Show inhabits a more tuneful and human place even if studded with lines like 'Mama here comes midnight, with the dead moon in its jaw'.

Birddog was really Bill Santen, from Portland, and he/they recorded a mini album in 1997, *The Trackhouse, The Valley, The Liquor Store Drive-Thru*, with Charlie Campbell on cello. More recently, Paul Oldham, Will's brother and saviour, produced *Songs From Willipa Bay*, a lovely album as moody and bleak as its cover, a featureless grey sea, and with lyrics like 'sleeping in the arms of the devils and the lost stars'.

Let's look at three singer/songwriters brave enough to appear in public under their own names. Richard Buckner followed a boyhood spent in California with singing for tips on the streets of San Francisco, and a style learnt from his great hero Townes Van Zandt. His sombre, deep voice has been described as a cross between a 'keening Will Oldham and a trembling Jay Farrar'. A debut album in 1994 featured sparse backings from Butch Hancock on harmonica and Lloyd Maines on steel. But the real falling apart came on his 1997 masterpiece *Devotion And Doubt*, backed by members of Giant Sand. Buckner likes to write songs that capture people in crisis: 'they're just teetering and you get their experience just before they go over the edge'. This time round, Buckner himself was on the edge. His recent divorce was the real subject, told obliquely. This is a haunted album, full of slow chords and odd scrapings, plus a cricket chirping away on 'On Travelling', a sound imbued with 'warm, bittersweet darkness',* oozing out of the speakers like liquid.

The songs are given an even more unplugged setting on a live album recorded solo at the Blackeyed Pig. Buckner went on to make the 34-minute, one-track *The Hill*, a further raid on Edgar Lee Masters' *Spoon River Anthology*, cross referencing some of the key poems. The result is music that, like all the best alt country, comes on both 'quietly archival and utterly avante-garde'. And he is still exploring.

Neal Casal's work is lighter and more polished, less quietly desperate, reflecting his adopted home in California, though listen a little harder and you can hear his New Jersey roots coming through. His debut album, 1995's *Fade Away Diamond Time* was compared to early Jackson Browne, but then his record company dropped him. Like many another alt-country maverick, he found a saviour in the German record label Glitterhouse. My own favourite is 1997's *Field Recordings*, with a full band playing organic rock, and in once case 'extremely loud piano'. It holds together beautifully, which is odd when you come to realise it is really a collection of demos and outtakes.

All the sadder then that when *The Guardian* reviewed him at the Borderline, they found that after seven 'mostly impressive' albums in five years, all on tiny budgets, he remains grateful for a bar gig. He plays with a 'puppy-like enthusiasm', obviously in love with the fact of being a musician. Neal is symptomatic of so many in the alt country field, well respected by a specialist press and audience, producing solid work, yet still struggling to make a living.

* *No Depression*

And then we have Jim O'Rourke, who is quite another kind of artist. 'Don't believe a word I say' is the opening statement on his great album from 2001, *Insignificance*, lush and driving and evil. Jim formed alt rock act the Elvis Messiahs in Chicago in 1987, and has since worked with everyone from Smog to John Fahey, plus touring with Sonic Youth, which re-introduced him to playing electric guitar. His own woozy albums have long had the reputation for being difficult, right from his debut *Bad Timing*. O'Rourke clearly admires the films of Nic Roeg, full too of subtle dislocations: *Eureka* was described as like 'Burt Bacharach on drugs'. *Insignificance* shows an unexpected influence, that of Lynyrd Skynyrd, but uses hard-rock traditions as something to be manipulated, with the help of a crack band, which includes Jeff Tweedy.

Vic Chesnutt was born in small-town Georgia, playing in bar bands until at the age of 18, on Easter Sunday, he got drunk and crashed his car into a ditch, broke his neck, and has been wheelchair bound ever since. Not that he has lost his sense of humour, with lines like 'a chip on the shoulder usually means there is wood up above'. Vic re-learnt how to play guitar with a pick superglued to a plaster cast. Most of his CDs look as handmade and amateur – not amateurish – as they sound, and here is a man with time on his hands to investigate everything, particularly himself. 'I'm just pushing the paint around/on advice from your lying mouth.'

Vic's debut album *Little* (1990) was produced by Michael Stipe and exemplifies the 'old weird America'* of the Victrola age, as captured on so many Smithsonian anthologies. Except that they were largely unconscious of their artistry, whereas Chestnutt knows exactly what he is doing. No-one from 1930s Appalachia could have put together so ambitious a song suite as his 1998 masterpiece, *The Salesman And Bernadette*, with Lambchop acting as Vic's orchestra. It is an album with the aural sweep of *Sergeant Pepper*, and even fewer connections between songs, not that you mind with writing of the quality of 'I'm a sorry, sorry knight in a horrible castle/hoping to avoid certain societal hassles.' Caustic at all times, even if this is sometimes disguised by mindlessly happy music. Chestnutt is 'one of the most engaging suicidal depressives around'†. Many tracks feature disillusionment, but Lambchop can sound like an off-key Mexican band, and Vic slur his words like a woozy Chet Baker.

* *No Depression*
† *Uncut* magazine

The more recent *Silver Lake* is another fine album, all the better for employing a 'crack band honed on Victoria Williams'. Like Will Oldham, Vic is a strong enough individualist not to be swamped by a more polished production. Lines like 'the barn owl's white belly is like a flash bulb' still infiltrate their way through. Vic reveals that 'the record I really wanted to make was going to be exploded even more than this'.

When Vic played the Union Chapel in London, though, he turned up drunk and without a set list, and then turned on the audience: 'You people are sucking something from me.' 'He trampled one new song after another into the dirt, seeming to have no game face, or show-must-go-on mode.'* Just like his songs.

Earlier, a group of Vic's admirers made a tribute album of his songs, including everyone you would expect, like Sparklehorse, Victoria Williams and Nanci Griffith, and some you wouldn't, like Madonna and her brother in law Joe Henry. *Gravity Of The Situation: The Songs Of Vic Chesnutt* brings out the sly wit and sheer melodicism of the man, and explains that the wheelchair is a total side issue.

Kurt Wagner formed Lambchop largely as a result of hearing Vic Chesnutt's debut album *Little*. 'It spoke to me right away… It was finally hearing a voice that didn't seem strange to me at all. It made me realise I wasn't crazy.' Kurt saw Chesnutt in Nashville, of all places. There were only three people in the audience, 'I was one, the rest were cops.' Vic had a sign 'I suck. Tapes $5,' so Kurt bought as many copies as he could, then gave them away to friends, many of whom were later to be sucked into Lambchop, a band – to use the term loosely – named after a TV glove puppet. Built out of free improvisation, and never using set lists, just following Kurt into whichever song he chooses next, this 'sly, slippery' band might be sprawling in nature, but construct an extremely subtle soundscape, always subordinated to Kurt's quiet, near-spoken vocals, and the strange folk tales he invents. 'It's a positive thing that people can't describe what we do,' Kurt explained to Peter Doggett, and he is proud to have 'been able to create something unique in music – whether it's popular or makes money isn't the point. It's great to still wonder, to challenge yourself to articulate what you do, to understand just a little bit of the mystery'. And mystery is at the essence of Lambchop's appeal.

* *No Depression*

Kurt's band inverts 'all our expectations of how a band should be, behave and sound'.* It is no coincidence that he was at university while American academia was under the heady thrall of deconstruction, denying any sense of 'authenticity' or individual talent.

He rejects any simple-minded attempt to label what he does as 'alt country'. 'I've never been very fond of that genre of music. I never really understood it. It was like the bad bar-room rock I grew up with.' Kurt was born in Maryland, but his parents moved to Nashville when he was two, and he always felt like a fish out of water. The town that he got to know was a violent and troubled place. Kurt soon found out that 'Nashville's not all Buck Owens and Roy Clark – it's an absolute fantasy, that yee-haw portrayal.' If a hillbilly singer turned up on TV, he would go and play his Monkee albums instead. As a teenager, he listened to the likes of Gram Parsons and the New Riders, acts abhorred by Music Row. 'Cosmic cowboy stuff, not what we'd have called country back then'.

Kurt went off to study art in Memphis, where he would see Elvis going off to his karate class, or bump into Rufus Thomas in the street. 'Memphis had a punk factor and a groove thing. I could feel it everywhere – even the hillbilly guys blended right in. It was mindblowing.' He would play lap steel with local punk bands, supporting the likes of Panther Burns, even if he missed the gig when The Sex Pistols hit town. He later moved to Chicago, where he saw a gig by the Mekons that turned him round. 'Singing Hank Williams in a totally new way – that interested me.'

Then Wagner's life began to fall apart, and he moved back to Nashville, where he began writing songs straight into a tape recorder, and formed a three-piece band, Posterchild, 'funny and cool and angry and sad; it was like Neil Young jamming on acid'. Kurt came to realise that 'the music I thought as a kid was terrible was truly great, moving stuff. I'd been in the heart of its creation and never realised it'. The results are bewitching – pedal steel and strings and clarinet and all kinds of percussive clatter (including open-end wrenches) all merge into a rich syrup behind Kurt's quiet, slow-paced vocals and upsetting lyrics. Even when appearing to be self-revelatory, the words tremble on the edge of sense: 'I don't speak well I mumble/to life's little tragedies/if you touch me I crumble/with songs from the wishing you well'. The same song refers to 'spit on the

* *Uncut* magazine

ceiling', about to drop on the listener's head. He is indeed saying the unsayable. In more ways than one – 'the idea that the mundane can carry a full emotional weight, that these songs are here to make things better, get you through'.*

Lambchop gradually coalesced, with a largely anonymous bunch of locals taking time off from their day jobs. As well as singing, writing the songs and playing a vintage 1929 Gibson guitar, Kurt himself laid hardwood floors, which provided a great fund of anecdotes for his songs. Line ups change from album to album, but 'professionals' include Music Row recording engineer Mark Nevers on guitar, Paul Burch on vibraphone, and classically trained Deanna Varagona. The pedal-steel player Paul Niehaus also toured with Calexico. The size of the band ranges from 9 to 17, depending on who's available.

Onstage, Kurt acts unassuming, but he seems to operate much the kind of thought control that we saw with Captain Beefheart. Newcomer Matt Swanson comments 'Kurt never tells me what songs we're going to play – it's his way of keeping things interesting, and keeping me a nervous wreck.'† He was brought in to replace another bassist, who then turned up anyway, so both are on board for the tour. 'I play in a lot of groups, but in Lambchop there's so much going on that you play less to allow room for everyone else.'

Their 1994 debut *I Hope You're Sitting Down*, later retitled *Jack's Tulips*, establishes a spooky countrypolitan. It still sounds unlike anything else on earth. The band was expanded further for the next year's *How I Quit Smoking*, with a fully integrated sound, and a four-piece string section. Next came the ten-inch EP *Hank*, supposedly their most country-orientated record of all, recorded as a series of one-off takes on the 4th of July. You can't get more Americana than that.

The next full-length album was named after Michael Jackson's best selling *Thriller*, and lasts precisely 33 minutes and 33 seconds, in tribute to the vinyl album. This marked a shift in their music towards Memphis soul and Ben Thompson is surely right to call it the best white soul album since Orange Juice's debut, though where that was the sound of sexy young Scotland, this is the noise made by seen-it-all Nashville, watching itself on the dance floor. 'It's so simple, it's so stupid.'

* *New Musical Express*
* *Uncut* magazine

223

Perverse as ever, Kurt decided to call the obvious radio-friendly track here 'Your Fucking Sunny Day', thus assuring that it barely troubled the airwaves. The album features three songs by the elusive New Yorker Fred Cornog, aka East River Pipe. Overall, Kurt found the new album 'a bit more dynamic – if you can use that word with reference to Lambchop – a little more like a real record'. He still can't resist a slight Johnny Cash parody on the opening track, 'My Face Your Ass'.

What Another Man Spills is more what we treasure from Lambchop, with covers of songs by Curtis Mayfield and Dump, but still really only 'half a record', as Wagner himself acknowledges. One review found that the R&B is 'that bit more funky' and the late-night countrypolitan 'more plaintive', but the overall mood is that of a man defeated by life. '

The year 2000 saw the release of *Nixon*, praised by nearly everyone, and described as everything from 'Nashphilly' to an alt country Pet Sounds. Its risk taking is breathtaking, not least with the final track, the murder ballad 'The Butcher Boy', an unsettling conjunction of the Doug Yule era Velvet Underground trying to boogie with brass arranged by Burt Bacharach. A glorious mess ensues. There's even a lyric sheet this time round, but being Lambchop the words are all jumbled up.

It is on this album that Wagner's 'mastery of the twisted love song comes to some sort of a peak', awash too with sweeping strings, the Bobby Jones Gospel Choir, pedal steel and stabbing brass. A *Forever Changes* for blank times. Tom Cox fell asleep while reviewing this narcotic aural sweep, left feeling numb and ambivalent by a band that doesn't seem to care, and a singer who never changes tempo. And who exactly is singing falsetto? I can see his point, but that is all itself part of the record, a concept album about life in a cynical and fallen world where all illusions to anything better or more noble have been shattered.

And though false hope certainly isn't on the agenda here, there's a counterbalance in Kurt's voice, which sounds battered but determined to keep going. The album puts Lambchop up there with Mercury Rev and the Flaming Lips of 'what we might call nouvelle-America, a re-drawing of the musical topography of America',* reinventing its traditional music and creating from it 'something vibrant and new and unclassifiable'.

* *Uncut* magazine

On *Is A Woman*, the sound is gentler, with the horns quieted right down. It's a 'sound no louder than a light wind through a tobacco barn', built around Tony Crowe's piano, and Kurt's strummed acoustic guitar. The results are dreamlike, 'at once traditional and utterly modern'.* Wagner, now freed from his day job, sounds more accepting, here in 'the afternoon of the new cobweb summer'. Producer Mark Nevers 'didn't want any gothic shit on it', keeping things 'light and breezy', on the surface at least. And though Kurt describes the album as 'dark and breezy', there is at least the possibility of love , 'and you take her hand as you gesture towards the bed/I can't believe this feels this good'.

Wagner once said 'I am a bad storyteller, or at least one who can never remember the punchline.' But that is exactly the point of his songs, that the punchline never comes when you would expect it. Live, Lambchop are something else. At the LA Troubadour in 1999, joined by both Calexico mainmen for the night, Neal Weiss was entranced by 'a frail and lilting bit of aural cinema', spanning R&B, folk and jazz and alt rock in its 'quiet presence'. Alt country, as it should be. Here was a band as mesmerising as the early REM, or classic Cowboy Junkies.

They are the tip of a considerable iceberg. Take your pick. LA's Acetone reached some kind of pinnacle with 1994's *I Guess I Would*, with 'whispery vocals and spare accompaniment'†, and cover versions of Gram Parsons, John Prine and the Fugs, plus an '11-minute grungy' take on Kris Kristofferson's 'Border Lord', which opens with fuzz guitar, but eases down into a 'drowsy jam'. The self-titled follow up was released on Neil Young's own label, more drone with a touch of twang, courtesy of Greg Leisz on pedal steel. A harder listen comes courtesy of the Black Boot Trio from Ottawa, and albums like *Blood* (1996) have been reviewed as 'acid and western'. Bloodshot describe Trailer Bride, a band they signed from Chapel Hill, as 'somnambulistic country', even if Melissa Swingle had formerly played bass with all-girl band Pussy Teeth. *Smelling Salts* is a particularly eerie listen, following on where songs like 'Graveyard' led on their 1996 debut. Then there are the aptly named Low, from Missouri, of whom has been written 'as much as they bathed us in light, the songs were edged in demonic darkness, funereally slow, gloriously sparse, and strangely uplifting'.**

* *No Depression*   ** *Maverick*
† *Modern Twang*

Grandaddy come from Modesto, California, and are alt country enough to have been recently chosen for the album of the month spot on Virgin's *Captain America* show, but spunky enough to rouse an audience, not embalm them– 'a warm and fuzzy sun seems to come out whenever Grandaddy are on the turntable'. To me they sound like a less mysterious and quieter Mercury Rev.

The Sophtware Slump (2000) uses decaying technology as a metaphor. 'Jed The Humanoid' drinks the family's booze, and wrecks his own circuit boards as a result. These boys relish mispellings, and the follow up album *Sumday* is a warmer affair, with Jason Lytle's tremulous quiver even more appealing as a result. Here is the magic in the everyday: 'Becky wondered why she had never noticed dragonflies'. He demands of himself, too, to 'be as creative as possible, stretch the boundaries'.

San Francisco's Granfaloon Bus follow on from the work of '80s bands like American Music Club. Lead singer Felix Costanza was once a member of the Lords Of Howling, based in New Mexico. *Good Funeral Music* (1998) was issued by a record label in Dusseldorf, though the songs themselves sound as if translated from a foreign language, and badly at that. Macabre too: 'now that Helen's dead we can put a "for sale" sign on the hearse'. But the music itself can be quite cheery, even if it sometimes sounds like two separate bands playing at once, with military drums and metallic guitars rubbing up against tuneful and laid-back vocals. Weird stuff, which is never likely to hit the mainstream, so, if you don't categorise it under Americana, I hardly know where else to put it – its hardly rock music.

But what 'lo-fi' is really about is the manipulation of textures. Kurt Wagner is a master, and so, in a different way, is Daniel Lanois, who creates a magical alchemy down in his New Orleans nerve centre. State-of-the-art technology meets vintage instruments and lots of echo in the vocal booth. The results include works such as Emmylou Harris's *Wrecking Ball* and Dylan's double whammy of *Oh Mercy* and *Time Out Of Mind*, with Lanois prising every last nuance from that ruined voice.

Lanois started his professional career as a pedal-steel player in his native Quebec. His solo debut, 1989's *Acadie*, ranges from gospel hymns and Aaron Neville singing 'Amazing Grace' to French language songs and is the sort of album The Band might have made 'if their studio had been a city art gallery rather than a rustic Woodstock homestead'.*

This personal variant of Americana continues into the wider sound palette of *For the Beauty Of Wynona*. Who could resist 'Death Of A Train', a slow lament with synthesised locomotive noises blowing around his quiet, solemn voice? The year 2003 saw the third in this loose trilogy, and *Shine* has a sparse and subdued beauty, laced with pedal steel, to demonstrate Lanois's 'conjurer's way with texture'. Lanois, although in his 50s 'continues to push North American music in new directions'†.

There is a whole bunch of lo-fi bands creating rich tapestries of sound, with the same kind of inner discipline as Lanois. Nebraska's *Lullabye For The Working Class* added cello, violin and trumpet to the alt-country sound, and their 1996 debut *Blanket Warm*, was slow-paced, mournful and slightly disturbed. Construction Joe came from Vermont, and Nelson Caldwell's electric cello threads its way through their 1997 debut of the same name, especially when it plays against clawhammer banjo or slide guitar. Then there was San Francisco's US Saucer, loading their solitude onto a series of albums starting with the 1992 LP *My Company Is Misery*.

The richest sound of all came from the Mary Janes, an offshoot of Bloomington's Vulgar Boatmen, whose lead singer Janas Holt has her voice framed in 'mesmerising tiers of electric violin and viola', as Goodman exclaims, playing a sort of 'country chamber music', though by the time of their first album *Record No 1* (1999), much of the magic was dissipated.

But if you want luxuriant misery, then go straight to Dakota Suite who are actually from Leeds: the name is taken from the brownstone block outside which John Lennon was murdered. More ex-new wavers discovering that quiet is the new loud, the band include a Richard Formby of Spacemen 3, on all kinds of stringed things, while singer, Chris Hooson, writes the words. *Modern Twang* get the band just right, with songs like 'Crippled World' interpreted through 'weary vocals, sullen violin, brooding cello and weepy lap steel', and at a graveyard pace.

A later album like *Morning Lake Forever* drives along a little harder. The requisite cellos and violins still give background resonance, while Phil Madeira contributes pedal steel from Nashville, and the lyrics are still glum, with Hooson repeating 'I must be evil', over and over.

* *Trouser Press*
† *No Depression*

The Scud Mountain Boys began by jamming informally around a kitchen table: Joe Pernice on lead vocals, Bruce Tull on guitar, and Stephen Desaulniers on bass. Their name was an in-joke. Then they began to provide a quiet – though still electric – opening act to their better-known incarnation as Massachusetts rock band The Scuds. Suitably encouraged they went on to record a brace of albums of glorified demos, later re-released on one CD as *The Early Years*. There are interesting cover versions of Jimmy Webb's ethereal 'Where's The Playground, Susie' and 'Wichita Lineman', plus some of their own, low-key songs.

The Scud Mountain Boys' 'moodily magnificent'* sound is best captured on *Massachusetts*, recorded in 1996 in a proper studio in Hartford, Connecticut. By now, they have added a drummer, and the album rings like a vintage bell, especially whenever Tull adds perfectly tailored guitar breaks. Joe sings like a bruised angel, and his brother Bob adds more guitar on three tracks. This is one of the great alt-country albums, mysterious at heart, effortlessly tuneful, with odd song titles like the driving 'Cigarette Sandwich' and the melancholic 'Scratch Ticket'. The country element comes in Joe's aching vocals and in the subject matter, but even so this owes more to early Beatles than to Gram Parsons.

In the summer of 1997, Joe left the Scud Mountain Boys. A lot of the new songs he was writing were suited for strings and piano. 'I wanted to expand the sound a bit and try different songs and really indulge myself, which I couldn't do in the Scud Mountain Boys.' So he put together the Pernice Brothers, Joe and Bob and hand-picked sidemen, and they released *Overcome By Happiness*, which Joe proudly describes as a 'pretty and mellow pop record'. This is the realm of pure tunefulness inhabited by Big Star and The Raspberries.

The sounds inside are sugar sweet, with a string quartet, three trombones and a flugelhorn, but no pedal steel. Even so, the lyrics are still oblique and there is something forever 'rural' in Joe's fragile vocals, wherever he comes from. And as to the closing track, 'Ferris Wheel', gently whispered to strummed guitar, you couldn't really have more 'Americana' a subject, a carnival attraction doubling as the wheel of life: 'oh I don't want to die/but you never know 'til you fail'. If The Jayhawks are still 'alt country' then so is this, pop music with depth.

* *Uncut* magazine

Joe Pernice admits that 'I just naturally move towards darker, more introspective themes than the run-of-the-mill pop song', even though he clothes them in 'celestial' harmonies and arrangements. *The World Won't End* is even more so, a classic example of harmony pop, with a choir of male voices. The Beach Boys meet the Left Banke, with the Zombies hovering in the background. Reviewers made much of Joe's supposed change of image, having 'hung up his stetson, put a flower in his hair and created a summer pop masterpiece', then noticed lyrics like an 'open wound'. It might sound summery, but there are storm clouds looming.

Uncut caught the Pernice Brothers live, and reckoned Joe the supreme salesman of 'heartbreak with harmonies', even if he had realised just in time that alt country was 'too constricting, its habitually melancholic lilt too glib for what he was trying to achieve'. Except that Joe still sounds melancholic, though never glib. Look closer at the backing musicians on *The World Won't End*, and you will find members of the Sadies and Whiskeytown, while Joe's low-key solo album *Chappaquiddick Skyline* is a collaboration with Jolene's John Crooke. You can take the boy out of alt country, but you can't take alt country out of the boy.

The Willard Grant Conspiracy come from Boston, and are something darker and stranger still, a loose collective who play a richly textured but deeply paranoid 'country noir', with lots of cello and violin and accordion framing Robert Fisher's deep baritone, but with an ominous undertow and occasional sonic distortions. Not to mention fire crackers.

The band honed their sound in an old shack on Willard Grant Street, a dirt road, but Fisher and the band's other mainman Paul Austin had met years earlier, in Maine. They had finally become tired of 'assault-orientated, abrasive rock', and gravitated towards the 'brilliant, chilly Eastern fringe of the neo-country map'.* As Paul explains, their new sound was just as uncompromising as grunge, in its way – 'it's unafraid to be direct'. The sound of mandolin is 'still direct emotion, unshielded by technology'. Even so, there is mutual respect between the two, and a changing cast of backing musicians. When they play folk clubs, people stare, and mutter that 'there's something seriously wrong with these guys'. They are probably right. But when they play rock clubs, 'we play so slow and quiet it drives them insane. The tension can be incredible'.

* *Uncut* magazine

Robert rejects the alt-country tag, though. He enjoys to listen to what he himself calls 'western music', but 'alternative country' is a label currently applied to 'things that aren't really alternative and aren't country either'.

The appearance on CD of their 1997 debut *3 A.M. Sunday @ Fortune Otto's* was an 'accident', having been put together to test out a friend's home studio. Early copies come in a handmade sleeve, with the simple credit that 'anyone who tells you they played on this, probably did'. Fisher sounds mournful, and seems to emerge from a litany of speaking voices between tracks, like a representative. And a pessimistic one. This is certainly the dark side of country, so that Mr Bojangles can no longer dance, and morning 'is the end of the day'. Here are songs about lost times, and absent friends. This extremely disturbing record closes on the seemingly interminable 'Chinese New Year (New York)', which is just that, the sound of endless firecrackers.

Flying Low saw Fisher deliberately going against the grain of good practice, recording tracks 'backwards' and 'wrong', and the drums last. It starts with traffic noise, then just piano and scraping fiddle, before the full band ease in for 'Evening Mass'.

Just when you thought you could pigeonhole this band, *Mojave* – drawing on Robert's time back in the desert – broke out with punky thrash amidst the slow-fi. The album 'gives off a shimmering but darkly dangerous acoustic vibe',* like lightning trapped in a bottle. The later *Everything's Fine* is anything but. 'They say that everything will turn out right/it never seems that way this time of night'. The whole thing 'inhabits a place where rootlessness has become a dull, aching necessity, and nostalgia is nothing more than the knowledge that you can never go back.† Not exactly light comedy then, with the opening track asking the listener to 'sing a sweet song when I'm dead'. Fisher recorded all his lead vocals in one day, even if he inhabits a different character in each, 'redemption songs, lyrically disparaging yet strangely uplifting'. It is this contrary quality that lifts the Willard Grant Conspiracy above so many others of the 'vaguely miserable' persuasion, and which puts this luminous record on a par with Nixon.

Paul Austin also put together *Come On Beautiful*, a tribute to American Music Club, with reinterpretations of their songs by his own

---

* *No Depression*
† *Mojo*

band, Calexico, Lambchop and Steve Wynn: 'perfect if you love Mark Eitzel's songs but can't stand his voice'.

Robert tries to make stage announcements without the benefit of a microphone: 'his intros provide a sense of the primitive, unseen America', which fertilises the band's music, backed up by keyboards, mandolin, guitar and viola. Elsewhere, he talks about using true, traditional music. 'Stripped down or not, I think there's a sense of narrative, a sense of the story itself being about specific things.' The result is possibly Willard Grant Conspiracy's best album, recorded in Slovenia with Chris Eckman of The Walkabouts, though Paul Austin is notable for his (near) absence.

Regard The End (2003) sees some spine-tingling duets with Jess Kline and Kristin Hersh, beautifully understated ensemble playing worthy of Lambchop, and a mix of desperate love songs and traditional murder ballads, some old as the hills, some newly written. Comparisons were immediately made with Nick Cave, but this lacks his actorly sense of performance. With a huge beard and dark glasses, Fisher now looks the very essence of a mountain man, slow of speech and deep of thought.

Like their debut, it was another album that almost came together by accident, and is 'really a case of me being in the studio having fun'. He took traditional songs, then fashioned new tunes and music to match. 'Beyond The Shore' is about falling for the caress of the 'long black veil' of death, but it is also a hymn to the human spirit, and its ability to transform itself. 'I'm bound to go beyond this shore/in glory I will be placed.' 'Twistification', first attempted with the Dutch band Telefunk, is a tale of a 'belle dame sans merci' in a maple swamp and has a hypnotism that draws you right into the water. The album closes with 'The Suffering Song', and its message that we are all going to weaken and expire, but things are redeemed by the sheer power of Fisher's huge vocal, unhurried and magnificent, a close cousin to Johnny Cash's 'brimstone holler'.

Rob Hughes reckons that this band has finally made an album you can fully immerse yourself in. Perhaps it is no coincidence that they have done this by getting back in touch with the deepest roots of American traditional culture. By fashioning music of redemptive grace from 'death, suffering, misery and hardship' they have tapped into a motherlode of the purest 'folk gothic'.

vii) Gothic Country

'Be content with your life/it may not get any better'
– Johnny Dowd

The term 'gothic country' was first attached to The Shivers, a husband and wife team from Austin who explored the back roads of America in their camper van. They stopped long enough to record two albums, *The Shivers* (1994) and *The Buried Life* (1996). There is something very odd about them, 'playing and singing each note as if the wolf was permanently at the door'. Kelly Bell retells grim fairytales for adults in her twangy voice: 'you're the earth, the sea, the sky my love and barely 17'.

The term 'gothic country' was then appropriated by Dave Goodman, to describe music that focused intensely on 'the supernatural, death and sorrow', often sung in a deceptively laid-back style. Tennessee Williams, with a rhythm section. This can be deeply scary stuff, about violent crime and incest and mental illness. The most on-the-edge performer of them all is Johnny Dowd. One of his later songs is called 'Woody Guthrie's Blues', and evokes the dust bowls. He recorded 1997's *Wrong Side Of Memphis* in his home studio, and it's a surprise the phone wasn't tapped.

The music is genuinely scary, rough and primitive with Dowd phoning in scene-of-crime reports in his horrible voice. 'A postcard from the last trailer park before hell'* It does indeed sound like something recorded in the old Sun studios, on Friday 13th during a full moon. The homemade quality of it all makes things worse, with plunking banjo and tubercular harmonica and Sir Douglas Quintet organ.

The Handsome Family have learnt the same trick of singing extremely quietly, so that you are drawn in, then sometimes wish you hadn't been. But, while Dowd's music grows out of true murder magazines and *crime noir* fiction, this couple are an appendage to the *Harry Smith Anthology*. They first discovered an original vinyl set in a public library in Michigan, and were particularly taken by the 'strange black humour' of his liner notes. 'Those dark, giggling comments intertwined with strange, primordial folk songs about shipwrecks, stabbings, hangings and run-away trains created a strange meditation on the mysteries of life.'

* *The Independent*

The Handsome Family have made it their mission to update these tales, while also covering 'The House Carpenter' in a particularly toneless way on an early album. Like Harry Smith, their message is truly subversive. Life is, and always has been, 'dark, violent and unfair', but it is lit up at times with a 'baffling and bittersweet beauty'. And Mr and Mrs Sparks are there to record such epiphanies.

Rennie plays bass and autoharp, sings call and response with her husband, and writes lyrics that employ the folk process in miniature, 'distilling her fables and laments from myths, legends and everyday events'. Brett writes the tunes, sings lead vocals and puts the backing music together in their home studio in Chicago. Dubbed 'countryonica' by Jon Langford, their music takes on board samples from the natural world, snatches of old recordings, and even stray sounds from the street outside. 'We don't rock in any shape or form. With the computer I can have harps, cellos, full string arrangements that creep in like a fog, stuff I never thought possible.'

He regards The Rolling Stones as being far more influential in 'introducing real country music to the world' than Gram Parsons. 'Far Away Eyes' is 'high lonesome' 'done before anyone in rock knew what that meant' while 'Dead Flowers' is the first 'alt country I tried to learn in a band'.

Having a master's degree in music helps Brett to gently parody country-music stylings, which unfold at an 'impossibly unhurried Nashville pace'. Jeff Tweedy got closest to describing this weird pairing as 'the two halves of a sick and beautiful brain. They're just about the only storyteller songwriters who don't make my stomach turn.' For Rennie, hearing the 'old story songs' inspired her: 'no extra words, no fat, just clean emotional scary things'. Their twisted view of their native land has made them a cult item in Britain, but induced paranoia at home. Brett recalls an audience member in Minneapolis saying that he loved their songs, 'except they all end with someone dying', when he replied 'yeah, just like in real life' the man looked terrified, and ran away. 'Americans are so afraid of even going to movies with unhappy endings, let alone hearing songs about murder, suicide, fear'. All of which are The Handsome Family's stock in trade.

On the duo's 1994 debut *Odessa*, 'a passionately slung together clarion (call) of punk angst' with Mike Werner on drums, things are not yet completely in focus. They quieten down a lot for *Milk & Scissors*, though there is still the odd blurt of distorted electric guitar noise. The lyrics start to cut deeper, for all their apparent kookiness, and Brett sounds like a comatose Leonard Cohen as he sings, without any apparent emotion, lines like 'and you remember how he cried when they strapped him to the stretcher/convinced his arms were burning with electricity from heaven'. *Down In The Valley* compiles the best of their early work.

By 1998 and *Through The Trees*, everything was in place, and the opening track 'Weightless Again' could sum up a whole genre – and almost does, so prevalent is it on alt country compilations. Cheerfulness has entered the equation, despite the ostensible subject of killing yourself. This is a new note in American music, from the oldest of sources: taking everything in your stride. Rennie plays smooth melodica, and her lyric seems a disconnected series of holiday snapshots, but it all comes together, about those times in life when you feel special. Jeff Tweedy sings and plays guitar on some tracks – some of the most 'beautifully dark American country folk music you're likely to hear this side of the Nick Cave and Johnny Cash "Together At Last" tour'.[*]

In The Air looked like a sequel, and was packaged like a New Age record, though here are more tales of the unexpected. 'The Sad Milkman' could almost be Hank Williams, until you listen to the words. It is another song about being stuck in life – 'he wanted to feel like a bucket of milk' – which leaves its protagonist literally in mid air. 'Welcome to the home of alt country's anti-Waltons' ran one review; another traced a direct line to here through Buell Kazee and Will Oldham: 'visceral, sinister but ravishing in its darkness'. Brett chews on vowels as if on tobacco – 'the violin wails and the plangent acoustic guitar hides a secret in every note'.

The opening track is a parody of The Eagles, and a clever twist on country music's love of the familiar, with a 'straight-faced injection of Gothic-tinged hyper-reality, so vivid that it's surreal'[†]. It is different from their earlier output in its 'lushness and delicacy'[**] of sound that makes it a counterpart of Lambchop. But sicker. This is Ray Bradbury, crossed with the Brothers Grimm.

[*] *New Musical Express*   [**] *Uncut* magazine
[†] *No Depression*

Twilight feels like the final album in a trilogy. The sound is smoothed out, and the overall feeling eerie: there is a sense of things running down: 'when they closed the last shopping mall, crickets sang in crumbling walls'. The line about 'the quiet sound when airplanes fall out of the sky' was written and recorded long before the events of September 11th. The couple ask fans to send 'dead birds or chocolates' to their website and few would disagree with Rob Hughes when he sees the album placing them 'atop the poisonous spire of alt country's twisted high tower'. There is a real sense of hope on 'Gravity' – the whistling saw presumably comes via Pro-tools – with Johnny Appleseed walking the city streets and planting trees 'because gravity is not the only force at work in this world'.

Brett sees now that for too long he has been trying to write 'alt country' songs, often at the expense of other material'. Now he is getting his Scott Walker albums out again. Not that you would notice from *Live At Schuba's Tavern* (Chicago, 2000), which captures a wilder sound than their home-studio output, so that Brett's guitar sounds 'desolate and outraged' and Rennie paints 'primary colours' on her bass, with a between-song commentary that captures the 'spark' in the Sparks' live shows.

They are now a cult act, at least in the UK, surrounded with plastic animals onstage and while Brett sets up his Macintosh G3 – 'I'm having a bad tuning experience' – Rennie passes the time by asking 'any questions about insects? Especially ants. I'm good on ants.' She hugs and strokes her autoharp 'as if was a kitten she'd just rescued from the river'.

At the 12 Bar Club, she invites the audience to her dressing room for shrimp cocktails, comments adversely on her lovelife with Brett, then suggests that the audience might be flesh-eating zombies. 'Kill all the people with glasses' she suggests, looking meaningfully at her bespectacled husband. For Gavin Martin, the live vaudeville that is The Handsome Family come on like an 'opposites attract attraction at an end of the century *Medicine Show*'. This is a live show 'as funny as fuck, as sweet as love and as serious as death – variety entertainment at its finest'.

So, in their own way, were Sixteen Horsepower, except that something genuinely primitive is going on here. Sixteen Horsepower were the most primeval force in alt country, a band who played with a rare sense of determination and passion. There was an emphasis on 'traditional instrumentation, sparsely applied', on 'antiquated phrasing' and on the more savage parts of the Bible. The man who imposed all this was David Eugene Edwards, grandson of a travelling preacher, and brought up strictly as part of the Nazarene sect. He played in a series of punk bands, until moving to Denver and founding Sixteen Horsepower, a band with a constantly changing line-up, until inner tensions blew it apart.

Edwards plays banjo, bandoneon – a precursor of the accordion – and lap steel. Sixteen Horsepower's full-length debut, 1996's *Sackcloth 'n' Ashes*, also includes Keven Soll on standup bass and cello, a drummer and a guest fiddler. The band exude 'darkness, desolation, grotesque-ness',* both live and on disc, and even fervid instrumentals are born 'more out of madness than out of joy'. Edwards sings like a cross between Patti Smith and Johnny Rotten at their most messianic, with not a hint of pity or pathos. Defiantly 'rock 'n' roll', it is like Dock Boggs with an electric amp, a weird and wonderful mix of 'Appalachian jigs and flatland reels laced with remnants of old country polkas and cabaret adagios.' A wonderful rich and driving sound, but rancid around the edges, somehow.

On *Low Estate*, the carefully laid out words are as uncompromising as the harsh banjo and distorted electric guitar chords: 'the train moves fast as I walk this track/carrying sin in my sack'. Its producer John Parrish reckons the band have a 'very, very definite sound'. Live, Edwards rarely varies his tone of voice, and there is little respite from the 'stomach churning dynamics': on disc at least you can turn it off.

Sixteen Horsepower use weird tunings, learnt from Edwards' dabblings in world music, and the words threaten retribution, without too much sense of joy. On *Secret South*, the lyrics are laid out like runes, and the acoustic lament 'Lost Wayfarer' sounds like a field recording from the '20s. No wonder that David Goodman sees the band as trans-porting the listener back to '19th-century mining camps, run down farms and urban slums'. This sense transferred over to live shows, as captured on *Hoarse*, 'pitched on the edge of hysteria'†. The band go for the jugular, and take their air of 'wild abandonment' with them when they cover songs by Joy Division and Creedence Clearwater Revival.

Playing live at Dingwells, Edwards sits near motionless and sings like a 'true fire-and-brimstone preacher': even a banjo becomes threatening

* *Modern Twang*
† *Uncut* magazine

in his hands. This is a man 'it might be wise not to mess with'. But the music he makes 'builds and broods' – mountain music for a new century – and can only be compared to a particularly malevolent Johnny Cash fronting Led Zeppelin. Now that the band is seemingly gone for good, we can only mourn what has gone – and wait for the bootlegs. There's a great review by Maddy Costa of a gig at the Borderline in 2000, with a five-piece band who sound like an avalanche, plus a fiddle 'like coffins breaking open'. Edwards rides the maelstrom, praising Jesus with a fervour that takes you aback. For a shuddering version of 'Harm's Way', the band 'attach bluegrass to a freight train, and play like they're hurtling down rusty, broken tracks'.

Sixteen Horsepower's greatest legacy is *Folklore*, with the amps turned right down, but still strange scrapings and howls proving this is certainly not CSN. One *No Depression* reviewer, is far from convinced by the band's apparent integrity, and compares the music herein to UK trip hop. Edwards himself admits to having listened recently to 'a lot of medieval music and Renaissance music and folk music from all over, not just Appalachian bluegrass music'. Though a verse like 'lost in my backwood/ you woke and found me there/running hard and dirt heavy/in the skin of a bear/all my harm/I shall wear' could only have been written by Edwards, it's a mixture of detailed imagination, and a metaphorical mind. Such things are balanced by songs from the traditional canon, The Carter Family and Hank Williams, and some spirited playing.

Well, even if still troubled by the 'truth' of Will Oldham, I find it very hard to believe that David Eugene Edwards was anything less than sincere. I see more sense in another complaint, that there are simply not enough tunes, but surely not here, the band's most open-hearted and accessible recording, 'three parts arcane Appalachia, one part Violent Femmes'.* Jean-Yves Tola – who has stayed the course somehow – and fellow European Pascal Humbert give sterling support, and there's a lot of Balkan-style chanting, and mournful cello.

Edwards went on to make a solo album *Woven Hand*, which is as bleak as can be, but he does not discount the chance of becoming suffused with happiness and well-being. 'I believe in God, and however God wants me to be, I want to be. If I do go through a time of just complete joy, I

* *Uncut* magazine

really wouldn't care what anybody else thought'. Don't hold your breath. My bullshit detector bleeps when I read Jim's stated intention to merge 'white trash hillbilly with Sufi music'. Chalk and cheese surely. The first is all of the body, the second a means to transcendence. When Dock Boggs or Doc Stanley sing about death our corporeal decay is all too real. The mystic side of Islam, whose fiercest adversaries include the likes of Bin Laden, sees life and death instead as an illusion, out of which we can lift ourselves if we work and pray hard enough. Even so, one man did come as close as possible to fusing East and West, but that was Gene Clark on *No Other*, and poor Gene's own demise was far short of noble.

So, what I hear on Jim White's *Wrong Eyed Jesus* (1997) is some beautiful, soft-voiced laments, lots of wilful weirdness, some nice banjo and pedal steel, and lots of parody. Not least the halo painted around his stetson on the back cover, or the vocal imitation of a hillbilly on 'When Jesus Gets A Brand New Name'. Eleven 'dark little songs' as White himself describes them, and 'fables of bizarre enchantment'.*

Perhaps Sixteen Horsepower are genuine, but this is ersatz fun, which I for one would be quicker to put in the CD tray if I wanted some instant entertainment. It is no coincidence that David Byrne signed White Up – Jim is exactly what Byrne thinks of as Americana: dime-store dada. True Americana is far stranger and more disturbing, not just a freak sideshow.

The critical success of *Wrong-Eyed Jesus* made White 'America's most adept savant', even if this did not really translate over into commercial terms. For a while Jim still lived in a trailer, and a rented trailer at that. Any shreds of authenticity fled with *No Such Place*, which is actually a far more honest and fascinating affair. How could you not fall for a track titled 'Handcuffed To A Fence In Mississipi' and its cheerful nightmares of 'squirrels and stigmata'. Morcheeba help out with electronic sound textures, and this could almost be the Alabama 3 in a sunny mood.

Jim once caught a rare backroom gig by Johnny Dowd, who looked up slowly and said 'Oh yeah, you're that kid who does what I do.' White adds that 'he feels like we're in competition and he might have to kill me'. This would be enough to have me running for the hills. The problem with gothic country is that if you get too close to it, you can become infected too. And there is no known cure.

* *Uncut* magazine

3 New Blossoms On An Old Bough

i) New Wave Bluegrass

'Bluegrass at its best is always coloured outside the lines,
but there are still very strict parameters'
— *Emmylou Harris*

When checking into hotels and the like, Nirvana would disguise themselves under the name the Simon Ritchie Bluegrass Ensemble. It's a good joke, but the anarchic spirit of Sid Vicious does indeed animate some of the more extreme examples of the form, then and now.

Bluegrass is a musical form that, for all its constraints – indeed, because of those constraints – is open to endless variation. The Austin Lounge Lizards were two Princeton alumni who declared 'guerilla warfare on the conventions of country music'. Except that no-one much cared anymore, except for the diehards who would spend their summers going from one old-time music festival to another. The Austin Lounge Lizards loved this music just as much, even if the dominant element on a span of albums that followed on from 1988's *Highway Café Of The Damned* was satire, with songs like 'Jesus Loves Me But He Can't Stand You'.

But the real breakthrough came through Killbilly. Originally from Dallas, they fused together bluegrass and thrash metal. Alan Wooley had played with new-wave rock band the White Shapes. In 1986, he put together a solo cassette in his bedroom, under the name Killbilly. A radio DJ called Craig 'Niteman' Taylor called his bluff, and then asked to join the band, which became a kind of forcing ground for new bluegrass stars, including two of Bad Livers, and Louis Myers, who helped establish 'South By Southwest' as a major festival. It all connects.

Killbilly soon gained a reputation for their 'scalding' sound, linking Bill Monroe to Motorhead, and kicked the door open for the likes of Uncle Tupelo. In 1990 they released the cassette-only album *Alive From The City of Hate In The Lone Star State*. Two years later, *Foggy Mountain Anarchy* came out on Flying Fish, to rave reviews, but they split up shortly after. Who else could write a tune like 'Mountain Dew Or Die'?

The Bad Livers 'play it old and raw'. In their defence against die-hard traditionalists, they quote Bill Monroe himself. 'If a man can take a little bit of my music and put a little bit of himself in, and come up with something of his own, well that's all right by me.' It was what Bill himself did to string-band music. And what the Bad Livers first put into the equation was punk rock, gaining instant notoriety as a novelty band who would rip through 'goofy, high-speed renditions' of Iggy Pop and Motorhead tunes with bluegrass instrumentation'. But there was a certain bravery attached to playing Iggy's 'Lust For Life' at a bluegrass festival and then performing 'Crying Holy Unto The Lord' at a punk club. As Mark Rubin puts it, 'basically we would do music we respected. We would do Johnny Cash numbers. We would do Motorhead numbers. We would play Miles Davis and Charlie Parker. And then we'd do "Beaumont Rag".' They attracted 'shavehead punks, pipe-smoking professors and cowboy-hatted folkies' alike, 'Then we thought about John Hartford saying "Don't get famous doing something you hate".'

So, their debut single aside, the Bad Livers set out to build a career – almost by accident – in which the punk-rock attitude was internalised into a music that both respected the heritage of bluegrass and gospel music, and added a new chapter to it, through their own compositions – 'their performances crackle with energy and humour and give an old music a very new and long overdue lustre'.* The Bad Livers are emblematic of all the pioneers we are dealing with in *South by Southwest*, from The Carter Family to Snakefarm, non-conformists who bring something new to the tradition, while still respecting it.

Certainly the Bad Livers were not prepared to play anyone else's game. Mark Rubin comments: 'there's certain little hoops that you have to jump through in order to be a bluegrass band. We've probably violated quite a few of them. No tubas, no short pants on stage.'† Not to mention

* *New Country*
† Mark Ruben, *No Depression*

his being Jewish. 'The accordion is a certain no-no,' Danny Barnes adds. 'Because we played to kids and to people that didn't really have an education in bluegrass music, we were free to do whatever we wanted.' Danny Barnes is a superb banjo player, gifted on mandolin and guitar, and a wonderful singer, in a rough-voiced, honest kind of way. 'Even though we grew up in Texas, I was always inundated from a very early age with *Grand Ole Opry* acts, Bill Monroe and Lester Flatt, all those kind of guys.' But he is more influenced by the likes of Captain Beefheart than Sam Bush, much as he admires both. Danny played in a punk combo, and a mainstream country band, before turning off his amp.

Mark Rubin set himself up for a career as a classical tuba player, but 'I was getting really involved with punk-rock music and I'd got an electric bass and hung around the punk-rock scene up in Oklahoma City, bands like the Flaming Lips came out of that little bag.' When he moved to Dallas, 'I bought a string bass and joined them. The way I play bass is a lot different than 99 per cent of the bluegrass players out there. I play a lot more percussively because we have a trio and everybody's got to work extra hard.' For the Bad Livers, he also resumed playing the tuba, and sang back-up vocals. The trio was completed by Ralph White, III on fiddle and accordion, the mystery man of the band.

It is no coincidence that it was the sound of the Bad Livers that inspired Grant Alden to whisper to a friend, 'Let's start the magazine we've been talking about'. This being *No Depression*. He later wrote, the Bad Livers found a way to expand the 'hidebound traditions of bluegrass', looking backwards and forwards at the same time, and 'with tremendous joy'.

Danny compares the Bad Livers' direction to the super-technically competent pickers of the new-grass scene. 'We're more interested in organic grooves and relationships between the instruments, rather than creating scenarios whereby you can take good solos.' Mark Rubin is less interested in bands who take an existing idea and force it into life than in music that 'just kind of happened'. He also asks why you have to be a Christian to sing gospel. Danny Barnes adds that one of the things he most enjoys about gospel is 'just this incredible groove and vibe' whereas 'so much of our music today doesn't really help you out much in terms of spirituality or philosophy. If you read interviews with Bill Monroe and Ralph Stanley, they certainly respected the power of gospel, in that it has levels of communication in it that are beyond mere music and lyric.' For Rubin too, this is why he got interested in music in the first place, 'because it seems to do things you can't touch'.

But the real catalyst came late in 1991, when the band sent out a cassette tape cheekily labelled *Dust On The Bible* as a Christmas gift. It has the same kind of feel as The Byrds' *Sweetheart Of The Rodeo*, half serious, half in fun. Just listen to the way they almost crack up on one harmony vocal. Then remember that Mark is of another faith completely, and that Danny was brought up in the Church of Christ, a faith that did not even allow musical instruments in its services. There are no punk-rock songs, just all the old gospel classics, played simply but luminously, 'Farther Along/Further Along', and 'I'm Using My Bible For A Roadmap', plus a medley of 'I Saw The Light', 'Will The Circle Be Unbroken' and 'I'll Fly Away'. Danny explained the whole process when years later, the album finally appeared on CD, augmented by a wondrous take of Danny's own composition 'How Dark My Shadow's Grown', recorded six months earlier on KUT radio. Barnes had begun to hang around with Paul Leary of the Butthole Surfers, and had long been interested in recording demo tapes. He finally procured a four-track machine, though the band were so broke that they had to rent it from a local music store.

'*Dust On The Bible* started out as a collection of Gospel pieces I had sung, sitting next to my Grandma in church. I added a few pieces I had learned from some older guys in my hometown of Belton. The music just grew from the influence of old people in my life'. Most of the music here is by Danny – including his debut on fiddle – with Mark contributing bass and tuba, in a wonderfully 'oom pah' way, and Ralph playing accordion on just one track. Although only ever intended as a Christmas gift, Mark sent it off to local press and radio, and some mistook it for the band's debut record, as by now they had already been gigging for a couple of years. 'Folks started asking for it at our gigs. It was the only thing we had to offer the A&R guys who came sniffing around the "South By Southwest" conference in 1982. You can imagine the response when they got an all-gospel effort from a supposed "punk bluegrass" band. It kept us in groceries for years.' And changed the musical landscape, too.

What the Bad Livers became was something else, best verbalised by Danny. 'It's like this hillbilly orchestra that lives out in the middle of nowhere and is totally cut off from media. But this band has a big record collection and has been to the big city, and knows what's going on. A band that knows all kinds of music, but is still isolated. That's us.'

Paul Leary of the Butthole Surfers produced their 1992 debut CD *Delusions Of Banjer*. It appeared on Quarterstick, an offshoot of Chicago's art-punk label Touch And Go, which issued the Jesus Lizard and other such bands. They sounded like a 'pre-bluegrass string band'.* There is an amazing 'free bluegrass' break on 'Crow Black Chicken'. The same year saw *The Golden Years*, an EP of radio sessions, which contained a Johnny Cash/ Motorhead medley.

Their second CD *Horses In The Mines* (1994) included 'Puke Grab' and 'Chainsaw Therapy'. This album is designed just like the old Folkways albums, and sounds just as weird and deep as the real thing, with lots of tuba, and elements of blues and New Orleans jazz.

The Bad Livers moved on to Sugar Hill, a 'real' bluegrass label, and *Hogs On The Highway* sees them rampage through a 'deceptively experimental' set, with Bob Grant flatpicking his guitar. He has 'hardened the Livers' rhythmic attack, bringing wood and ballast to their sound'.* Ralph White III dropped out at this point, tired of life out on the road.

Folk Roots admired the band for playing their bluegrass 'old and raw, with none of that new grass widdling', and *Industry And Thrift* adds drums and electric guitar for 'Doing My Time'. There's even some klezmer, 'A Yid Ist Geboren Inz Oklahoma', reflecting Mark's roots, and a sparkling version of Merle Travis's 'Cannonball Rag'. Producer Lloyd Maines gives them a fuller sound than every before, though the band are now essentially a duo of Mark and Danny, plus a full supporting cast who layer in snatches of pedal steel, bottleneck, clarinet and fiddle.

Which brings us to *Blood & Mood* (2000), and something else entirely. 'You don't have to get over and figure out what that's all about' a voice whispers over banjo and odd noises, then we're straight into a rap, about the perils of being a banjo player. Their own record label pegged this as a 'post-everything soundscape', and 'down-home trip-hop' music. It is certainly exciting, with wild electric guitar, heavy drums and weird

* *New Country*

243

electronic bleeps, plus lots of samples. Surely it is just the logical development of what Danny was doing nine years before on his rented four track.

Grant Alden wrote a lead review in *No Depression*, claiming that through 'the new sterility of their sound, the Bad Livers have chosen to alter the dialogue they have enjoyed with their audience for the last decade'. Here was a band who were once advocates for acoustic music, but now 'Danny's got a brand new bag and it involves a drum machine and a sampler and his joyful embrace of the sounds made available by that technology.' No matter that with outfits like Thee Old Codgers, Danny continued to release strict bluegrass albums like the following year's *Things I Done Wrong*. Like Joe Henry and Beck they have found ways to 'incorporate traditional American music within the new textures of electronic sounds'. But didn't a previous hippie generation do just the same with country rock?

Alden's real gripe is that the Bad Livers have lost touch with their roots, and with a 'song-driven music', but *Blood & Mood* contains some of the best songs Danny has ever laid down. Barnes states that 'if there's an agenda involved, it was only to make a record the way people make records these days – the way the Eminem record got made'. *Folk Roots* found that half the tracks 'actually sound like songs' while the rest 'seems as if it was banged together on the spur of the moment'. Exactly the same description applies to David Bowie's *Low*, perhaps the most influential album of the last quarter century, I would argue. 'But when it comes together, as on "I'm Losing" with electric guitar thrashing behind drums, they make it sound like true newgrass'.

Meanwhile, back in the cosy world of bluegrass, a band like the Lost And Found favoured 'restraint and clarity over rock 'n' roll energy or the high lonesome sound'. When asked why, the affable Allen Mills, bassist and lead singer, pointed out that 'I made a vow that I was going to make a living playing music or starve to death, and this morning when I weighed myself, I'm down to 210 pounds.' An album like *It's About Time* proves that devotion to one's cause is enough for any lifetime.

As to New Grass Revival and their likes, Danny Barnes comments 'I think those guys are great players, especially Sam Bush, but that music is a kind of pitch that I never swung to. It reminds me a bit of Al DiMeola. You can't deny that it's great music, or good picking, but it doesn't really speak to me personally.'* His fellow banjo player JD Crowe had founded the New South in the early '70s, with the likes of Jerry Douglas on dobro, Tony Rice on Martin acoustic guitar, and Ricky Skaggs. Their debut album *JD Crowe & The New South* was issued in 1975, and established the template for a whole new generation of 'progressive bluegrass'.

Tony Rice went on to help found the David Grisman Quintet in 1979, where he incorporated jazz, swing and 'hornlike solos' into his flatpicking style, then set up his own Tony Rice Unit. As a boy, he had known Clarence White, but found it impossible to play like him 'What happened was that I developed a unique sound, both rhythmically and harmonically. Trying to sound like him opened up a whole new world'.

Rice freed up his instrument from the need to play scales or modes, almost like a fiddle, or a banjo. 'Every note is like a bell.' And every solo like a series of words that add up to sentences, paragraphs, whole novels. As fellow guitarist John Carlini put it: 'we discussed the use of musical space and the concept of how a solo should breathe. It's the same way you speak; you don't let go this rapid flow of words without breathing.'* Just listen to an album like *Unit Of Measure*, for a blend of folk, jazz and bluegrass, all strictly acoustic, which Tony himself termed 'spacegrass'.

Jerry Douglas, plays on many of the best albums of the last 30 years, *Copperhead Road*, *Infamous Angel*, *The Grass Is Blue*, *Roses In The Snow* and *Interiors*, plus jamming with everyone from Phish to Bela Fleck. Jerry was brought up in Ohio, the son of a steelworker, but dreamt of playing bluegrass, then moved to Washington DC to join the Country Gentlemen. More recently he joined Alison Krauss & Union Station.

Alison is a German immigrant's daughter from Illinois who was 'Most Promising Country Fiddle Player (Midwest)' age 12, then developed into a fine a vocalist, sweet yet sassy and able to act heartbroken like 'a young Dolly Parton or a melancholic Emmylou, yet wholly her own'. With the acoustic Union Station, Krauss has resisted the temptation to get sucked into the Music Row machine. When she made a solo album, *Forget About It*, most of Union Station are along for the ride, and one track has Willie Nelson and Dolly Parton singing vocals in the background.

* *No Depression*

Union Station are as flexible an unplugged band as could be imagined, and the recent double album and DVD *Live*, recorded at an April 2002 'New Favorite' show from the Palace Theatre in Louisville, Kentucky is stunning. Strictly no overdubs. With Douglas on dobro, Barry Bales on string bass, Ron Block and Dan Tyminski on guitars, banjo and vocals – and horror of horror for some traditionalists, Larry Atamanuk on drums for part of the set, plus Alison singing and playing up a storm on her fiddle, this is a marvellously flexible unit. They switch effortlessly from pop ensemble to hoedown band, gospel quartet to driving bluegrass.

The set list runs the gamut of country: Carter Stanley's arrangement of 'Man Of Constant Sorrow' to traditional chestnuts like 'The Boy Who Wouldn't Hoe Corn', the string-band favourite 'Cluck Old Hen', the Louvin Brothers' 'Tiny Broken Heart', a Bad Company song (!), Gillian Welch's 'New Favourite' and the best of the contemporary Nashville songwriting production line, plus instrumentals written by the band. Somehow, they make it all flow as one.

A particular delight is the singing of Dan Tyminski, clear as a mountain stream and 'a blend of up-against-the-wall intensity and bluegrass polish'. It was Dan's voice that came out of George Clooney's body whenever he stepped up to the microphone in *O Brother, Where Art Thou?* Here, his party piece is just part of his 'flawless instrumental work, exquisite ensemble singing and impeccable sound that let every woody tone and every sighing vocal nuance saturate a concert hall',* livened by Alison's chirpy comments between songs.

Says Alison, 'Our live show is pretty loose. Everyone improvises on their solos and no one is required to play a solo or sing just like it's done on the record. It's much looser than that', even though the band plays the same set list every night. Krauss also 'discovered' the strictly traditional Cox Family, who worked with her on *I Know Who Holds Tomorrow* (1994), and young, wild bluegrass combo Nickel Creek.

This is a band that make the Dixie Chicks seem old, with Chris Thile, Sean Watkins and his sister Susan Watkins, all still in their mid 20s. They began playing together in Southern California, inspired by new-wave bluegrass musicians such as Mark O'Connor and Bela Fleck. Their self-titled debut became the best-selling album ever on roots label Sugar Hill.

* *Maverick*

Ex-Long Ryder Sid Griffin was among those most impressed: 'live they can throw a hip-hop version of 'Subterranean Homesick Blues' or a Bach partita into the middle of a traditional tune and get away with it – and they don't have a banjo player. They blend together jazz, folk, classical and indie rock, and their blistering playing and energetic singing energised a recent edition of *Later*. It was like watching Bill Monroe's grandchildren. Their second album, 2002's *This Side* has plenty of 'modal changes, time signature experimentation and inventive orchestration', plus some electrics, and a cover version of Pavement's 'Spit On A Stranger'.

Other people were giving bluegrass a much-needed kick up the behind. *One Riot, One Ranger* would feature the odd song by Pere Ubu or Roky Erickson, though their use of male harmony singing is strictly traditional. Earl Lee Grace was another persona for Blag Dahlia, lead singer of the Dwarves, an extremely unpleasant hardcore punk band. In 1995, he released Blackgrass, because 'I got sick of rock 'n' roll, I couldn't do hip hop, and new country sucks.'

Mike Seeger, David Grisman and John Hartford joined together as Retrograss, who described themselves as 'music shifted back in time'. They performed classic rock 'n' roll bluegrass style, so here the likes of 'Maybelline', 'Hound Dawg' and 'Maggie's Farm' are taken back in time. A neat idea, but very much a one-off, just like the Anachronistic Jazz Band, who play John Coltrane Dixieland style. And it is in connections with jazz, rather than rock music, that bluegrass takes its most interesting conceptual leap.

Alison Brown was born in Connecticut, raised in California, and studied at Harvard, where she joined the Northern Lights bluegrass band. After business school, she began working for investment bank Smith Barney. Like Cantrell, the lure of music eventually proved too great, and Brown gave it all up to play the 5-string banjo, and join an early line up of Union Station. She also served as musical director for Michelle Shocked and used her experience as an MBA to set up the Compass record label. Her 1998 album *Out Of The Blue* sees Alison's playing veering closer towards cool '50s jazz, Wes Montgomery style.

Alison Brown live is quite a different proposition, and she also adds some stellar banjo to New Grange – one of the best recent string band projects. Lead vocals are taken by the light-voiced Tim O'Brien, the very model of a modern bluegrass player.

Tim moved to Colorado, where he founded Hot Rize, which lasted through the '80s. The name came from the flour mill who sponsored the *Grand Ole Opry*, and the music was to match – 'we looked for old songs and made them relevant to the current day'. In 1996 he made *Red On Blonde*, reversing the process by treating Bob Dylan songs done string-band style. On 'The Wicked Messenger', the original bassline turns into a Bill Monroe mandolin riff. Three years later, Tim took Appalachian music back to its Celtic roots on *The Crossing*, affable but melancholy, and a transatlantic meeting between the likes of Earl Scruggs and Del McCoury on one side, and De Danaan on the other. On 'Talkin' Cavan', Tim ends his quest with a Woody Guthrie-style ramble, about going back to his ancestral home, and finding the natives far from friendly.

The same year, O'Brien released *Songs From The Mountain*, an album based on Charles Frazier's novel, and featuring traditional fiddle tunes brought over by the area's Scotch-Irish immigrants in the late 1700s. It ties in with Martin Carthy once telling me that such roots music is part of the living heritage of American musicians, in a way that it no longer is in Britain. 'We went to see the Flying Burrito Brothers play a set of bluegrass, and what they did was entirely in context, it wasn't like putting silly hats on.' As to the roots of such things, 'If you look in the collections you will find Scots tunes from Aberdeenshire falling over the feet of Appalachian tunes, a tune like "Shady Grove", Fairport Convention recycled it back for "Matty Groves" on *Liege And Lief*.'

Bela Fleck, a banjo virtuoso from Manhattan sounds as much at home playing bebop as playing in the Earl Scruggs style, but peppers his albums with the likes of 'Amazing Grace' and 'At The Hoedown', even 'The Ballad Of Jem Clampett' on the extraordinary double album *Live Art*, and still admits that 'when I play with Doc Watson, I find myself straightening right out'. His band the Flecktones feature funk slap-bass, a Synth-Axe Drumitar, keyboards and electric banjo.

New Grass Revival, which he joined in 1981, were always constricted to one musical genre, and thus never able to break out and open for rock bands like the Allman Brothers, which they had once hoped for. Now the Flecktones were getting a far wider audience 'because we so clearly were not a bluegrass band. Even though the banjo was in there, we were able to be just a weird band.'* It gave them options that New Grass Revival had never had, like jamming with Chick Corea, or having their video for 'Sinister Minister' played on *MTV*.

Slaying with such variant musicians has slowed down his bluegrass licks, as Bela 'applies the rhythmic and harmonic liberties of a jazz piano to his instrument'. The results, as on 1995's *Tales From The Acoustic Planet*, are strangely 'rural' – time signatures may shift, and chord patterns shift 'into shapes never heard in an Appalachian hollow but everyone, even the jazz and pop guys, uses the circular phrasing of bluegrass'.

The people who really took this forward were bunched around a small scene in Seattle. The prime movers are three members of the New York avante-garde jazz scene in the '80s – guitarist Bill Frisell, singer and pianist Robin Holcomb and her husband Wayne Horvitz, all of whom would perform at a performance space called Studio Henry, where the likes of Eugene Chadbourne would also appear when in town. But the fourth of this Seattle gang of musical terrorists is no less than Danny Barnes, having closed down the Bad Livers, and moved west.

Country jazz might well be 'the most innovative hybrid of all'†. Jazz can offer new harmonics and the ability to improvise to an increasingly hidebound country-music scene, much as rock music did 30 years earlier. This rather undervalues the conceptual leaps made at the fringes of alt country, as opposed to the dark heart of Music Row, where music is literally a cash crop. Even so, there is certainly a fellow spirit shared by 'the unresolved harmonies of Ornette Coleman's 'Lonely Woman' and the unsoftened truth of Dock Boggs' – some of us call it Americana.

The catalyst for the Seattle scene was probably Bill Frisell's 1997 album *Nashville*, which he recorded in Tennessee with Alison Krauss, Jerry Douglas and other members of Union Station. 'Go Jake' is a 'chuggling hoedown', played straight, and Robin Holcomb joined in to reinterpret songs by Hazel Dickens and Neil Young. Strangest of all is her take on Skeeter Davis's 1962 hit 'The End Of The World', with Frisell and Douglas playing long, sustained notes 'in counterpoint' to the jog-trot rhythm.

* *New Country*
† *No Depression*

Holcomb comes from Georgia, and she had already recorded some experimental keyboard pieces that incorporate snatches of traditional songs from her native South like 'Oh Susanna', in much the same way as Charles Ives or Aaron Copland. On her own recent album *The Big Time*, she makes 'experimental art songs' out of two tracks from the *Harry Smith Anthology*. On The Carter Family's 'Train Song Engine 143', and 'A Lazy Farmer Boy' Holcomb and Danny Barnes's harmony vocals 'stretch and twist the melody', while Frisell 'constructs nervous guitar figures that occasionally burst into cathartic roars'.

These were the two songs that she chose to sing at the Harry Smith tribute, but Horvitz recalls his wife singing these same songs – relatively straight – 25 years before, long before she ever performed professionally. 'But as is my wont, I fooled around with the songs,' Robin adds, putting 'perky ostinatos under the melody'. Barnes points out that on Carter Family recordings there are a lot of rhythmic shifts, 'there'll be a 5/4 bar here and a 3 /4 bar there. The post-war guys rounded off everything into groups of four, but Robin taps into that Carteresque way of shifting the rhythm around.'

A recent album on Nonesuch, *The Willies*, is played by a trio of Frisell, Barnes and bassist Keith Lowe, reinventing tunes like 'Cluck Old Hen' and Hank Williams' 'Cold, Cold Heart'. *Folk Roots* admires the way they go back to the 'naked song', and abandon any preconceived ideas. So, on The Carter Family's 'John Hardy Was A Desperate Little Man', they slow the thing down to the point of desperation. Then Bill starts playing 'substitute chords', and the atmosphere becomes ominous . Again, on Dock Boggs' 'Sugar Baby', Frisell plays electric lead against Barnes' bouncy riff on banjo, so that as the two melody lines split apart, it sounds like John McLaughlin jamming with Bela Fleck.

Bill had turned up on Danny's doorstep asking for guitar lessons, after hearing him support Del McCoury at a Seattle club. Having teamed up with Keith Lowe on bass and fiddler Jon Parry from the Goose Creek Symphony, Horvitz and Frisell both guested on Thee Old Codgers' *Things I Done Wrong* (2001). Here is old-string-band music, updated, and songs by Barnes that borrow themes, tunes and words from the Harry Smith project. 'But the tonalities are darker than your usual old-time effort.'

Out on the road with Frisell, plus the likes of bassist Dave Holland, who once played with Miles Davis, Danny realised that 'jazz players have the facility to take the weirdness of old-time songs even further'. He has learnt a wider range of rhythm and harmonies, as has Frisell. 'I spent 30 years of my life trying to play Scruggs banjo, while Bill was transcribing all those Theolonius Monk solos. We both did our homework, but it was in different classes. Now we're exchange students.'

Bill Frisell found it particularly interesting when he couldn't tell if a singer was black or white. 'I like it when our assumptions get messed up. The deeper you look into American music, the more the names, boundaries and all the racial stuff just melts away. It just becomes music.'

ii) Renewals

'A crackpot is usually only a few steps sideways from a visionary'
– *The Handsome Family*

Nick Cave might have started his career screaming at the top of his voice and rolling around the floor, allegedly stiff with heroin, with the Birthday Party, transplanted from Australia to post-punk London. Now he is a much respected author, and festival director, as well as a singer of rare power and terror. He tends to dress in black, like an old-time preacher, but even grimmer of aspect.

Cave's latest songs are fuelled by two main obsessions, apocalyptic passages from the Bible, and the savage murder of young girls. Pure Harry Smith. 'I've always enjoyed writing songs about dead women. It's something that crops up that still holds some mystery, even to me.' Though maybe not to the poor, murdered women. By turns horrific and comic, *Murder Ballads* – laid down in 1996 with the Bad Seeds – is the logical extension of one aspect of the *Anthology*, although in the traditional song 'Henry Lee' it is the woman who wields the knife, and PJ Harvey joins in with relish.

In July 1999, Cave put together an evening at the Royal Festival Hall in celebration of 'The Harry Smith Project'. It was the culmination of his stewardship of the Meltdown Festival that summer, which had featured evenings with Lee Hazlewood and Will Oldham. Running at almost four hours, it was an uneven, varied and at times utterly shambolic event. This was more about discipleship than discipline, and some interesting conjunctions occurred, almost by mistake. Harry would have approved.

'Pyschedelic grandad' Van Dyke Parks made his first stage appearance in London, with Syd Straw singing harmonies, and a string quartet as he chuckled through 'East Virginia'. He was followed by Nick Cave, as 'serious as cancer in a button-upped three piece',* singing apocalyptic gospel. Former Beefheart guitarist Gary Lucas 'taps into uncharted psychedelic C&W waters'. Beth Orton glows with pathos. Bryan Ferry croons his way through 'John Henry'. Bob Neuwirth sang about wanting to become a mole in the ground, while looking like a Las Vegas cowboy.

Descriptions of Mary Margaret O'Hara ranged from 'hyperactive toddler' to 'distracted', and as she sang 'The Ship Went Down', about the sinking of the Titanic, Mary frolicked like an 'embarrassing aunt at a wedding'. One reviewer found the song choice particularly appropriate. Mary had the misfortune to follow Jimmy Scott and his scalding version of 'Motherless Child'.

The man who stole the show was Jarvis Cocker, with his versions of the 'Coo Coo Bird' and the Masked Marvel's 'Mississippi Boweevil Blues', delivered with a metaphorical limp wrist. At one point he departs from the original lyrics to shout 'I shat in your ciabatta'.

Another unexpected triumph was the showing of two cartoons made by Harry Smith, which can now be seen as an inspiration for Terry Gilliam's early Monty Python animations, 'more mind-altering than any of today's club visuals'.

Almost two years earlier, in October 1997, two evening concerts and a day-long symposium in Washington DC at the Smithsonian Institute's National Museum of American History – where better? – had marked the re-release of the *Anthology* as a 6-CD box set. Here were some of the survivors of the great 'folk scare', which the Harry Smith had wished into being in the early '60s, the likes of the New Lost City Ramblers and Dave Van Ronk and John Sebastian duetting with Geoff Muldaur. It was a great night for nostalgia.

* *New Musical Express*

Key performances were captured as *The Harry Smith Connection*, but much here sounds too respectful in the cold light of day, and certainly not in the spirit of 'God's own guest DJ', a man who in Peter Stampfel's words, wanted to 'shove the world up his – ears'. Or the spirit of alt country, for that matter. Even so, there is a dream combination of Roger McGuinn, singing with rare passion on 'East Virginia Blues' with lively acoustic backing from Jeff Tweedy and Jay Bennett of Wilco.

When Ginny Walker, a traditional singer from West Virginia, who grew up singing hymns in a Primitive Baptist church, attacks 'The Butcher Boy', it raises the hairs at the back of your neck. And the stars here are those once regarded as wild mavericks. Stampfel debuts a tribute in song, 'His Tapes Roll On', while the Fugs update 'Nothing', a Tuli Kupferberg lament from their first album, produced by Smith.

The best tribute of all was the *Harry Smith Project*, held in California in 2001, and again tied in with an academic symposium at the Getty. Here the chosen songs come mainly from the fourth volume of the *Anthology*, which has only recently been issued, years after its compiler's death. Now a live album of this gig would be something very special.

'Harry Smith's shining down on us' exclaims a stately Marianne Faithfull early on in what turns out to be a five-hour marathon. By now the organisers have got things right, cutting across musical genres to forge new connections. Just like the *Anthology*. One sequence starts with David Thomas backed by Van Dyke Parks and bluegrass fiddler Richard Greene, reworking Uncle Dave Macon's 'Way Down The Old Plank Road'. The crowd clap along in time. Then straight into Steve Earle, with rough-and-ready covers of Dock Boggs and Blind Lemon Jefferson. Philip Glass follows, with his very smooth and repetitious piano playing, as a soundtrack to three of Smith's short experimental movies.

It is the sort of show where Elvis Costello joins Bill Frisell and Martin Carthy's daughter Eliza. Faithfull's rousing 'John The Revelator' has a celebrity chorus of Earle, Todd Rundgren and Beck, with David Johansen wailing away on harmonica, who later showcases his own barrelhouse singing on 'A Lazy Farmer Boy'. Bob Neuwirth talks about his own memories of Smith. Costello returns with the McGarrigle sisters, on a two part 'Omie Wise', with Elvis adding a modern sequel.

Best of all are the three actors who became forever Spinal Tap, here parodying the 'Folkmen', whose 'clean style was the antithesis of what Smith was all about'. *No Depression* claims their version of the Flashdance song 'What A Feeling' would have made the Kingston Trio proud.

But the real jaw-dropping moment was no less than Garth Hudson's keyboard gymnastics on a revival of The Carter Family's 'No Depression', while his wife Maude sings with 'unadorned elegance'. It hushes the packed hall. As the clock approached 1:30am, Hudson played the crowd out with a rambling but energetic recessional on the pipe organ.

In 2000, Revenant issued this long missing fourth record to complete Harry Smith's original plan. The alchemical pattern was at long last complete, and the original take of 'No Depression' by The Carter Family is now available at the click of a play button. Sara sounds as truly depressed as ever, though she gets almost exultant at the economic downturn, and a midnight storm bringing 'millions to their doom' (this was recorded in 1936, with the death camps less than a decade away). Even so, no one here sounds exactly convinced by the vision of 'that bright land' they are supposedly transfixed by. What really cuts through is the misery of the present world in which they are singing, with 'orphans crying for bread'. I love the way they sing the word 'where' as only Appalachian natives can, more like 'whur'.

Even so, there is something disappointing about *Volume Four*. The packaging is sumptuous, but it doesn't connect with the Folkways reissue of the original *Anthology*, or indeed the design of that 1952 vinyl box set. There are no less than five essays, and as Smith's original notes to what was originally planned as a survey of 'rhythm changes between 1890 and 1950' are long lost, the critical notes here are more 'scholarly' and less wilfully eccentric – or funny – and seem to overwhelm the actual music. With its 'dark brown, ersatz faded, recycled paper', the package looks like a reissue of something that never was.

All is explained in a letter from Paul Vernon to *Folk Roots* magazine. The track listing here does not cohere with Harry's list as kept at the Smithsonian. Some of these 28 tracks appear here, some not. Vernon asserts that those responsible for compiling *Volume Four*, none of whom were connected with the Folkways reissue, had circulated that list to collectors and researchers, 'asking them what they would have liked to have seen on the set instead'. The 'new' compilation was based on their response. If true, this is disgraceful, as it is certainly not mentioned on the packaging. The whole point about Harry Smith is his weird sense of authenticity. Even so, Vernon admits that the Revenant issue is 'actually a much better collection than the one Harry nailed together'.

It certainly sounds of a much higher aural quality than volumes 1–3, because the compilers have gone to better source tapes. This 'secret volume' covers 78s recorded between 1928 and 1940,and the shadow of the grinding poverty of those years lies dark across the songs here. Smith omits vital new forms like western swing, early honky tonk and cowboy songs. That wild exuberance that makes the original *Anthology* so wonderful has largely fled.

It has fled only so far as those now picking further at the rich musical seam somewhere between blues and country and folk opened up by Smith. David Johansen even named his band The Harry Smiths, in homage for what was at first intended as a one-off gig at the Bottom Line. But the mask stuck, and now David comes on like a mountain man, hollering out in a gravelly voice and gutbucket style the white man's blues.

You could really get no more authentic, nowadays, than the way David urgently reinterprets 'Oh Death' on their first album from 2000, which reworks four songs from the *Anthology*, or sings Gillian Welch's 'My Morphine' on their second, a slightly rockier affair. Both could as easily relate to the late Johnny Thunders, and the junkie chic that killed him, as to any traditional model.

Geoff Muldaur's *The Secret Handshake*, from 1998, is a relaxed and tuneful recreation of some of the bluesier songs chosen by Harry Smith. Muldaur is the corn to David Johansen's husk. He plays banjo on 'Mistreated Mama', with fiddle and dobro, and sweet brass. Geoff actually saw Dock Boggs, who himself learnt the song from 'a coloured girl with a piano', live at the Newport Festival in 1963. All of us Cambridge folkies had heard him on the *Smith Anthology*, but there he was, living history'.

The follow up, *Password*, was described as reworking 'gems from the Aladdin's Cave of musical Americana'. Those involved were a similarly eclectic mix from Dave Alvin to Van Dyke Parks, on pump organ.

Kelly Joe Phelps comes from Washington State, and via the jazz world. He plays acoustic guitar flat across his lap and uses a solid-steel bar in his left hand to control the sound, picking with his right. Live, he seems to expend little digital effort for the extraordinary sounds he makes, though he is intensely visual, throwing his head back, jerking his knees and elbows as if in some kind of trance, and scraping, tapping and banging his guitar. As he told *Folk Roots*, 'music is a very mystical experience for me. It almost becomes a Zen thing. How good are you going to get at opening yourself up?' On a good night, the music comes through him.

Kelly Joe pulls old time songs from Appalachia into country blues settings, making a brand new sound out of combining elements from the *Anthology*, like an alchemist. He sees no great divide. 'You can take the music of Roscoe Holcomb and put this alongside Skip James, and there's a certain correlation'.

The results on an album like 1999's *Shine Eyed Mister Zen* are much like early John Fahey, acoustic guitar ringing clear as a bell, but with intimate, slurred vocals on top, all set to a shuffle. 'Dock Boggs' Country Blues' is a slow, bottleneck stomp, sung with huge tenderness. But since then even his agent jokes that Phelps has 'gone weird' and the music on *Slingshot Professionals* is awesome, with Bill Frisell, and Jesse Zubot on fiddle and mandolin, and Kelly Joe singing surrealistic words and playing subtle guitar, with lots of space round the edges.

Recent live gigs have been mesmeric. At the Jazz Café, he complains about the UK's chaotic rail system, before his own train song, 'almost crashed there, almost crashed', as his guitar vibrates like 'whipping power lines'. He strokes it, karate chops it and beats it like a drum. Over in Belfast, he plays a 'mind-blowing' first set, then calms things down with gentle ballads and 'a smouldering Appalachian-trilogy featuring guest fiddler Tim O'Brien'.

One young band from New York went even further, and the Boggs named themselves after the master. Their 2001 album *We Are The Boggs, We Are* is an extraordinary recreation of a lost time and place. As *The Guardian* puts it, 'they sound as if they dragged themselves out of a graveyard in Appalachia', brought back from the dead by moonshine whisky. Singer Jason Friedman sings in a 'petrified scarecrow croak', over an eerie and clattering background of banjo, fiddle, accordion and slide guitar, with not a hint of delicacy. It was recorded only a few weeks after the band was formed, so this is fresh and pungent as bear shit. The nearest comparison is the early Pogues, so that you can hear not a word, and everyone sounds like they're either dead drunk or on speed, and playing in boxing gloves. All recorded in mono, for extra authenticity.

This is string-band music, back with a vengeance. Solo banjo pieces and primitive hollers, all with inner propulsion: Will Oldham with a rocket up his arse. The band are far more clever than they try to make out, and themselves call it 'archival no-wave'. Friedman describes how 'multiple folk sources are folded in on each other – a telephone game of culture'. Just like Harry Smith.

The Boggs might convincingly ape the scratchy shellac of 78rpm discs, but songs like 'Hard Times' are about modern day Brooklyn, not the past. Everything here is newly written by Jason, about night burials and the like. *The Independent* praises Emily Jane Oviatt's vocal on the duet 'Emily O Emily' as 'capturing the authentically thin, reedy quality of Sara Carter'. Ian Anderson admires Friedman's dedication to stump-toothed mumbling, too. This vocal sounds like he phoned it in. 'There are dark, spooky bits, distantly recorded where the spirit of old Dock himself is lurking somewhere in the dark corners of the studio'. Even so, recent songs played live seem to be moving towards alt country territory.

Back with *Volume Four* of Harry Smith's great project, young listeners would immediately spot the links with Smog or Will Oldham, or even be convinced the whole thing was newly cooked up in a studio by some revivalist pranksters. The Boggs, say. Smith's artful segues make him less of an archivist and more like a 'modern, mood-spinning DJ'.

If Harry Smith was the prankster in the DJ booth, then the likes of Alan Lomax were earnest ramblers, with a tape recorder bulking out their knapsack as they trawled the South for remnants of folk culture. The turn of the 21st century saw a niche market opening up to supply vintage Americana on CD. It was an adjunct of the 'world-music' craze. Here were sounds as weird as anything you would find in Tibet or the Congo, and you too could play at being Cecil Sharp and play this rough, outlandish music in the comfort of your living room.

Labels like Rounder and Smithsonian Folkways and Yazoo brought out collections of rare string-band music, or a 13-volume set of Alan Lomax's *Southern Journey*, or Mike Seeger's collecting trips in the '50s and '60s. As with Harry Smith, there was no hidden colour bar – Appalachian folk merged into rural blues, and the only criteria was authenticity. The most startling recent discovery comes via two CDs on Appleseed gathering highlights of reel-to-reel tapes made by Anne and Frank Warner, who with what Lomax calls a 'continuous act of unpaid, tender devotion' made regular songcatching trips from their New York home to capture poor mountain folk singing and talking, with rare intimacy. At the time, these tapes fed into the '60s folk revival, through Frank's own singing, and books like *Anne's Traditional American Folksongs*. Now here they are, real as life, and young musicians like Cordelia's Dad have mined them for diamonds.

But questions of appropriation intrude, as they did even with Cecil Sharp (who copyrighted to himself the material he was given free). When Frank Noah Proffitt brought one of those new-fangled television sets back to his log cabin in Pick Britches Valley, North Carolina. 'One night I was looking at some foolishness when three fellers stepped out with guitar and banjer and went to singing 'Tom Dooley' and they clowned and hipswinged. I began to feel sorta sick, like I'd lost a loved one. Tears came to my eyes. I went out and balled on the Ridge, looking towards old Wilkes land of Tom Dooly.' No wonder, for it was Frank who had passed this song to the Warners, from whence the Kingston Trio picked it up. 'I looked up across the mountain and said, Lord, couldn't they leave me the good memories.' Then Warner wrote explaining the song's popularity and 'the shock was over and I went back to work. I began to see the world was bigger than our mountains of Wilkes and Watauga. Folks was brothers, they all liked the plain ways... Life was sharing the different thinking, the different ways. I looked in the mirror of my heart – You ain't a boy no longer. Give folks like Frank Warner all you got. Quit thinking of Ridge to Ridge, think of ocean to ocean.' But there is a happy outcome, as not only did the Proffitts finally benefit from a cut of the royalties, but Proffitt became a well-respected performer on the world stage, whose 'quiet, dry humour toppled old stereotypes'.

Tim Ericksen argues rightly that 'something like love radiated from the recordings – the Warners really, really listened'. The Warners' son Gerret still recalls his summer holidays in the mountains, far from their Greenwich Village home, distracted by 'the lack of toilet facilities and running water', and even more by these weird mountain folk who 'would sit and stare comfortably. Then somebody would speak or sing a song. They didn't fill in, the way all of us feel so comfortable with doing'. This sense of difference has fuelled a modern industry, with novels by Lee Smith and Sheila McCrumb, and movies like *O Brother, Where Art Thou?* and *Songcatcher*, and a renewed interest in old-time music, and the culture that envelops it.

iii) Oh Brother

'I just know that it's good music. I always saw it
in opposition to packaged music'
– *John Goodman*

The movie *O Brother, Where Art Thou?* (2000) was described by director Joel Coen as combining 'the three Stooges with Homer's *Odyssey*'. Heart-throb George Clooney plays against type as the vain and hair pomade fanatic Ulysses Everett McGill, on a quest taking him back home to Ithaca, in the deep South, not the Mediterranean.

Homer's narrative poem is updated to Mississippi in 1937, with John Goodman playing a one-eyed Cyclops. The Sirens who lured men to their doom are voiced by an alluring trio of Emmylou Harris, Gillian Welch and Alison Krauss, with an *a capella* version of 'Didn't Leave Nothing But The Baby'. Singers who actually appear on screen include two singing families, the Coxes from Cotton Valley, Louisiana and the Whites, while the Fairfield Four turn up as grave diggers.

Three prisoners escape from a chain gang and are saved from justice by their prowess as vocal act the Foggy Bottom Boys, who have a local hit with their rendition of 'Man Of Constant Sorrow'. This is the 'treasure' that an old blind seer tells them about: needless to say, they meet him on a railway track. The film is suffused with old-time music, both black and white. The Foggy Bottom Boys are racially mixed, which almost leads to a lynching – 'the music just became another character in the story. It began to take over the script as we went on, until the film became almost a musical. It establishes the tone and the flavour.'*

The guiding hand behind all this was that of T-Bone Burnett. T-Bone has had an interesting career as a kind of zelig of Americana, always just standing just a few yards off the main action. His first claim to fame was when he was running a tiny record label in Fort Worth, Texas, and recorded 'Paralysed' by the weird, hollering Legendary Stardust Cowboy. Burnett later joined Dylan's backing band on the *Rolling Thunder Review*, and has worked on albums by Elvis Costello, Peter Case, Jimmy Dale Gilmore and Gillian Welch. His own records are a tad anonymous, but one that stands out is the rockabilly influenced *Trap Door*, with Richard Thompson. But T-Bone's great ability is as a guiding spirit. It is no great surprise that the soundtrack album comes over like an addendum to the *Harry Smith Anthology*, and works perfectly in its own right.

When Dan Tyminski came to record 'Man Of Constant Sorrow', T-Bone told him 'You're hungry, you've just heard you can win $50 on a radio contest. You're trying to play rock 'n' roll, it just hasn't been invented yet.' The soundtrack links archive recordings to newly performed material, which is made to sound from '30s America. It opens with a chain-gang version of 'Po Lazarus', from 1957, and ends with the 1955 original of the Stanley Brothers' 'Angel Heart', like a benediction. On the earliest track sampled here, Harry McClintock's 'Big Rock Candy Mountain' from 1928, Grant Alden reckons 'you can hear the needle in the grooves'.

The emotional heart of the film is Ralph Stanley's unaccompanied 'O Death', which on screen is put into the mouth of a red-robed Klan leader. The Whites perform The Carter Family's standard 'Keep On The Sunny Side', while instrumental passages are supplied by modern maestros Norman Blake and John Hartford, who updates the old Holy Modal Rounders' fiddle tune 'n' wail 'Indian War Whoop'.

The CD went on to be a surprise hit. Homer on a railway truck spoke truer than he knew: the lost treasure was American roots music, and the shops filled up with all kinds of re-releases, like *O Sister*, a female

* *Joel Cohen*

equivalent. This all helped to kickstart a massive revival of interest in a musical form that Music Row in Nashville had thrown into the trash.

Needless to say, country music radio tried to ignore completely what was then a top-selling album. 'Pop stations considered it too country, and country stations too pop.'* Gillian Welch considers that the album has had little effect on the kinds of acts being signed up in Nashville, though they might put banjo on a track of their bland new albums. Everything else is a 'windfall'.

Even so, the mainstream music industry certainly sat up and took note. Suddenly, mandolins and fiddles were cool again. Before the flood hit, the musicians gathered in May 2000 at the Ryman Auditorium, original home of the *Opry*, to celebrate what they had done. Grant Alden was a bit bemused about how these songs would fit together in the forthcoming movie, and spoke about the 'inevitable soundtrack album', without knowing how it would change everything. He also mentions an 'unobtrusive documentary' being made that night by DA Pennebaker.

It is fascinating now to read Grant's account of a stage bare of drums or amplifiers, just a collection of 'vintage microphones', and a procession of musicians who 'though they came from old places, there is nothing of the museum in their presentation'. Indeed, 'that was the evening's chief joy, that this music – distant kin to what rides the radio – was yet so alive and vibrant'. Each artist does one song from the film, and one of their own, with T-Bone doing an 'extraordinary job pacing the show'. He prods vocals from Gillian Welch on 'Indian War Whoop' 'teasing her, bringing her closer to the microphone as if he were a snake charmer'.

A year later, after the flood had hit, much the same cast reconvened for a sell-out concert at Carnegie Hall. John Hartford can hardly be replaced, but Elvis Costello does his unobtrusive best as 'merely a member of the audience who got promoted'. The most spine-chilling moment is Krauss, Emmylou and Welch singing 'Your Long Journey', performed only a few days before at Hartford's funeral. As Gillian later explained, 'I've known that song for years. It's by Doc Watson's wife Rosalie, and it's one of the most beautiful songs about parting.'

Ralph Stanley closes the show, admonishing David Rawlings for an out-of-tune guitar, then launching into 'O Death', before returning for

* *The Coen Brothers*

'Man Of Constant Shadow' and a mass singalong on 'Angel Band'. Early in 2002, Ralph led a *Down From The Mountain* Tour, with Bob Neuwirth acting as compere, and Patty Loveless getting the crowd going on 'Shady Grove'. She describes Dr Stanley as 'the father of mountain soul'. Best of all is Emmylou Harris, backed by Buddy and Julie Miller.

DA Pennebaker's film of the original concert appeared as *Down From The Mountain*, and its blend of on-stage and backstage footage proves mesmerising. The setting of the Ryman, an old wooden church, merely adds to the sense of ghostliness, with Ralph Stanley in old age, but straight backed and proud, a visibly dying John Hartford, Gillian Welch looking as if she should have been born back at the time of The Carter Family, and Emmylou holding it all together.

The documentary opens with Dr Stanley being driven down from the hills into Nashville in the back of a limousine, like royalty and as if he has never been there before. There is also some precious footage of him and Carter, back in 1965. It culminates with his pinched voice singing 'Oh Death'. Grant Alden treasures both the rehearsal footage and 'tight shots of performance', notably the 'instant smiles' that flash between the Cox family as they sing close harmony, the Peasall Sisters' youthful mixture of nerves and composure, and 'especially in Gillian Welch's eyes as she follows Hartford's fiddle during "Indian War Whoop".'

Pennebaker captures the warp and wooft of live music as it happens, plus the action off stage. Here it is John Hartford who catches the camera most strongly, seemingly dancing in his bowler hat and glasses perched on the edge of his nose, racked with illness but almost burning up as you watch. Offstage, he talks quietly about his parallel life as a steamboat skipper, and the cancer that is taking both his lives away.

Pennebaker intercuts a radio interview in which Ralph Stanley sternly argues that one must have Appalachian blood to sing this music properly, with people like Hartford and Emmylou and Gillian Welch, who obviously don't, but are infused with its true spirit. And by the strangest irony of all, Pennebaker is actually older than Ralph Stanley. He knows well where this music is coming from. 'I've been in those mountains – you may as well be on the moon. Those people carry that music along like luggage, generation after generation.'

At the age of 75, Ralph Stanley won a Grammy for Best Country Vocal Performance, beating the likes of Ryan Adams and Johnny Cash. 'I'm real proud of it. It makes me think that maybe I haven't wasted 55 years.' He has always called his style 'old-time mountain music, it's more farther back, down-to-earth than bluegrass'. And if *Clinch Mountain Country* (1998), where he was joined by luminaries like Dylan, Alison Krauss, Ricky Skaggs and BR5-49 seemed at the time like a stately farewell, now he has a new lease of life. Even then, *No Depression* noted how Ralph's singing voice seemed to have strengthened with age, and he agreed. 'I didn't want to lose nothing, and I guess I just put out more.'

The set list has been chosen from hundreds of murder ballads, love songs and hymns, plus a Hank Williams number and Ralph's own 'Great High Mountain'. Ralph sings with throaty eloquence, plus a relentless determination, and musicians from *O Brother*, like Norman Blake, add a 'tender melodiousness to these songs of revenge, anger and lost love'. And redemption. He is 'capable of singing of incredible violence without betraying any weak sentiment',* relating over a droning fiddle accompaniment how Lord Darnay drags his wife by the hair, cuts off her head and 'kicked it against the wall', with quiet relish. The entire album has 'the smell of death, largely because the folk canon is so inescapably bloody'†. These songs were, after all, the tabloid newspapers of their day, and nothing sells like murder and sex. Just listen to the matter of fact way he sings 'and Matty lied dead in his gore'. But what cuts deepest of all is Ralph's voice stripped naked of all instrumentation, with the final allelujah in 'Twelve Gates To The City' both sad and triumphant.

Stanley has recently collaborated with the relatively youthful Jim Lauderdale, with Robert Hunter providing some of the songs. Thus does the circle turn, but things stay much the same up at Dr Ralph Stanley's Memorial Bluegrass Festival, remembering Carter, held each May in Ralph's family cemetery Here, Stanley is playing to the converted, and only a smatter of applause follows his mention of *O Brother*, while wild whooping greets 'Angel Band'.

Gillian Welch often quotes something that Townes Van Zandt once told her, that there are only two kinds of music, 'there's the blues and there's 'Zip-A-Dee-Doo-Dah'. Her own music definitely veers towards

* *The Guardian*
† *No Depression*

the former, as mindless joy is hardly on the agenda. Dressed in '30s chic and looking as if she just walked out of a Walker Evans photo – with music to match – Welch is about as far from a Spice Girl, or even a Dixie Chick, as you could imagine. 'She ought to come sepia tinted.'*

Gillian started singing Carter Family songs at the age of five, but never heard the originals until she went away to college in Santa Cruz, and met a bluegrass DJ. 'When I heard the Stanley Brothers, I was doomed. It was so raw and exposed.' She had played in a garage band, and back home was well aware of the Blasters and Maria McKee, but this was something else. It had 'the same degree of grit, as tough as any rock 'n' roll I had ever heard. I knew what I had to do.'

This consisted of studying at Boston's Berklee College of Music, where she met up with David Rawlings and found their voices fitted well together. 'We're a band, a little band.' 'Welch wrings untold emotion out of her lyrics in much the same way that Linda Thompson's stately vocals do on *Bright Lights*.'† And Rawlings' guitar work is 'strikingly similar to Richard Thompson's modal excursions of the mid '70s'.

The pair moved to Nashville in 1992, and scuffled for gigs and open-mic sessions, while Gillian worked as a hotel maid. Barney Hoskyns recalls seeing them early on, with Rawlings' 'soft tenor exquisitely shadowing Gillian's stark, vibrato-less alto', while their vintage acoustic guitars intertwined, a 1935 Epiphone for him, a Guild for her. Emmylou Harris was an early supporter, and included 'I Am An Orphan' on *Wrecking Ball*. Then T-Bone Burnett caught a 20-minute set when they were opening for Peter Rowan at the Station Inn, and the result was their 1996 debut album, *Revival*, recorded largely in mono.

The follow up *Hell Among The Yearlings* had been intended to feature just the duo, plus veteran bass player Roy Huskey Jr, 'and then he died. It was a dark year. I guess some of that stuff worked its way out into the songs'. The result is an even more stripped-back sound, with producer T-Bone joining them for 'Whiskey Girl', on keyboards. Saddest of all is 'My Morphine', with its yodel and love song to dope.

Time (The Revelator) is bleaker still, and the duo now seem to sing and play and write songs as one. They also produce the album themselves this time round, in Presley's favourite studio, RCA's Studio B in Nashville.

* *Uncut* magazine
† *No Depression*

This is music on the edge of trance, and 'Dear Someone' virtually slows to a halt. The best description of what Gillian's voice has evolved into comes in *Mojo*, 'its starkness muted by a kind of airiness like a small rip in a concertina'. *No Depression* reckons that Welch and Rawlings have gathered 'fragments from across the rich history of American music' and then reset them as 'small, subtle jewels adorning their own keenly observed, carefully constructed language'.

Of course, some people objected to what this was, a construct. Gillian's Appalachian accent in 'Red Clay Halo' bears no relation to her personal history. But just like Harry Smith, they blended disparate fragments into something genuinely new: 'Our palette is a little more constricted, so we're pretty careful about sequence, plus those tiny connections that happen from song to song.'

Live in Toronto, Welch actually warns the audience about her morbid streak. 'So far we've been light on the killing songs. We usually lose two per set.' At the Barbican, playing live lends their performance a 'thrilling improvisatory edge'. They are joined by Buddy Miller, and later join him as he plays an electric set in the foyer, for gutbucket versions of Dylan's 'Wallflower' and Chuck Berry's 'Nadine'. Rawlings blasts out guitar lines 'like Eddie van Halen, with a grin as wide as the Grand Canyon'.

Soul Journey (2003) is looser and more personal, with drums whacked hard, 'scrunched' electric guitar and bass, scrapy fiddle and dobro, leading Gillian towards a 'more rockin' Basement Tapes-ish Americana'.* It is their first album in colour, so to speak. The traditional 'Make Me A Pallet On Your Floor' is just Gillian and guitar, recorded at home. It is as if the couple have been through the valley of despondency, and come out the other side. 'No One Knows My Name' starts starkly, about 'just another baby born to a soul lost and gone', but light breaks through as a banjo chuckles. Gillian herself describes the writing here as 'super straightforward. The whole record is super-revealed. So the recording was done the same way, though some of it was unintentional'.

She was influenced by John Hartford's *Aero-Plain*, played live in the studio without listening to playbacks. It gets away from the notorious self-criticism musicians can be prey to. Gillian has also at long last recorded one of her happy songs, previously confined to her notebooks. On 'One

* *Uncut* magazine

Little Song', 'it's got that nursery-rhyme thing where the words just kind of roll along'. She is much influenced by Roger Miller – 'he gets played at my house a lot'.

For *The Observer*, Gillian surpasses her genre to become a chronicler of a 'different, contemporary America, one lived in strange, unsuitable places, and above all, internally'. But what exactly is that genre? When she toured with Son Volt, they found 'we have the same record collections'. So are they alt country? 'We're probably over on one edge of it. What Dave and I do is as stripped-down as that spectrum gets. 'It's good to feel you are not alone on the moon in what you do.'

But she is, really. As she told *The Guardian*, she might still look like a '30s throwback, but 'the same shit still happens, the dying, the sickness, the morphine addiction, the shooting, everything. It's right there out on Hollywood Boulevard.'

Gillian also appears on the soundtrack album for *Songcatcher*, a movie set in the 1900s, starring Janet McTeer as a professor of music who resigns and moves to the mountains and begins to collect folk songs, recording them onto wax cylinders. 'Barbara Allen' runs throughout the movie, there is some lovingly photographed North Carolina scenery, and a token Hollywood happy ending. It feels a bit formulaic, but the soundtrack doesn't, with all the actors doing their own vocals. The writer and director Maggie Greenwald is married to David Mansfield, like T-Bone a veteran of the *Rolling Thunder Review*, and has left him to put together the score. Iris Dement and Hazel Dickens even appear on screen.

Things were tidied up for the indispensable album, of 'music from and inspired by the original motion picture', with the added help of just about every contemporary female icon you would expect, Emmylou to Dolly Parton, Deana Carter to Maria McKee and Julie Miller. There is even a second volume, which goes back a generation to the likes of Doc Watson and Maybelle Carter. If this is a cynical marketing ploy, then let's have lots more of it. Even the UK alt-country magazine *Maverick* finds it 'in all honesty quite hard work', but praises a 'rare opportunity to hear some ancient ballads sung in a style that has largely passed out of existence', often a 'plaintive, sing-song style'. But in the latest twist of the kaleidoscope, this style is again in fashion, among a whole new generation of old time singers, most of them barely out of their teens when *O Brother* or *Songcatcher* hit the screens. The circle turns once again, and we will leave it just about where we began.

iv) New Old Time

'I made up every one of these songs, in as much as you can "make up" anything' – *John Hartford*

There is something in the mournful Appalachian voice that Greil Marcus once described as 'saying everything while seeming to say nothing'. Underneath all the packaging and TV appearances and stage persona, nobody sings – or writes – it better than Dolly Parton.

Dolly is part Scots/Irish, part Cherokee. She was born up on Locust Ridge in Tennessee, in an old log cabin. Her grandfather was a fiddle-playing preacher, and she first sang in public in her local tabernacle. 'Our services would be mostly music. The old hymns. They were just about the biggest things we did, recreation-wise'.

As a songwriter, Dolly has made rich use of her poor rural upbringing, and a fund of memories, from which she constructs stories with a moral. As a singer, Parton seems to be able to radiate pure joy or bleak despair, seemingly at will. Her voice is unusually flexible: it floats and trills and pierces and aches and giggles. One thing it will never do is lull you to sleep. She yodels, too.

Parton first emerged on the *Porter Wagoner* show in the late '60s, when Music Row was already trying to distance itself as quickly as possible from such rural corn (and great music). Dolly made a series of wonderful albums for RCA under Porter's jurisdiction, culminating in *My Tennessee Mountain Home* in 1973, a concept album about living and working in Nashville, yet feeling the pull of the mountains. The music is made to match, with the greatest Music Row session men, and lots of dobro, electric banjo and fiddle, plus Charlie McCoy on harmonica, always a mark of authenticity. While so much of Nashville was yielding to the blandishments and sweeping strings of 'countrypolitan', Wagoner kept things downhome. As a result, her albums from the early '70s sound timeless, as do the songs. Dolly's vocals start to shine with a 'singular, disarming brilliance; she skips and soars with effortless grace'.*

If anyone claims they cannot stand country music, I play them the recent Raven compilation *Mission Chapel Memories: 1971–1975*, which gathers highlights from her early years. Then she broke free of Porter and all that he represented, but only managed to escape into showbiz.

After years of LA bombast and albums stuffed with filler, with her best performances confined to the movie screen and TV talk shows, Dolly Parton's voice began to recover its original twang and snap. On the aptly named *Hungry Again* she soared like a lark ascending, having retreated to her Smoky Mountain home to fast and pray for guidance, plus write a new batch of songs. Her cousin recorded the album in the basement studio of his Nashville home using roots-rock band Shinola and his own acoustic combo, Richie Owens And The Farm Bureau. As Owens said, much of the music that she recorded in California showcased 'great production instead of Dolly Parton. It overwhelmed this beautiful Appalachian voice. I'm glad if maybe the different mindset of Hungry Again maybe helped pave the way for the bluegrass record, because that is the best way to record her. Back off. Let her do her thing.'†

The record was finally released in August 1998. Shortly thereafter, Universal shut down Decca and left Parton without a label. She went off to the specialist label Sugar Hill in North Carolina, and made *The Grass Is Blue*, a year later. It opens with a brief passage of sad and lonely fiddle, then we're into banjo time and the upbeat 'Travelling Prayer', and Dolly sounds electric. That song is by Billy Joel no less, but even choosing a song by someone well outside the bluegrass scene, and making it go native is all part of the tradition. Just think back to all those Beatle songs reinterpreted by the likes of The Dillards. Parton herself provides some of her best new songs for years, done old style.

Recording sessions saw a supercharged acoustic combo, including Jerry Douglas on dobro and Sam Bush on mandolin. There is not a hint of crossover; no drums, no electric instruments. The age of each instrument used here is proudly announced – a century old German fiddle, a 1937 Gibson mandolin, a 1934 Gibson banjo. Only Dolly's voice is undated.

* *Rolling Stone*
† *No Depression*

Backing singers include Alison Krauss and Patty Loveless, but it is Parton who startles most, attacking each song, and by turns ferocious, sassy and aching. Dolly told *No Depression* that 'what brought me out of the Smoky Mountains was the fact that I loved songs and wanted to sing', and it is as if she has suddenly rediscovered all that early passion. She made a guest appearance at the CMA Awards, 'all those Dixie Chicks and one old southern hen'. They wanted an uptempo song to keep the show moving'. 'Train, Train' was an inspired choice. Parton had picked the song from her husband's record collection, a 1979 album by the Southern boogie band Blackfoot, an offshoot of Lynyrd Skynyrd.

Sessions for *The Grass Is Blue* intersected with those for *O Brother*. Something was definitely in the air. But Dolly moved on again, and Grant Alden reckoned that the follow up, *Little Sparrow* veers away from 'hard bluegrass' towards the 'smooth, cocktail bluegrass of *IIIrd Tyme Out*'.

Dolly might wrest back 'Seven Bridges Road' from The Eagles, and bluegrass-up Cole Porter, but the heart of *Little Sparrow* lies in the trio of songs beginning with 'Mountain Angel'. Dolly has taken up Steve Earle's challenge on *The Mountain*, and dared to write new songs for the canon. 'Mountain Angel' is a whole novel in a song, told at a distance and with hints at dark forces lurking in those hills.

As if reborn, Dolly set out on her first live tour for a decade, and when she hit the 9.30 Club in Washington DC, she drew a strange crowd of city hipsters and long-time fans. As she sang, 'her face would grow thoughtful',* but when she reached the end a switch would flip and the 'incandescent personality would come on again'.

Halos And Horns is much the same, an aural counterpart to the Blueniques stage attire, denim and rhinestone vests, a 'close harmony singing that JS Bach wouldn't look down his nose at'.† The Oakridge boys, neither. The emphasis is on country gospel, and she even turns Led Zeppelin's 'Stairway To Heaven' into a back-porch hymn. In 'These Old Bones', Dolly plays both a young girl and her cackly, hillbilly mother, to suggest a bond between them that survives death. On such songs, Parton taps into something primeval and witchy in the Appalachian mindset. Others have dipped their bucket into this deep, deep well of music, to whom it will always be a matter of cultural tourism, and not a birthright.

* *No Depression*
† *The Guardian*

Laura Cantrell was brought up in Nashville, but the old Nashville of wealth and power. Her father was a judge, her mother a lawyer. She went to Columbia University, and was amazed to find New York bar bands 'playing the Dolls and Johnny Cash in the same set'. It was a 'neat discovery, I thought I could fit in', so she formed her own band. Laura also began to present an alternative music show on WFMU in New Jersey, and then hooked up with the independent Scottish label Shoeshine, who brought out *Not The Trembling Kind* (2000). Despite the tough title song, Laura comes over as sweet-voiced and vulnerable, especially on her own songs, heartfelt and poignant. 'Queen Of The Coast' pictures a fading country singer, which Cantrell must have seen all over Nashville, 'with a catch in her voice and a beehive on her head/do you remember anything she ever said?'. It is sweet but sharp. The backing musicians are understated, with gorgeous dollops of pedal steel, mandolin and 12 string, all courtesy of Jon Graboff: this is essentially country-flavoured pop, with a melancholy edge. And strangely addictive.

Reviewers and DJs fell at her feet, and the finest of them all, John Peel, confessed that 'I love this album to the point of madness.' For long-time adherents of his programme, Laura's clear diction and gentle emotion certainly came as a culture shock in the midst of noise epics and bratty teens, like a queen amidst malcontents.Which, in effect, Cantrell was until recently, as an investment banker working on Wall Street. You'd never guess it from this luminous record.

When the Roses Bloom Again again relies chiefly on New York-based songwriters like Amy Allison and George Usher, Amy Rigby and Joe Flood. There is a retro feel, from the cover to the opening line 'I've been sitting all night listening to my records', and there's a '50s-style train song, while the title track comes straight from AP Carter, via Wilco.

Laura's has 'vintage and plain-sung sincerity',* but like the best of the music she recreates, there is something darker underneath here too, a 'murky undercurrent'. It surfaces on 'Conqueror's Song', by Dave Schramm, but worthy of Richard Thompson at his bleakest and best.

Bleak is not a word one would immediately associate with the Be Good Tanyas, three young women from Vancouver, but it is there too, throbbing underneath. It is in country music's water, like it or not.

* *No Depression*

No Depression found what was so exciting about this stripped-down string band, complete with three-part harmonies – and a male drummer – was 'the way they can get so much going in a song and yet still keep things so quiet'. They come out of an oral tradition of home singing, just like The Carter Family. 'We started really young with our siblings, singing *a capella* and working out harmonies, and you really have to listen.'

Their 2000 debut *Blue Horse* has an appealing mix of new songs and traditional, like the 'Coo Coo Bird': truly these are Harry Smith's children. As Frazey Ford puts it, 'we were all the rejects. But in the hippie movement you weren't allowed to be angry, and in the punk movement you weren't allowed to be tender. That's why I was drawn to old country and blues tunes, because it allowed you to be both.' Samantha Parton concurs. 'It made me want to find the real roots of American music. I wanted to hear harmonica. I wanted to hear banjos. I wanted to hear women singing.'

Blue Horse had a strange genesis. A local music lecturer saw the girls busking around town, and asked them to come into the studio so that he could teach his students how to record acoustic instruments. *Folk Roots* likes the way the vocals seem to meander at will, and the band's 'lethal cocktail' of charm, sadness, elegance and pain.

The Arlenes could be straight out of the '50s, judging from the cover of *Stuck On Love*, even though the music inside has more than a touch of late '60s country rock. 'Big Steve' is English but sounds like a 'cross between Gram Parsons and Glen Campbell'. Stephenie Arlene is a transplanted American who sings mainly vocal harmonies, as she did in another life for LA punk band the Flesheaters.

Together, 'we range from the hardcore country Hank Williams thing to dreamy stuff like The Byrds or Neil Young'. They have been rightly described as the best (half) British alt-country act, and go down a storm live, but the album reveals some neat picking from the likes of pedal-steel player Melvyn Duffy, on loan from Robbie Williams.

Patty Loveless is just about as authentic as you can get, born in Pikeville, a small mining town in Kentucky. Her voice is to match, and it can whoop and ache, seemingly at will. Her father had worked at the coal seam, and played Stanley Brothers records and the like at home, and Patty herself started to write her own songs in the old style. The first thus was 'Sounds Of Loneliness', a mature composition, which she wrote when just 14 and which appeared both on the *Songcatcher* soundtrack, and as the final track on *Mountain Soul* (2001).

With two fiddles droning under her vocal, Patty sounds 'as old as loneliness itself',* while the 'loamy arrangements', rich in traditional banjos and mandolins, summon up the 'looming hills and dark hollers' of her childhood. The old Appalachian song 'Shady Groves' is updated as 'Pretty Little Miss', while the newly famous 'Man Of Constant Sorrow' becomes 'Soul Of Constant Sorrow'. The album is generally mournful in tone, but such music 'gave my parents a way to escape. It spoke to their souls'. And to ours.

Patty cites the 'old line' singing at the church she attended as a child – a Baptist preacher would sing each line in turn, *a capella*, for the congregation to repeat, and worshippers would build up to a fever pitch. 'He would preach hellfire and brimstone. I mean stomping and yelling.' But Patty did not remain in the backwoods. She auditioned for Porter Wagoner, and went out on the road with him and Dolly Parton: they would sing trios, which must have been a treat.

But she couldn't make a living on Music Row until the '90s, with a less 'authentic' but punchier sound than her material for MCA, and produced by Emory Gordy Jr, Patty's husband and former bass player with Presley and Emmylou. A duet with George Jones on 'You Don't Seem To Miss Me', described as reaching 'heights of obsession' worthy of Roy Orbison was dropped by some in the marketplace as 'too country for country'. *Mountain Soul* was her riposte, giving them real country music with both barrels blazing. Patty had always tried to 'put a song or two in the mountain vein on each of my albums', so now she devoted a whole album, with family photos in the CD booklet, and her own tour band playing the sessions.

Kristin Hersh was still in her early teens when she founded the Throwing Muses with her half sister Tanya Donnelly, plus a rhythm section. 'We were kids. Our demos were like our heroes – the Meat Puppets, X, Violent Femmes, REM.' Jerky guitars, fronted by Kristin's 'hiccuping vocals', and dealing noisily with teenage traumas, though this soon became a formula, and subject to diminishing returns.

* *No Depression*

Hersh's best work appeared on much folkier solo records like *Hips And Makers*, starkly framed with piano and cello, and like a Pre-Raphaelite painting given voice. *Murder, Misery And Then Goodnight* (1998), which she sold via the internet, is a childrens' book illustrated by Arthur Rackham. It was a bare, largely acoustic and deeply sinister album of Appalachian ballads, as taught to her in childhood, a deeply troubling catalogue of murder and dismemberment, but sung in apparent innocence and a little girl voice. Apart from her finger-plucked guitar – 'you don't have to play blandly behind lyrics: a guitar is percussive, and there's rawness here' – the only accompaniment comes from Hersh's husband Billy O'Connell on piano and kitchen implements. Plus some vocal overdubs, which find Kristin singing with herself.

'When I began to compile some old family songs in the hope of giving a taste of my warm, fuzzy childhood, I was intrigued to find that my soundtrack had been – evil. The chick always dies. She's stabbed and poisoned and drowned.'* Cue songs like 'Down In The Willow Gardens' and 'Pretty Polly'. Her versions have none of the relish that Nick Cave brings to such material. This is even more unsettling, with a kind of emotional blankness, like the voiceover to the movie *Badlands*.

A showcase at the Borderline showed Kristin getting back to writing her own songs, which reflect the tiny but telling details of American urban life, like 'Raymond Carver miniatures'.† Hersh had just moved back to Rhode Island from the desert near Joshua Tree, where her neighbour was Victoria Williams – 'she wears big hats'.

But the songs accessed on *Murder, Misery And Then Goodnight* are a rich repository, to be rediscovered by each generation. As Dave Alvin wrote in the sleeve note to *Public Domain*, they are 'spirits', which 'live in the silences of the mountains and deserts. Such songs are 'hard, sad, rowdy, tender and joyous images of who we were, where we come from – a lot of what is good, and bad, about us in these songs.'

A traditional singer like Jody Stecher might come from New York – just as Martin Carthy, his nearest English equivalent, comes from London and was trained as a boy chorister. Even so, Jody is about as close as we can now get to old Appalachian balladeers, with his high-pitched, matter-of-fact vocals and dexterity on banjo and mandolin. Then he adds oud,

* *No Depression*
† *Uncut* magazine

to show that the essence of continuity is change: he has long flirted with Indian classical music, then combining it with Appalachian laments.

Stecher first appeared in the '60s, as a boy prodigy, and was part of long-lost combos like the Greenbrier Boys and the New York Ramblers. Later albums like *Snake Baked A Hoecake* from 1974 have proved quietly influential. There is an intensity to Jody's performances on *Oh The Wind And Rain: 11 ballads from 1999*. Many are sourced from American variants of 'original' British versions. 'Young Rapoleon' started life as 'Bonny Bunch Of Roses', mispronounced by the Tennessee mountain man who first sang it, thus renaming the would-be conqueror. As Jody's wife and singing partner Kate Brislin puts it, 'our renditions of old songs aren't a recreation of the past. The songs feel very immediate to us'.

Another hero of vintage Americana is Mike Seeger, who, after all those collecting trips and concerts with the New Lost City Ramblers and duets with his sister Peggy, finally takes centre stage on *Third Annual Farewell Reunion*, from 1994. Needless to say, the result is a series of collaborations with just about every great figure of the folk revival, from Maria Muldaur to Ralph Stanley.

But the greatest American traditional singer of them all has still to be Doc Watson. There is a wonderful album, *Remembering Merle,* of live duets from the early '70s with his son on nylon-strung guitar – a proud dad comments that 'I wondered what kinds of things he'd come up with, you have to let a fellow figure out what he's going to do with something once he gets a hold of it' – plus slide guitar and banjo. Just listen to the way the two generations come together on the timeless 'Omie Wise, And Its Pre-naturally Calm Murderer'. It is the folk process in action.

Then Merle tragically died in a tractor accident in 1985. The Merlefest established in his memory and held each April in Wilkesboro, North Carolina, has became one of the major Americana events. Gillian Welch won the first Merlefest songwriting competition, and now 14 stages are needed to fit in all the guest acts. The 2003 line up included The Nitty Gritty Dirt Band, Bela Fleck, Vassar Clements, Guy Clark, Peter Rowan, Asleep At The Wheel, Emmylou Harris and Jerry Douglas. Not much 'alt country', though, but Ralph Stanley and the Clinch Mountain Boys earn a respectful standing ovation.

Classical cellist Yo-Yo Ma along with fiddle player Mark O'Connor and Edgar Mayer on double bass, plus guest vocalists James Taylor and Alison Krauss, all joined in a concert at the Lincoln Centre to promote the *Appalachian Journey* CD. Here are songs and instrumentals either taken directly from or inspired by American traditional music and reinterpreted by a string trio. But still fully alive and emotionally engaging. As O'Connor points out, Americana is a national music 'which comes from everywhere else, from Africa, from Europe, from Asia', and which Mayer sees as 'fundamentally hybrid', neither purely classical or country, but something 'the three of us make when we get together'. It bends back.

A whole bunch of young American musicians started to rediscover their national music, while learning not to take it too solemnly. The Freight Hoppers came out of Bryson, North Carolina, and invested string-band music with high energy, 'the Pogues of old time'.* Frank Lee was hired to play banjo on the Great Smoky Mountain Railway, and met like minded revolutionaries who took the music of their childhood, and gave it a good kicking. As their singer Cary Fridley puts it, 'there were old bands who were just as wild as us . Listen to the Skillet Lickers. They were wilder than we could ever be'. Bassist Jem O'Rourke adds that 'we don't get bogged down in the idea of trying to play like they did on the record'. *Modern Twang* describes their 1996 debut *Where'd You Come From, Where'd You Go* as a 'non-stop, full-speed train ride'. Appearances at 'South By Southwest' won over a new generation to old time, done new style, all the old chestnuts like 'Little Sadie' and 'Cotton Eyed Joe', but done 'because it's natural, not as some academic revivalist crusade'.

Portland's Golden Delicious picked up where the Holy Modal Rounders left off. Check out 'Get the Hell Out of Your Sister's Dress', which it is difficult to imagine in the mouth of Bill Monroe. The band split up after SXSW, then mutated into Bingo, which adds sitar and ragas and a collaboration with Cornershop. The Asylum Street Spankers came from Austin, and local legend Mark Rubin produced their 1996 debut *Spanks For The Memory* at home and on one mic. Here are song titles like 'Startin' To Hate Country'.

The Red Clay Ramblers come from Chapel Hill, led by Debby McClatchy on lead vocals and banjo, and are a gentler proposition,

* *Folk Roots*

though they worked with everyone from Eugene Chadbourne to Michelle Shocked, and more recently on Kudzu: The Southern Musical, based on a comic strip. Not to be confused with the Red Mules (devoted to preserving Ohio's old-time heritage), the Red Mountain White Trash (who double harmonica with fiddle as lead instruments just like the Carolina Tar Heels once did), the Volo Bogtrotters from Chicago, the Hypnotic Clambake from Boston (who add klezmer on albums like *Ken The Zen Master*, 'like a bar mitzvah on acid), or the Strapping Fieldhands (whose albums are not so much produced as thrown together, and whose debut EP *The Demiurge* 'lies squarely on the creepier side of the tracks').

Darkest of all are the Deliberate Strangers who take their name from a TV movie about mass murderer Ted Bundy. Violent death is a constant theme, sometimes lightened by redemption, and the two come together on the album *More Music for Snake Handlers* (1998), which singer Tom Moran, once a Pittsburg punk, describes as 'like Dock Boggs meets Throbbing Gristle'.

A far quieter but no less unsettling combo are the Old Joe Clarks, a semi-acoustic combo formed in San Francisco, and named after a vintage fiddle tune. Though the band are basically a three piece, clarinet and melodica and autoharp join fiddle and banjo. Mike's wife Jill comes from an avant-garde background, so that too feeds into the pot. *Town Of Ten* saw general release in 1997, and a new song like 'Welfare Hotel' sounds like something out of the Great Depression. *Metal Shed Blues*, issued two years later, was even moodier.

Other bands have been inspired by this same idea, to create a contemporary mood of alienation and doubt using old-time elements. Last Forever describe what they do as 'new and old songs out of the American tradition' and their 1997 CD debut is rich and stately, a collaboration between Harvard-educated composer Dick Connette and the singer Sonya Cohen, John's daughter and Mike Seeger's niece. There are lots of violins – definitely no fiddles – and cellos and spinets, and some polite banjo. The slower the tempo, the more resonant the music.

This is beautifully thought through – just compare the version of 'Po Lazarus' here, sonorously arranged, with polite percussion, with the wild recording that opens *O Brother*.

A more recent exercise in rural nostalgia is *The Creek Drank The Cradle* by Iron & Wine. Soft, whispery male vocals, a handmade CD booklet, and songs like 'Muddy Hymnal', all written and performed at home by Sam Beam in Miami. Another one to watch is yet another luminous newcomer from Seattle, Laura Veirs, whose recent album *Troubled By The Fire* includes Bill Frisell on guitar, and Danny Barnes on backing vocals, plus subtle electronics from producer Tucker Martine. For once the claim pasted onto review copies that these are 'folk' songs that twist into 'uncharted territories' is justified.

Noah John flits between about five categories in *South By Southwest*. It is as if every kind of music celebrated here – old time, western swing, punkabilly, bluegrass, country rock – were all jumbled together, then played backwards. 'Post-modern hillbilly' is what that singer Carl Johns himself calls it. As Maddy Costa puts it, 'there's no melody to his voice, but it stretches across each song like a sheet of silver'.

Tadpoles joins this doleful voice to accordion, cello and pedal steel, on songs like 'Bullshit Games'. But the real meat is to be found on 2001's *Had A Burning*, where Carl fronts a five-piece electric band. Though not as you have ever heard before. All the praise falsely heaped on Jim White applies to Noah John, a form of postmodern music where the listener feels completely disorientated, yet strangely thrilled.

On *Water Hymns*, recorded in Chicago on one hot summer day, viola and cello now set the mood, with the 'prairie wobble' of a musical saw just to add a hint of unease. Carl Johns still cannot sing by any measurable definition, but his voice is questing and ornery and given to strange utterances. 'My mouth's too dry for your lips.'

The band that best recreates the spirit of old-time music is Freakwater, two women singers from Louisville, Kentucky, plus rhythm section. This is the same town that produced Will Oldham. Freakwater have been described as a 'post-punk Carter Family', and as reminding their small but rabid audience of 'churchyards, grandparents and the dust that comes out of 19th-century bibles'. There's something almost primeval about the way their two voices intertwine and react off each other.

Catherine Irwin has the deeper, smokier vocal cords and tends to take the melody line – she does pathos real good – while Janet Beveridge Bean has a sharper, higher tone, and floats and stings and sings descant all around her. At times it sounds as if they are being recorded in separate rooms, without being able to hear each other. Then suddenly they harmonise like angels. The words are always graphic and to the point, 'the twin anti-Shanias of country music, more partial to adenoidal twanging harmonies, pedal steel and fiddle than rock guitars'.* This is music not yet fully formed, and all the more affecting for it.

Freakwater is slang for moonshine whiskey, up in the hills. Catherine says made Janet 'sing my songs in a Tammy Wynette style because I thought it would contrast with my voice'. And it did. Catherine talked her into joining her at an open-mic night at the Beat Club: 'It was in an area downtown where there were a lot of strip clubs. We did 'Pistol Packing Mama' and 'D.I.V.O.R.C.E.' Then they spent months 'ploughing through Louvin Brothers and Carter Family records and harmonising around a basement four track.' Janet moved to Chicago but stayed in touch. She and Catherine would sing duets on the phone before officially forming Freakwater in 1989. Irwin's songwriting was developing into something genuinely new. 'Catherine is never the victim,' says Janet. 'Some of her songs are full of venom and can be really caustic, but it's never this "pity me" sort of thing'. As to 'alt country', Catherine reckons 'I don't know how mass a movement it is. It's certainly not going to change anything. Whenever we play Nashville, we get a good crowd, but we never hear from that side of the industry'.

Freakwater were wooed by E-Squared, and suddenly found themselves in a world of limousines and corporate lawyers, but they felt that Steve Earle's advisors wanted too polished a sound, and went back to cult label Thrill Jockey for *Springtime* – more songs about death, salvation in the blood of the Lord and hard drinking. It was recorded virtually live in Chicago, in eight days. This upped the cheerfulness stakes from their earlier album *Old Paint*, largely thanks to the presence of Max Johnston, from Wilco and the like, who even gets a lead vocal on 'Harlan'. Catherine refutes the charge that the band might be going soft. 'I don't think this record is any less evil.' That's a relief, then.

End Time (1999), a pre-millenial special, richly melodic thanks to a string section, pedal steel and organ, plus drums for the first time. Some

* *The Guardian*

of the trance rock of Janet Bean's earlier band Eleventh Dream Day has seeped in, and muted electronics serve as a rich backcloth for the Appalachian abandon of the two voices. Whatever category you put it in, this album aches and exults and chills.

The same applies to Cordelia's Dad, a wild, electric trio founded by college chums in Amherst, Massachusetts, who then toured with the likes of Nirvana. They apply a thrash-and-grunge style to folk songs as if cheerfully smashing up the family china. Lead singer and banjo player Tim Eriksen had played in hardcore bands, and was turned on to the English traditional singer Martin Carthy by his bandmate Tom King. He even sounds English on Cordelia's Dad's 1989 self-titled debut, made in 12 hours. On *How Can I Sleep?* everything comes together: 'we started listening to a lot more American music' and the sleeve notes namecheck the Warner field recordings, to which Eriksen was given access. Then the Warner family themselves became excited about this 'goofy rock band doing songs from their collection'. No wonder.

These boys have learnt well from the likes of Fairport's 'Sloth', recorded during the first flush of folk rock over in England, that sense of wildness restrained, but ready to break out any second. 'Bend To The East' could also be straight off *Full House*, except that Tim is as fluent on banjo as Dave Swarbrick is on mandolin. Eriksen later reworked 'Farewell To Old Bedford' as the opening track on his first solo album, recorded live and acoustic, and reminisced how the band would start with it during support slots for the likes of Weezer and The Dead Milkmen.

That side of their heritage comes over loud and clear on *Road Kill*, a messy compilation of various live shows from the early '90s, taped live on two track. Proudly labelled 'obscurity! tape hiss!' it is ominous and joyful and low-down dirty and tuneful. But the very opposite of genteel. By now Cath Oss had taken over on bass, and Tim moved to lead guitar.

An appearance at 'South By Southwest' saw the new line up of Cordelia's Dad move towards what you would least expect from *Road Kill*, a purely acoustic sound, or 'extreme modal music' as Eriksen calls it. *Comet* (1995) is still percussive and rough, it is just that someone has turned the electricity off. Somehow the unaccompanied songs sound the loudest, and much like the sonic assault of the live album.

The amps were still turned off for *Spine*, now with Laura Rusk on fiddle, and produced by grunge merchant Steve Albini.

It all seems a long way from CBGBs, though a short step to Dock Boggs, but 'within the sharp, sometimes brittle, folk geometry on *Spine* moves the ardent, volatile spirit of alternative country. 'Hard-core folk music',* an 'American folk suite, flowing with melancholy fascination'. Having taken traditional folk just about as far as it can go, the next Cordelia's Dad album, *What It Is*, saw Tim Eriksen beginning to write his own songs, in the same folky vein as Richard Thompson's early 'brooding self-examination'

A handful of key bands from the eastern seaboard have attacked string-band music from the south with the same hi energy that Cordelia's Dad use on traditional folk. The Tompkins County Horseflies were a largely traditional and acoustic bunch who added reggae to the musical equation. Then they hatched out as The Horseflies, and shared an album – *Old Time Music: Chokers & Flies* – with fellow iconoclasts the Chicken Chokers. On *Human Fly*, released two years later, The Horseflies had fully developed their 'neoprimitive bug music', like a cross between the Holy Modal Rounders and LaMont Young. 'Demented, post-modern mountain music' as one reviewer put it.

As they told *Folk Roots*, it was when 'Oh Death' entered their repertoire that The Horseflies 'started seeing ways of really letting ourselves branch out'. Claus explains that 'for a long time, I've heard connections between traditional music and contemporary minimalist composers who I remember hearing in the early '70s. Philip Glass, Steve Reich, Terry Riley and the rest. The essence lies in the use of repetition, over a changing ground. Add to this 'lyrics of desperation, but not in a blues way. It's the white boys' whine. REM do it brilliantly, and the Violent Femmes too.' But neither of those bands dare to reinterpret Dock Boggs' version of 'Rub Alcohol Blues', and alter both the music and some of the words.

In 1996, they took their sound further by adding three percussionists playing African rhythms, along the lines of the Rail Band or Jali Musa Jawara, so that uke and bass double as balafon, and banjo and fiddle as the kora, in a kind of dialogue. The spirited results were recorded at the 6th Annual Fingerlakes Grass Roots Festival, and later appeared as *In*

* *Folk Roots*

The Dance Tent, by which time bassist John Hayward had passed away. One reviewer reckoned that if whirling dervishes suddenly sprung up in the Appalachians, 'this is the type of music to which they probably would have danced'. It certainly got the tent shaking that day.

The sound was refined on a studio album *Two Traditions: Balaphon, Banjo, Fiddle And Drums*, largely instrumental, and bringing together string-band music with talking drum, conga and kalimba, on tunes such as 'Hangman's Reel'. Often less is more, and by cutting down the number of musicians playing, the band attain a haunting quality all their own. Another Dock Boggs classic, 'Sugar Babe', is played on banjo and electric mbira, and this 'minimalist approach' works beautifully.

Again from the Finger Lakes region were the Chicken Chokers, who also updated traditional soongs, though with more humour and a lighter touch. Their 1987 debut *Shoot By Your Radio* updated songs like 'Shady Groves', and has an Uncle Dave Macon 'rap' song 'Worthy of Estimation'.

The Hix come from Philadelphia and are a more arty, slier combo, led by banjo player Keith Brand. They first came together to play at a square dance in New York, having met at various 'old time festivals down South'. On albums like *Sweet Sunny South*, they weld influences from Henry Cowell to Laurie Anderson, Tom Waits to Talking Heads onto a solid base of string-band music. Brand reckons that 'what old time has taught us is the groove. I think the groove is more apparent in old-time music. The instruments come together and they're all one thing'. It worked at back-porch get-togethers, and it works too on the contemporary dance floor. 'I don't think we're expanding the tradition. We're borrowing from it. When we're playing a bar in Philadelphia, I don't consider us to be an old-time band.' At the time of this interview, they were recording a new album in Crumm's home studio, one song at a time as they all have full-time jobs. 'I think there'll be a few influences from the new Beck record, which just knocked us out.'

And there is no more controversial musician in the whole alt country continuum than Beck, a man who doesn't so much combine his old-time leanings with a musical palette that brings together hip hop, grunge and electronics as alternate between the two. Alienating both of his audiences in the process.

v) Electronica

'Set your guitars and banjos on fire, smoke a pack of whiskey
and it'll take care of itself'

– Beck

Beck is a musical magpie, cutting and pasting elements of old-time country, rural blues and '60s funk. It's all about being inauthentic: 'The acceptable side of Americana pressed up against acts like Pearl Jam, who stay yankee-doodle dandy.' Beck has 'skirted across the surface of every native, North American pop idiom, sampling from all but committing to none'. Though every now and then Beck will plunge back into an acoustic-roots project.

Born Bek Campbell in 1970, he was a white kid living in downtown Los Angeles with his Mexican step-father. Even so, 'the bedrock of art theory, the breakbeat fixation, the multi-cultural montage, the edge of European-style irony – all are more East Village than West Hollywood'. His grandfather was Al Hansen, who trained with John Cage and helped form the anti-art art movement Fluxus, whose ideas influenced much new wave music. From him, Beck learnt that 'in the most beatific peacefulness there's complete chaos and maniacal laughter. Music that doesn't reflect that is boring'. His other granddad was a Presbyterian minister in rural Kansas, where the young Beck would spend his summers. 'It was as far away from my normal environment as it could be'. Beck's mother was a young actress who ran with the Andy Warhol crowd. She married David Campbell, a bluegrass violinist who arranged strings for the likes of Linda Ronstadt and The Rolling Stones, and later for his son.

Beck began as a folk musician, first rediscovering the rural blues, and then The Carter family – they had 'these really strange, really beautiful harmonies'. He immersed himself in the *Harry Smith Anthology*, and 'that faraway strange quality is definitely something I gravitated towards.' He also became immersed in the remnants of the LA punk scene, with bands like Pussy Galore and X. Noise became a drug for Beck – 'once you start doing it, you can't stop' – and he began to realise that 'purism is a dead end'. 'Every few years some band comes along and connects to the primal violent energy that is the essence of rock.' He would be next.

In 1989, a teenage Beck arrived in New York. 'There was what I'd call a free-form, punk-rock, folk scene. It was our reaction to the whole '60s and '70s folk thing.' He would play Woody Guthrie songs at open-mic sessions, though not those of Dylan. 'There was a real anti-Bob Dylan feeling in that scene. There was this need to move on, and not linger in his shadow'.

Hansen busked on the street, and fell in with the 'Anti Folk' scene, updating the chaotic stagecraft of the Fugs. Performers like John S Hall and Roger Manning 'shouted and yelled'. Manning remembers that seeing Beck perform was 'like seeing the ghost of Guthrie'. In 1990, Beck distributed a rough-and-ready tape called *Banjo Music* putting new words to old songs. 'Everybody was writing songs, and those people were breaking into rap stuff, and hip hop was coming in, all kinds of things.' Beck would take old folk songs and mix them up with rap and punk.

Songs could be about 'waking up after having been sawn in half by a maniac – stuff like that'. Beck notes that 'a lot of us were playing folk music because we couldn't afford all the instruments'. Then he began to put all this to a hip-hop beat. By 1991, the New York anti-folk scene was dead. Back in LA, Beck briefly formed Ten Ton Ltd, specialising in Carter Family/Louvin Brother songs. He began to improvise, first jokes and then 'I'd make up these ridiculous songs just to see if people were listening. "Loser" was an extension of that.' A limited edition single of 'Loser' came out on Bong Load just as the LA riots hit town: suddenly Beck was at the cutting edge – 'It dissolved the past into the future, to make a wholly new sound.'* Beck had bought himself a four-track recorder, and his first album, the cassette-only *Golden Feelings* issued by Sonic Enemy (1993), described itself as 'genuinely fucked up, straight from the heart of spooky folky noisy unaffected tales of poverty and lucklessness'.

But Geffen – the record label formed out of the very LA '70s scene that Beck most despised – signed him up for a multi-album deal, with the strange proviso that anything they considered too uncommercial could come out on independent labels. As a result the funky *Midnight Vultures* came out first as a digipack 'limited to half a million copies', while his folkier side surfacing on vinyl and cassette only, in runs limited to a few thousand. Gradually, the two have drawn together.

* Nick Tosches

After *Mellow Gold* (1994), Mike D of the Beastie Boys remarked that Beck's hip hop 'legitimised *Public Enemy* as the real folk music of the '80s. Even so, Beck wanted the follow up, *Odelay* to be 'the kind of album they made in the '60s, when people experimented with whatever they felt like – folk, country, chamber music, Eastern sounds'.

One Foot In The Grave was a full-size album, issued the same year. Beck's lyrics have often been compared to mid-'60s Dylan, that same kind of illogic, 'when they ask for credit, give them a ranch'. But there is a sense here too of someone on the edge of a mental breakdown, Syd Barrett or Skip Spence. 'There's blood on the futon, there's a kid drinking fire.' There is a lot of rough-and-ready bottleneck guitar, some equally rough vocal duets, and songs that just tail off. One review described this album as 'mounds of twaddle surrounding the odd gem'. Woody Guthrie, though, would certainly respond to the songs about hard travelling, times when 'it's getting hard to think/my clothes are starting to shrink/and the moon is sagging down like a metal bar'.

What isn't present is much country, either alt or old time. The connection is one of spirit, not slavish imitation. 'That Appalachian stuff is still something I love doing… I guess another time I could have gone that way, but here I am in 1997 and I don't want to be a revivalist. Living in the past is really…a pale version of what's already been done perfectly.'*

A sequel entitled *A Tombstone Every Mile* was never completed but several songs from it showed up on *Mutations*, an album about decay, where everything is 'corroded to the bone'. The lovely finger-style guitar and harpsichord only adds to the darkness of lines like 'night birds will cackle/rotting like apples on trees/sending their dead melodies to me'.

It was also largely recorded direct to tape, and live. As a result, Beck suddenly sounds human, for maybe the first time. He also cuts down on the break beats, 'as Beck's ancient voice becomes all the more intimate, tapping into a timeless mythology of melancholy'.†

Beck reckoned 'it's a singer/songwriter album essentially, but there'll never be the purity of a folk song like one that was written by The Carter Family or Jimmy Rodgers. It's like the folk revival of the '60s wasn't – could never be – like Woody Guthrie, because all those kids had already heard rock 'n' roll.' In turn, though, Beck had got sick of 'all this drum

* Beck
† *New Musical Express*

'n' bass stuff'. 'I felt it was becoming a little gratuitous. I started off playing folk songs...and I still believe in the tradition'.

Sea Change came out in 2002 and took as its subject Beck's split with his long-time girlfriend Leigh Limon. He at last seems to be singing from the heart. It opens with strummed guitar and pedal steel – synthesised, of course – and suddenly Beck does indeed sound like a country singer.

There is something almost narcotic about this record, sung at a sloweddown tempo, and seemingly irony free, with lyrics like 'days turn to sand/losing strength in every hand', rendered in a lugubrious baritone. 'Up to now I've never really written albums for my own singing voice, I've always covered my vocals with gunk. But on this album I've really been able to give it some white man's underbite'.

Massive string arrangements by David Campbell and others touch the same musical vein of glorious sadness as Mercury Rev or late-period Sandy Denny, just hanging there while the singer throbs beneath them. Beck's quiet and melancholic side is just 'as skilful as the clever one we all know',* but then is this 'sincere desolation' just another mask?

Well, if so, Beck would earn a fortune in Hollywood. 'I live in a desert. I took a trip out there right before I wrote these songs. If there's a terrain to this record it's the desert or the open sea, a place where it feels like you're in some kind of void.' One thing that helps fill the void is the music he fell in love with as a kid in downtown LA. 'The simplicity of that songwriting is a big influence. That's something I go back to.'

Beck toured with the Flaming Lips as his backing band, and they do an amazing live approximation of *Sea Change*, with Beck crooning like a new-wave Sinatra. 'Audiences would often leave my gigs feeling molested. Now I let the Flaming Lips do the molesting.' For their own set, the band had an army of volunteers dressed as rabbits, bears and dolphins, egging on the crowd while Wayne Coyne would sing tenderly about everyone having to die some day – a trick they repeated at Glastonbury.

Beck himself then went back to basics, touring Europe solo, and playing intimate venues, for his new intimate songs. A gig at the Union Chapel was filmed by the BBC, and Beck darted between his instruments, strumming guitar like a boy-man possessed, plunking at an old upright piano and giving way to sudden yelps on 'Debra'. *The Observer* reviewer

* *Mojo*

warmed to this 'grown-up Beck', while a gig at the Grand Rex, Paris was the 'most surprising and moving performance I've seen in a long time'.

Comparisons have been made between Beck's verbal oddity and 'fellow LA misfits'. He concurs. Tom Waits is one of those 'rare products of Los Angeles who has an interest in the history of the place. LA is a city that kind of hates itself: Tom represents a part of LA that died a long time ago and he keeps it alive for us.' Captain Beefheart too makes sense 'as someone coming from LA. The town can be like a wasteland, but it forces you to use your imagination.'

Julian Palacios was there to witness a historic show at the Ryman in the Spring of 1997. He opens with 'Devil's Haircut' with a wild young band, and DJ Swamp at two Technics turntables and a mixer. His voice 'crackles with laconic intensity', and he shakes and shimmies, as the band break into dance moves. It's like bringing Harlem to Nashville, and Beck 'shouts himself hoarse between harmonica blasts, his voice over-amplified until the stained-glass windows shake with dissonance'. 'I never rocked the pews before', he gasps, launching into a solo version of Jimmie Rodgers' 'Waiting For A Train' on acoustic guitar and bringing the crowd to its feet. No wonder that no less than Johnny Cash considers that Beck has got 'that mountain music in his blood'.

Others have fused old-time music with modern technology. Greg Garing fell in love with bluegrass in his native Pennsylvania, then moved to Nashville to 'look for Bill Monroe'. He took a job at Opry Land, and ran into the likes of Jimmy Martin: 'the rocker of bluegrass singing, he jumped around and screamed like no-one else'. Greg himself became a mainstay of the Lower Broadway scene, and led a honky-tonk band that played Tootsie's Orchid Lounge. But then he went strange.

Garing began to experiment with tape loops. 'To me, trip hop has that same lonesome sound. Tricky meets Hank Williams.' The first fruits of this new approach appear on the 1997 album *Alone*. Greg sings with spirit and determination – and a real twang – over strong electronic rhythms, samples of old 78s, odd industrial noises and disco whistle. Adding to the sounds here are the cooling breeze of Irish folk and Peter Rowan guesting on mandolin for 'Where The Bluegrass Grows'. The two styles don't quite jell, but there are times when it hits the spot, with old and new technology coming together in a kind of catharsis. One reviewer likened this album to 'Bill Monroe and John Cage meeting at the end of the century'. It certainly rubs away at something already deep in bluegrass music, like an itch. 'A good bluegrass band has a really repetitious groove and I would get my band to play a riff for each section of a song and just play that in the background over and over again'. Then legendary scene maker BP Fallon pointed out that modern bands like Garbage did exactly the same, with machines. Greg recently relocated to New York, and set up shop in a club in the East Village, just as Beck had done a decade before.

Moby was born Richard Melville in New York, a distant relation of the man who wrote that cornerstone of Americana, *Moby Dick*. Hence his nickname. As fervent a Christian as The Carter Family, though a little more energetic on stage, he formed the Vatican Commandos when he was 15, and a string of hardcore bands followed. As a solo artist, he brought mixing to a fine art – his first hit single 'Go' is based around a sample from *Twin Peaks*. But where he interests us here is the 1999 album *Play*, largely based around samples of rural blues drawn from the John and Alan Lomax archive. Vocals by the likes of the Shining Light Gospel Choir were welded to acid house, and the results became a favourite both on the dance floor and as soundtrack to countless adverts.

Moby's near namesake but far weirder UK counterpart Momus, just a boy christened Nick Currie and his computer, released *Folktronic* in 2000. It opens with 'Appalachia', a love song to an imagined hillbilly girl: 'won't you come and comfort me, electronically?'

Then things get really bizarre with 'Mountain Music'. '"Moon of Alabama" is my favourite country tune/it's got lyrics by a communist and music by a Jew.' Written in Berlin, too. You can hear the history of country music in just over two minutes – 'Johnny Cash, casio, Dylan and Beck' – learnt 'yesterday' from a CD-ROM and recreated with tinny samples of banjo and fiddle. Through cheap technology, Appalachian music is as available to a Pakistani as to a native of Tennessee. 'When I press the play button I hear the music start.' As to the diaspora of the Scots Irish, 'they travelled round the world and never stayed where they belonged/and if they had we'd never have these lovely mountain songs'.

Momus gave the album a fresh lease of life as *Folktronia*, an installation in a smart New York gallery. Members of the public sang their own misheard, mis-remembered or improved versions of some of these songs, putting them firmly back into the oral tradition.

Uncut reckons Momus a master at spreading cultural confusion. He filters Americana through a 'tacky synth pop sensibility', as if Stereolab chose to produce Smog. These songs find the exact point where the authentic becomes 'showbiz', and ripe for plunder. 'Folk music, the bloody world's mine.' Thus can the 'great despoiler of all that is cherished' mix c&w melodies with lyrics about his favourite body part in 'The Penis Song', or deride Shaker furniture.

The year 2003 saw Natalie Merchant's album *The House Carpenter's Daughter* appear on her own 'Myth America' label. Natalie is backed by The Horseflies, and the album includes an 18th-century hymn 'Weeping Pilgrim'. Merchant's 'rich, expressive voice is imbued with all the awe, dread and authority the material requires' while subtle arrangements prove these 'timeless treasures are still capable of revealing previously uncharted mysteries'.* Then there is Venus Hum's *Big Beautiful Sky* – a combo in the Morcheeba mould, with two computer nerds laying down a backdrop for torch singer Annette Strean, who grew up in the Northwest. Her lyrics are shot through with natural imagery, and she has also acquired a country twang, as a result of relocating to Nashville.

And then there is Snakefarm, with their 1999 album *Songs From My Funeral*, 'acid-laced hip hop collides with coffee-house troubadour'.* This was as much a cultural shock when it appeared as when Fairport Convention put a rock rhythm section to British folk music on *Liege And Lief* 30 years before. According to the singer here, who goes under the name of Anna Domino, 'using traditional instruments such as banjo and dobra with programmed sounds isn't unusual, it's just folk music for our times'. And you can dance to it, just like the old string bands.

Billboard once wrote of Anna as 'the spearhead for all singers of the trip-hop scene', Portishead and the like. Her languid, almost disconnected vocal style as she tells of murder and savagery stretches back in time too, to Sarah Carter and the like. Anna's husband, Michel Delory – an emigree from Belgium – plays the aforesaid banjo and dobra, and programs

* Peter Stampfel

keyboard and drums on his computer. He had, had no idea how the album would be received. 'Here we are in the Mojave desert, thinking we're in some vacuum, but of course we're not.' The story of alt country in a nutshell.

The repertoire is roots Americana, but never heard like this before. Dance beats have freed things up. 'Black Girl' is better known as 'In The Pines', and was covered respectfully by an unplugged Nirvana. The Snakefarm version starts with Anna humming to a banjo, but after the first verse a shuffle beat comes in, and her voice is distorted almost beyond recognition. 'Banks Of The Ohio' starts with sonorous cello, then Anna sings and mix maestro Delory makes his guitar shimmer.

Anna first heard these songs from her parents, and found them 'spooky, the…sense of longing and loss are so strong'. As she told *Folk Roots*, 'my record is what happened to songs after they got to America, when they sat around the Appalachians and got bent out of shape for a few hundred years'. Actually, this is the standard '50s revival take on old time, 'Tom Dooley' and the like, and many of the songs here were translated into UK skiffle, courtesy of that old pedlar of Americana Lonnie Donegan. This is just as 'inauthentic' as Momus, though easier on the ear.

The album came together with a worrying ease. 'Every song that I tried, even when I tried to make it difficult – okay, let's try 'Pretty Little Horses', that'll be impossible – they all worked.' The couple had previously lived in New York, and she gave a tape to Matt Johnson of The The. No stranger to the power of electronica himself, he took it straight to a local record label.

There were plans for her to take this set of songs on the road with a DJ/soundman and a specially filmed video. It all seems a very long way from Dock Boggs and his banjo. But maybe Dock will have the last laugh: little has been heard of Snakefarm since, and their album already sounds of its time, in a way he doesn't.

It awaits the next generation to decide where to take this ancient music next – whether deeper into electronica, or rediscovering Eddie Arnold, or even back to '70s-style country rock (as Josh Rouse seems to think). One thing is sure: the next big thing will come from somewhere completely unexpected. And I can't wait.

Epilogue

Johnny Cash: The Final Train Ride

'People say, well, he wore that body out. Well, maybe I did. But it
was to a good purpose.' – *Johnny Cash*

Johnny Cash died on 12 September 2003 in Nashville's Baptist Hospital,
at the age of 71. It had been an epic life, a constant battle against his inner
demons, matched with a deep love of the roots of country and an intense
love for his native land. Just listen to *America: A 200-Year Salute In Story
And Song*, from 1972, one of his pageants of US history, which takes the
listener westward and 'southwestward', as the new nation adds on states,
goes to war, and reaches for the stars. It is all somehow ludicrous, yet deeply
affecting. No wonder Bono once described that voice as 'all wailing freight
trains and thundering prairies, like the landscape of his beloved America.
He had a soul as big as a continent.' One of Johnny's own final comments
was the somewhat double edged, 'I'm thrilled to death with life.'

In the wake of 1994's *American Recordings*, Cash went on to record
three further albums with Rick Rubin, for which this phrase could now
be an epitaph. None are exactly easy listening, but they each exude an
urgency and majesty which belies his years. Denied a live audience now
that ill health had stopped him being able to go on the road, this is music
as dark and serious as death itself. Cash's voice wavers and goes off key
– 'flat and almost impossibly low' – while the backings are deliberately
low. However, taken with his recordings for Sun back in the 1950s, these
albums now bookend a life 'as dark and as luminescent as America itself'.

They look interchangeable. All four feature virtually monochrome
shots of Johnny, with not even the hint of a smile. This was not a man
trying to ingratiate himself or sell you anything. Rubin keeps the backing

musicians anonymous – despite their celebrity – and well in check. Acoustic guitars predominate. Cash sings as if alone in his own world, as he prepares to leave this one. Forget the joys of the consumer society, or happy-clappy Christian faith: this is all about sin and redemption. It is a vision which Dock Boggs and AP Carter testified to. It is present in the very grain of Ralph Stanley's pinched voice. It is what Gram Parsons died for. And it is the lonely, hard place which a visibly ageing Bob Dylan also now inhabits every time he takes the stage. Guilt and bitter regret, and forgiveness and a refusal to forgive.

Thus does country music come full circle, with the young rockabilly star of Sun now married into the ancestral Carter family, and himself a patriarch, free to bless the wildest young men from the alt-country rebel movement by using the best of their songs. *Unchained* came out in 1996, following a serious illness, and features songs by Beck, Soundgarden and Tom Petty, plus Johnny himself, but he rises to an emotional crescendo on Josh Haden's 'Spiritual': 'Jesus, I don't want to die alone ... all my troubles, all my pain will leave me once again'. But *Unchained* is a garden party compared to the 'punishing intensity' of *American III: Solitary Man*, which emerged four years later. This is a bare-knuckle ride, opening as it does at the 'gates of hell' and with an even more stripped-back sound. The first song is co-written with Jeff Lynne, and the second with Neil Diamond, but by the time Cash has finished with them they are just as 'authentic' as such traditional fare as 'Mary Of The Wild Moor' or 'Wayfaring Stranger'. On U2's 'One', he rises to an emotional crescendo of bitter exultation: 'Have you come to raise the dead? Have you come here to play Jesus to the lepers in your head?' He fully responds to the Old Testament vengefulness of Nick Cave's 'The Mercy Seat': 'And I'm not afraid to die'. On Will Oldham's 'I See A Darkness', Cash conveys authenticity on a song that, in the hands of its author, 'could be construed as mere melodrama'. Sepulchral piano chords, and a raw-voiced, half-spoken account of things that come 'blacking in my mind'. And yet this is also a song about friendship. Bonnie Prince Billy himself joins in on the chorus.

Cash resurrects David Allen Coe's 'Would You Lay With Me (In A Field Of Stone)' and 'That Lucky Old Sun', the song with which he won a talent contest 'when I was young', but surely not by singing like this.

June Carter Cash brings a touch of brightness on the love lyric 'Field Of Diamonds', but this song – like much of her family's own repertoire – is about a better land beyond (or, in this case, above), not here on earth.

As *No Depression* puts it, the key to this terrifying album lies in 're-imagination', the remaking of old and new songs, country standards and alt-rock anthems. Johnny has the alchemist's touch to turn even contemporary rock songs into 'something that sounds as old as the hills'. Cash himself wrote that 'this record has been a long time coming, and I feel another in there somewhere'. Just one, perhaps. The album in question was *American IV: The Man Comes Around*, which came out shortly after his 70th birthday and already had the feel of a last will and testament. After two sapping bouts of pneumonia, automatic neuropathy had 'stripped some of the bulk' from Cash's voice, suddenly making him seem humble, fragile even. But as *Uncut* puts it, once that voice comes up centre stage, 'suddenly any technical shortcomings seem like virtues'.† Johnny describes the music behind him as 'not so much production, as kind of cushioning for my ragged voice. There's much more instrumentation on this one, but it fits. It works'. This is a man looking back on his life, as he prepares to meet his maker. He sings 'Desperado' in a 'way that makes The Eagles sound like a boy band'. In the words of Nick Tosches, Johnny gives the songs here 'the imprimatur of ageless cool'.*

The song selection is extraordinary. Depeche Mode's 'Personal Jesus' drives along, recreating that band's electronics with a small country band. Johnny sounds like a preacher, calling his errant flock home. Yet, on the hymnal 'Bridge Over Troubled Water', he sounds weary as hell, with Fiona Apple an angel singing him across the great divide. Then there is the dying cowboy song 'Streets Of Laredo', and the defiance of that old music-hall chestnut, 'Sam Hall'. The Beatles' 'In My Life' has never been sung so tenderly, or slowly.

Cash does not forget his country music history. Hank Williams' 'I'm So Lonely I Could Cry' is described by *Mojo* as an 'affecting duet with country crooner (honest) Nick Cave'. Again, it is taken at a funereal pace, and that 'midnight train' has almost slowed to a stop. Marty Robbins' 'Big Iron' closes the album with an outlaw song, an old man at 24, and a final shoot-out – we're almost back with Leon Payne.

† *Uncut* magazine   * Chris Morris, *Billboard*

Most affecting of all is that Second World War song 'We'll Meet Again', which would win Johnny no prizes at a singing contest, but which goes straight for the heart, with clarinet, dobro and fiddle, a spoken passage and a singalong at the end. It already sounds downright spooky. June Carter Cash died a few months after the CD release, and it was a shock that Johnny never seemed to truly get over. As one review at the time put it, 'if this is to be Cash's last album then what a magnificent way he has chosen to say goodbye'.

The MTV award-winning video for 'Hurt' has the air of a proud farewell, filmed at the singer's home with archive footage cut in of Johnny playing San Quentin and jumping trains. The dying Cash sings with an epic grandeur, and June Carter Cash watches her husband with 'sadness, pride and love'. As one obituary put it, 'tenderness on that level is a power that knows no master'.

Cash made a surprise appearance at the Americana Music Association Awards in Nashville that same year, to receive the first-ever Spirit Of Americana Free Speech Award, 'for his lifelong commitment to voicing the struggles of those who languish on society's margins'. He brought June and other members of the Carter family onstage with him. Indeed, Johnny now had the same sense of innate authority as old AP himself: 'He was selling fruit trees sometimes, and he'd trade a fruit tree for a song. I've followed in that tradition of singing and writing. You never know where you'll find a good song.'

As he told Sylvie Simmons, 'I don't know if it's because of my age, but the songs just keep coming round about pain and death, so I keep singing about it. I had pneumonia twice while doing this album. And I'm not a good patient. I haven't been touring, so all the energy went into the album.' Does the album have a theme? 'No, it just kind of happened that way. If it has a theme then it's the strength of the human spirit.'

And Cash's music will continue to celebrate that each time we get it down off the shelf and have a listen. As to the place where his spirit has now ventured, well if we can trust the music of The Carter Family and Dock Boggs, Ralph Stanley and the Louvin Brothers, and all of those who have followed in their musical footsteps, then it is a place even more huge and unknown than America itself.

Useful Information

AMERICANA: FURTHER READING

Alden, Grant and Blackstock, Peter: *No Depression: An Introduction To Alternative Country Music (Whatever That Is)* (Dowling Press) 1998

Artis, Bob: *Bluegrass* (Hawthorn) 1975

Asch, Moses and others (ed): *Anthology Of American Folk Music: Songs Transcribed From Recorded Performances That Appear On The Renowned Folkways Recording Anthology Of American Folk Music*, with historical and folkloric commentary on each song (Oak Publications) 1973

Body, Sean: *Wish The World Away: Mark Eitzel And The American Music Club* (SAF) 1999

Burt, Olive: *American Murder Ballads And Their Stories* (OUP) 1958

Cantwell, Robert: *Bluegrass Breakdown: The Making Of The Old Southern Sound* (University of Illinois Press) 1984

Cantwell, Robert: *Smith's Memory Theatre: The Folkways Anthology Of American Folk Music*, New England Review (Spring/Summer 1991)

Cantwell, Robert: *Ethnomimesis, Folklife And The Representation Of Culture* (University of North Carolina Press) 1993

Cantwell, Robert: *When We Were Good: The Folk Revival* (Harvard University Press) 1996

Dawidoff, Nicholas: *In The Country Of Country* (Pantheon) 1997

Doggett, Peter: *Are You Ready For The Country* (Viking) 2000

Earle, Steve: *Doghouse Roses* (Secker and Warburg) 2001

Escott, Colin: *The Story Of Country Music* (BBC) 2003

Folk Roots/F Roots, various issues

Fong-Torres, Ben: *Hickory Wind: The Life And Times Of Gram Parsons* (Omnibus) 1994

Goodman, David: *Modern Twang: An Alternative Country Music Guide And Directory* (Dowling Press) 3rd ed, 2000

Griffin, Sid: *'Sin City' In Love Is The Drug: Living As A Pop Fan*, ed John Aizlewood (Penguin) 1994

Guralnick, Peter: *Lost Highways, Journeys And Arrivals Of American Musicians* (Godine) 1979

Guthrie, Woody: *California To The New York Island: Being A pocketful Of Brags, Blues, Bad Man Ballads, Love Songs, Okie Laments And Children's Catcalls... Woven Into A Script Suitable For A Concert, Clambake, Hootenanny Or Community Sing By Millard Lampebell* (Oak Publications for the Guthrie Children's Trust Fund) 1958

Harris, Stacey: *The Carter Family* (Lerner Publishing) 1978

Heatley, Michael: *Ryan Adams* (Omnibus) 2003

Helm, Levon and Davis, Stephen: *This Wheel's On Fire: Levon Helm And The Story Of The Band* (Plexus) 1993

Heylin, Clinton: *Behind Closed Doors: Bob Dylan – The Recording Sessions 1960–1994* (Viking) 1995

Hoskyns, Barney: 'Redneck Soul, George Jones And The White Man's Blues' in *From A Whisper To A Scream: The Great Voices Of Popular Music* (Fontana) 1991

Hunter, Robert: *A Box Of Rain: Lyrics 1965–1993* (Viking 1990, 2nd ed with extra lyrics, Penguin) 1993

Igliori, Paola (ed): *American Magus, Harry Smith – A Modern Alchemist* (Inanout Press) 1996, includes interview with John Cohen

Jovanic, Rob: *Beck! On a Backwards River* (Virgin) 2000

Klein, Joe: *Woody Guthrie – A Life* (Knopf) 1980

Laws, G Malcolm Jr: *Native American Balladry: A Descriptive Study And A Bibliographical Syllabus* (University of Texas Press for the American Folklore Society) 1950, rev ed 1964

Lomax, Alan: *The Folk Songs Of North America In The English Language* (Doubleday) 1960

Lomax, John: *Cowboy Songs And Other Frontier Ballads* (Macmillan) 1918, rev ed 1938

Lomax, John and Alan: *American Ballads And Folk Songs* (Macmillan) 1934

Lomax, John and Alan: *Our Singing Country: A Second Volume Of American Ballads And Folk Songs* (Macmillan) 1941

McNeil, WK: *Appalachian Images In Folk And Popular Culture* 1995

Malone, Bill: *Country Music: USA* (University of Texas Press) 1985

Malone, Bill: *Singing Cowboys And Musical Mountaineers: Southern Culture And The Roots Of Country Music* (Univ of Georgia Press) 1993

Marcus, Greil: *Mystery Train: Images Of America In Rock 'n' Roll Music* (EP Dutton) 1975

Marcus, Greil: *In The Fascist Bathroom: Writings On Punk 1977–1992* (Viking) 1993

Marcus, Greil: *Invisible Republic: Bob Dylan's Basement Tapes* (Picador) 1997

Mojo, various issues

No Depression, various issues

Palacios, Julian: Beck: *Beautiful Monstrosity* (Boxtree) 1999

Perry, Tim and Glinert, Ed: *Fodor's Rock And Roll Traveller USA* (Fodor) 1996

Porterfield, Nolan: *Jimmie Rodgers: The Life And Times Of America's Blue Yodeler* (University of Illinois Press) 1979

Price, Steven: *Old As The Hills: The Story Of Bluegrass Music* (Viking) 1975

Ritchie, Jean: *Folk Songs Of The Southern Appalachians* (Oak Publications) 1965

Rogan, Johnny: *The Byrds: Timeless Flight Revisited – The Sequel* (Rogan House) 1997

Rosenberg, Neil (ed): *Transforming Tradition: Folk Music Revivals Examined* (University of Illinois Press) 1993

St John, Lauren: *Walkin' After Midnight: A Journey To The Heart Of Nashville* (Picador) 2000

St John, Lauren: *Hardcore Troubadour: The Life And Near Death Of Steve Earle* (Fourth Estate) 2002

Sandburg, Carl: *The American Songbag* (Harcourt Brace) 1927

Sandburg, Carl: *Carl Sandburg's New American Songbag* (Broadcast Music) 1950

Scarborough, Dorothy: *A Song Catcher In The Southern Mountains: American Folk Songs Of British Ancestry* (Columbia University Press) 1937, repr 1966

Sharp, Cecil J (comp): *English Folk-Songs From The Southern Appalachians, Comprising 274 Songs And Ballads With 968 Tunes, Including 39 Tunes Contributed By Olive Campbell*, ed Maud Karpeles 2 vols (OUP) 2nd ed 1932

Silber, Irwin and Robinson, Earl: *Songs Of The Great American West* (Macmillan) 1967

Smith, Harry: *Think Of The Self Speaking: Selected Interviews*, ed R Singh (Elbow Press) 1999

Smith, Henry Nash: *Virgin Land: The American West As Symbol And Myth* (Harvard University Press) 1950

Smith, Lee: *The Devil's Dream* (Putnams) 1992

Thompson, Ben: *Seven Years Of Plenty: A Handbook Of Irrefutable Pop Greatness 1991–1998* (Gollancz 1998)

Tichi, Cecelia: *High Lonesome: The American Culture Of Country Music* (University of North Carolina Press) 1994

Tosches, Nick: *Country: The Biggest Music In America* (Stein and Day) 1977, reissued in Britain as *Country: Living Legends And Dying Metaphors In America's Biggest Music* (Secker and Warburg)

Uncut, various issues

Unterberger, Richie: *Music USA: The Rough Guide* (Rough Guides) 1999

Warner, Anne: *Traditional American Folk Songs: From The Anne And Frank Warner Collection* (Syracuse University Press) 1984

Wootton, Richard: *Honky Tonkin': A Travel Guide to American Music* (Travelaid) 3rd ed 1980

RECOMMENDED MAGAZINES
No Depression, 5816 Ninth Ave NW, Seattle, WA 98107
www.NoDepression.net
Uncut, 24th Floor, King's Reach Tower, Stamford St, London SE1 9LS
wwwallan.jones@ipcmedia.com
Mojo, Mappin House, 4 Winsley Street, London W1W 8HF
www.mojo4music.com
Maverick: the new voice of country music, AAG Publishing, 24 Bray Gardens,
    Maidstone, Kent ME15 9TR

RECOMMENDED UK AMERICANA BROADCASTS
Captain America, Virgin Radio, Sunday night 22:00
www.virginradio.co.uk/djsshows/djs/captain-america.html
Bob Harris Country Show, BBC Radio 2, Thursday nights 19:00
Bob Harris, BBC Radio 2, Saturday nights 22:00

RECOMMENDED CD COMPILATIONS
*Another Country: Songs Of Dignity & Redemption From The Other Side Of The
    Tracks* (Agenda)
Are You Ready For The Country (Warners) 2-CD
Beyond Nashville, The Twisted Heart Of Country Music (Manteca)
    2-CD
Both Sides Now: The Spirit Of Americana (Gravity/BMG) 2-CD
Cowpunks: 24 Trailblazing Tracks (Vinyl Junkie)
Come Fly With Me (Glitterhouse)
*Further Beyond Nashville, Welcome Back To The Twisted Heart Of Country
    Music* (Manteca) 2-CD
Global Roots Americana (Spectrum) 2-CD
Howl, a farewell compilation of unreleased songs (Glitterhouse)
Loose, New Sounds Of The Old West (Vinyl Junkie)
Loose, New Sounds Of The Old West, Volume Two (Vinyl Junkie)
Loose, New Sounds Of The Old West, Volume Three (Vinyl Junkie)
Sounds Of The New West, The Best Of Alternative Country 1998 (Uncut)
More Sounds Of The New West, The Best Of Americana 2000 (Uncut)
Sounds Of The New West, The Best Of Americana 2001 (Uncut)
This Is Americana, Vol One: A View From Sugar Hill Records (Americana Music
    Association)

RECOMMENDED DVDs
American Roots Music (Palm) 2-DVD
Heartworn Highways (Catfish)

RECOMMENDED VENUES AND FESTIVALS
The Borderline, Orange Yard, Soho, London
Borderline Radio (www.borderline.co.uk)
Merlefest, Wilkesboro, North Carolina (www.merlefest.org)
North by Northeast, Toronto,
South by Southwest, Austin, Texas (www.sxsw.com)
Twangfest, St Louis, Missouri (www.twangfest.com)

AMERICANA MUSIC ASSOCIATION
The Americana Music Association, PO Box 128077, Nashville, TN37212
info@americanamusic.org

RECOMMENDED WEBSITES
Almost all the bands referred to in this book have their own website, accessed through any good search engine. Key examples include:
www.gumbopages.com (Uncle Tupelo)
www.wilcoweb.com (Wilco)
www.hollywoodtownhall.com (Jayhawks)
www.geocities.com/-wolf-eyes/sparkly.html (Sparklehorse)
www.morebarn.com/hazeldine (Hazeldine)
www.steveearle.net (Steve Earle)

General websites include the following, correct at the time of writing:
www.alternativecountry.com
www.americanauk.com
www.americanaCDs.com
www.americanamusic.org
www.country.com/music/news/feature/twang.html
www.lancnews.com/moderntwang/
www.ursasoft.com/bob/

RECOMMENDED UK AMERICANA RECORD DEALER
Rear View Mirror, 8 Town Meadow, Little Torrington, Torrington, North Devon
      EX38 8RD, UK. Tel/Fax 01805 624589. Email: rear.view.mirror@btconnect.com

Index

Spyboy 74
Stafford, Jim 62
Stampfel, Peter 44–5, 48, 49, 253
Stanley, Carter 37
Stanley, Dr Ralph 36, 37, 49, 59, 206, 238, 241–2, 260, 261–2, 263, 274, 290
Stanley Brothers 37, 61, 260, 264
Starkweathers 185
Stecher, Jody 28–9, 273–4
Stewart, John 17, 88, 129–30
Stipe, Michael 129, 220
Stirratt, John 163, 165
Stoneman, Scotty 80
Stoneman's Blue Ridge Cornshuckers 26
Strapping Fieldhands 276
Strean, Annette 288
Strummer, Joe 118–19
Stuart, 'Big Daddy' Dan 130, 131, 132, 134–5
Stuart, Mark 157
Stuart, Marty 36, 38, 147
Supersuckers 188–9
Swanson, Matt 223
Swenson, Roland 10

Take It To The Limit 177
Talking Heads 113
Talton, Tommy 90
Tarnation 194
Taylor, Chip 102, 157
Taylor, Earl, and his Stony Mountain Boys 86
Taylor, Eric 149, 150
Texas Jewboys 102
Texas Playboys 33
The, The 39
Thee Old Codgers 244, 250
Thin White Rope 134–5
Thomas, David 207, 208, 253
Thompson, Ben 210, 212, 215, 223
Thompson, Linda 114, 179, 207, 264
Thompson, Richard 114, 179, 260, 264, 280
Thorns, The 190
Throwing Muses 272
Timmins, Margot 211, 212
Timms, Sally 121, 173, 174, 214
Tobler, John 46, 72

Tolman, Russ 133, 134
Toomey, Jenny 174
Torgerson, Carla 186, 187
Trailer Bride 225
Traum, Happy 47
Travis, Merle 38, 46
Triffids, The 137, 212
True West 133
Tucker, Tanya 100
Tull, Bruce 228
Tweedy, Jeff 35, 160–3, 165–6, 167, 168–71, 176, 177, 220, 233, 234, 253
Tyminski, Dan 246, 260

Uncle Tupelo 25, 113, 115, 125, 158, 160–4, 165, 167, 176
Union Station 245–6, 247, 249
US Saucer 227
Utah Carol 176

Van Zandt, Townes 103–5, 143, 146, 150, 212, 263
Van Zant, Ronnie 99
Vassal, Jacques 23
Veirs, Laura 277
Veitch, Doug 120
Venus Hum 288
Verlaine, Tom 102
Vernon, Paul 254–5
Victims Of Society, The 183
Violent Femmes 137–8, 207

Waco Brothers 121, 171–3, 174
Wagner, Kurt 173, 183, 221, 222–4, 225, 226
Wagon 171, 185
Wagoner, Porter 267–8, 272
Waits, Tom 12, 96, 105, 130, 150, 173, 205–7, 286
Walkabouts, The 84, 186–7, 189
Walker, Ginny 253
Walker, Jerry Jeff 103, 110
Ward, Ed 83, 216
Ward, Matt 190–1
Warlocks 79–80
Warner, Anne 47, 258, 259
Warner, Frank 23, 47, 258, 259
Warner, Gerret 259

Watson, Arthel 'Doc' 29, 43–4, 47, 93, 94, 103, 274
Watson, Dale 196–7
Watson, Merle 44
Webb, Jimmy 57, 184, 228
Welch, Gillian 21–2, 28, 59, 73, 113, 147, 152, 165, 192, 259, 261, 262–6, 274
Wessom, Steve 107, 108
Westerberg, Paul 136, 160, 166
Whiskeytown 70, 124, 137, 159, 164, 229
White, Clarence 62, 65, 66, 69, 77, 89, 245
White, Jim 213, 238
White, Ralph, III 241, 242–3
Whiteley, Keith 59
Wilco 34, 35, 70–1, 112, 136, 165–71, 179
Wilheim, Mike 79
Willard Grant Conspiracy 229–30, 231
Williams, Hank 25, 38–9, 51, 83, 114, 140, 237
Williams, Hank, III 142
Williams, Hank, Jnr 39–40
Williams, Lucinda 10–12, 39, 40, 56, 73, 74, 97, 104, 109, 146, 153–6
Williams, Victoria 70, 156, 179, 198, 199, 201, 221, 273
Williamson, Nigel 71, 169, 181, 199–200
Wills, Bob 33, 98, 157, 196
Winchester, Jesse 95, 116
Wooley, Alan 239
Wynn, Steve 77, 84, 134–5, 231

X 122, 123, 160, 164, 197

Yoachum, Iggy 172
Yoakam, Dwight 59, 122, 144, 196
Young, Neil 73, 84, 85, 105, 130, 163–4, 185
Young, Rusty 85–6

Zakinska, Annette 127
Zellar, Martin 142, 177, 182
Zevon, Warren 17, 92
Zollo, David 182
Zoom, Billy 122, 123